SHAKESPEARE & COMPANY

Shakespeare & Company: When Action is Eloquence is the first comprehensive insight into this internationally acclaimed company founded in 1978 in Lenox, Massachusetts, by actor-director Tina Packer and voice pioneer Kristin Linklater, with the transformative power of Shakespeare's language at its heart.

Why act Shakespeare? What's his relevance in the twenty-first century? Compelling answers to these questions lie at the center of this highly accessible journey into Shakespeare & Company's aesthetics and practice. Drawing on hitherto unpublished material – including notebooks, lectures, interviews, rehearsal diaries – and the Company's newly collated archive, this book provides insight into a working theatre company and sheds light on the role Shakespeare plays in our modern world. It also details:

- Shakespeare & Company's founding and early history
- Its aesthetic based on the Elizabethan theatre's principles of the *Art of Rhetoric*; *Structure of the Verse*; *Voice and Movement*; *Clown*; *Fight*; and *Actor/ Audience Relationship*
- Vocational components of its *Training* Intensives
- Practical pedagogy of its *Education* programs
- Insights into its unique approaches to *Performance*
- Impact and legacy of its three lifetime founding members: Dennis Krausnick (Director of Training), Kevin G. Coleman (Director of Education) and Tina Packer (founding Artistic Director).

Actors, directors, students, educators, scholars and theatre-lovers alike will find practical acting strategies, inspirational approaches to theatre making and lively insights into the sustaining of a unique and robust theatre company that has been thriving for over 40 years.

Bella Merlin is an actor, professor of acting at the University of California, Riverside, and the author of six books on acting, including *The Complete Stanislavsky Toolkit* and *Facing the Fear: An Actor's Guide to Overcoming Stage Fright.*

Tina Packer is the multi-award-winning founding Artistic Director of Shakespeare & Company, and has acted and/or directed all of Shakespeare's plays as well as touring her original take on Shakespeare's women, *Women of Will.* Her book of the same name was a *New York Times* Editor's Choice.

SHAKESPEARE & COMPANY

When Action is Eloquence

Bella Merlin and Tina Packer

LONDON AND NEW YORK

First published 2020
by Routledge
2 Park Square, Milton Park, Abingdon, Oxon OX14 4RN

and by Routledge
52 Vanderbilt Avenue, New York, NY 10017

Routledge is an imprint of the Taylor & Francis Group, an informa business

© 2020 Bella Merlin and Tina Packer

The right of Bella Merlin and Tina Packer to be identified as authors of this work has been asserted by them in accordance with sections 77 and 78 of the Copyright, Designs and Patents Act 1988.

All rights reserved. No part of this book may be reprinted or reproduced or utilised in any form or by any electronic, mechanical, or other means, now known or hereafter invented, including photocopying and recording, or in any information storage or retrieval system, without permission in writing from the publishers.

Trademark notice: Product or corporate names may be trademarks or registered trademarks, and are used only for identification and explanation without intent to infringe.

British Library Cataloguing-in-Publication Data
A catalogue record for this book is available from the British Library

Library of Congress Cataloging-in-Publication Data
Names: Merlin, Bella, author. | Packer, Tina, 1938- author.
Title: Shakespeare & Company : when action is eloquence / Bella Merlin, Tina Packer.
Description: Abingdon, Oxon ; New York, NY : Routledge, 2020. | Includes index.
Identifiers: LCCN 2019053983 (print) | LCCN 2019053984 (ebook) | ISBN 9780367086848 (hardback) | ISBN 9780367262556 (paperback) | ISBN 9780429292231 (ebook)
Subjects: LCSH: Shakespeare, William, 1564–1616–Dramatic production. | Shakespeare & Company (Lenox, Mass.) | Theatrical companies–Massachusetts–Lenox.
Classification: LCC PN2297.S53 M47 2020 (print) | LCC PN2297.S53 (ebook) | DDC 792.09744/1–dc23
LC record available at https://lccn.loc.gov/2019053983
LC ebook record available at https://lccn.loc.gov/2019053984

ISBN: 978-0-367-08684-8 (hbk)
ISBN: 978-0-367-26255-6 (pbk)
ISBN: 978-0-429-29223-1 (ebk)

Typeset in Bembo
by Swales & Willis, Exeter, Devon, UK

**For
Kristin, Dennis, Kevin
and Miles**

CONTENTS

List of figures	*ix*
Foreword – Allyn Burrows	*xi*
Preface	*xiii*
Acknowledgments	*xvii*
Abbreviations	*xix*

Prologue: 'To unpath'd waters, undream'd shores' 1

ACT I
History and roots **7**

1 Visions and revisions: The Company is formed 9

2 Bricks and mortar, trellis and trees: An aesthetic is realized 38

3 Talk #1: Function of the Theatre 63

ACT II
Training **81**

4 Evolution and influences of the Month-Long Intensive 83

5 Talk #2: Actor/Audience Relationship 107

viii Contents

6 Voice Work and Basics — 116

7 Text Work and Dropping In — 132

8 Body Work and bringing it all together — 148

ACT III
Education — **169**

9 Practical pedagogy — 171

10 Shakespeare in the Schools — 190

11 Shakespeare on the campus — 209

12 Shakespeare in the Courts — 223

ACT IV
Performance — **237**

13 The art form of performance — 239

14 Talk #3: Theatre, Therapy and Theology — 264

15 *Cymbeline*: A performance case study — 274

Epilogue: 'On such a full sea are we now afloat' — 296

Appendix 1: An abridged performance history — *302*
Appendix 2: An abridged dramatis personae — *309*
Appendix 3: A potted plot of Cymbeline — *312*
Index — *314*

FIGURES

Unless otherwise stated, all photographs are copyright of Shakespeare & Company and reproduced by kind permission.

1.1	Kristin Linklater teaching a workshop in the early years	15
1.2	John Broome teaching first Intensive, January 1979	21
1.3	Dennis Krausnick, Tina Packer and Kevin G. Coleman, 2016	31
2.1	Mainstage at The Mount: *The Merchant of Venice*, dir. Tina Packer, 1998	42
2.2	Corinna May as Edith Wharton, The Mount, 1985	44
2.3	*A Midsummer Night's Dream*, dir. Tina Packer, 2000, Mainstage at The Mount	48
2.4	Aerial view of Kemble Street campus	50
2.5	Tina Packer Playhouse: break in rehearsals, *The Merchant of Venice*, 2016	53
2.6	(a) Rose Playhouse and Renaissance Village model and design, Payette Associates; (b) Rose Playhouse composite image, Payette Associates	57
2.7	Roman Garden Theatre: *The Tempest*, dir. Allyn Burrows, 2017: (a) Ella Loudon (Miranda), Deaon Griffin-Pressley (Ferdinand); (b) Josh McCabe (Stephano), Martin Jason Asprey (Caliban)	59
3.1	Tina Packer, London, 1972	64
3.2	Rehearsal of *The Merchant of Venice*, dir. Tina Packer, 2016: John Hadden (Antonio), Jonathan Epstein (Shylock) and Tamara Hickey (Portia)	76
7.1	Dennis Krausnick, *Sonnet* session, STI, 2014	136
7.2	*Dropping in*: Allyn Burrows, Tina Packer and Timothy Douglas, 1988	140
8.1	Karen Beaumont, with participant Ray DuBois, STI, 2017	150

x Figures

8.2	Susan Dibble's Storm Dance, Month-Long Intensive, 2018	151
8.3	'Protect the Cookie,' with participants Rebecca Poretsky and Bob Wicks, Month-Long Intensive, 2016	154
8.4	Tony Simotes in *Fight* session, STI, 2016. The participant is making the sound of the physical blow with a clap or 'nap'	159
8.5	Final scene-sharing with participants Shirong Wu (Kate) and Maeve Hook (Petruchio), Month-Long Intensive, 2019	164
9.1	Kevin G. Coleman in an *Education* workshop, 1997	182
10.1	*Love's Labour's Lost*, dir. Kelly Galvin, 2018, at the Dell at The Mount	191
10.2	*SLaW*, dir. Jenna Ware, 2013: Ryan Winkles, Enrico Spada, Kelly Galvin, EBT	192
10.3	'Air broadswords' in *Stage Combat* common class, 2017	200
10.4	Fall Festival, 2017: *As You Like It*, dirs. Lezlie Lee and Ellie Bartz with Springfield Central High School	203
11.1	Riotous Youth rehearsing, 2016	218
11.2	Summer Conservatory 2019: *King John,* dirs. Caroline Calkins, Rory Hammond, Tom Jaegar, with participants Ashli Funches (King John) and Eliza Carson (Queen Elinor), Rose Footprint	220
12.1	Jennie M. Jadow (Education Programs Manager) and MaConnia Chesser (Administrative Director of Training) in *The Merry Wives of Windsor*, dir. Kevin G. Coleman, 2019	234
13.1	Tina Packer and Nigel Gore in *Women of Will*, dir. Eric Tucker, 2011	244
13.2	Miles Anderson (Malvolio) and Cloteal L. Horne (Olivia) in *Twelfth Night*, dir. Allyn Burrows, 2019	258
13.3	(a) Kevin G. Coleman as Touchstone (*As You Like It*), dir. Eleanor Holdridge, 2004; (b) as The Fool (*King Lear*), dir. Tina Packer, 2003	259
14.1	Dennis Krausnick as King Lear, dir. Rebecca Holderness, 2012	267
14.2	Allyn Burrows (Coriolanus) and Tina Packer (Volumnia), *Coriolanus* workshop production, dir. Daniela Varon, 2019	271
15.1	Dead Family and Jupiter visit Posthumus, sleeping	287
15.2	Tamara Hickey (Imogen) and Thomas Brazzle (Posthumus Leonatus)	289
15.3	Opening storytelling tableau	291
15.4	Final revelations	292
E.1	Allyn Burrows as Henry V, dir. Jonathan Epstein, 2002	298
E.2	Gala 2018: Kenneth E. Werner (Chair), Kevin G. Coleman, Tina Packer, Michael A. Miller (longtime Chair), Annette Miller (Company member), Dennis Krausnick, Adam Davis and Allyn Burrows	299
E.3	Cast of *Lovers' Spat: Round Two*, dir. Allyn Burrows, 2018	300

FOREWORD

Imagine you are walking through the woods along a river and at a bend in your path you discover a pool of water that could serve well as a swimming hole, deep, clear and inviting. You dive in and the bracing plunge takes your breath away, making you feel startled, alive and inspired to dunk yourself again. Such is the experience of the introduction to Shakespeare & Company, and its window into the myriad of possibilities waiting to be unlocked for an actor in the language of the company's namesake author.

I inherited a love of Shakespeare from my father, who as a small boy on the farm entwined his chores with the rhythm of the words. Plow a row, read a scene. Plow a row, learn a sonnet, for the recitation of which he would be given a nickel at family gatherings, no small sum for a boy in the 1920s. I also had long admired Shakespeare's pragmatism, in the accounts of his life as a theatre producer and in the structure of his verse. So when I first landed at Shakespeare & Company some 30 years ago I was moved to throw my shoulder into what was a collective effort to enliven the experience of the poetry for the artists and the audience alike in order to strike a common chord, a harmonic that resonated to the bone. As I went on to help create the 'artist manager' structure, and became an artistic associate, board member, and now these many years later, Artistic Director, I've encouraged us here to continually hearken back to the original, rabid curiosity on which Tina Packer and others founded this tireless effort: how to dig into yourself and the language, and bring the result of that endeavor up and out into the air that others breathe. This book is an opening, an overview of not just this company's history, but a record of what happens when hundreds of artists are driven to work on exceptional material, hammer and tongs, to illuminate the value of what it means to be human: to speak and to celebrate the simple, profound experience of that action.

xii Foreword

Bella Merlin and Tina Packer are exacting practitioners of their craft. As witnessed in this account they thoroughly embrace the rigors of the work, are fascinated by a person's inner workings, and are ever intrigued by the dynamics of a group, be it an audience or a company of artists. Consider these pages an invitation to experience an immersion into the invigorating pool that is Shakespeare & Company.

Allyn Burrows
Artistic Director, Shakespeare & Company
Lenox, 2019

PREFACE

Nestled in the small town of Lenox, Massachusetts, is a hive of creative activity. Shakespeare & Company (S&Co.), as this story will detail, was the brainchild of British-born, actor-director Tina Packer. Tina and I first met in 2012 at the Colorado Shakespeare Festival where I'd been hired to play Margaret in her production of *Richard III* with Nigel Gore. Having recently emigrated from the UK, I was new to the American acting scene and hadn't yet heard of Shakespeare & Company. But soon after meeting Tina, I discovered we were both from the Midlands of England (my mum was born in the same town of Wolverhampton a month before Tina) so we kind of 'knew' each other's pragmatic, 'risen working class' stock. And I instantly loved her searing intelligence, nononsense truth-telling and mischievous laugh. When she discovered I wrote books on acting, she gently suggested that I write one on Shakespeare & Company. Because my ignorance of the Company at that time was embarrassing, I declined. She also gently suggested that I take their 'Month-Long Intensive' training for mid-career professionals, held every January at their campus property in Lenox. Although I'd been working as an actor for 20-odd years at that point (including five years' training in the UK and Moscow), I'm always curious to re-tune the 'instrument.' And although Tina gave no hard sell, her voice resonated in my head for the next three years. In 2016 I took the Month-Long Intensive. That transformative month made such an impact that, at the end, I declared unequivocally, 'I'd be honored to write your book.' Later that year, I was cast in S&Co.'s summer season (no doubt a pertinent Packer-ploy to have me on site for 14 weeks); thus, I was somewhat ethnographically embedded in the Company, putting their *Training* into practice, experiencing their *Performance* processes and gaining insights into their *Education* programs. I also encountered the elephant in the room …

xiv Preface

Over the years Shakespeare & Company had apparently acquired something of a 'cultish' reputation, with the bothersome, 'Have you drunk the Kool-aid?' all too frequently asked by those 'on the outside,' so to speak. This was curious to me. Personally, I'd found the training to be wholly complementary to the training I'd received both in England and Russia (which brought together Lecoq, Brecht, Stanislavsky, Cicely Berry, Michael Chekhov, Laban, Grotowski, Keith Johnstone and many others). Likewise S&Co.'s training drew on multiple influences and was specific, playful and rigorous. Sure, the isolation in the Berkshires of New England – into which participants and artists descend for a while before returning to the world at large – might give the Company a certain mystery. Yet many a director and/or company 'retreats' into the countryside, from Staniewski's Gardzienice (founded the same year as S&Co. in 1978) to Phillip B. Zarrilli's Llanarth Group in Wales, not to mention Stanislavsky's Moscow Art Theatre and Lee Strasberg's Group Theatre during their respective evolutions: and all those (male) directors and/or their companies now feature on university curricula. Sure, some S&Co. personnel have stayed with the Company for years and actors are often hired from within the ranks: so too with, say, Steppenwolf (Chicago) or Kneehigh (Cornwall), as you can be more time efficient and creative when you share a methodology. Perhaps the root of Shakespeare & Company's 'cultish' reputation was their interest in all aspects of Shakespeare's world – including the spiritual, philosophical and emotional hardcore of human behavior. In the 1970s, Tina had been an inquisitive seeker. 'Meditation, mysticism, rebirthing, Rolfing, past lives therapy, est, primal screaming. If it was on offer,' she said, 'I'd try it – not drugs or alcohol – but any investigation into the way the mind and/or body worked.' Lots of these practices were just that – practical. est, for example, was very pragmatic:

> 'There is no Promised Land,' they told us. 'This is it.' And I got it. And it was such a relief. It's 45 years ago now, but it stayed with me through my working life, both artistically and as a manager.
>
> *(Packer discussion with Merlin, September 2019)*

With all this in mind, I wanted to do my bit in this book to unpack and clarify some of the more esoteric or immersive aspects of S&Co.'s work, which are no more unusual than many processes employed by artists curious about the human condition. Tina is (thankfully) a zealot for good theatre: she's an intellectual firebrand with passionate viewpoints and a drive that is enviable and inspiring. She's also highly irreverent as much as she is reverent. Without that zeal and irreverence she might not have survived as a female artist in the 1970s, let alone built and sustained an ever-expanding theatre institution. It's a zeal and irreverence she shares with current Artistic Director Allyn Burrows. And it's a zeal and irreverence without which they wouldn't have garnered and held the loyalty of audiences, artists, donors and volunteers.

Preface **xv**

Indeed, in a blessed synchrony, in 2016 – the year I started researching this book – a valiant team of volunteers had initiated an Oral History Archive Project. Enthused by Tina's vision, they were recording interviews with Shakespeare & Company members, sorting through carrier bags bursting with press cuttings, saving boxes of invaluable papers from moldering basements – and their task had only just begun. Without their extraordinary work my own task would have been impossible. Even then the labors have proved daunting …

First of all, Shakespeare & Company has been in existence for over 40 years. There are hundreds of performances, classes, workshops, reviews and experiences that form its history. Scores of dedicated theatre makers, educators, managers and administrators comprise its *dramatis personae*, including Kristin Linklater, who left in 1992 to pursue her pioneering voice work. There are anecdotes, personal insights, scribbled notebooks, published articles, interviews and philosophies. Where to begin? What to omit? And how to avoid inadvertently committing *lèse-majesté* by leaving someone out? How to emphasize that documents written in the twentieth century using 'mankind' and 'he' or 'him' refer in intent to the broader landscape of all human identities? And then, how to construct a linear narrative for work that is three-dimensional and experiential?

As I was grappling with these questions, I actually met Kristin Linklater in November 2018 at the Shanghai Theatre Academy where we were fellow presenters at their Second International Actor Training Forum. One poignant evening we split a pint of wine and she shared heart-warming tales of Shakespeare & Company. At the end of the evening, she said, 'When you wander down Memory Lane, you stumble across a few potholes.' And this wouldn't be a truthful tale if it didn't place a few cones around the potholes on S&Co.'s path. That said this book is *not* a history of the Company (though someone should write one very soon). It's an attempt to give a perspective (unavoidably mine) on the three pillars upon which it is built: *Training, Education* and *Performance*. This is only one perspective, of course: others in the fullness of time will write their own. This really is just the beginning.

Very early on I asked Tina to co-author. While I was happy to do the lion's share of the writing, the contents inevitably and appropriately hold large swathes of her story. Furthermore, I wanted the immediacy of her voice to appear in written versions of the 'lectures' that she has shared with training participants for years (see Chapters 3, 5 and 14). When we convened in August 2018 to consolidate the book's material, I stressed my need to have the endorsement of those concerned, particularly the three lifelong Company members, Dennis Krausnick, Kevin G. Coleman and Tina herself. She looked at me quizzically. 'Don't you realize, Bella? We give our knowledge away.' In that quizzical moment I understood why to date there is no comprehensive book on the Company. On the one hand, they've been too darned busy actually *doing* the work. On the other, they don't necessarily 'lay claim' to their wisdom. Hence *this* book (which has been described by an outside eye as 'an unabashed love letter to Shakespeare & Company,' a description I happily embrace). I'm striving xvi Preface

to fulfill in a tiny way what Packer, Coleman and Krausnick have yet to do themselves, and to flag up what the Company will continue to do under the vibrant auspices of Allyn Burrows and Managing Director Adam Davis and longtime General Manager Steve Ball.

At the end of the day, however, theatre and actor training are experiential, which is also why the founders have been nervous over the years about committing their practices to paper. So in no way is this book a replacement for that live experience. Rather, it's an open invitation for you, the reader, to find out more about the Company if you wish, through *Training*, *Education* or *Performance*. Be that as it may, we ultimately hope you'll find these words thought-filled. After all: 'Words without thoughts never to heaven go.'[1]

Bella Merlin, Ph.D.,
Los Angeles, 2019

Note

1 Shakespeare, W. (1599–1601), *Hamlet*, Act III, Scene iii, line 98, Claudius. (Line numbers will vary slightly according to which edition you use: throughout this book I have used a treasured *Oxford University Press* edition.)

ACKNOWLEDGMENTS

This book owes much to many. First, the artists, managers, administrators, technicians, grounds-people and creative beings, who run Shakespeare & Company and have sustained its 40-plus-year history providing Tina with unfathomable amounts of creativity and practical research (not least the contents of this book). With particular gratitude to Kristin Linklater, Dennis Krausnick, Kevin G. Coleman, the Board of Trustees including Chair (at the time of writing) Kenneth E. Werner and Rhea Werner, Michael A. Miller (longtime Chair) and Annette Miller (Company member), General Manager Steve Ball, the Advisory Board, Elayne Bernstein and her generous family, and all the brave-hearts who have contributed to the Company, enduring every weather at The Mount and beyond, including lifelong Company member Martin Jason Asprey, and Artistic Directors Tony Simotes (2009–2014) and Allyn Burrows (2016–present).

For this book in particular, thanks to those who gave interviews: Allison Galen, Andrew Borthwick-Leslie, Ariel Bock, Caitlin Kraft, Caroline Calkins, Chase Hauser (STI 2016), Claire Warden, Cloteal L. Horne, Dalton Hedrick (STI 2016), Dave Demke, Elizabeth Aspenlieder, Gwendolyn Schwinke, Jane Nichols, Jenna May Cass, Jenna Ware, Jennie M. Jadow, John Hadden, Jonathan Croy, Jonathan Epstein, Josh McCabe, Kholoud Sawaf, Kristin Wold, Leslie Field (STI 2016), Mariana Peters (Month-Long Intensive 2016), Michael F. Toomey, Nehassaiu deGannes, Nigel Gore, Noa Egozi, Raphael Massie, Rory Hammond, Sarah Weatherwax, Shahar Isaac, Tamara Hickey, Tom Jaegar and Victoria Rhoades. To those who offered insights for chapters, including Kelly Galvin, Ryan Winkles and Susan Dibble (who also kindly shared emails and notes). To those who read drafts of chapters, including Bessel van der Kolk, Carol Gilligan, Charline Su, James Gilligan, Lezlie Lee, Michael Nott and Kevin Vavasseur. To the S&Co. artists with whom Bella worked over the three years of writing, including Bob Wicks, Deaon Griffin-Pressley, Diane Healey, Ella

xviii Acknowledgments

Loudon, Gregory Boover, Hope Rose Kelly, Kate Abbruzzese, Kathleen Soltan, MaConnia Chesser, Steve Barkhimer, Mark Zeisler and Thomas Brazzle.

To Sarah Hancock who has filled the mightiest of roles in the Company, yet was also willing to make sense of Tina's 'terrible scrawl' while providing notes, insights and reactions on draft chapters. And to Anna Kritikos for meticulously transcribing hours of interviews.

To Catherine E. Wheeler, Jenne Young, Molly Merrihew and Katie McKellick for their abundant administrative assistance, not least with the illustrations. Photographs are reproduced courtesy of Shakespeare & Company, with thanks to Laurie Asprey for the photograph of Tina (Figure 3.1). And to MaConnia Chesser for her invaluable, eagle-eyed proof-reading.

To the extraordinary volunteers who created – and systemically sustain – the Oral History Archive Project at Shakespeare & Company. Without the tireless work of Sarah Lytle, Kristen Lochrie, Melody Mason, Sandy Bourgeois, Gail Kotler, Selina Morris, Julie Quain, Nancy Walters and their team, the writing of this book would have been impossible.

To Stacey Walker and Lucia Accorsi, our indomitable editors at Routledge/ Taylor & Francis, for their enthusiastic support and unremitting rigor in bringing this book to life so swiftly, as well as the insightful and thorough commentaries from the two anonymous reviewers. And Tina's invaluable literary agent James Levine at Levin Greenberg Rostan and Bella's ever-patient theatrical agent Natasha Stevenson at StevensonWithers Talent.

And finally to Miles Anderson – who read endless drafts; fed and watered Bella and Tina when they were deep in the throes of writing; and brought his own artistry to Shakespeare & Company in *Twelfth Night*, 2019. 'Jove and my stars be praised!'

ABBREVIATIONS

ACT	American Conservatory Theatre
ART	American Repertory Theatre
ASP	Actors' Shakespeare Project
EBT	Elayne Bernstein Theatre
est	Erhard Seminars Training
EWR	Edith Wharton Restoration, Inc.
F1	First Folio
LAMDA	London Academy of Music and Dramatic Art
NEA	National Endowment for the Arts
NMF	National Music Foundation
NYU	New York University
PIP	Performance Internship Program
RADA	Royal Academy of Dramatic Art
RILKO	Research Into Lost Knowledge Organization
RSC	Royal Shakespeare Company
SLaW	Shakespeare and the Language that Shaped a World
SPI	Summer Performance Institute
SSI	Summer Shakespeare Intensive
STI	Summer Training Institute
TPP	Tina Packer Playhouse

PROLOGUE

'To unpath'd waters, undream'd shores'[1]

We're about to embark on an adventure. One that will take us deep into the heart of a theatre company forged from a love of language and an ambitious hope that Shakespeare can contribute to the 'healing' of society, the 'feeling of positive joy'[2] (Packer). Part history, part actor-training textbook, part guide to educational pedagogy, and part performance-making manual, we're going to cover much terrain from many perspectives, as we explore what happens when words and actions align. Or in the words of Volumnia in *Coriolanus*: when 'action is eloquence.'[3]

Our story begins with two British-born females: actor-director Tina Packer and voice pioneer Kristin Linklater. They both emerged as creative spirits in the 1960s, when women's voices in British theatre had limited authority, so they each crossed the Atlantic to pursue their respective visions in the nearly New World. In the early 1970s their paths formally crossed. And their collaboration fully ignited in 1978 when they co-founded Shakespeare & Company in Lenox, Massachusetts. Their aim (as we'll see) was to manifest an inclusive, classical actor training that would unite American psychological openness with British attention to text, and where 'the voice would be restored to its rightful place as the core element in the art of acting'[4] (Packer). At that time there was no specific training in the United States for classical theatre, where the disciplines of movement, voice and text were all aimed 'at the release of the passions [...] on a larger level than domestic, everyday contemporary realities'[5] (Linklater). So Packer and Linklater would create one and infuse it into a multi-racial, multicultural theatre company.

That was over 40 years ago. The ensuing narrative surrounding Shakespeare & Company plays out like its own Renaissance drama – comedic, tragic, historical, pastoral and combinations of them all. And the *dramatis personae* exude artistic

2 Prologue

vision, political passion and romantic idealism. So, the intent here is to let myriad voices speak. Although 'Act I' sets some historical context, this book isn't a comprehensive compendium of events. Rather it's an exploration of an early 'Statement of Values that Unite Us': 'The symbiosis of performance, training, and education creates a clarity and deepening of experience critical to a healthy company, and enhances the creative impulse.'[6] So we'll look in depth at the three pillars supporting Shakespeare & Company: namely *Training*, *Education* and *Performance*.

Because the story we're embarking upon is so multi-faceted, here are some plot points to navigate the voyage ahead.

Act I: History and roots

'Act I' features the challenges (frequently faced and often overcome), the dreams (fulfilled and sometimes lost), and some of the key players, notably Kristin Linklater whose voice work infuses the Company's practice. Chapter 1: 'Visions and revisions: The Company is formed' looks at the birth of Shakespeare & Company in the 1970s, when Tina Packer brought together – in a ten-month, Ford-Foundation-funded experiment – five master-teachers steeped in the fundamental disciplines of Elizabethan theatre: namely Structure of the Verse; Voice and Language; Dance; Fight; and the Actor/Audience Relationship. Chapter 2: 'Bricks and mortar, trellis and trees: An aesthetic is realized' looks at how the places where Shakespeare & Company has lived (Edith Wharton's home, The Mount, and now the former Lenox Boys' School on Kemble Street) shaped their performance aesthetic. Chapter 3: 'Talk #1: Function of the Theatre' offers the first of three written versions of lectures – or rather 'Socratic discussions' comprising questions and answers – offered by Packer during the annual training intensives. We'll then scale the Company's first pillar: *Training*.

Act II: Training

Grow. Evolve. Advance. Become. Flourish.
Dare. Explore. Risk. Confront. Defy. Venture. Brave.
Learn. Acquire. Attain. Peruse. Uncover. Master.
Rejoice. Celebrate. Delight. Enchant. Exalt. Triumph.

These calls to action have appeared on the publicity for Shakespeare & Company's *Training* programs. And they celebrate the way in which training (beginning with Packer's Ford Foundation experiment) has always held a central place in the Company's existence. So too has the Director of Training for nearly three decades: Dennis Krausnick. Krausnick appreciates that, to the outsider, the *Training* department, 'is the most mysterious part of Shakespeare & Company's three main pillars.'[7] While *Performances* are obviously public and *Education* programs are witnessed by teachers and parents, *Training* typically happens behind closed doors. And yet, at Shakespeare & Company, it informs every level of performance. So, 'Act II' puts the *Training* center stage. It has taken various forms over the years, such as weekend 'Intensives'; workshops on *Rhetoric, Clown* and *Public Speaking*; and the Summer Training Institute. And it has attracted participants including Anna Deavere Smith, John Douglas Thompson, Keanu Reeves and Sigourney Weaver. The focus here is on the Month-Long Intensive for mid-career professionals. So in Chapter 4: 'Evolution and influences of the Month-Long Intensive,' we look at how the first iteration (initially a 'Linklater Workshop') sprang into being in December 1978, and how the pedagogy has continued to evolve ever since. Chapter 5: 'Talk #2: Actor/Audience Relationship,' offers the second of Packer's talks, looking at the heartbeat of Shakespeare & Company's aesthetic. And in Chapters 6–8 we unpack the disciplines of the core curriculum comprising *Voice Work, Body Work* and *Text Work*, and revealing how the deep veins of *Training* pump through the more visible limbs of *Performance* and *Education*.

Act III: Education

In 'Act III' we enter the award-winning world of Shakespeare & Company's *Education* department where Shakespeare's 'old English' language is seen to be '"younger" English – more outrageous, insulting, dangerous, risky, in-your-face, sexy, and playful'[8] (Coleman). Chapter 9: 'Practical pedagogy' unpacks the underpinnings of the *Education* programs, including the work of Kevin G. Coleman, longtime Director of Education. Chapter 10: 'Shakespeare in the Schools,' looks at programs including: the Northeast Regional tours; the schools residencies; the Fall Festival of Shakespeare; and the professional development workshops for teachers. Then we head out of the schools for Chapter 11: 'Shakespeare on the campus' (their summer program Riotous Youth and Shakespeare & Young Company Conservatories) and Chapter 12: 'Shakespeare in the Courts' (their celebrated program for juvenile offenders). Through these chapters we trace how *Voice Work, Body Work* and *Text Work* are explored in the *Education* programs.

Act IV: Performance

And so to the third pillar: *Performance*. Shakespeare & Company was founded as a professional entity to mount moneymaking productions. And all three lifelong Company members – Packer, Krausnick and Coleman – along with current Artistic Director Allyn Burrows, act in plays as well as directing, teaching or managing. In Chapter 13: 'The art form of performance' we ask questions about rehearsing and directing; since Packer has sustained the role of theatre director throughout the Company's 40-year existence, the meat of this chapter focuses on her idiosyncratic directing process. We revisit *Voice Work, Body Work* (including *Fight* and *Clown*) and *Text Work* (including Packer's original practice

4 Prologue

of *dropping in* a text) within the context of professional *Performance*. Chapter 14: 'Talk #3: Theatre, Therapy and Theology' comprises the last of Packer's three talks, in which she takes us on a mini-journey into theatre's significant, spiritual aspect, as celebrated by the ancient Greeks and beyond. *Spiritus* for the Elizabethans referred to 'an aerated fluid,' which did 'the work of intercommunication among the body's parts': so for Shakespeare and his contemporaries the 'soul' 'was as much physical as spiritual.'[9] This propels us into a world, both esoteric yet practical, fairytale yet politically resonant, in Chapter 15: '*Cymbeline*: A performance case study,' which in 2017 completed Packer's cycle of directing and/or acting in all of the Bard's canon.

Throughout the book, we'll see how practices and principles in *Training*, *Education* and *Performance* are continually passed on through dedicated mentorship, along the lines of Elizabethan apprenticeship.

Epilogue: 'On such a full sea are we now afloat'

Shakespeare's plays have five acts. However, Act V of Shakespeare & Company is only just beginning under the auspices of newly appointed Artistic Director and Managing Director – Allyn Burrows and Adam Davis – alongside longtime General Manager Steve Ball. In fact, it's really Act I of a whole new play. As the Company evolves into its next iteration, there promises to be many more books, articles, papers and presentations across the globe on the resilience of Shakespeare & Company, especially as their Oral History Archive Project is digitized. This volume (we repeat) is only one possible voyage into their work.

Before heading out on our adventure, a quick question that may be pricking young readers …

Why Shakespeare?

Or perhaps more specifically: 'Why should I train in Shakespeare if I really want to do television and film?' Because: 'Once you can do Shakespeare, you can do anything.'[10] Training and performing any one of his works is like running an emotional and physical marathon. Indeed, actors famed for their screen work – including Viola Davis, Tom Hanks, Helen Mirren and Chiwetel Ejiofor – return to Shakespeare to fine-tune their skills. There's a power in Shakespeare's language that can rarely be found in other scripts. And it starts with his *specificity*. As S&Co. actor Rory Hammond describes

> the specificity of thought and language makes the actor's work simple. Not *easy*. It's never easy! – But simple. What an amazing exercise you're giving your brain and your acting instrument! In fact, you're cheating yourself as an actor if you don't immerse yourself in the greatest poetry ever written, exploring all the extremes of the human condition.
>
> *(Hammond interview, August 2016)*

Prologue **5**

And those extremes exponentially expand your acting *range*: 'There is not a single emotion, a single act of love or violence that Shakespeare does not explore'[11] (Packer). Psychologically, emotionally, intellectually, 'Shakespeare goes further than anybody else – and not only that, he goes to tragic heights and comic depths.'[12] So why would you want to do anything less as an actor – on stage or screen? Whether you're striving to keep your imagination active with green or blue screen; sustaining your emotional availability between multiple takes; or searching for the stories worth telling a twenty-first-century spectator – the tools implicit in playing Shakespeare are surprisingly transferable.

Time to embark on our journey, beginning with a moment's breath …

While we were writing this book, on 26 November 2018, Dennis Krausnick died. We've chosen to keep his voice in the present tense whenever relevant, as his role in Shakespeare & Company – and especially his shaping of the *Training* – has been inspirational and instrumental. Wherever he may be in 'the undiscovered country,'[13] his presence at Kemble Street remains keenly felt, not least beneath the dogwood tree in the corner of the meadow …

Notes

1 Shakespeare, W. (1611), *The Winter's Tale*, Act IV, scene iii, line 580, Camillo.
2 '[W]hat I mean by "to heal" […] is to bring those things that are unconscious into consciousness, or those things that can't be said *to be said* in a public place, collectively, where everybody can *hear* them. So it's actually to try and *focus* what the issues are that a community needs to deal with, and within that, of course, is what […] the *individual* needs to deal with, because what happens to individuals is *reflected* in society, and how society conducts itself gets *reflected* within the individual – the microcosm of the macrocosm, as the Elizabethans would have said. What I mean when I'm talking about *healing* is that there is a feeling of positive joy.' Packer, T. (1996), 'The Function of Theater is to Heal,' transcription of Tape #1, 27 February 1996, Stockbridge, Massachusetts. S&Co. archive.
3 Shakespeare, W. (c.1609), *Coriolanus*, Act III, scene ii, line 76, Volumnia.
4 Tina Packer notebooks, 1986. S&Co. archive.
5 Linklater cited in Fuller, B. (1989), 'Actor-Centered Training,' *The Paper*, 3 August–6 September 1989, p. 23.
6 'Statement of Values that Unite Us,' c. 2000. S&Co. archive.
7 Krausnick cited in Goodwin, J. D. (2012), 'To Act, One Must Stop Acting,' *The Advocate*, 4 October 2012.
8 Coleman cited in Verzi, D. M. (2003), 'Shakespeare Through the Ages: Company Invites All to Learn,' *The Paper*, 1–15 August 2003, p. 16.
9 Smith, B. R. (ed.) (2001), *Twelfth Night: Texts and Contexts*, Bedford/St Martin's: Boston and New York, pp. 188, 187.
10 Lindsay, B. (2017), 'Why (and Where) You Should Study Shakespeare,' *Backstage*, 14 June 2017. The Month-Long and the Weekend Intensives are recommended in this article along with Juilliard and the Shakespeare Society.
11 Packer cited in Gudeon, A. (1997), 'Tina Packer,' *The Artful Mind*, April 1997.
12 Packer cited in Sanders, V. (1997), 'The Passion of Tina Packer,' *The Boston Globe*, 17 August 1997.
13 Shakespeare, W. (1599–1601), *Hamlet*, Act III, Scene i, line 80, Hamlet.

ACT I
History and roots

1

VISIONS AND REVISIONS

The Company is formed

Kristin Linklater and Tina Packer are creative powerhouses. And when they met in the 1970s, they had much in common. Both were born into a world on the brink of war and subsequently fostered pacifist perspectives. Both received progressive educations. Both knew frustration as young actresses at drama school. And both seemed fascinated with bigger-picture questions about the purpose of theatre and the process of acting. While the nuts-and-bolts of their practices form the substance of 'Acts II' and 'IV,' here we set the historical scene …

Tina Packer: 'an alchemist of intellect and emotion'[1]

Born on 28 September 1938 in a Wolverhampton workhouse-turned-hospital, Tina Packer's modest upbringing in the Midlands of England was steeped in intellectual curiosity and socio-political engagement. Edwin (a probation-officer) and Phyllis (a schoolteacher) encouraged a strong work ethic and a love of learning in their four children, who benefited from the 1944 Education Act. (Which provided education to all children through to college level at the government's expense.) Christina (Tina) – the Packers' second daughter – received a scholarship when she was 11 for a Quaker boarding school not far from Stratford-upon-Avon. And before long the school trips to the Royal Shakespeare Company made their impact, as did the Quaker qualities of non-judgment, non-violence and social justice. Then when she turned 18, her romantic idealism erupted and she ran away to Paris to be a writer. There she captivated (and was captivated by) thrice-married, American painter and sculptor Bill Waldren. The next two years were filled from dusk till dawn talking love, art and poetry, and Packer's favorite haunt became the Parisian bookshop, Shakespeare and Company. Founded in 1919, Shakespeare and Company was

10 History and roots

re-envisioned in 1964 by another American – George Whitman – as a haven for creative spirits. On benches that doubled as beds at night, writers and artists slept between the books in a 'socialist utopia masquerading as a bookstore.'[2] By definition, sadly, utopias aren't real and two years later Packer returned to London, broken-hearted. The West End theatres soon became her new haunt and an ardor for acting emerged.

From her first steps along the acting path, Packer had a vision of how impactful theatre could be. Yet her experiences didn't always match her expectations. This was poignantly true at two of Britain's most prestigious theatrical institutions: the Royal Academy of Dramatic Art (RADA) (where she was accepted as a student in 1962) and the Royal Shakespeare Company (RSC) (where she was hired as an actor in 1964).

At RADA Packer was honored with the Ronson Award for Most Promising Actress, though her experience came at a cost. While RADA is now one of the most progressive actor-training establishments in the world, much of the teaching at that time seemed stuck in tradition. The *Voice Work* emphasized rib reserve (where you expand your ribs to maximum capacity), bone props (where you literally prop your jaw open with a bone to create rounded vowels) and Standard English: yet Packer was proud of her Midlands accent and her 'risen working class' roots. The *Shakespeare Work* was lodged in what her teachers had been taught some 30 years earlier, so students were told how a speech should be spoken: yet Packer was brimming with her own ideas. The *physical training* focused on posture and poise: yet Packer sought a robust realism. While working on *As You Like It* she said to her teacher,

> 'Celia's exhausted so why don't I (as Rosalind) carry her in on my back and dump her on the floor?' My teacher thought that was a terrible idea because it was unladylike and not the way an elegant Shakespearean actress would behave.
>
> *(Packer, T., 'Training Shakespeare Actors in A Modern World: Tina Packer Talks to Helen Epstein,' 24, January 2007: 4. S&Co. archive)*

Two years later, at the RSC, Packer was working alongside such iconic actors as Paul Schofield and Ian Richardson, and she quickly became a favorite of director-scholar John Barton. In almost daily sonnet and text tutorials Barton guided her toward an understanding of humanity, and unlocked for her the vibrant structure of Shakespeare's verse. While these lessons were certainly life changing, Packer's yearning for emotional connection wasn't fulfilled at the RSC, which was generally considered 'Shakespeare Heaven' – '*the* place and *the* way to perform Shakespeare'; yet somehow it all seemed a little 'off-kilter.' At first she thought it was her own fault and she wasn't a good enough actress. Then she began to sense that maybe the rehearsal process was just too cerebral for her. Most directors were Oxbridge graduates[3] (where the Shakespeare tradition was literary, rather than visceral) and actors were rarely asked to connect the text to the inner life of the human being. And, for her, this intellectual approach seemed to be at odds with Shakespeare's heritage as an artist working right at the heart of the theatrical event. To compound the situation, she found few opportunities in the rehearsal room to offer up her own ideas: actors in general had little authority – and females even less (their chief leverage was 'tits and teeth').[4] Then, when she was playing the Princess in *Love's Labour's Lost*, Packer had an epiphany. The Princess is going through a profound transformation in her final speech when, on receiving the sudden news of her father's death, she sends the King and his chums off for years of study, and in a matter of moments evolves from a flighty, young thing to a thoughtful adult. Packer, as the actress, wasn't sensing any of this transformation beyond an intelligent delivery of the lines. And this disconnect bothered her. (It was actually while she was in India a few years later with the Jatra Group that she got to perform the Princess's speech to a packed house of non-English speakers – and then she had 'a real experience of the desire to speak …'[5] But that's another story …)

Packer left the RSC aged 26 and was cast as Dora Spenlow opposite Ian McKellen in *David Copperfield* (BBC, 1966). During early filming, she discovered that she and her husband Laurie Asprey were expecting a baby, and on 2 November 1966 their son Martin Jason was born. Within months, she was back at work playing leading roles in towns around Britain and at London's Royal Court. She also starred with Cliff Richard in the musical film *Two a Penny* (1967) and endured a yeti attack as scientist Anne Travers in the hit series *Doctor Who* (1968). And while a lucrative career was burgeoning, nothing satisfied her creatively on screen or stage:

> Once you get over the thrill of being on the telly and people congratulating you the next day and being at the Royal Shakespeare [Company] I came up against the question of *what theatre is about*. And it wouldn't go away. I had to just keep on asking it.
>
> *(Packer cited in Goodwin, J. D., 'Tina Packer: A Most Remarkable lady [sic] in Good Company,'* Shakespearescene, Summer 2008)

To get to the bottom of that question she would need to escape – from popstars and yetis, and everything in between.

In fact, Packer reached saturation point while filming Henry James' *The Heiress*, and she realized that she either had to get out of acting entirely '*or stop complaining and do what you want to do.*'[6] So she left both acting and husband to contemplate her real dream: How to create theatre that honors its transformative potential. She knew the source material had to be Shakespeare, as his plays address the most profound questions about being human. But since she hadn't been able to probe those questions deeply enough at the RSC, she would have to develop her own approach to the texts. And that meant creating a dedicated ensemble of which she would be the director, so that her thoughts about the

12 History and roots

power of theatre might actually bear some authority. It was time to learn how to direct …

In 1971 Packer approached the London Academy of Music and Dramatic Art (LAMDA), and despite her nascence as a director, they hired her for 12 plays in two years, including six Shakespeares. Thus she taught herself to direct *in* the studio *with* students in one production, wham-bam, straight after another. And this intensity led her to several epiphanies (all of which would impact on the ethos behind Shakespeare & Company). First of all, she realized the *interdependence of actor training and rehearsing*, since – in between rehearsals – her students were taking parallel classes (in disciplines including fight and dance) (see Chapter 8).

Her second epiphany was *the actor/audience relationship*. In the intimate theatre at LAMDA, Packer could focus on what was actually 'happening to the human beings up there *on stage*.'[7] Which in turn sharpened her attention to what was happening (or not) to the human beings *in the auditorium*. And it dawned on her how challenging it had been in the immense auditorium at the RSC to reach the back row with any nuance (see Chapter 5).

Packer's third epiphany entailed the *voice*. She had always felt that actors 'should be able to use their voices far more presciently' than was often the case.[8] And in this respect, LAMDA proved to be the ideal laboratory, as it was the practical-research environment for voice guru Iris Warren and her talented student-turned-teacher Kristin Linklater. Although Linklater had moved to the United States by the time Packer arrived at LAMDA, she nonetheless found herself alongside vocal teachers David Smuckler and Karen Grassle, who were likewise exploring how to free the natural voice. (More anon.) And through her self-created, director training here at LAMDA, Packer began to find her *own* voice, as a director and an actor trainer, both of which would be invaluable skillsets for her envisioned theatre company. The next step in realizing her dream was to seek out Kristin Linklater.

Kristin Linklater: 'the finder of hidden depths, laughter and magic'[9]

Kristin Linklater's seminal 'Voice progression' has redefined the teaching and practice of voice work across the globe. It's vibrantly detailed in *Freeing the Natural Voice*[10] and taught extensively via her rigorous, designation program.

Born on 22 April 1936 to literary giant Eric and actress-turned-activist Marjorie in Scotland's Orkney Islands, Linklater attended the progressive St. Leonards School, Fife (established in 1877 so that girls might receive as good an education as their brothers). She first went to LAMDA to train as an actress; then in 1957 began Voice Production training under the tutelage of Iris Warren. Warren's coaching was revolutionary. She taught voice from the inside out rather than the outside in: in other words, how do we *hear the person*, rather than *listen to the voice*? It was 'the emotional roots of voice'[11] that interested her, and this was a provocative, new way of approaching the discipline. Previously, voice coaching was more or less technical and straightforward: you needed enough *volume* to be heard on the back row; crisp *articulation* to convey text; and a *range of dynamics* so that the audience could enjoy listening to you. The actor's voice was considered 'a musical instrument to be well managed and expertly played. But [Warren] was dealing with successful actors on the West End stage who were losing their voices through the effort and strain of pushing for those desired effects'[12] (Linklater). Clearly, the human instrument wasn't being played properly: so Warren set about figuring out its proper use. It was apparently while working with a Freudian analyst in the 1930s that she discovered a direct connection between breath, body and emotions: if we hold our breath and tense our bodies, we restrict our voices and suppress our emotions. (And *vice versa*: if we suppress our emotions, we constrict our breath.) In fact, she discovered that our voices actually *change* when we're given permission to connect breath to sound to vocal expression. Warren's exercises encouraged actors to find the origins of their words deep inside their *emotional bodies* rather than regulating them through their abdominal and intercostal muscles.[13] And thus, she refocused voice training *away* from the technical apparatus of the human body and *toward* the psychological underpinnings of why we trap our voices in the first place.

These were the principles that Kristin Linklater would further evolve. Training first under Warren and then working as a voice coach in her own right, she taught at LAMDA for six years. During which time she crafted her practice-based research into human communication. And for 15 years – between 1963 (when she moved to the States) and 1978 (when she co-founded Shakespeare & Company) – she investigated ways of freeing the natural voice, by working with students and professionals in a variety of American venues.

In fact, Linklater's emigration to the USA was full of opportunities. The day after arriving in New York City she was hired by the new Lincoln Center's repertory theatre, and soon thereafter created her own studio. Given the dearth of good voice teachers, the theatre industry was hungry for her skill and vision, not least because several large American theatre complexes were built in the 1960s and 1970s using concrete and fabrics that were utterly unsupportive of the actors' voices. (Just like London's National Theatre, which was built in 1976.) So Linklater's understanding of the human instrument was vital for actors to do their job in these challenging venues without wrecking their voices. At the same time she was spurred by the revolutions emerging in American acting styles, which lined up physically and aesthetically with freeing the natural voice:

> Iris's emotion-based voice work spoke the same psycho-physical language as the Method and over the next years, I developed her techniques in the rich climate of psycho-physical exploration that became the human potential movement of the 1960s, 70s and 80s.
>
> (Linklater, 'The Art and Craft of Voice (and Speech) Training',
> *www.linklater.com*)

14 History and roots

The United States was certainly a propitious home for Linklater. She was inspired by the political movements that activated the era and she accelerated her research into human communication. In 1964 she secured a Rockefeller Foundation award to formulate a one-year Voice Training program. And a year later in 1965, leading actor trainer Ted Hoffman invited her onto the faculty at New York University, where she remained Master Teacher of Voice until 1977. Throughout these years, she made a major impact on American and Canadian theatre, training actors in venues such as the Denver Center (Colorado), Stratford (Ontario), the Guthrie Theatre (Minneapolis), the Negro Ensemble Company, La MaMa and the Open Theatre (all in NYC). Within each environment she was able to refine her way of systematically releasing actors – physically and psychologically – so that they could inhabit their own bodies and actually *experience* sound and word. In 1972 the Ford Foundation funded her to write what would eventually become *Freeing the Natural Voice*. (And she also met Tina Packer.)

Never ceasing to explore, Linklater founded a three-year program in 1975 with experimental theatre maker Joseph Chaikin and leading actor trainer Peter Kass. It was called the Working Theatre, and here she shifted her focus from coaching *actors* to training *voice teachers* through movement, voice and text. For many years Linklater maintained her connection with Peter Kass, who, of Russian descent, was credited with bringing Stanislavsky's psychological 'system' to the NYU graduate theatre program,[14] where he taught during the 1960s and 1970s. Through his teaching he provoked depths of emotional truth and self-questioning in his students, among whom were two young Jesuits (both crucial players in our unfurling narrative): Dennis Krausnick and Kevin G. Coleman.

And so it was that in 1972 Kristin Linklater first encountered Tina Packer, who had crossed the Atlantic to meet her. Six years later they co-founded Shakespeare & Company in Lenox, Massachusetts, at which point Linklater left New York and moved with her young son Hamish to the Berkshires of New England. There, the two feisty females shared their passions about acting, which included a mutual fascination with ancient Greek theatre. For the Greeks

> the job of the actor was to go onstage and, by creating harmonious sounds, reinforce the harmonies of the spheres. This is a role that involves far more than telling stories or enlightening people or serving as a vehicle for their catharsis. It can be achieved only by *the alignment of the body and the soul*.
>
> *(Linklater cited in Epstein, 1985: 40, (my emphasis))*

Indeed, acting for the Greeks was a kind of 'physio-spiritual practice.' And the way the actors used their bodies and voices worked directly on the audience, helping them to heal themselves (through *catharsis*) by experiencing particular sound vibrations. Linklater and Packer applied these ancient Greek principles within the burgeoning Shakespeare & Company, as they investigated the *function of the theatre* (see Chapter 3) and *the actor/audience relationship* (see Chapter 5).

Kristin Linklater spent 14 years at S&Co. (where the work remains infused with her practices). In 1992, as her son grew older and she sought new schooling possibilities, she left to take senior positions at Emerson College (Boston) and then with Columbia University's graduate acting program. After 50 years in the States, she returned to her roots in the Orkneys to establish the Kristin Linklater Voice Centre in 2013. There, in the remote beauty of the Scottish Isles, she teaches voice teachers to teach actors and become Designated Linklater Teachers. A fiercesome intellect and an exacting practitioner, she – like Packer – has devoted her life to probing the big questions about human interaction:

> Why does the voice not do its communicative job better? Why is there such interruption and restriction in the neuro-physiological pathway between brain and body? Where is the prohibition stored in the brain? Why can't I, the teacher, intervene more directly to clear the tangled paths between emotion, breath and voice so that dramatic communication is filled with authenticity?
> *(Linklater, 'The importance of daydreaming,'* American Theatre, *January 2010)*

It's small wonder that, in 1972, something synchronous should happen between these two artists, both battling with complex questions about the nature of authentic expression …

FIGURE 1.1 Kristin Linklater teaching a workshop in the early years

16 History and roots

The British-American fusion

Among Tina Packer's students at LAMDA in the early 1970s were several Americans on a Fulbright 'study abroad' program, and she appreciated their direct, emotional response to plays without the edge of irony that so often laced British acting at the time. Growing increasingly confident in her evolving methodology (as a director and actor trainer), she started seeking financial backing to launch her dream company. 'Why don't you come to America,' said student Dion Anderson, 'and see if you can get money there? My ex-wife works at the Ford Foundation. She'll introduce you.'[15] Within days, the 34-year-old Packer was on a flight to NYC, where she aimed to meet with the Program Officer for the Division of Humanities and Arts, Richard Kapp, and the primary, potential master-teacher for her company, Kristin Linklater.

On a crisp, autumn evening, Packer arrived at Linklater's East Village apartment wearing an orange, ankle-length, Laura Ashley dress. With her infectious laugh and unshakable belief that her project should be funded, she convinced the somewhat skeptical Linklater that – *sans* contacts, celebrity or American citizenship – she would secure a Ford Foundation grant and found her own Shakespeare company. Linklater flagged up the obstacles that stood between an unknown British director and American money. But she was intrigued by Packer and struck by 'her energy, her intelligence, and perhaps most of all, by her drive.'[16] As a result, Linklater agreed to serve as one of the British master-teachers 'in the unlikely event that a company was formed.'[17]

That unlikely event would, indeed, come to pass. Although Packer had no idea how tough it was to win Ford Foundation funding, she set off to see Richard Kapp, who advised her that he couldn't do anything for her without seeing her work. Undeterred she sent him her 'Idea Behind the Plan,' in which she articulated more cogently her British-American vision:

> American and British theatres dominate the world. As a generalization, the great strength of the American theatre lies in its energy and the directness with which it uses speed, violence and uncomplicated moral argument, all grounded in an ever-present promise of material wealth. The British strength is laconic use of form, accurate study of character and verbal agility.
>
> *(Packer, 'The Idea Behind the Plan,' 1971, S&Co. archive)*

Contemporary theatre, she argued, merely titillated the audience's sensory perceptions rather than seeking out the depths of the human soul. And if the theatrical experience had any chance of making a more profound impact – if theatre makers had any desire to 'make conscious the unconscious, to reveal the emotions and name their source'[18] – then both the *voice* and the *ear* had to be engaged. That meant the *actors' language* had to ignite the *audience's listening*. And

Visions and revisions   **17**

at the heart of such dynamic communication lay the vibrational impact of both raw sound and spoken words:

> Sound is transitory and emotive. [...] It acts upon the whole body and aligns, vibrationally *that without* with *that within.* [...] The only way to free ourselves from our suppressed or unconscious emotional states is through [spoken] *words*; the only way to define, as best we can, our philosophical positions and be understood by others, is through [spoken] words.
>
> *(Packer, 'The Idea Behind the Plan,' 1971)*

With this in mind, Packer's 'Plan' laid out her British-American fusion. While American theatre acknowledged 'mankind's' need to make its mark upon the world, European theatre celebrated classical form and values:

> By classical *form*, I mean balance and harmony in relation to the physical and spiritual dimensions of man [*sic*]; by classical *values*, the acknowledgement that all men are on a journey, are part of a greater whole, and are driven by forces larger than the smaller self.
>
> *(Packer, 'The Idea Behind the Plan,' 1971)*

Yet British theatre, mourned Packer, seemed to have lost its connection with those classical ideals, falling instead into semantics, irony and understatement. If she could bring the American and British cultures together – digging deep into the differences and exposing the common ground beneath – she might (she proposed ambitiously) create a regenerative theatre that could eclipse 'all other moments or effects,' because every actor would then be a 'teacher of the world':

> It is at the point where an actor can consciously create himself [*sic*] to be a human being on all levels that *he becomes a great teacher*, and that *the role language plays in our lives becomes apparent.* [...] It comes when an actor is so focused in his energy, so totally in touch with his thoughts and emotions, when he has a body and voice attuned to expressing his state, words to express his purpose, that he takes away all resistances from the beholder and recreates within [the beholder] a comparable state. The power of the word, then, is uniting and total. If, at this point, insight to the nature of man is accurately offered, *the only completion possible for the beholder is to look at the content of his own life.*
>
> *(Packer, 'The Idea Behind the Plan,' 1971, (my emphasis))*

This was no small ambition. For Packer, the entire *raison d'être* of the theatrical event would be nothing less than the empathic unity of actor and audience as a means for social change. And the words through which this far-reaching ambition could be achieved would be Shakespeare's:

18 History and roots

> He holds the new perceptions of time and space; he writes in classical
> form; he combines aggression and poetry; not least, he is our roots. [...] It
> is only within the truth and physical immediacy of Shakespeare's language
> that an actor can find the atavistic depths of his [sic] self. Shakespeare is
> the marathon of theatre – the supreme test emotionally, physically,
> spiritually.
>
> *(Packer, 'The Idea Behind the Plan,' 1971)*

'The time is propitious for such a venture,' she urged, 'especially in the new
world. [...] If the company can remain truly honest with itself and its audience,
it will become a court for playwrights, scriptwriters, T.V. stars, teachers and
philosophers ... and a joy for people.'[19] This 'Plan' wasn't just a letter for funding. It was an ardent call to action. And Packer was addressing the very question
that had been haunting her for years: *What is theatre about?*

Kapp was hooked. A musician himself, he understood how Packer was working with the impact of sound. So he arranged to meet her next time he was in
London and see her work at LAMDA. Which he did. Thereupon, he swiftly set
about helping her craft an application to the Ford Foundation. They reconfigured some of the ardent ambitions in her initial 'Plan' and reframed them as
a practice-based experiment. Packer's fundamental research question would be:
*What made the Elizabethan theatre so vibrant that it could endure for four hundred
years?* And to answer this question, she would explore five key elements from
Elizabethan theatre: (1) structure of the verse; (2) voice and language; (3) fight;
(4) movement; and (5) the actor/audience relationship. She would be the Principal Investigator, working as the director of a British-American company
(which eventually would also include a South African and a Canadian). And she
would conduct her experiment by combining the rehearsal and performance of
Shakespeare plays with actor training led by invited master-teachers. The experiment would be carried out over ten months: four months' training in the War-
wickshire village of Alcester (near the RSC in Stratford-upon-Avon, so that
John Barton could be among her master-teachers, and the actors could experience the atmosphere of Shakespeare's rural stomping ground). Then to America:
first to the O'Neill Center in Waterford, Connecticut; and then to East Hamp-
ton in Long Island, to prepare a production of *The Taming of the Shrew* for the
Performing Garage, NYC. And Packer's referees in the grant application were
Peter Hall and Trevor Nunn, directors of the National Theatre and the RSC,
respectively. If her application were successful, the Ford Foundation grant
would afford her the time, energy and physical bodies with which to experiment
and, thereby, develop contemporary training methods for acting Shakespeare
that might reignite theatre's potential to improve (if not 'heal') society. Kapp
knew that the funding application would be unusual for the Ford Foundation, as
they typically support established American theatres and practitioners. Yet the
selling point was Packer's compelling case for creating a classical actor-training
system for Americans.

She submitted her application to the Ford Foundation in October 1972. And sure enough: she was awarded $142,000 (the equivalent of nearly $854,000 in 2019). This princely sum was 'testament to her passion, vision, persuasiveness and fearlessness of risk, and to a willingness to surrender her life to an all-out involvement in her artistic goals.'[20] Only four months later in February 1973, a team – comprising 15 actors, three stage managers, and five professional instructors led by Kristin Linklater – began their work in Alcester, training from dawn to dusk to find their personalized way of 'owning' Shakespeare's language.[21] In June 1973, they moved to Connecticut for the American stint of the experiment. And thus it was that Shakespeare & Company began to forge its idiosyncratic blend of *Training* and *Performance*, created by the disciplines of the *five master-teachers*.

The master-teachers

Joining Kristin Linklater were Packer's colleagues from the RSC and LAMDA: John Broome (choreographer and movement teacher); B. H. Barry (fight director); and John Barton (Packer's mentor in text analysis). And, completing the circuit, was Linklater's colleague from LAMDA, Trish Arnold (pioneering movement practitioner). All of them were artists in their own right and could, therefore, take the training in whichever direction they chose, like 'streams coming from disparate sources to form a river'[22] (Packer). The disciplines are detailed in 'Act II': here are the *dramatis personae* ...

John Barton and Structure of the Verse

John Barton had also co-founded a theatre company: it was the Royal Shakespeare Company with Peter Hall in 1960. He was renowned for his insightful love of language and structure, the roots of which could be traced back to 1948 and his student days at King's College, Cambridge. Among his English professors was the literary critic F. R. Leavis, who had inspired the idea that literature exists in the invisible world between the writer's words and the reader's imagination. Barton's main mentor was George 'Dadie' Rylands (the then unusual hybrid of professional actor and university don), who had written an influential publication, *Words and Poetry* (1928), flagging up the way in which words play off each other in Shakespeare. Inspired by his mentor, Barton's own passion for Shakespeare soon escalated from his first major role as Sir Toby Belch at Cambridge (1950) to his co-founding of the RSC ten years later.

Barton devoted his life to unlocking Shakespeare. He recognized all too clearly how panic-stricken actors become facing the poetry, and he understood 'the habit of mind' needed by directors in 'the hurly-burly' of a rehearsal room: 'It is not enough for a director to speak true. He must reach and help the actors with whom he is working, and if he does not do so then he fails them'[23] (Barton). So instrumental was Barton in Packer's understanding of verse

20 History and roots

structure that she wanted him to teach her experimental theatre company in 1973 how to spot 'the clues in the written text by speaking the verse and examining the implications of punctuation, line endings and meter.'[24] To this day, John Barton's approach remains a critical part of Shakespeare & Company's methodology, the baton passing to Packer, who has been disseminating the knowledge for decades through actors in the rehearsal room and students in the studio.

John Broome and Movement/Dance

Barton's colleague at the RSC was choreographer and movement teacher John Broome, who had also taught Packer at RADA: he was, therefore, another top choice for master-teacher. Dance and music are fundamental parts of the Elizabethan World Picture: 'Nothing exists without music; for the universe is said to have been framed by a kind of harmony of sounds, and the heaven itself revolves under the tones of that harmony.'[25] In the 'cosmic dance' Elizabethans believed that all beings (mortal, celestial and divine) are carefully choreographed in the motion of life: 'The path of each is different, yet all the paths together make up the whole'[26] (like Packer's cadre of master-teachers). While directing at LAMDA, Packer had witnessed how a dance changes the energy on the stage. So she turned to Broome as a natural master-teacher for the Ford Foundation experiment because, fueled by his exuberance, actors forgot whether or not they could dance: they simply celebrated the movement of their bodies through space.

Broome had been a classical dancer at Sadlers Wells and the Royal Ballet from age 15, before training with Sigurd Leeder from the Ballet Jooss in Weimar Germany. And here he transitioned from ballet to modern dance, which for him was closer in style to the actor's art, requiring 'a more expressive view of the body'[27] (Broome). Through the Jooss–Leeder training, he recognized how *structured form* actually leads to *free flow*. In fact, you could say a choreographed dance is a kind of physical equivalent of Shakespeare's iambic pentameter: both have a very disciplined form, which (paradoxically) then allows the performer to be spontaneously free. When Broome formed his own company in 1950, he faced a dearth of trained dancers, so he added drama students to the ensemble. And lo! – He began his particular style of 'actors dancing.' Instead of dwelling on correctness, he would 'hand out the steps inch by inch,' giving actors a chance to excel in each moment until eventually, by means of his mischievously 'sneaky approach,' they were performing entire dance pieces[28] (Dibble). From 1969 to 1974, he served as movement director at the RSC, where productions included Buzz Goodbody's *King John* with Patrick Stewart (1970) and John Schlesinger's *Timon of Athens* (1965), in which Broome had Packer prancing on a table as the Courtesan as if she'd been dancing all her life!

Broome's contribution to Packer's Ford Foundation venture has shaped Shakespeare & Company's aesthetic enormously, with dance as *storytelling*;

FIGURE 1.2 John Broome teaching first Intensive, January 1979
Photo: Joel Librizzi

reenactment of the Elizabethan *social structure*; and *release*. To this day, performances in the *Training* and *Education* programs, as well as the mainstage productions, often end with a dance to uplift the spirit and restore social order. Broome passed the baton to colleague Susan Dibble, who in turn shares the work with faculty members Victoria Rhoades and Kristin Wold.

B. H. Barry and Fight

Violence in Shakespeare's plays is everywhere, as it is in society. Therefore, stage fight was an essential component in Packer's 1973 experiment. And the natural choice for master-teacher was B. H. Barry, with whom she had worked at the RSC and LAMDA. She knew that (as with dance) something 'changed in the energy of theatrical experience when you added fight, and the energy that the good fighter needed was the energy that a good actor needed'[29] (Packer).

Barry Halliday (B. H.) trained at London's Corona Academy of Stage Training, where he studied mime. Mime revealed to him the power of the body to convey character and emotion, and this became the basis of his Fight Work. Having learned swordplay from Errol Flynn's stunt double Patrick Crean, Barry had been working on fights since 1959. There was a tendency at that time for stage fights to be 'stuck on' to the dramatic narrative in order to ratchet up the audience's excitement: 'the play stopped, the fight took place like a cabaret piece, then the play went on.'[30] While teaching at Central School of Speech and Drama, however, Barry met Bill Hobbs (with whom he created the fights for Roman Polanski's 1971 film *Macbeth*). And together they intricately wove fight sequences into dramatic narrative, so that no longer were fights 'just for

22 History and roots

show, now they would drive story and character.'[31] This evolution completely changed the way that 'fight coordinators' or 'fight arrangers' were appreciated in British film and theatre. Their titles changed to 'fight directors' and, led by Henry Marshall (a fencing master at RADA), Hobbs and Barry established the Society of British Fight Directors. As well as working at various drama schools (including LAMDA and RADA), Barry was fight director at the RSC between 1968 and 1973: 'Shakespeare never, ever puts in a fight unless there is some reason. Either it will be to further the story or the characters.'[32] Which raises the essential questions: How are the fights an extension of dialogue? What happens to a character when words no longer serve them and they transmute their thoughts into violence? And therefore, 'If you *remove* the fight from the play what would be missing from the plot? Or, if you remove the fight from the actors which facets of their characters would be missing?'[33]

Packer's belief that the function of theatre was to regenerate and heal convinced her that actors needed to explore the extremes of Shakespeare's violence while remaining wholly safe. Barry's own interest in the project was piqued by the idea of forging a British-American training: 'There's a kind of urgency [in America], everything is quicker. The American actor is more available physically than the English one.'[34] And yet the psychological truth of the American Method at the time wasn't always conducive to safe fights: 'The popular American acting process is to act from inside of the body. If you can feel it, then the audience will believe you are "for real." Unfortunately, [...] one cannot perform a stage fight "for real."'[35] And so – like Barton (with the structure of the verse) and Broome (through dance) – Barry foregrounded dramatic *form*, one of his mantras being 'Through form there is freedom.'[36]

Since emigrating in 1973, Barry has had a wide-ranging impact in the USA. He influenced the creation of the American Association of Fight Directors, and was one of two directors petitioning American Actors' Equity Association for designated fight directors and daily fight calls. He mentored ten actors in the early days, each of whom studied with him for three to six years to direct fights and teach safely. And one of these mentees was original S&Co. member and then Artistic Director Tony Simotes, who in turn mentored fight teachers (in *Training* and *Education*), including Martin Jason Asprey, Corinna May, Claire Warden and Edgar Landa. The baton passes.

Trish Arnold and Movement

Completing the team of master-teachers was movement pioneer, Trish Arnold. Arnold followed a similar career trajectory to Broome, training at Sadler's Wells Royal Ballet School and performing with the Royal Ballet, before working closely with Jooss and Leeder's company. In 1955, Arnold joined the staff at LAMDA just as the 'angry young men' of British theatre were shifting contemporary styles toward something more emotionally connected.[37] In a physical manifestation of the 'angry' movement – and working alongside Iris

Warren as voice coach – Arnold evolved a new technique specifically for actors, which became known as 'Pure Movement.' Pure Movement encouraged actors to use their breath, follow their impulses, free their bodies from their daily habits, liberate their imaginations, and thus find all manner of new ways of expressing themselves. At the heart of this technique is a series of physical stretches and swinging movements (in which you simply give in to gravitational swings from your shoulder joints, hip sockets, etc.). And these swings (the physical counterpart to Linklater's 'Voice progression') 'begin to loosen the muscles of your throat and open your throat for a much larger expression of yourself'[38] (Krausnick). And herein lay the synergy between Arnold's approach and the other master-teachers, as she strove to *free the natural human being*:

> movement can be one of the hardest parts of training for an actor [...] and TV gives the young aspirant the idea that to appear 'natural' is all that is needed. Actually, no acting is natural. I believe to appear 'natural,' actors have to give up some of the habits they have accumulated. The posture is hard to change because what is habitual is safe. They have to unlock their expressive, imaginative body.
>
> *(Arnold cited in Snow, 2017)*

Arnold's Pure Movement 'is now the basis of movement departments in many major British and US drama schools,'[39] and her impact on directors and choreographers on stage and screen has been significant. She remained senior faculty at S&Co. for many years, also teaching mask work and passing her baton to faculty members including Karen Beaumont, Charls Sedgwick Hall and Kristin Wold. In 1978 she brought to S&Co. her colleague and clownmaster Merry Conway, whose work linked voice to text to the animated body.[40] (More anon ...)

And thus in 1973 the five master-teachers of Linklater, Barton, Broome, Barry and Arnold were recruited by Tina Packer to contribute to the five major elements of Elizabethan theatre in the first iteration of Shakespeare & Company. Packer herself completed the circuit as director, connecting Shakespeare's texts to the actors' own experiential repertoires. And in the fullness of time, other influential teachers joined the core faculty, including Neil Freeman with the First Folio (see Chapter 4). And the Company's training remains ever evolving.

The slings and arrows of the 1973 experiment

There were many successes arising from Packer's ten-month Ford Foundation experiment, not least the synergetic, practice-based research between the master-teachers. As they took part in each other's workshops, they collectively discussed how their respective pedagogies integrated to make Shakespeare come alive in every moment on the stage. And they made some valuable discoveries:

24 History and roots

First of all, Linklater evolved her approach to *Sound and Movement*, a series of classes that coupled Arnold's Pure Movement with her own process of 'freeing the natural voice.' Her aim was to help actors experience their voices throughout their whole bodies and vibrate sound through their bones (see Chapter 6).

Second, Packer experimented with ways of *planting language in the body*. To which end, she and Linklater cut up Shakespeare's sonnets – 'William Burroughs style' – and explored how an actor's breath can connect images to feelings in a free-associating manner, rather than the linear, logical context of a line.[41] And thus were sown the first seeds of her original practice *dropping in* (see Chapter 7).

Third, the troupe tested *the actor/audience relationship*, giving public performances in villages outside Stratford-upon-Avon with little more than actors, audience and Shakespeare's words. And answers began to emerge to Packer's primary research question: 'What made Elizabethan theatre so vibrant that it could endure for four hundred years?' One crucial answer was: the ability to *reveal* yourself through language and voice, and experience how that revelation reverberates in your listener.

All in all, the four months of training in the UK were very productive. The work was invigorating and the methodological discussions were lively. It was when the troupe moved from Alcester to America that the cracks began to show …

Tina Packer has always been egalitarian by nature. Her distaste for authority and a potent anti-establishmentarianism spring deep from her 'risen working class' upbringing. So, as the team's leader, she encouraged lots of collective decision-making. Yet a leader has to lead. But because she had little experience of group dynamics at that time, she found the more democratically she tried to run the company, the more the company rebelled. It was almost as if the act of freeing the human voice – without demanding people take the responsibility that comes with that freedom – was a double-edged sword.

Then came the professional pressures. The minute the troupe left the comparative safety of the experiment and headed out toward commercial venues, typical actorly anxieties arose. For some of the Americans in particular, it was now a question of who had which role? What would the critics say? And would they secure an agent? When one company member quit a month before going into New York, Packer's two mentors – George White at the O'Neill Center and Lloyd Richards at the Playwrights' Conference – encouraged her to cut the collective meetings and just get on with the play. In fact, her decision to seize the leadership was to everyone's relief. And the prototype Shakespeare & Company stayed together to perform *The Taming of the Shrew* at four American venues, opening at the O'Neill Center, Connecticut, to a positive reception and closing at the Performing Garage, NYC. Then, at the end of the funding period, the troupe disbanded.

Despite the critical success, Packer was disillusioned with human behavior: 'Here were the people I was working so closely with to do the thing dearest

Visions and revisions **25**

to [us] – destroying one another.'[42] And, 'I just couldn't bear this idea that what I perceived to be a socialist model didn't bloody well work.'[43] Utopias – particularly socialist ones – don't by definition exist. And depressed by the breakdown of the company's communication, Packer flew back to London in November 1973 to deal with family matters, not least the untimely death of her lover Austin Hyslop. There followed a winter of deep discontent, a 'fallow' period in which she hid out with her young son in Suffolk and ruminated upon the whole experience:

> I had had my opportunity to experiment with the kinds of things I thought would work in theater and they did. But the things that I thought about life didn't work at all.
>
> I thought that if you gave an individual the tools of his [sic] trade, good living conditions, and the opportunity to speak his mind, happiness would automatically ensue. Those ten months had shown me that was not true, that unconscious drives were far more powerful in everyone – including myself – than any idealistic vision of human behavior.
>
> *(Packer cited in Epstein, 1985: 50–51)*

Most of us learn by failing, and Packer was certainly willing to learn: 'I smacked my face so hard, but I would never have given up that kind of idealism and become much more pragmatic if I hadn't gone to the Nth degree on it.'[44] It was once again the combined forces of Richard Kapp at the Ford Foundation and Kristin Linklater in NYC that provided catalysts in Packer's life. And the fallow months ripened into fecund years ...

Fecund years of global voyaging

Underpinning Shakespeare & Company is a deep desire for fathoming human behavior. Sometimes those on the peripheries have viewed this search for knowledge as suspicious: were they actually a bunch of hippies dancing naked in the moonlight? (see Preface). In fact, the search is no more mystical or strange than any detailed text analysis or creative fascination, and it comes with a whole bundle of playful rigor and natural curiosity. It's also a search for knowledge that's best explored by simultaneously and contrapuntally *voyaging out* into the world and *reflecting in* on yourself. And for the next two years, this was precisely the voyaging on which Packer embarked. To shed some light on a few myths, we should understand (albeit briefly) the context of that voyaging ...

In 1974, Packer returned to NYC to see Kapp, who was helping her craft a Travel and Study application to the Ford Foundation. She had been inspired to make the application by Head of the Arts and Humanities Division, W. McNeil Lowry, an instrumental force in American theatre who had been impressed by Packer's *Taming of the Shrew* and wanted her to pursue her research.[45] In order for her to understand more rigorously other world views

26 History and roots

and cultures, her Travel and Study proposal included stays in: India (to explore the correlation of Sanskrit texts to music and rhythm); Israel (to meet movement specialist Moshe Feldenkrais); Italy (to study *commedia dell'arte* and clowning traditions); France (to witness Peter Brook's multi-ethnic, multi-national company in action); Denmark (to understand more fully the integration of professional practice and multi-cultural training as modeled by Odin Teatret), a return to the United States; and then onto Brazil (to experience the burgeoning political theatre with its interactive actor/audience relationship). While she and Kapp were working on the application, Kristin Linklater reached out to her about weekend workshops that were sweeping America known as est training. Around this time, Packer also met Feldenkrais teacher Ruthi Alon, 'and she said, "Let's do it together." So we did.'[46]

Although est has received controversial press over the years (and we'll look at it further in Chapters 4 and 5), Packer found its immediacy and pragmatism very useful at that time in shifting her creative tectonic plates: 'They take you on a huge journey, unpacking the way the psyche and body work. Then they say, "This is it. This is life. Stop looking for a magic answer. Here and now: that *is* the answer!"'[47] (Packer). This pragmatism was liberating: she'd felt creatively 'stuck' since the failure of the 1973 experiment and est 'unstuck' her. And this change in perspective altered her journey over the next two years. She took many paths – esoteric, philosophical and artistic – not so much to 'achieve enlightenment,' but to be curious. She screamed in Primal Therapy. She communed at séances. She scribbled at automatic writing sessions. She learned more about the ancient Greeks and the way in which amphitheatres brought communities together in dancing and chanting, and how they connected to the gods through the vibrations of special brass urns.[48] She found herself in the Research Into Lost Knowledge Organization. She was rebirthed (literally and metaphorically). And she became (in her own words) a 'New Age junkie.'[49] All of these experiences were not only vibrant aspects of living on the planet in the 1970s, but also informative ways of exploring the bodymind union. What's more, they gave Packer insight into the power that language has to move energy *through* people's bodies. And this in turn emboldened her understanding of how actors might breathe life into a playwright's words in the actual process of *Performance* (as we'll see throughout this book). Near the start of her *inner* voyaging, Packer's Travel and Study grant was successfully awarded and, in mid-1974, she set off on her *global* voyaging. She began her trip in India – in Swami Muktananda's ashram – and ended it in January 1976 in the diverse Theatre Department of New York University.

The meeting of soul mates: NYU

The faculty at NYU was dynamic: Kristin Linklater taught voice; Ron Van Lieu, Olympia Dukakis, Harold Guskin and Peter Kass were among the acting masters; and there was a lively exploration of Stanislavsky's psychophysical truth.

But there was no Shakespeare component. So Packer was invited as a 'cutting edge,' Shakespeare-based director to work on a project surrounding violence. She chose to stage *The Wars of the Roses* (a four-and-half-hour adaptation of the *Henry VI* trilogy, with some bits of *Richard(s) II* and *III*).[50] B. H. Barry was hired to stage the fights. (There were no fight directors in the States at the time.) And within the MFA cohort were three young actors by the names of Tony Simotes, Gregory Uel Cole and Kaia Calhoun, and two Jesuits fired up for theatre: Dennis Krausnick and Kevin G. Coleman.

Dennis Krausnick: 'a force of good'[51]

Most people training with Shakespeare & Company over the past few decades have found themselves in the presence of longtime Director of Training, Dennis Krausnick. Krausnick was born on 8 July 1942 in Cedar Rapids, Iowa, and raised Catholic on a small farm in the tiny town of Scottsbluff, Nebraska. While his siblings were sent to Catholic school, he attended public school where he studied Latin and French, and acted in plays. In 1961, he was on the brink of going to college to double major in theatre and journalism when he suddenly felt that life was unfulfilling and he 'needed to lose [himself] in something bigger than [himself]': 'I just decided to become a – Jesuit.'[52] For Krausnick the Jesuits modeled radical ways of looking at the world, with a commitment to intellectual rigor. So he pursued two years of monastic training as a novitiate and several years at St. Louis University, Missouri (where Jesuits came from all over the world for an intensive undergraduate program). He studied Latin and Greek drama, as well as French theatre in Canada and Spanish theatre in Mexico. And then in 1973, aged 31, he was ordained. Krausnick remained in the Jesuits for 15 years (a priest for four), counting among his closest allies a fellow Jesuit by the name of Kevin G. Coleman (whom he met in 1968):

> I think that Kevin and I both ended up in the Jesuits because we were drawn to people who wanted to be in service, and to living in a community. We're attracted to the idea that people working together can create more than the sum of their parts.
>
> *(Krausnick interview, July 2016)*

With a BA in Philosophy and an MA in French,[53] Krausnick was permitted by his superiors at the Wisconsin Province of the Society of Jesus to go to NYU to register on the MFA acting program – provided he took another Jesuit. (Coleman was his escort.) In New York, he also studied at the Manhattan Project with André Gregory and Richard Schechner, and appeared at the Public Theater in *Henry V* featuring a young Meryl Streep. And in his final semester at NYU, he chose to work on *The Wars of the Roses* with a visiting director by the name of Tina Packer.

28 History and roots

Love can be complicated for a Jesuit priest, as indeed it was for Krausnick. (So too for Coleman, who took a year's absence from his MFA after falling in love and needing to sort out his spiritual priorities. Hence, he wasn't on campus for Packer's *Roses*.) Krausnick 'fell in love with several things' at NYU, 'none of which were in keeping with my vows of chastity and poverty.'[54] And among them was Tina Packer. Arriving late to her very first class, Krausnick found her 'talking about love and hate' and 'how the function of the theatre was to heal. I fell in love with her.'[55] At the end of 1978 (by which time he had joined Packer and Linklater to form Shakespeare & Company), he had to decide: 'Should I leave the Jesuits and pursue a career in theatre? I believed I could better serve the goal of all endeavors, *the redemption of the world*, in theatre [rather] than as a Jesuit.'[56] Before long he moved in with Packer and 20 years later, in 1998, he married her. As lifelong partners he declared, 'What I find striking about Tina [...] is a profound and abiding connection to her own sense of inner truth.'[57]

Krausnick has remained one of the three lifelong members of Shakespeare & Company (minus a brief spate as Managing Director of the American Stage Company in St Petersburg, Florida, and as a realtor in the Berkshires during leaner times). Among his many stage roles – including Polonius (*Hamlet*), Menenius (*Coriolanus*), myriad Edith Wharton characterizations particularly Henry James – Krausnick appeared in S&Co.'s debut season as Theseus in 1978, and in 2012 as King Lear. Much of his vast contribution to the Company has been offstage: writer, director, managing director (11 times, from three months to three years), annual adapter of Edith Wharton's short stories into one-act plays from 1978 to 2002 (and beyond), and perhaps most importantly Director of Training. When Kristin Linklater left in 1992, Krausnick trained as a designated Linklater teacher in order to take on her mantel and honor her voice work as the basis of the *Training*. Thereafter he led many workshops – from the Month-Long Intensive (detailed in 'Act II') to weekend intensives around the country. And his benign smile belies his searing intelligence, quick wit and penetrating understanding of human interactions. Not to mention his devotion to serving his global citizens. To which end, his belief that actor training goes beyond vocational preparedness into deeper resonances for human communication has underscored the ethos of S&Co.'s Center for Actor Training for many years: 'I think that that attachment to the expression of language – in love with poetry and the mysteries of the universe – was one of the first statements of what we wanted out of the actor training.'[58]

It may be that Krausnick's commitment to the mysteries of the universe is a reason he has been described as 'the balancing rod' in Tina's life.' In fact, the jest sometimes goes that Packer is Elizabeth I in the court of Shakespeare & Company: if Krausnick is perhaps the spiritual advisor, Kevin G. Coleman is the court jester (though, as far as she's concerned, they've regularly swapped roles!).

Visions and revisions **29**

Kevin G. Coleman: 'S&Co.'s man for all seasons'[59]

The accolades for Kevin G. Coleman are multiple (see Chapter 9). Yet – like Packer and Krausnick – his background is humble. He was born on 15 November 1950. After his mother died in childbirth, he was raised by his grandmother on a farm in Clare (a tiny town near Fort Dodge, Iowa). He milked dairy cows before and after school, and played baseball under the yard light once the chores were done. At age 13, he went to Jesuit boarding school in Wisconsin, where – after he was injured playing football – he spent his time in the school library devouring the poetry section. It was while reading Shakespeare one afternoon that he had an epiphany:

> It was a little frightening because I realized, 'I'm thinking in a way that I've never thought before … I'm thinking thoughts that are very different than what I've been told, or what I'm supposed to think or believe. Now I'm thinking thoughts that seem to be coming from who knows where? But they're my *own* thoughts …
>
> *(Coleman interview, August 2016)*

He started to see that *his* thoughts – provoked by Shakespeare's words – were different from the thoughts that had been put into his head by parents and priests: 'It was a kind of waking up and being curious about "Who am I? And what is it I think? What is it I want? Who is it I want to be?"'[60] Shakespeare's words seemed to open up a whole universe for him, and the ideas that he'd been told all his life might not be the ideas that he wanted to think or believe any more.

On graduating from high school Coleman entered the Jesuits, devoting himself to the spiritual exercises of St. Ignatius Loyola with a *bona fide* desire to be of service in the world.[61] He enrolled in two Jesuit universities (Marquette University in Milwaukee and then St. Louis University, Missouri), and he met Dennis Krausnick (who was teaching Creative Writing and French). Majoring in English and Philosophy, Coleman lived as a novice in the Jesuit community at St. Louis, praying for hours each day, taking many philosophy classes and gaining an expansive exposure to the humanities. And at night he independently studied acting and improvisation with two actors from the New York Actors Studio. This fueled his love of theatre and, after an extensive stint teaching on Rosebud's Pine Ridge (a Sioux reservation in South Dakota), he headed to NYU with Krausnick.

Coleman's time there was bumpy. After failing his audition into the MFA acting program, he worked for the summer with André Gregory, who championed his late acceptance into NYU. Certainly he had a penchant for the edgy physical work of Jerzy Grotowski and Ryzard Cieslak, into which he could throw himself with the same energy that he'd used on the sports field. And, when he finally met Packer in winter 1978, his reputation as the 'mysterious Kevin Coleman'[62] (who did new plays, behaved outrageously, had a nervous

30 History and roots

breakdown, bit one of his teachers, was kicked out of NYU and was then unprecedentedly invited to complete his degree) preceded him!

After his MFA, Coleman directed and taught a little, before being urged by Krausnick in December 1978 to join him with Packer and Linklater in Lenox. The following summer, he was cast as Mercutio in S&Co.'s *Romeo and Juliet*, and through this experience he realized fully the enormity of Shakespeare's thoughts:

> Even though I'd had wonderful actor training, it was like Shakespeare wanted to go to a deeper place in myself than I was able to allow that actor training, or my work on contemporary plays, to go. There were too many habits, too much fear, too much patterning – not enough deep thinking.
>
> *(Coleman interview, August 2016)*

And as Shakespeare's world opened up to him, he saw so much more going on in the plays than he had ever imagined. After that summer at S&Co., he bade farewell to his girlfriend, loft apartment and New York City to immerse himself in Shakespeare and the potential of live theatre.

Immediately, Coleman joined the Company's nascent *Education* team touring schools with five other actors in 'An Actor at Work' (an hour-long program which gave students insights into the mysteries of the actor's art). But really it was the adolescents' own participation in Shakespeare that fueled him. He believed Shakespeare could be of serious use to them, given the wealth of extreme experiences expressed by 'intimately personal people as eloquently and insightfully as the characters express themselves in Shakespeare's plays.'[63] And very soon the *Education* department became Coleman's fiefdom and forte (as we'll see in 'Act III.') He also performed many roles in the Company's seasons, including Ethan Frome (1996) and the Fool to the Lears of both Jonathan Epstein (2003) and Dennis Krausnick (2012). A walking paradigm of contradictions – perspicacious yet consciously maverick, intellectual yet playfully dumb, teasing yet profoundly serious about human potential – Coleman is rarely seen without a luminous smile and a baseball cap.

The other crucial player to join the team of master-teachers in the Company's early days was (as already mentioned) clownmaster, Merry Conway.

Merry Conway and Clown

Clowns were an important part of Elizabethan theatre, particularly with their vivid actor/audience relationship. And *Clown* was a part of Shakespeare & Company's aesthetic from the very early seasons, not least because there were lots of funny actors around (including Tony Simotes, Rocco Sisto and Erick Avari). Furthermore, B. H. Barry's tumbling classes created a physical, performance vocabulary that ranged from bloodcurdling violence to silly slapstick. And into this environment Trish Arnold and Kristin Linklater introduced Merry Conway.

Visions and revisions **31**

FIGURE 1.3 Dennis Krausnick, Tina Packer and Kevin G. Coleman, 2016
Photo: Enrico Spada

Conway had trained under Jacques Lecoq in Paris in the disciplines of mask, clown and buffoon; she had also studied *commedia dell'arte*, as well as training with Arnold at the School of Movement, Mime and Mask. During the early 1970s, she taught at four British drama schools, and her discipline quickly intertwined with Arnold's Pure Movement, from which she created Mindbody Perception and Physical Awareness. As a clownmaster, she taught the first five years of S&Co.'s January Intensive (see Chapter 4) and guided actors in 'the ferocious joy of play' for productions including *The Comedy of Errors* (1983). In fact, her pedagogy evolved in response to S&Co.'s vast Mainstage at The Mount as well as the big canvas of Shakespeare's texts (see Chapter 2). And her teaching method has always been 'committed to bringing truth to large physical expression [...] in the contexts of physical character work, actor-audience relationships, character analysis and creating emotion from sensation.'[64] (Conway). Through the Company she received a Directing Fellowship in 1984 from the National Endowment for the Arts to study fool and clown in Shakespeare's canon, and develop a basic lexicon for the language of fool.[65] Thereafter she created a progression that led from (a) actors accessing their personal clowns, to (b) an examination of the traditional clown in Shakespeare, to (c) the crucial difference between clown and fool (see Chapter 13). Conway's impact on S&Co. has been extensive. And *Clown* has remained an intrinsic part of *Training*, *Education* and *Performance*, with key faculty including Jane Nichols, Kevin G. Coleman, Michael F. Toomey and Karen Beaumont,[66] each bringing different traditions and emphases to the task of playing 'in the moment.'

However ... to return to *this* moment in our narrative ...

32 History and roots

While the story of Shakespeare & Company is the story of many, it simply wouldn't have happened without the tenacity of its founding artistic director …

From Ford Foundation to company foundation

It was January 1976 when Tina Packer directed the graduate students at NYU in *The Wars of the Roses*. In 1977 she led a series of Shakespeare workshops at the Riverside Studios, London, culminating in a 'bare-boards' production of *King Lear* with Roger Lloyd Pack,[67] where everyone 'worked collaboratively. Several of us had taken the est training, so we said what we felt without "dumping emotions" on each other or expecting others to "put it right" (all pointers from est)'[68] (Packer). And through this honest, respectful collaboration, she regained her nerve as a director. The knowledge she had garnered from her years of creative and personal voyaging reignited her conviction that she had to create her own company; otherwise, her directing career was destined to hop from one freelance project to another – and that simply wouldn't enable the knowledge to build. Added to which, her work at NYU and the Riverside Studios had given her a clearer understanding of management structures and how to avoid the emotional mayhem of the 'democratic' 1973 experiment.

Between January 1976 and March 1978 Packer's plan gestated. Initially her vision was for a multi-racial, classical company based in New York City, as there lived her chief collaborators Linklater, Barry and Krausnick (with whom she was now romantically involved). She had kept in close contact with her master-teachers following the 1973 experiment, and was honing her directing skills through various avenues, including a production of Molière's *The Learned Ladies* at Smith College, Northampton, Massachusetts. She had also kept in touch with Richard Kapp, the Ford Foundation Program Officer for the Division of Humanities and Arts. And in March 1978 she wrote to him, sharing the findings of her five years' practice-based research.

Her major finding inevitably went back to the spoken word: 'Obviously with Shakespeare the verbal must have ascendancy over the visual.'[69] And yet during the 1973 experiment, she had rubbed up against actors wailing, 'It's the words […] we can't deal with words':[70] the very thing that should be liberating them in Shakespeare was in fact stymying them. As she had tackled the practicalities of guiding them through that process, a light bulb had illuminated for her: she had started understanding – on a social and philosophical level – that all too often as human beings we actually *disconnect* from our language:

> It was in getting actors to own the words and give them full power that I began to see how we, as a culture, have cut ourselves off from the verbal. […] We use words to pass information, to intellectualize, words even as weapons, or to mask our purpose; but *communion between people* happens rarely.
>
> *(Packer letter to Kapp, 1 March 1978, (my emphasis))*

The ten-month, practice-as-research – plus the two years' Travel and Study plus the two years' working as a director – had brought Packer to the realization that:

> as [humankind] passed from the Renaissance into the era of individualism, the Newtonian mechanistic world of cause and effect, industrialization and the break down of society, it became too painful and inefficient to use *language as experience*. *Abstraction* is easier to deal with than *empathy*. As we divided and fragmented ourselves, we divided our voices from our bodies.
>
> Theatre [...] lost the communion of words [and] became a visual medium, dividing actors and the audience, finally inventing TV and films where they don't meet at all.
>
> *(Packer letter to Kapp, 1 March 1978, (my emphasis))*

The Elizabethans, on the other hand,

> must have used *words as experience*. For in order to get [my] actors to release the words in a way that theatre becomes electric I had to get them to pass the words *into their bodies*: they 'became' the words, so to speak (as a musical instrument is its notes). There was no separation between them and the words they were speaking.
>
> At this moment, the whole atmosphere in the theatre changed. I suddenly saw that *words as experience* tap into all dimensions of time – past, present, future, conscious and unconscious, individual and collective; and the barriers between actors and audience melt. *Theatre becomes a verb.*
>
> *(Packer letter to Kapp, 1 March 1978, (my emphasis))*

With this discovery in hand, the next 'evolutionary cycle,' wrote Packer, '(already on its way) is about finding some kind of unity, empathy and harmony: and in order to express ourselves we need *experiential words*.'[71] The birthing chamber for that next evolution would, of course, be theatre: 'Theatre can return to its role (usurped by the printing press) of informing people about themselves.'[72] But because theatre had lost the communion of words and awareness of its own potential, it needed to regain '*knowledge and responsibility of what it is.*'[73]

And so it was that, during her complex years of creative searching, Packer acquired her own experiential knowledge, much of it from collaborating with her master-teachers as well as observing her actors and students. And this practical, hands-on knowledge enabled her to formulate a particular approach to acting that could potentially reverse her actors' lamentation of 'how do we deal with the words?' Instead: 'words will become the backbone of a classical company.'[74] While that may not necessarily be novel in its own right, Packer's understanding of what had happened to people's connection to language over

34 History and roots

400 years – not least in the theatre, where women's voices had yet to bear much authority – was certainly innovative. And her vision for her company was (again) ambitious:

> I want to gather together the best young American actors, have them supported by some British (the company should be multi-national, multi-racial – for to recognize cultural characteristics and go beyond them is the essence of classicism [...]), put them through my own version of a classical training [...] and open a season of plays in the heart of New York.
>
> *(Packer letter to Kapp, 1 March 1978)*

Packer's ambition went beyond professional *Performance*. There would be expansive programs in *Training* and *Education*:

> I also want a classical training programme [*sic*] for young actors [...] and a summer academy where we can teach teachers, playwrights, anyone who wants to learn, about *language as experience*. [...] That would run in conjunction with a summer season of plays.
>
> *(Packer letter to Kapp, 1 March 1978)*

At the time she was formulating this fervent letter – and inspired by the collective practice-based research – Packer met up one evening with Linklater in the kitchen of the Manhattan loft that Linklater was subletting to John Hadden (a young actor) and his girlfriend Susan Dibble (a young dancer). Both Hadden and Dibble quickly became enthused by Packer's visions combined with Linklater's encouragement, and were eager to become part of a potential company.

Events now moved very quickly. And in April 1978, Packer visited Kapp in Chappaqua, New York. Their plans included a mini-conference between Packer's proposed company and the Freedom Theatre of Philadelphia and the National Black Theatre of Harlem to investigate deeply what it meant to have a classical, multi-racial company. (In time, they would define it as one having 'the highest truths, universally told, with healing powers.') And as they chattered animatedly in the kitchen, a man whom Packer took to be the plumber was advising a workman on some repairs. When she and Kapp moved to the living room, the plumber followed them and sat in on their in-depth discussion. 'Why is the plumber coming?' she thought. 'He never said a word.'[75] A few days later, the 'plumber' telephoned her to say he would help her start her theatre company and they should do it in the Berkshires. This was no plumber: this was Mitchell Berenson. Packer had no idea who Berenson was or where the Berkshires were, but she was running a workshop at Smith College, Massachusetts, and 'he said, "I'll come up there and watch you do the workshop, then we'll drive over to the Berkshires." I thought, "Well, let's not look a gift horse in the mouth."'[76]

Mitch Berenson was actually a celebrity in his own right. A former long-shoreman turned New York real-estate developer he was also a staunch union man, wholly simpatico with Packer's democratic ideals.[77] Berenson (who would become a lifelong champion of Shakespeare & Company) had left school at 15 and worked as a union organizer in New York's Garment District. In 1937, he was jailed for his activism and on his release spent the summer reading Shakespeare: 'the language, the beauty of the language!'[78] (Berenson). Thereafter, he had been endlessly disappointed by the productions he had seen to date. Yet, as he watched Packer direct the students at Smith College, he was struck by her no-nonsense approach to Shakespeare, and he was determined to help her realize her dream. He suggested the Berkshires as a base, because of the number of New Yorkers and Bostonians, who have historically kept summer homes there and particularly love their culture. And he also understood the gravitational pull to the area for artists, with Jacob's Pillow for dance and Tanglewood for music.

It was a chilly April evening when Berenson drove Packer through the Berk-shires to look at potential properties. They viewed the former gymnasium at Foxhollow School in Lenox – owned at that time by real-estate entrepreneur Donald I. Altshuler – before traveling down an unlit, dirt road that crosses the former Foxhollow property toward Route 7. Through the bare branches of pine trees in the snow-laden twilight, Packer caught sight of a derelict mansion, its myriad windows boarded up: 'It was huge and romantic, like [Daphne du Maurier's] Manderley. The driver said, "That's Edith Wharton's house, and no one has lived there for years."'[79] Immediately Packer knew that she had found the home for Shakespeare & Company …

Notes

1 Nehassaiu deGannes interview with Bella Merlin, August 2017.
2 shakespeareandcompany.com (accessed 17 September 2019).
3 Graduates of Oxford and Cambridge Universities.
4 Actress Janet Suzman's advice to Packer at the RSC.
5 Packer, T. (2000), Interview with KB, PM, 11 May 2000, Subject # TH-004, transcription, p. 21. S&Co. archive.
6 Epstein, H. (1985), *The Companies She Keeps: Tina Packer Builds A Theatre*, Massachusetts: Plunkett Lake Press, p. 30.
7 Packer cited in Gudeon, A. (1997), 'Tina Packer,' *The Artful Mind*, April 1997 (my emphasis).
8 ibid.
9 Testimonial from K. F. on www.linklatervoice.com: 'Not only does Kristin push you in the studio to find the hidden aspects of yourself, but she fills you with laughter, friendship, magic and culture' (accessed 17 September 2019).
10 First published by Drama Publishers, New York in 1978, then expanded and republished by Nick Hern Books in 2006.
11 Linklater, K. 'The Art and Craft of Voice (and Speech) Training,' see 'Resources' at www.linklatervoice.com (accessed 17 September 2019).
12 ibid.

36 History and roots

13 ibid.
14 Named Tisch School of the Arts in 1966.
15 Packer interview, 11 May 2000, p. 25.
16 Epstein (1985), p. 10.
17 ibid.
18 Packer, T. (1971), 'The Idea Behind the Plan.' S&Co. archive.
19 ibid.
20 Nesbitt, C. (2000), 'Tina Packer's Bard-Tending,' *TheaterMania.Com*, 11 March 2000.
21 The actors included most of Packer's American students from LAMDA, plus R. H. Thompson from Canada; Wilson Dunster from the Market Theatre, South Africa; and actor-teacher Karen Grassle. The stage managers included Francine Stone and Barry Grove, who both went on to have illustrious careers.
22 Tina Packer interview with Bella Merlin, August 2018.
23 Barton, J. (1984), *Playing Shakespeare*, London: Methuen, p. 3.
24 Epstein (1985), p. 45.
25 Isidore of Seville cited in Tillyard, E. M. W. (1943), *The Elizabethan World Picture: A study of the idea of order in the age of Shakespeare, Donne and Milton*, London: Chatto and Windus, p. 94.
26 Tillyard (1943), pp. 94–95.
27 Broome cited in Davies, J. T. (1980), 'Relief from the Classical Hangover: Interview with John Broome,' *The Berkshire Eagle*, 20 June 1980.
28 Susan Dibble Notes on John Broome, June 2018.
29 Packer cited in Nesbitt (2000).
30 Barry cited in Bass, R. (1979), 'Director with Punch,' *The Berkshire Eagle*, 12 August 1979.
31 Barry, B. H. (2013), *Fights for Everyone: The Performer's Guide*, Self-published, p. 15.
32 ibid., p. 77.
33 ibid., p. 77, (my emphasis).
34 Barry cited in Bass (1979).
35 Barry (2013), p. 12.
36 ibid., p. 13.
37 As epitomized by the character of Jimmy Porter in John Osborne's *Look Back in Anger* (1956).
38 Dennis Krausnick interview with Bella Merlin, July 2016.
39 Snow, J. (2017), 'Trish Arnold: Pioneer of Movement Training for Actors,' *The Guardian*, 27 February 2017.
40 Susan Dibble Notes from Merry Conway's reflection, May 2018.
41 Packer in 'Training Shakespeare Actors in A Modern World,' p. 10.
42 Packer cited in Epstein (1985), p. 47.
43 Tina Packer interview with Bella Merlin, August 2016.
44 Packer interview, 11 May 2000, p. 23.
45 Lowry had supported regional repertory theatres including Arena Stage (Washington, DC), A.C.T. (San Francisco), the Mark Taper Forum (Los Angeles) and the Denver Center.
46 Packer edit, September 2019.
47 Tina Packer interview with Bella Merlin, September 2018.
48 Kristin Linklater cites the first-century Roman architect, Vitruvius – who is linked to the 14,000-seater auditorium at the outdoor theatre at Epidaurus – in her paper 'Our Vocal Heritage' (www.linklatervoice.com): 'let bronze vessels be made, proportionate to the size of the theatre, and let them be so fashioned that, when touched by the voice, they may produce with one another the notes of the fourth, the fifth, and so on up to the double octave. Then, having constructed niches in between the seats of the theatre, let the vessels be arranged in them, in accordance with musical laws.' As Linklater states, these sound-waves 'carried the story horizontally to the audience'

and 'vertically upward to nourish the harmonics of the music of the spheres' (accessed 17 September 2019).

49 Tina Packer interview with Bella Merlin, April 2018.

50 The project was inspired by John Barton's epic (and highly politicized) adaptation of Shakespeare's *Henry VI* trilogy and *Richard III* (and including 1,450 of Barton's own lines), directed by Barton and Peter Hall at the RSC in 1963, and subsequently, filmed by the BBC in 1965.

51 Bass, M. (2001) 'Getting Comfortable with Will Shakespeare,' *Berkshires Month*, 15 November 2001. Dennis Krausnick is 'a force of good and in this world today there can be no higher talent than that.'

52 Krausnick cited in Caffrey, B. (1982), 'Dennis Krausnick, Director, American Stage Company,' *St Petersburg Independent*, 26 May 1982.

53 MA from McGill University, Montreal.

54 Krausnick cited in Caffrey (1982).

55 Krausnick cited in Epstein (1985), p. 59.

56 Krausnick cited in Caffrey (1982), (my emphasis).

57 Krausnick cited in Cahill, T., Nunley, R., Sokol, F. and Banner, M. (2000), *Muses in Arcadia: Cultural Life in the Berkshires*, London: Frontlist.

58 Dennis Krausnick interview with Bella Merlin, August 2016.

59 'Ten People Who Made a Difference: Bringing Shakespeare into the Schools: Kevin Coleman,' unnamed author, *Berkshire Eagle Magazine*, 12 January 1990.

60 Kevin Coleman interview with Bella Merlin, August 2016.

61 Coleman interview with Sarah Lytle and Sandy Bourgeois, November 2017, with Packer and Krausnick.

62 Packer cited in ibid.

63 Coleman cited in ibid.

64 www.merryconway.com (accessed 17 September 2019).

65 ibid.

66 Longtime Company member, Karen Beaumont sadly died during the writing of this book on 19 January 2019. She had been associated with S&Co. since 1983 and a professor at Bard's College, Simon's Rock, MA, since 1989.

67 Along with Shakespeare scholar John Russell Brown and BBC trainee-director Kenny McBain, Packer's team also included actors Hilton McCrae and Nicholas Clay (Edmund and Edgar), Lorna Heilbron and Petra Markham (Goneril and Regan), and Stevie Williams (the Fool).

68 Packer edit, September 2019.

69 Packer letter to Richard Kapp, 1 March 1978. S&Co. archive.

70 ibid.

71 ibid., (my emphasis).

72 ibid.

73 ibid., (my emphasis).

74 ibid.

75 Packer interview 11 May 2000, p. 22.

76 ibid.

77 The character of the lawyer Charley Malloy played by Rod Steiger in Elia Kazan's 1954 film *On the Water Front* is based on Mitch Berenson, though Budd Schulberg's rendition is apparently radically different from Arthur Miller's original portrayal.

78 Berenson cited in Kelly, K. (1993), 'Shakespeare & Co. raises money merrily,' *The Boston Globe*, 18 June 1993.

79 Packer cited in Mead, R. (2008), 'Life and Letters: Restoration Drama: How did Edith Wharton's Home End Up Being Threatened with Foreclosure?' *The New Yorker*, 28 April 2008, p. 19.

2

BRICKS AND MORTAR, TRELLIS AND TREES

An aesthetic is realized

In a symbiotic relationship, theatrical styles have always evolved hand-in-hand with theatre architecture – from the vast Greek amphitheatres to the intimate blackbox to site-specific performances. And so with Shakespeare. He started out writing for 'outdoor theatres in the less salubrious parts of London catering per performance to 2,500 spectators from all strands of society.'[1] And by the end of his career he was writing 'for a wealthier and socially more acceptable group of 700 per performance in an indoor theatre in the better part of the City.'[2] When outbreaks of the plague closed the playhouses, Shakespeare played 'on the road' in constantly differing venues – from lords' houses to guildhalls to open-air spaces. And each venue impacted his style. So it stands to reason that, in 1978, the newly formed Shakespeare & Company would be shaped by their performance space. But little could they anticipate just how much personality their first home held …

The morning after Packer and Berenson sighted The Mount, they headed back to the property to look at it properly. The windows were covered with 12-foot conifers. The shutters had been closed for almost two years. 'There was ice all over the floor from a hundred different leaks in broken pipes. The library was knee-deep in books and there wasn't a room without plaster out. […] It was filthy and freezing cold.'[3] Yet Packer remained convinced that this should be their home. A week later Krausnick arrived to make a floorplan, only to find moldering food amid the plaster, a dead pizza in the fridge and a ghost or two in the attic.[4] With its tattered stables and overgrown gardens, the property's state of disrepair belied its former glory.

The Mount: 'surrounded by every loveliness of nature and every luxury of art'[5]

Pioneering women weave the fabric of this story, not least when it comes to the history of The Mount. From 1901 (the beginning of its construction) until

Bricks and mortar, trellis and trees **39**

1911, this imposing, white stucco mansion was home to the iconic, American novelist Edith Wharton (1862–1937).[6] She also loved architecture and intricately influenced the plan and construction of her 130-acre property with its 22-roomed Mount. She designed the floorplan as a fluid configuration, so that people could move from almost any room in the house to almost any other without going through the main quarters. Here she wrote one of her most famous novels, *The House of Mirth*, and here she lived with her husband Teddy until his mental health deteriorated and Edith could bear it no longer. Soaked in sorrow, she sold The Mount in 1911, fled to France and filed for divorce.[7]

Thereafter, The Mount embraced a series of owners, beginning with Mr. and Mrs. Albert Shattuck (who occupied the house from 1911 to 1935, and both died there. Were they the ghosts in the attic?). After three years' probable vacancy, Louise and Carl Van Anda (editor of the *New York Times*) bought it at auction, but soon found the furnace didn't work well enough for them to live there in the winter. With other expensive repairs overlooked, The Mount was woefully deteriorating barely 40 years into its existence. In 1942, the Van Andas sold the house with furniture and outbuildings for just under $24,000 (worth in total over $100,000) to Aileen Farrell, the headmistress of nearby Foxhollow School – and a new life for The Mount began.

There's a belief that the walls of a house hold the energy of those who lived there. It's no surprise, then, that – given Shakespeare & Company's love of language, education and the female voice – the nascent company should find itself in a domicile infused with the energy of a famous *literata* followed by a bevy of schoolgirls. Headmistress Farrell was British, like Packer and Linklater, with a similar revolutionary vision. Sadly, that vision didn't incorporate The Mount's maintenance. And by 1970 Foxhollow School had a deficit of nearly $30,000, with restoration costs estimated at $400,000. Fortunately in 1971, Farrell's successor Hilda Mumford did have the foresight to secure The Mount as a National Historic Monument. Unfortunately, that didn't prevent Foxhollow School closing in 1976 after almost 35 years as The Mount's longest owners. By now the mansion was seriously suffering: 'A burst pipe in an attic bathroom caused so much water damage that the plaster ceiling in the drawing room – ornamented with garlands of fruit and flowers and stylized rosettes – collapsed.'[8] At the same time, heavy rain caused the north wall of the forecourt to fall, and Wharton's beloved statue of Apollo toppled from its niche. Maybe it was time for Apollo, the god of reason, to make way for Dionysus, the god of theatre?

There was a chance The Mount might be saved in January 1977, when Connecticut real-estate developer – Donald I. Altshuler – offered $600,000 to buy all of Foxhollow School's property.[9] He planned to turn The Mount into a French restaurant during the summer and a special events venue in the winter. Later that year, however, his plans changed. And when he tried to sell off The Mount with some acreage, no offers were forthcoming. As the chill of winter descended, the property again stood hauntingly empty. Until a former

40 History and roots

longshoreman drove past with an enterprising, young theatre director. Dionysus was on the move …

Shakespeare and The Mount

Only a month after Tina Packer first saw The Mount, Shakespeare & Company became tenants on 22 May 1978. Lured by this house of mirth and in her own age of innocence, Packer again approached the Ford Foundation, who contributed $5,000 toward the Company's establishment. Berenson negotiated the rent down with Altshuler from $8,000 to $4,000 in light of the vast amount of work they would have to do just to make the house habitable. And by June, Packer and Linklater had assembled the first intrepid ensemble of 35,[10] several of whom bought international flights at their own expense. Packer had just enough money to keep the Company going for three weeks, so they rapidly had to mount a show and bring in box-office takings. And on $50 pay a week, they set about their monumental, two-fold task: to restore The Mount so that they could live in it, and to create a classical theatre company.

And they did it. On 21 July 1978, *A Midsummer Night's Dream* opened to several hundred spectators.[11] And there was no stopping them this time. Through the summer months, Packer assembled a board including Maria Cole (widow to Nat King Cole), Joyce Crane (of the Crane Paper Company, who made dollar bills for the Treasury), Herb Halpern (a close friend of Berenson), and Leila Berhle (a former pupil at Foxhollow School). On 15 September – just as their first, summer season closed – Shakespeare & Company signed a contract to actually purchase the property from Altshuler for $200,000. And on 10 January 1979, they became the official owners of The Mount. Within a mere nine months, they had saved Wharton's dream home from dire dereliction.

Committing to the bricks and mortar of The Mount was a galvanizing experience. The team scrubbed grime off the moldering floors. They pulled up weeds – both indoors and out. They plastered water-damaged walls (with materials donated by Berenson). They broke the ice in the lavatories each morning during their first winter. (Was that furnace ever repaired?) And in the fullness of time, they built screens for 75 windows, re-painted 150 weather-beaten shutters and renovated the gardens. This restoration of The Mount wasn't just practical: it was a manifestation of the Company's philosophy. Among the trees and the trellises, they were embodying the Elizabethan ideals of harmony and balance in connection with the cosmos. In fact, they were living the 'earthly existence' of the Renaissance Chain of Being:

> First there is *mere existence*, the inanimate class: the elements, liquids, and metals. [...] Next there is *existence and life*, the vegetative class [...] Next there is *existence, life and feeling*, the sensitive class. In it there are three

grades. First the creatures having *touch* but not hearing, memory or movement. Such are [...] parasites on the base of trees. Then there are animals having *touch, memory and movement but not hearing,* for instance ants. And finally there are the higher animals, horses and dogs etc., that have *all these faculties.* The three classes lead up to man, who has not only *existence, life and feeling,* but *understanding*: he sums up in himself the *total faculties of earthly phenomena.* (For this reason he was called the little world or microcosm.)

> *(Tillyard, E. M. W.,* The Elizabethan World Picture, *London: Chatto and Windus, 1943: 25, (my emphasis))*

In this earthly existence – out in the Berkshires and away from the metropolis – S&Co. were in contact with all the links in the Great Chain of Being. Had they been based in New York City – as was Packer's initial dream – their history would've been quite different. As it was, the environment itself shaped their vision and aesthetic.

The Mainstage: 'wild but civilized, open yet contained'[12]

In the open-roofed playhouses of Elizabethan England, the sky was literally the limit. And Shakespeare's stories fill that space. His canvas of emotions is big; his expression of human nature is expansive. And so it would be for Shakespeare & Company.

On arriving at The Mount in May 1978 they had to identify a suitable performance space. With no time or money to build a stage, they roamed the grounds calling out to each other until they found a hollow with the best acoustics on the southwest side of the mansion.[13] The clearing was backed by tall fir trees, with an overgrown Italian garden to 'stage' right and a grassy bank to the front that raked up toward the mansion. (An ideal 'auditorium.') Here was Shakespeare & Company's Mainstage. A year later, wooden platforms would be built, but for the first *Dream* they performed with a carpet of fir needles beneath their feet and a roof of stars above them.

Indeed, the Mainstage was huge. So the actors needed a matching performance style, one that was sweeping and outwardly focused: in other words, the complete opposite of the introverted halftones of the popular American Method. To help them create an appropriate aesthetic, the master-teachers were vital during the early years. As veteran actor Jonathan Croy recalled, the work of 'Broome's dance, Arnold's movement, Linklater's voice, Tina's text, Barry's fight work were all specifically formulated to allow us to expand into a space that had enormous size and natural resource.'[14] And it demanded that you 'take the tiger by the tail' as seasoned actor Jonathan Epstein put it. He was among the physically and creatively imposing 'tiger-grapplers' recruited in the early years, along with Rocco Sisto, Kevin Coleman and Peter Wittrock, and later joined by Malcolm Ingram, Joe Morton and John Douglas Thompson (among many others). And it wasn't

42 History and roots

necessarily physical stature that was needed to fill the Mainstage's vast canvas: the energetic feistiness of Tod Randolph, Fran Bennett, Kaia Calhoun, Natsuko Ohama and Midori Nakamura (also among many others) was a potent ingredient in creating the robust acting style that has come to characterize the Company. Nature and nurture, body and spirit, all melded to realize an aesthetic.[15] And with this immediate connection to nature, they soon found that the Elizabethan rhythms sounded particularly vibrant in the wild. Which in turn nurtured that all-important feature of the Elizabethan playhouse: *the actor/audience relationship*. Indeed, as the Company's reputation quickly grew, so too did the audience from its initial 500 spectators on blankets and picnic chairs. And within a matter of summers, the car park had to be extended, ergo the 'auditorium' widened and the stage lengthened. So now the actors had to send their voices and emotional connections even further out to Mother Nature. And although the size of the Mainstage brought certain challenges, it was an essential and exciting component in the exploratory process:

> There was an understanding that we were all trying to achieve a powerful, collective resonance through an authentic connection to Shakespeare's language. So while Tina was directing a rehearsal, Kristin would run up onstage as you were speaking and shake your jaw or check your diaphragm and make sure you were dropping your breath into your body. This navigation happened in real time *through* the material and *in conjunction with* the director. And we were all trying to solve onstage – in front of an audience – our own individual interpretations of this dynamic methodology.
>
> *(Allyn Burrows interview, July 2017)*

FIGURE 2.1 Mainstage at The Mount: *The Merchant of Venice*, dir. Tina Packer, 1998

The Salon

At the other extreme was the Company's second performance space, the 90-seater Salon Theatre, where manners, etiquette and emotional containment created quite a different aesthetic. Indeed, Edith Wharton's Salon bore its own history. On many an afternoon, she had served high tea there to her literary friends including Henry James. On many a balmy evening, she had traversed onto the terrace to gaze at the stars and sense the music of the spheres. So, from the moment they arrived at The Mount, S&Co. planned parlor performances of her stories, staged in a site-specific way, with actors intimately close to the audience, who would be served tea and biscuits as part of their immersive experience. Actually Wharton's stories were out of print in 1978, so 'We went down to Scribners and said, "We're going to start doing her work. Can you start thinking about bringing these books out again?"'[16] (Packer). And the lot fell to Dennis Krausnick to adapt them to the stage. Krausnick wholly understood Wharton's understated charm. And that first summer he wrote 'an evening's entertainment' entitled *Three Voices of Edith Wharton* focusing on, 'the private Edith, the literary Edith, and the society Edith [...] through vignettes from her novels and stories, mixed with biographical material.'[17] With actress Gillian Bargh and Packer herself playing Edith in various years, Krausnick's one-act and full-length dramatizations counterpointed the expansive, outdoor Shakespeare with delicate irony and pithy dialog. And so it was that, along with R. W. B. Lewis's *Edith Wharton: A Biography* (1976 Pulitzer Prize-winner), Krausnick and Company contributed significantly to putting Wharton back on the literary map. Although their tradition of staging her stories subsided somewhat after they had to leave The Mount in 2001 (a sorry saga for another time), it reemerged in their 40th-anniversary season, when longtime Company members Diane Prusha, Corinna May and David Joseph performed in Krausnick's adaptation of *The Fullness of Life*.

Expanding the playing venues

In the fullness of life and the fullness of time, other performance areas were added, including Oxford Court, a 200-seater outdoor space to the northeast of The Mount, where the training programs (the Summer Performance Institute and the Summer Training Institute) would perform. Then in 1991 – a year when statewide cuts rocked the arts leaving S&Co. on their beam ends – Packer seized the bull by the horns and, instead of cutting back, the Company added more performances in more playing venues. So a 108-seater studio was created in the Stables, where they mounted three 'Bare Bard' productions (small-budget, small-cast stagings) and five contemporary plays. The risk paid off, and that summer they thrived.

The range of site-specific venues meant that a panoply of human experience could be expressed: from the largest of Shakespeare's cosmic realm to the intricate femininity of Edith Wharton to the immediate 'rough theatre' in the

FIGURE 2.2 Corinna May as Edith Wharton, The Mount, 1985

Stables. Despite their eventual departure from The Mount, the Company remains closely connected to the property. Most summers, young actors mainly from the *Education* program's Northeast Regional Tours mount a Shakespeare production in an outdoor performance area behind the Stables called The Dell (see Chapter 10). In fact, The Dell's configuration echoes that of the original Mainstage, with a wide, natural playing area, a wooded hill as the backdrop and lively interaction with a picnicking audience. And so it was that the architecture, atmosphere and geography of The Mount's haunting premises impacted the Company's very being and mission.

The mission

Inquiry. Balance. Harmony.

This triad lies at the heart of Shakespeare & Company's mission, which holds many binaries at its core. It's anchored in Elizabethan values while celebrating contemporary perspectives. It honors each individual's evolution while foregrounding the ensemble. And it invites Company introspection while reaching out into the community. The early Mission Statements emerged in many respects from discoveries made by Packer during the 1973 experiment.

The main mission was 'to create a theatre of unprecedented excellence in *Performance, Training,* and *Education.*'[18] Inspired by 'classical principles' and 'classical standards,' Shakespeare & Company 'aspire to perform as the Elizabethans did – in love with poetic language, visceral experience, and the mysteries of the universe, while rooted in the classical ideals of inquiry, balance and harmony.'[19]

Classical principles means 'the highest truths told in a universally accessible form with an impact that is healing for society.'[20]

Classical standards means 'being able to go beyond our individual social and cultural backgrounds, and [...] use those backgrounds in creating that which is universal in all of us.'[21]

Inquiry means 'the practice of questioning from an attitude of honesty, curiosity, and courage.'[22]

Balance means 'welcoming and deeply considering other points of view.'[23]

Harmony means 'incorporating ethical behavior and aesthetic sensibility in all our work and creations.'[24]

And the way to galvanize these practical philosophies is through *Training, Education* and *Performance*. In a document crafted toward the end of 1978 (simply titled 'Shakespeare & Company'), the framework of the three-pronged company is set out:[25]

First, they envisaged a year-round Conservatory Training Program with Kristin Linklater as Director of Training for young actors, bridging the gap between university teaching and the industry. Since all too often practitioners are seen as poor cousins to scholars, Packer and Linklater also wanted to mirror the early days of classicism, where scholarship and practice were mutually valued. (See 'Act II.')

Second in their mission was an Outreach Study Program. Embedded in Shakespeare & Company's DNA is a commitment to lifelong learning – from 7-year-olds to 99-year-olds. So, from early 1979, they offered classes to the general public and to teachers, as well as taking programs into schools. (See 'Act III.')

Third in the mission would be the formation of a British-American professional performing company, playing on both sides of the Atlantic. As African American, founding member Gregory Uel Cole described it, 'What really fascinated me was that this was a company interested in transcending stereotypes, crossing barriers, being international and multi-racial *without any fuss*.'[26] (See 'Act IV.') (As it happened, the British-American part never fully came into being because of the actors' unions, though British-born, American-based actors still feature regularly each season.)

Interestingly, the 1978 Mission Statement also makes the role of the *director* very clear. In place of director-*auteurs*, the emphasis would be

> on the *actor's* art, and on the direct relationship between *actors and audience*. While the directors realize this philosophy in production, the master teachers provide training that develops in the actors the necessary power and insight to fulfill a classical text.
>
> *(Shakespeare & Company' overview document, c.1978, (my emphasis))*

46 History and roots

Indeed, the Company's commitment to the ensemble has always been part of their *modus operandi*. While stars have occasionally been brought into the mix including André Gregory and Olympia Dukakis[27] (who both played Prospero in 1989 and 2012, respectively), the leading actors usually arise from within the Company. If this commitment has inadvertently contributed to the 'cult' myth (see Preface), it's ultimately a compassionate nod to the loyalty of those who have stuck with the Company in an industry fraught with disposability. 'I created Shakespeare & Company as an ensemble,' wrote Packer in an early 'Artistic Director's Statement' for an ensemble grant:

> It has operated against all odds as an ensemble. And will come to true fruition only as an ensemble [...]. I want to create an institution which will serve the world's greatest playwright long after I have disappeared; an ensemble which generates itself; a home where classical principles can be nurtured, experimented with, and manifested from decade to decade. [...]
>
> For us ensemble does not mean that all company members have to work together all the time; it does mean a critical mass has to be present in any given project and that new blood comes in to inspire and be inspired. Therefore, the principles of the ensemble should, of themselves, attract other artists to want to work with the group. Thus, knowledge is easily absorbed and passed on without ever becoming stagnant.
>
> *(Packer, 'Artistic Director's Statement – Ensemble Grant':*
> *c.1984, S&Co. archive)*

The ensemble aesthetic and the basic principles of the Mission Statement have essentially remained the Company's bedrock. Each successive decade has shaped the mission. And by the time the Company celebrated its 40th anniversary in 2017, the Mission Statement bore the addition that 'by its commitment to the creative impulse' Shakespeare & Company might be *'a revolutionary force in society.'*[28] In light of the hundreds of thousands of students whose lives have been touched by its *Education* programs, the thousands of audience members who have shared the *performances*, and the thousands of actors from around the globe who have experienced their *Training*, 'revolutionary force' is arguably a fair description.

While over the years the details of Shakespeare & Company's 'Statement of Values that Unite Us' have also morphed (into what's now called 'Values and Ethic'), it's always underscored by the core questions of: 'What does it mean to be alive? How should we act? What must I do?' Or as King Lear asks, 'Who is it that can tell me who I am?'[29] In their 2019 online Mission Statement, they overtly include 'generosity' and 'ethical action' as well as 'fiduciary responsibility' and 'consensus as the foundation of decisions.' Company members are encouraged to voice their ideas and take artistic risks 'for the creation and sustainability of great theatre and great teaching.'[30] And anyone who has passed

Bricks and mortar, trellis and trees **47**

through their studios and theatres is welcome to share the Company's technique, build audiences and expand the work through experiment. With an unrelenting belief that the art of acting can change the world, they invite their performers and participants to use Shakespeare *to reveal human truths to an audience*.[31] That's no small mission and no insignificant statement.

When Shakespeare & Company moved from The Mount in 2001 to their current home, they continued to adapt to their environment. But before we look at the new property's impact on their aesthetic, a quick historical sidebar as to how this move came about. Trigger warning: this touches upon the 'sorry saga' to which I alluded earlier.

The move from The Mount

Shakespeare & Company's mission document created in the fall of 1978 includes the ambitious but necessary, 'Project to Restore "The Mount."' This both cemented a dream and conjured a nightmare ...

To fulfill their obligations of restoring The Mount, Packer, Berenson and Krausnick legally incorporated Shakespeare & Company at the same time as creating a separate entity: Edith Wharton Restoration, Inc. (EWR). This was a not-for-profit company manifested to be the ultimate guardians of The Mount. And the process was very pragmatic: a theatre company could access funding opportunities that weren't available to architectural restoration projects – and *vice versa*. And should one entity fail, they wanted to protect Wharton from Will, and Will from Wharton. The deed of trust for The Mount was put in the name of EWR, with Shakespeare & Company as the rent-paying tenants for a lease of 25 years (though 'in perpetuity' was the expectation). Although both entities initially shared six of the same board members,[32] that set-up shifted within the first few years to prevent confusion and conflicts of interest when it came to fundraising. New administrators were gradually brought in, and in the fullness of time the two entities became increasingly disconnected: it was always somewhat idealistic to believe that a newborn theatre company could also restore an unwieldy stately home.

It's beyond our remit here to chart the unhappy demise of the relationship between Shakespeare & Company and Edith Wharton Restoration, Inc. The potted version is that, despite S&Co.'s exhaustive fundraising to take ownership of The Mount in the first place – as well as the blood, sweat and tears expended in bringing it back from the brink of dereliction – EWR were the legal owners. Preserving a National Historic Monument while it was occupied and professionally used by actors (however well-intentioned they may be) became as unpalatable to EWR as Lear and his retinue were to Goneril and Regan. Despite its 22 rooms, 'This house is little: the old man and his people/Cannot be well bestow'd.'[33] As the years progressed the relationship deteriorated. Ugly court battles ensued and in March 2001 – two years before their 25-year lease was due to expire – S&Co. decided to leave The Mount.

FIGURE 2.3 *A Midsummer Night's Dream*, dir. Tina Packer, 2000, Mainstage at The Mount

The departure was heartbreaking, not least for Packer: 'Our style has evolved because of this space. It's more than a theater; it's a home, a physical living space that's in our bodies and in our cells.'[34] It made sense, therefore, to close the chapter at The Mount with the same play with which they had opened it: *A Midsummer Night's Dream*. Packer revealed her romantic soul and her practical drive, when she voiced, 'The spirits of these woods, of Edith Wharton, who has looked after us these 25 years, we feed off their energy. And we're not stopping. We're just taking all that energy down the road.'[35]

Indeed, the place to which the *Dream* was propelling them was literally half a mile down the road, to a property they bought in April 2000 for $3.6 million: 70 Kemble Street.

70 Kemble Street: 'the indomitable spirit'[36]

Kemble Street was named after another British actress, who had once lived nearby: Fanny Kemble (1809–1893), a famous 'Juliet' and a prominent abolitionist. Number 70 was essentially a 64-acre campus with 23 (mainly derelict) buildings. It was no run-of-the-mill place and came with its own colorful history and heritage, which (just like The Mount) had led to its physical demise over the years.

Lenox Boys' School

The campus originally comprised three estates amalgamated to form Lenox Boys' School, founded in 1926 in the manner of an English public school. Its motto was *Non ministrari, sed ministrare*: 'Not to be served, but to serve.' Its patron saint, St. Martin, 'manifested humble self-service, fiery zeal and whole-hearted devotion to all he undertook.'[37] And the school's mascot, the little martin bird, stood 'for the indomitable spirit ... humble and moving in a spirit of perfect love for all men.'[38] This was uncannily appropriate for the three life-long, S&Co. members, Packer, Krausnick and Coleman, with their respective Quaker and Jesuit backgrounds. Equally appropriate was the school's strong Drama Club, devoted to the educational purpose of self-expression. In 1971 financial issues closed Lenox Boys' School. And for the next few years, the property remained in the hands of Lenox Savings Bank, before being bought in 1976 by the controversial ministry *The Bible Speaks*.

The Bible Speaks

The president of The Bible Speaks was (former bakery-truck driver) Pastor Carl Stevens, who operated the ministry's international headquarters from 70 Kemble Street. Stevens' tactics as 'God's authority' were persuasive, to say the least, and he soon gained the attention of the Christian Research Institute. Their investigations suggested that spiritual, emotional and financial havoc was being wreaked on the parishioners' lives. Dozens, it seems, had sold their homes to give thousands of dollars to the ministry. Widows had donated their life savings, with the promise of a better life if they lived in Lawrence Hall (the humble accommodation of Lenox Boys' School, now used by S&Co.'s seasonal artists and interns). It was when 33-year-old American heiress Betsy Dayton Dovydenas donated $7 million that blind eyes could no longer be turned. In 1986, the Doveydenas family brought a $5.5 million lawsuit against Stevens for 'undue influence and fraud.'[39] At which point The Bible Speaks declared bankruptcy, abandoned the Kemble Street campus (apparently overnight, leaving cups on the tables and dishes in the sinks), assets were liquidated and Stevens relocated. Betsy Doveydenas retained ownership of the campus from 1987 to 1993, when Kemble Street was sold to another colorful enterprise: the *National Music Foundation*.

The National Music Foundation

Incorporated in Florida in 1987, the NMF had previously changed its name twice from 'Starlite Starbrite Foundation' to the 'National Foundation for the Love of Rock'n'Roll.' And they planned to turn Kemble Street into a $30 million National Music Centre, with museum and retirement homes. But within a few years an audit revealed that NMF managers had engaged in 'questionable, ineffective, and inefficient' practices.[40] Furthermore, it transpired that they had entered into a Purchase and Sale agreement to sell the property to another not-for-profit organization (Shakespeare & Company, as it happens) which, 'if finalized, could result in a gain of over $3 million on this sale. Our analysis indicates that this gain is attributable to the $3,660,000 of taxpayer-funded grants that the NMF has received.'[41] The National Music Foundation was ordered to repay the hefty government grants as well as nearly $300,000 in potential lost-interest income. This

FIGURE 2.4 Aerial view of Kemble Street campus

was, of course, impossible: they were not-for-profit! They likewise disappeared. And so it was that, in 2000, Shakespeare & Company became the owners of 70 Kemble Street, with a mortgage financially arranged by the First Massachusetts' Bank and a big fundraising campaign to boot.

Shakespeare & Company's new home

10 April 2000 has been described as the most important date in Shakespeare & Company's history. With 16 months between purchase and move, there was plenty of time to contemplate the future at the new premises. Inevitably, the move would involve psychological, aesthetic and managerial transformations as the Company continued to expand its visions (if not always its bank account to the same degree).

The first vision was, of course, the property itself. And Packer's imagination was ablaze. She pictured a 'veritable [...] theater wonderland'[42] that would incorporate and expand all three strands of *Performance, Training* and *Education*. After all, Shakespeare & Company now had a physical plant with buildings, which could be converted into theatres, administrative offices and rehearsal spaces. There was also living accommodation not only for summer-season actors, but also for all the people who could now come to Shakespeare & Company for *Training* and *Education*. And if the teachers came during the summer – when performances were happening – they could see the work in action and then take it back into their communities. As for the enormous ice-hockey stadium – built by Lenox Boys' School and used by The Bible Speaks for large baptismal dunkings! – S&Co. could use this to make films of their workshops and intellectual properties, which could then be put online to develop distance learning. Packer pictured dance studios, outdoor performance areas, craft shops, coffee shops, restaurants: she had a plan for almost every inch of the property. Even as she was being ousted from her creative and spiritual home at The Mount, her mind was working overtime on new ventures: 'I've got this picture of what it's going to look like when it's all complete. [...] I'm very excited about it. It just means – it's a hell of a lot of work to raise this money.'[43] As well as a hell of a lot of institutional and organizational building.

Visions are one thing. Practicalities are another. And both are vital for an institution to evolve. The money to be raised was not just to launch these visionary projects: it was to salvage the buildings already on the campus, most of which were dilapidated and defunct. If Shakespeare & Company thought they had a Herculean task with The Mount, there were even more Augean stables to clear out at Kemble Street ...

Kemble Street performance spaces

The campus was (and remains) an architectural montage, including two farmhouses with Tudor-style barns, the ice-hockey rink (built during the 1960s and 1970s), the 1950s dormitories of Lawrence Hall, an adjacent Italianate mansion known as Spring Lawn, the colonial Clipston Grange, and the impressive St. Martin's Hall with its white cupola designed by the famous architectural team McKim, Meade and White. Of the 23 buildings only 6 were usable in 2000 (all of which had to be upgraded). Others were fenced off due to holes in the roofs, damaged foundations and faulty wiring. The marshy land was overgrown with reeds and grasses. And St. Martin's Hall sported a mossy, green carpet with puddles on the floor and pigeons in the attic. An estimated $17 million at that time would be needed to upgrade the whole site.

Yet the Company wasn't discouraged. Under the auspices of then Managing Director Christopher Sink, the administration moved into the 1950s library renamed the Miller Building (after Michael A. Miller, then Chair of the Board, who led the fundraising drive to make the move and has been a loyal supporter for many decades, along with his wife and longtime Company actress Annette). Immediate work began on consolidating possible performing venues to sustain the current repertoire while also having year-round, all-weather, moneymaking capabilities.

Spring Lawn

As one of the most magnificent and complete buildings, Spring Lawn was more or less usable (but not habitable) as-was. Built in the same year as The Mount – and architecturally and aesthetically similar – the Italianate mansion was the ideal replacement for The Salon to stage the Wharton plays. There was also the potential for outdoor Shakespeare performances on the mansion's sweeping lawn. And for several years, Spring Lawn provided a summer venue for Shakespeare & Company,[44] until 2007 when they had to sell off the property (along with Clipston Grange) to free up some much-needed capital.

52 History and roots

Founders' Theatre, or the Tina Packer Playhouse

If Shakespeare & Company were to generate income all year round, they would need an indoor theatre as quickly as possible. And the obvious choice for major development was a concrete 'Quonset' hut that had served as a gymnasium and cabaret venue for the erstwhile Lenox Boys' School. Packer wanted to manifest a theatre space 'in which people can let their hair down a bit but also create some mystery about the place.'[45]And because the Company was basically building a theatre from scratch, they could make every decision, including the choice of architect. (Mothers Nature and Necessity had called the shots at The Mount: now it was S&Co.'s turn.) To blend the mysterious and the mechanical, they sought the architectural skills of two key players. British theatre designer Iain Mackintosh had designed the Tricycle Theatre in Kilburn, as well as being part of the team who built London's Globe and the Cottesloe auditorium at the National Theatre, and author of the much-acclaimed *Architecture, Actor and Audience* (1993). His collaborator – architect George E. Marsh – was based at Boston's Payette Associates, a company renowned for reconfiguring campuses.

The first thing to consider was *the actor/audience relationship*. Rather than mourn the loss of the outdoor expanse at The Mount, they decided to celebrate the enclosed intimacy of the Quonset hut. Every audience member would be close to the stage, so the actors could directly impact each spectator with their energy. So a versatile performance space would be created whereby the intimacy could be experienced as *thrust* (three-sided actor/audience configuration); *arena* (four-sided actor/audience); or *traverse* (audience everywhere as the actors walk between them). Even if it were configured as *proscenium* (traditional two-way actor/audience), there would be a gallery on three of the four sides ensuring that the audience was above, as well as around, the actors at all times. In fact, this would emulate the Elizabethan playhouse much more closely than The Mount's Mainstage. That said there was a twist on the intimacy, which would retain some of The Mount's magic. There would be 'backstage' corridors running along the inside of the building's walls; thus, the audience would be enveloped by the actors, as much as the actors were surrounded by the audience. And footsteps might be heard or bodies might be glimpsed – just as they had been glimpsed through the trellises at The Mount. Though they still had to turn the actual concrete into magic ...

The previous 'mystery of the outdoors' is in many ways conjured by the materials of the theatre's construction. Using canvas and scaffold, the bones of the space are constantly on show (like the trees of the Mainstage). And the canvas sections of the construction move as the actors run about, which means that – be it *on*stage or *back*stage – you're 'never completely *off*stage'[46] (Krausnick). This aliveness in the materials suggests a hint of the wind that the great outdoors allowed, a contradiction of spaciousness and intimacy, airiness and enclosure. There's also a 'mystery' in the theatre's actual dimensions, which incorporate three overlapping circles extending from the lobby (with its large bay frontage), through the main auditorium and into the backstage area. These three overlapping circles are based on the *vesica piscis* (from the Latin 'fish bladder,' associated with the 'unconscious mind,' where the higher self meets the lower self). It's an image used in ancient wisdom traditions as well as freemasonry, ecclesiastical seals, the 'Flower of Life,' and Celtic, Roman, Islamic and Gothic art. Basically, the perimeter of one circle crosses the center of the next circle (as in a Venn diagram) and these three circles contribute to the symbolically feminine flow of the building.

Then there are the seats themselves … Part of the magic of *the actor/audience relationship*, and of the actual theatre space, is the dynamism of the *audience/audience relationship*. Not only can the spectators see each other across the intimate space, but they're also seated on fabric bench-seats *sans* arms. These were specifically designed to be comfortable, while at the same time rendering each spectator physically very close, ergo, emotionally available – both to each other and to the story.

Initially known as the Founders' Theatre (in honor of the twelve donors who each gave $250,000 for its completion), it was renamed in 2012 by the Board of Trustees as the Tina Packer Playhouse, to celebrate the community's appreciation of Packer's extraordinary impact.

However, it's not the only on-campus playhouse to be named after an impactful female.

The Bernstein Center for the Performing Arts

Elayne Polly Bernstein Schwartz (1924–2011) was a generous, longtime supporter of Shakespeare & Company and the primary donor for creating the

FIGURE 2.5 Tina Packer Playhouse: break in rehearsals, *The Merchant of Venice*, 2016.
Photo: John Dolan

54 History and roots

building on campus initially known as the Berkshire Center for the Performing Arts, renamed in 2009 the Bernstein Center for the Performing Arts. Through her generous philanthropy and deep understanding of the Company's mission, Bernstein and her family enabled the conversion of the vast, indoor hockey rink and its accompanying field house (a 72,000-square-foot structure) into S&Co.'s creative nucleus. It comprises scene shop, costume shop, prop shop, armory, rehearsal studios and an intimate 180-seater space: the Elayne Bernstein Theatre, which provides a venue for contemporary repertoire (in the manner of the Stables at The Mount). In fact, the layout of the whole building is designed like The Mount, with rooms fluidly connecting to each other. The local master-architect Stefan Green[47] designed an indoor, spiral configuration, so that the production departments have easy access to each other as well as to the rehearsal rooms. And the building was completed on time and within budget thanks to the project's manager, Executive Director Nicholas J. Puma. Puma had been brought into the Company by Mark Jones, the then Managing Director. No strangers to turning companies around, Jones' and Puma's arrival in 2007 was a major turning point for Shakespeare & Company. Until then, an 'artist management' structure had endured (whereby the actors also had administrative responsibilities). Remarkably successful in many respects, the model demanded unconscionable working hours from Company members, and as S&Co. expanded, the model was quickly outgrowing itself. To this day 'the artist manager model' is an important aspect of S&Co.'s ethos, though it was Puma's level-headed, no-nonsense background in finance, administration and law that galvanized the Company at that critical moment. And by completing the building on 26 December 2007, Puma consolidated their physical nexus. EBT (as the whole complex is affectionately known) brings together under one roof the *Training, Education* and *Performance* programs in a hubbub of year-round activity. And whenever the studios are free, actors can work independently from dawn till dusk till dark and beyond: there's no clocking-off time for the Muse.

There are two more noteworthy 'contents' in EBT. An exhibit of the Lenox Boys' School history can be found in the lobby. Meanwhile, the remnants of a display in a back corridor show the models and ground plans of another ambitious plan …

The Rose Playhouse

When S&Co. originally bought 70 Kemble Street, the lure for Packer was largely the chance to realize many dreams in one location. Her biggest dream was an American Center for Shakespeare Performance and Studies. This would be an epicenter of enquiry drawing practitioners and scholars from around the world for creative stimulation and personal regeneration. Here, the Elizabethan principles that underpin S&Co. (the historical, social, spiritual, political and philosophical ideas) could be shared and debated. And Packer believed that bringing together the intellectual rigor of scholars and the creative aspiration of

Bricks and mortar, trellis and trees **55**

artists could reignite and repurpose Renaissance ideals. Not only for the mutual inspiration of each other, but also for the 'betterment' of the world.

Every aspect of this vision was huge. Exhibitions in this Center would connect 'modern America to Elizabethan England and Renaissance Europe.' These exhibitions would emphasize artistic and scientific revolutions; lawyers and the common law; the art of rhetoric and America's founding documents; sea voyages and the beginning of the slave trade; 1492 as the year Columbus and the expulsion of the Jews began in Spain; the printing press and the computer; timber framing, thatching, stonemasonry and other building methods; and the role of Shakespeare in America today.[48] And the vision didn't stop there …

The Center would be part of a whole 'Rose Renaissance Village.' The village would embrace the global and the local community, benefiting both scholarship and tourism. And the vision didn't even stop there …

When the purchase of the Kemble Street property was announced in April 2000, Packer shared:

> we're going to build the Rose Theater, which is the precursor to the Globe. We'll do an absolute replica, […] that is the shape and space that the plays were written for. The young directors can direct in there; they can do what they like. They can deconstruct, because […] it will come from knowledge and not from ignorance. […] So I want a Rose Theater. I'd build a Globe, but they've built it already. It's a huge thing that I have to do, institutionally.
>
> *(Packer interview, 11 May 2000: 28)*

The original Rose Playhouse had been built around 1587 on the banks of the Thames. It was a 14-sided polygon, 72 feet in diameter with a thrust stage, a timber frame, plaster-and-lathe exterior, thatched roof, and an architectural design that incorporated all kinds of esoteric principles. The acoustic chambers built into the structure enabled the actors' voices to bounce off the audience, 'sending the energy into the skies to serve [the Elizabethan] God and see his greatness. The theatre was a spiritual place, however bawdy the pit might be!'[49] (Packer). And thus the acoustics of the building 'strengthened the vibrations between the actors and the audience so that the space became a true debating chamber.'[50] If S&Co. could build a Rose to the actual dimensions, incorporating the practical and 'spiritual' architecture of the original, they would bring Packer's and Linklater's initial dream of the potency of live theatre to unimagined fruition. Indeed, Packer's passion to build a replica in New England was feverish. It was almost as if the inner ire of being expelled from The Mount ignited an inferno in her to put Shakespeare & Company on the map in a bigger, better, more holistic and coherent way than might ever have been possible while shackled to EWR.

Within a year, the Company had raised $5 million. Indeed, senator Ted Kennedy granted them $1 million to expand the *Education* programs and hold two

56 History and roots

conferences on the feasibility of creating the Rose. By 2002, they had $100,000 from the National Endowment for the Arts and $1 million from an anonymous donor. A team of experts comprising international consultants and architects was brought in to investigate many of the historical questions plus a burning contemporary one: 'how can an authentic Elizabethan theater be made to conform to modern building codes?'[51] After all, the aim was to use entirely original materials and construction methods: as Berkshire County was the American center of the timber framers' guild, there was a goldmine of local knowledge. And in all these discussions, the chief authority was Peter McCurdy, the timber framer who had built the Globe in London and was subsequently both the architect and timber framer on the Wanamaker Theatre.

The footprint of the Rose Playhouse was identified on a large, grassy area (in a low-lying field at the foot of the incline down from the Founders' Theatre). Local geometer Rachel Fletcher assessed the best location by aligning all the buildings on the property and finding the water and energy lines, all according to the principles of balance and synergy. 'Geometry' (stemming from the Greek words for 'earth' and 'measuring') is

> a technique for spatial organization evolved in western culture from ancient Egyptian sages and surveyors and from Greek philosophers. It was preserved by master builders of Gothic cathedrals and later revived by humanists and artists of the Renaissance. It continues to influence the way we see the world today.
>
> Geometry informs the perennial question of unity in a complex world. Regular geometric figures – the triangle, the square, and the pentagon – contain specific ratios and proportions which can mediate diverse elements and quantities.
>
> *(Fletcher, R., 'Introduction to the Geometer's Angle,' Nexus Network*
> *Journal: Architecture and Mathematics, Vol. 6, No. 2,*
> *October 2004: 93)*

Thus, Fletcher's plan would unify the diverse perspectives of the architects, designers and artists into one, practical location.

By August 2001, the selected site had been marked out with colored tape to define the entrance, gallery, stage and courtyard. And a groundbreaking was set for the fall of 2003 with a completion date of 2007. That would be just seven years from the seed of a thought to its final construction. (About a quarter of the 27 years taken to finance and build London's replica Globe!) Yet Packer was convinced this project would propel Shakespeare & Company from a regional entity to a national and international platform, drawing Shakespeare lovers from around the world, truly rendering 70 Kemble Street a theatre 'destination.' This was clearly a massive plan. Especially given the immediate renovation of buildings needed just to make the campus habitable and workable. Not to mention the proposed demolition of the derelict buildings beyond repair.

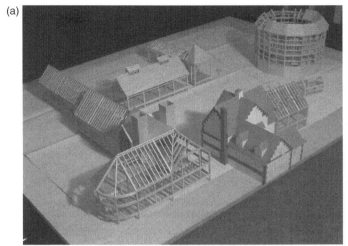

FIGURE 2.6 (a) Rose Playhouse and Renaissance Village model and design, Payette Associates; (b) Rose Playhouse composite image, Payette Associates

To date there is no American Center, Renaissance Village or Rose Playhouse. The upkeep of the campus proved to be much higher than the calculations provided by the National Music Foundation, and the previous annual budget of $2 million at The Mount immediately doubled to $4 million at Kemble Street. Although two fundraising campaigns garnered $16 million, which pretty much covered the move to the property and the upgrade to existing buildings (converting the Quonset hut and the ice-rink into theatres, bringing the internet into the administrative building and replacing windows in the living spaces). The Rose's tented 'footprint' does, however, remain on the intended spot as an outdoor performance area. Here Riotous Youth and Shakespeare & Young Company Conservatory programs perform in the summer days, and the odd actor may be found in

58 History and roots

the wee small hours rehearsing a favorite monologue. It also serves as the 'wet weather option' for the Company's most recent space created to sustain its aesthetic. But before we head to that location, a managerial sidebar ...

A managerial sidebar

In 2006, the Board of Trustees asked Tina Packer to step aside as Artistic Director on the promise of $1 million of shares offered by a benefactor, essentially because the Board needed to understand the Company's long-term survival without Packer at the helm.[52] For much of the previous decade, she had been assembling 'Associate Artistic Director' teams: each team comprised two people, who in Year 1 would take on the planning of a projected season and in Year 2 would execute that season; in other words, they would be responsible for programming, casting, budgeting, etc. This strategy provided a means of fathoming who might follow in her stead. It was always clear, however, that she wasn't 'standing down' but rather 'stepping aside': while the day-to-day running of an ever-expanding company was exhausting, her creative drive was unflagging. So she would remain a very active part of the Company, sharing her office as 'Founding Artistic Director' (so-named by the Trustees) with the various 'Associate Artistic Directors,' among whom were Allyn Burrows, Jonathan Epstein, Michael Hammond, Cecil MacKinnon, Gary Mitchell and Tony Simotes.

There followed several turbulent years. Some of the associates, including Burrows, moved on to other artistic ventures. For a while, it seemed that Hammond might be a strong candidate, before Simotes took on the mantel; however, he was quickly hampered by ill health, leaving Packer still handling many of the managerial tasks. Then Executive Director Rick Dildine stepped in and took the reins for six months, before longtime Company members Ariel Bock and Jonathan Croy were temporarily appointed joint Artistic Directors. And in 2016, Burrows returned to Shakespeare & Company after seven years running Actors' Shakespeare Project (ASP) in Boston, and Adam Davis[53] was appointed Managing Director. The turbulence subsided. And one of the first visions that Burrows realized was a new performance space ...

The Roman Garden Theatre

Allyn Burrows had first joined Shakespeare & Company as an actor in 1989. He worked for 18 seasons at The Mount, where he experienced the symbiotic relationship between Shakespeare's language and performing outside – especially in the beauty of the Berkshires. His muscle memory of S&Co., therefore, included the way in which their style and aesthetic were defined by the great outdoors. And so he wanted to take his audiences back to the magic of Mother Nature, Father Time and the 'cosmic design' of Shakespeare's imagination. In collaboration with Berkshires-based, scenic designer Jim Youngerman – and underwritten by a generous, local sponsor (from whom the letters Ro- and -man form the theatre's name) – Burrows created an intimate, open-air venue at Kemble Street.

The 280-seater theatre nestles across from the Tina Packer Playhouse in an enclosed garden carefully tended by the committed volunteer gardeners. With St. Martin's Hall as an imposing backdrop (including its myriad windows and fire-escape) and in the midst of some mighty pines, Burrows made his Artistic Director debut with *The Tempest* in 2017. Thus, he restored to S&Co.'s home its immersion in nature and its legacy of outdoor Shakespeare. Youngerman's set included a wooden stage structure, bulrushes, platforms in the various trees for

FIGURE 2.7 Roman Garden Theatre: *The Tempest*, dir. Allyn Burrows, 2017: (a) Ella Loudon (Miranda), Deaon Griffin-Pressley (Ferdinand); (b) Josh McCabe (Stephano), Martin Jason Asprey (Caliban)

Photo: Stratton McCrady

60 History and roots

Tamara Hickey's Ariel and a fire-escape look-out for Nigel Gore's Prospero. As Trinculo the jester, I can attest that Mother Nature became another character in the cast: with performances starting at dusk, each show was accompanied by twittering birds and whittering critters, a rabbit that hopped onto the stage one night and the stir of the breeze in the trees. The lighting designer was also Mother Nature, contributing her many shades of sunset as the evening fell.

In 2018 and 2019 S&Co. staged four more outdoor productions. Longtime education artist Kelly Galvin directed *Love's Labour's Lost* (2018) (see Figure 10.1) and *The Taming of the Shrew* (2019) at The Dell with artists and interns from *Education*. A second Burrows–Youngerman collaboration in the Roman Garden Theatre was *As You Like It* (2018), and Kevin G. Coleman directed *The Merry Wives of Windsor* (2019) with Youngerman incorporating St. Martin's Hall as Windsor Castle. By recreating an open-air space at Kemble Street, Burrows is revisiting and reinvigorating the expansive aesthetic first germinated by Shakespeare & Company over 40 years ago in the fir forest by The Mount. When actors have the opportunity to raise their voices to the skies and stir the audience with breath and body, the true function of the theatre perhaps becomes most apparent.

Notes

1 Freeman, N. (2001), *The Applause First Folio of Shakespeare: Comedies, Histories & Tragedies*, London and New York: Applause, p. vii.
2 ibid.
3 Packer cited in Epstein, H. (1985), *The Companies She Keeps: Tina Packer Builds A Theater*, Massachusetts: Plunkett Lake Press, pp. 66–67.
4 Krausnick cited in Epstein (1985), p. 70.
5 Henry James cited in Marshall, S. (1997), *The Mount: Home of Edith Wharton*, Lenox: Edith Wharton Restoration, Inc., p. 55.
6 Wharton was the first woman in history to receive the Pulitzer Prize for Fiction with *The Age of Innocence* (1921) and the second woman ever elected to the American Academy of Arts and Letters in 1930.
7 Wharton returned to the States only once to receive her honorary doctorate from Yale.
8 Marshall (1997), p. 135.
9 Including The Mount, the Vanderbilt Westinghouse, the farmhouses and stables.
10 Mitchell Berenson was Chair of the Board, with Bill Lieberman as Managing Director. There were artists from Packer's production of *The Learned Ladies* at Smith College (including Andrea Haring, Noni Pratt, Jeff Deutsch, Gina Weiss, and Bill Balou); Linklater's associates (including John Hadden and Natsuko Ohama); colleagues from England (including Gillian Bargh and Lorna Heilbron); graduates from NYU (including Gregory Uel Cole, Tony Simotes and Kaia Calhoun); and recent collaborators at Smith College (including costume designer Kiki Smith). Later, 'Resource People' (as described in a 1978 'Argument and Rationale for Shakespeare & Company: An American/British Classical Theatre Group' document, S&Co. archive) were listed as Tina Packer (Artistic Director), Kristin Linklater (Director of Training and Education), B. H. Barry (Stage Fighting and Tumbling Master), John Broome (Master-Teacher for Movement), Dennis Krausnick (Director), Kenny McBain (Associate Director – and 'British liaison') and Peggy Marks (Managing Director).

Bricks and mortar, trellis and trees **61**

11 Bill Balou was technical director and lighting designer. Brian Miller was sound designer. And the cast featured Krausnick as Theseus, Bargh as Hippolyta, Heilbron as Hermia, Cole as Oberon, Simotes as Puck, Haring as Titania, Hadden as Thisbe, and Ohama, Weiss and Pratt as the fairy band.

12 Jonathan Epstein cited in Garcia de Rosier, T. (2001), 'New stages of life: Shakespeare & Company troupe savors final days at Wharton estate,' *Times Union*, 12 August 2001.

13 Epstein (1985), p. 73.

14 Jonathan Croy interview with Bella Merlin, August 2016.

15 Eric Booth, Allyn Burrows, Joseph Marcell, Corinna May, Barry Primus, Harris Yulin and Kristin Wold could also be added to the tiger grapplers of the early years.

16 Tina Packer interview with KB, PM, 11 May 2000. Subject number: #TH-004, p. 27. S&Co. archive, (my emphasis).

17 S&Co. Welcome document, 2002. S&Co. archive.

18 Mission Statement, undated c.1998 reflecting on the Company's creation in 1978. S&Co. archive, (my emphasis).

19 www.shakespeare.org (accessed 17 September 2019).

20 'Statement of Values that Unite Us,' c. 2002. S&Co. archive.

21 Tina Packer, 'From the Artistic Director,' season program 1979. S&Co. archive.

22 www.shakespeare.org

23 ibid.

24 ibid.

25 'Shakespeare & Company' overview document, c. late 1978. S&Co. archive.

26 Cole cited in Epstein (1985), p. 94, (my emphasis).

27 Dukakis also played Mother Courage in 2013 directed by her erstwhile student Tony Simotes.

28 www.shakespeare.org, (my emphasis).

29 Shakespeare, W. (1606), *King Lear*, Act I, Scene iv, line 252, King Lear.

30 www.shakespeare.org

31 ibid.

32 They were Berenson, Krausnick, Packer, Berhle, Cole and Crane.

33 *King Lear*, Act II, Scene iv, lines 291–292, Regan.

34 Packer cited in Garcia De Rosier (2001).

35 Packer cited in Borak, J. (2001), '"All's Well that ends Well": Curtain Falls at The Mount,' *The Berkshire Eagle*, 4 September 2001.

36 Lenox Boys' School exhibition, S&Co., EBT.

37 ibid.

38 ibid.

39 https://law.justia.com/cases/federal/district-courts/BR/81/750/1,821,797/ (accessed 21 October 2019).

40 https://www.mass.gov/files/documents/2016/08/qa/199943973.pdf pp. 1–2 (accessed 15 September 2019).

41 ibid. pp. 1–2.

42 Packer interview, 11 May 2000, p. 28.

43 ibid., pp. 26, 28.

44 Productions included David Egan's *The Fly-Bottle* with Michael Hammond, Dave Demke and Dennis Krausnick in 2003, and Tina Packer and Diane Prusha in Peter Shaffer's *Lettuce and Lovage* in 2004.

45 Packer cited in Borak, J. (2001), '"All the World's a Stage": An International Team Readies the New Founders' Theatre at Shakespeare & Co.' *Berkshires Week*, 14 June 2001.

46 Krausnick cited in ibid. (my emphasis).

47 Chosen by George E. Marsh at Payette Associates, designers of the Founders' Theatre.

48 'Shakespeare & Company: Mission Statement, Statement of Values, Statement of Vision,' undated, c. 2000. S&Co. archive.
49 Packer notes, April 2019. How the Elizabethans defined 'God' and how a twenty-first-century artist and audience might, can be configured wholly compatibly. But that's another book …
50 ibid.
51 Gaines, J. (2001), 'Renaissance Woman: Stage Impresario Tina Packer has no Small Dreams. Her latest is to Re-Create an Elizabethan Theater in the Berkshires,' *The Boston Globe Magazine*, 12 August 2001.
52 Unfortunately the investment did not come to fruition as intended and $1 million manifested as $300,000.
53 Longtime Managing Director at the Los Angeles County Arts Commission.

3

TALK #1

Function of the Theatre

[*This chapter (along with Chapters 5 and 14) is a written version of a talk – or 'Socratic discussion' – presented by Tina Packer during the Month-Long Intensive described in 'Act II.' Function of the Theatre is typically given during Week 1.*]

I noticed in my teen years, when I found I really liked to be on stage, I was always asking myself, 'Yes, but why?' I liked playing hockey, too, but I never thought to ask why. It was great, running up and down the field, whacking the ball, seeing where everyone else was, passing off the play. And the goal was to win! And then pretend to be modest about it. Physical exertion, a struggle, belonging to a tribe, and a result.

But performing in a play was different. Why did I like being up there in front of others? Why did I like expressing the emotions of someone who was not me? Why did I desire to play more and more kinds of people? To get into the minds of murderers? Whores? Pathetic underlings? And why did I want people to watch me? And why did I never feel real, unless the audience was present? And what was it all for, anyway?

Those were the questions I carried with me. And when I finally put together my own company – and, therefore, could play a leadership role in where the artistic emphasis of the company would go – I started to get insights into what it was all about.

I'd been frightened in my teens and twenties that it was about showing off my physical attributes. After all, page 3 of *The Sun* newspaper each day had another 'actress' revealing enough of her goods to inspire masculine desire and sell more newspapers.

But the older I got and the less likely to fill those pictorial desires, the more I knew there was something far more important about one group of people enacting a story in front of a much larger group of people. In fact, I was fairly

FIGURE 3.1 Tina Packer, London, 1972
Photo: Laurie Asprey

sure our psychological and social selves *depended* on it. And the less popular theatre seemed to become – with fewer and fewer people attending live performances – the more urgent it became for me to understand *why* the stories that theatre was telling were not important to the community, and *why* people didn't want to gather together ritually in one place to hear those stories anymore. We were losing theatre at our peril. And my desire to articulate its purpose became central to all the work I was doing in the theatre.

In order to articulate this purpose I'm going to tell a story. The story may or may not be true. It's *based* in truth (as far as we know it) but its real function is to give a framework, within which we can posit certain truths. And the story's purpose is to arouse sensations, to ask the brain to think, to connect ourselves to our ancestors, and to see how we are all part of the human race.

Where did theatre begin? There are usually two answers. It began with the Rain Dance when the tribe was desperate for water. And it began with the story of the hunt when the tribe needed the meat of the Woolly Mammoth. Both are essential to our story now.

Let's start with the Rain Dance.

If you're a small, insignificant mammal desperate for food or water in a huge, uncontrollable world, it's a good idea to think you can do something about it, rather than think, 'I'm insignificant on the face of this earth, so I'd better just lay down and die!' No! You make up a story about a god or gods or goddesses,

Talk #1: Function of the Theatre **65**

who have control over the wind and water and sky and harvest. And you get into relationship with them. You send them offerings to placate their rage. You sing them songs to let them know that you know they're all powerful. You say you're sorry for any sins you might have committed. You might even offer up some virgin as a sacrifice (page 3 of *The Sun* again) to placate the gods and beg of them, 'Please don't kill us all with this heat!' If that doesn't work, you start the Rain Dance that goes on for three days and three nights to alter the energy of the earth and the sky and the moon until the rain comes. (And often it *does* come, thereby proving the dance is effective.)

Whatever the ritual might be, it's done with great reverence, and it *puts us into relationship* with those elements in our lives over which we have no power. Not to be in relationship with our natural world was the most terrifying prospect for our ancestors. So they made up rites and rituals to put them into relationship. And they designated the shamans to hold the knowledge of the ways of the gods, and perform the rites and rituals that would placate them. It's all about relationship: the only antidote to excruciating odds.

Now to the second part of the origins of theatre – the Hunt of the Woolly Mammoth – which is perhaps even more important than the rites and rituals to the Rain God.

What's the difference between a storyteller telling the story of the hunt around the campfire and the re-enactment of the hunt by the warriors of the tribe? Well, the storyteller might be a great storyteller, but it's not actually happening in the present moment. When groups of men get up, however, and a couple of other men dress themselves in furs and become the Woolly Mammoth, and they actually go through the tracking, stalking, calling, baiting, slaughter of the Woolly Mammoth … Now we're really talking about excitement *in the here and now*! Added to which we're passing on crucial knowledge *in the body and mind* to the young men who have not yet been on the hunt, but will go on it the next time. And if we can enact it again, and even put those novice hunters into the action, then their chance of survival – when the Woolly Mammoth directly charges them – is multiplied many times, because they've performed the dry-run first. They know how to be *with* their fear. They know how to stand their ground and throw their spear only when the beast is close enough for their aim to land accurately. They're trained to judge beyond the primitive fight-freeze-or-flight mechanisms. They can know the smell, taste, sound of slaughter *before* they actually go to the theatre of slaughter. (The army knows the benefit of rehearsing battles and they enact several mock battles before they ask their recruits to go into the real 'Theatre of War.') And as every good actor knows, the make-believe event is just as alive as the event itself – perhaps even more so because the make-believe event allows for a kind of 'consciousness' (as we'll look at again in Chapter 14: 'Theatre, Therapy and Theology'). The real-life event goes so fast, but in the staged event we can be aware of what we're saying and doing, and then we can be aware of the

66 History and roots

repercussions of our actions. And, in many ways, rehearsals comprise the layering-in of those levels of consciousness.

I think these two functions of theatre remain the essence of theatre. The *rites and rituals* allow us to create relationships, both with each other and with the gods (in other words, with the conscious and unconscious forces in our lives). And then *the enactment of life-threatening circumstances* (whether comic or tragic) allows us to gain insight into what life is all about, without actually having to suffer the consequences. It also allows us to live out our personal tragedies and understand the consequences of our violent actions (consequences, which we so often ignore or brush aside in daily life, as we'll again come back to in Chapter 14). And, thereby, we can build a bigger picture of humankind's suffering and humankind's collective responsibility.

Above all, we need to have *the audience* – a community – present while these rituals and enactments are taking place. The actors are acting for the audience. And they couldn't do what they're doing *without* the audience. They couldn't do it because the attention of the audience gives the energy boost to the actors. Also, if the audience weren't there, there would be no point in telling the story in the first place!

So the audience attends to the action. They connect their bodies and minds to the events on stage. And the energy of their focus and attention acts as a magnifier for the actor, in that the actor's body, mind and voice are injected with the spiritual focus that comes *from* the audience. By being a 'witness' the audience gives authenticity to the action. And the actor's job is to be able to *harness this energy* coming from the audience; *enhance the collective imaginative acts* created by and for the gathering; and then *give larger significance* to the actions of the play. It's an expanded awareness that everyone takes part in. The actors are the guides – or shamans, if you will – but the communion cannot nor will not take place anywhere but in the ritual space of the theatre. Acknowledging that the audience is key to the act of acting – and that the acting will be expanded, influenced and changed by the audience – is the essence of live theatre.

This doesn't happen in television or film, as the audience isn't directly affecting the actors in the moment of performance (and *vice versa*). It does happen in stand-up comedy and with some performance art. But the live nature of theatre inevitably builds community between the people actually watching it and the people actually performing it. And because of that community, live theatre can penetrate a deeper place in our collective psyches than television or film can allow. To some extent in 'the old days' – when the whole country was watching the same shows at the same time on a limited number of television channels – there was, in a way, a space for collective conversation, even though the art form itself couldn't directly affect the audience. But now there's such a barrage of content, our sensory perception is overwhelmed. And since there's no live audience to affect the creative act of acting or storytelling, there's no ritual space in television and film.

Even so, we pay not nearly enough attention to the ritual space of *theatre*. All too often we want something to take our minds off events happening in our lives, rather than plunging us more deeply into questioning why as human beings we behave the way we do. Great comedy can certainly relieve us for a while of the tension of our industrialized and computerized lives. Television can certainly give us respite from the tedium of our overstimulation by inconsequential 'stuff'; but because television lacks a collective audience – all sitting in the same place, focused toward the same atrocity – it allows us to feel safe in a violent world without questioning our participation in *creating* that world. Film's primary function is to entertain, rather than change, its viewer. And while it may provoke big emotions, there's no shared place for that message to go: no ritual space, no audience energy that can (however temporarily) allow a sense of collective power. Therefore, live theatre is the best place we have to explore – whether it's comically or tragically – the egregious stupidity of mankind, and to have some insight about it, and to *know* that we all know it! Only in theatre is the audience essential to the enactment of the story. Only in theatre is there enough energy to create a *transcendence*. Only in theatre is it possible to tap into the power of the gods and know that, in our individual and collective souls, we can be in touch with the art that expands our consciousness and leads us to action.

So what training does an actor need to be able to work openly and vulnerably with the audience? That's the subject of 'Act II' of this book. For some reason (as I'll touch on in Chapter 5: 'Actor/Audience Relationship'), drama schools and conservatories in the Western world ignore this facet of actor training. Some go as far as to pretend there's a 'fourth wall' between the actors and the audience, and try to ignore the audience altogether: 'Oh, those 500 people are not there! I'll shut them out and shut them off!' This is stupidity in the extreme and one of the reasons why theatre is dying. In the quintessential English pantomime, you end up dead if the audience doesn't tell you that the villain is there. 'He's behind you! He's behind you!' the children scream to stop the villain from perpetrating his evil acts. The audience has a major role to play, as everyone knows, in the telling of stories of good and evil. And to be saved from evil is one of the most important functions of theatre.

But before we go to 'Actor/Audience Relationship,' I want to skip through the history of Western theatre: in part to strengthen my thesis and in part to offer some suggestions as to why we've got ourselves into a weak position as far as theatre's function in society is concerned. I also want to make some general observations about where we might go.

Human consciousness and theatre go hand in hand. The storytelling of Homer (possibly one person; possibly many; possibly women – but most likely men) is around 800 BCE. *The Iliad* is a story about war and it's a written version of an oral story, passed down through generations. So, whenever it began, it involved a storyteller(s) and an audience. It's not until around 400 BCE that the first great construction of amphitheatres begins

68 History and roots

where audiences can go to hear a play. And the structure of these theatres is important. They're in *places of great physical beauty* where the mountains, the sky, the crevices in the rocks, the relationship to the heavens are of seminal importance: we're in the presence of the gods. The theatres are *large enough to house the whole community* (women and slaves included). And they are *acoustical chambers*: so the dimensions of the seating tiers (possibly with brass urns built into the ascending stairways) amplified the notes of the human voice, so that every person could hear what was being said.[1] The singing, the vibration of the voices and the dancing kept the order of the universe in place. The altar of Dionysus in the center of the playing area was both the fulcrum of chaos and the restoration to order. The three actors wore archetypal masks with a hole for speaking which amplified their voices. And the voice was primary. The plays were written in poetic form, and there are many descriptions of the voices hovering between singing and speaking – so it's an elevated sound (it's not conversational). The actors' faces and bodies were essentially the 'local habitation' and the 'name'[2] to which the audience could attach their imaginations as the characters moved between the heavens and the earth.

But for me, the aspect I'm fascinated by is the *content of the stories* they told. So let's tell the story of Oedipus …

A child is thrown onto the hillside by his parents because of the prophecy that he'll kill his father and marry his mother. The child doesn't die: he grows up. And he does kill a stranger at the crossroads (who will turn out to be his father) and he does marry a queen (who will turn out to be his mother). And they have children. Now all of society is suffering from the plague: Oedipus sets out to discover why they're suffering. He discovers it's because he has married his mother and, indeed, killed his father. In grief he blinds himself and has to be led around for the rest of his days by his daughter, Antigone.

Now let's tell the story of Medea …

A king is in captivity and is rescued from his fate by a woman, who forsakes her own country and family to free him and live with him in a strange land. They have children. But then the king tires of her and wants to make a second, more prestigious, marriage to a younger bride. His wife is so enraged that she kills their young children and sends a poisoned robe to the young wife. The king is left with nothing but his guilt. The gods, meanwhile, take Medea up to the heavens to be with them.

These are the stories that the whole of Athens or Thebes would see enacted. Not naturalistic acting, but huge, bold strokes. The sounds of the voices, the rhythms of the poetry, the comments of the chorus (a group of citizens), the rhythmic dancing: all these elements combined to create a story of human error, including transgressions and family dynamics that society hasn't yet understood. These are stories about the universals of human behavior. Do sons want to usurp their fathers? Marry their mothers? Do wives want to kill their husbands' children? Kill their competitors in love? And why would a city-state come together to explore these dramatized narratives?

Well, before the birth of the city-state, people lived in tribes. Then the city-state drew many tribes together for protection and commerce. And suddenly it was necessary to learn to live with people who weren't the same blood type, nor kith and kin. So stories needed to be told to map the human psyche and to know that these stories are universal across all tribes. In other words, it's universal that *actions have consequences* regardless of our tribe. And if our tribes are now living side by side, we have to create a new ritual. And the ritual of theatre is almost a process of *building community* artificially. Let's take a look at how it does that …

It is thought by some (myself included) that the chorus of concerned citizens, as presented in the plays, is a derivation of women's lamentation rites for the dead, rites that were told within the tribe and were exceedingly powerful. It was the women who once owned the rites and rituals of both birth and death. When someone died, it was necessary that *catharsis* (a 'letting go') took place. And how you did this was by telling all the stories about the dead person – all the good stuff, all the bad stuff, and everything in between. This went on for days and the dead body was taken to the crossroads in the village so that more people could join the lamentation. The hair was torn, the thymus thumped, the skin lacerated, sometimes the lamenters even killed themselves. And – most importantly – *the truth was told*. The collective voices were taking the soul of the dead person from this world to the next. And you knew the soul had arrived when the mourners were exhausted: they had said everything that needed to be said, and catharsis (the 'letting go') had taken place. The whole action was predicated on *telling the truth* as far as those left behind were concerned: all the good stuff *and* all the shitty stuff. These rites were very powerful in Greece (and still are in some parts of the world today).

However, when the city-states of Greece started organizing themselves into armies – and the separate tribes were no longer fighting for their own tribe, but rather for a new collective concept called 'Athens' or 'Sparta' – different stories about death were needed. A soldier needed to die 'for Athens': he needed to die heroically with his wounds to the fore (to prove that he wasn't running away). So the lamentation rites – which were all predicated on the truth being told (the good, the bad and the complex) – were no longer such an acceptable idea. Instead, 'Athens' and the hero story had to take precedence. And so lamentation rites were officially banned. But they were still a powerful part of people's sense of the ritual of dying: so, they couldn't just disappear. Instead, they became elevated. The playwrights made them an integral part of the great, collective play festivals, with the chorus representing and reflecting the voice of the people. So now we can wail, say wise things, invoke grief – but within the structure of a play.

In fact, the authorities now made some rules. As an audience we can still lament in the old style – tear our hair, thump our thymus – but we're forbidden from killing ourselves in lamentation as we used to be able. And the whole thing will take place in the theatre where, as a community, we can hopefully get some perspective on events. We'll have playwriting competitions, so that the city-fathers can choose the best, most suitable plays. Which means there'll be some control over our emotions. We'll be in a contained space. And hopefully a new collective consciousness can come forth from these stories. And we can see that we have things in common with people who are *not* our tribe, but are actually part of 'Athens,' our new identity. And we'll tell stories that won't necessarily invoke 'the whole truth' anymore, but they'll present powerful, new relationships and build the kind of stories that the city-fathers deem best suited to our collective living.

Thus theatre begins its long journey of self-censorship, as well as its insights into human behavior and its attempt to develop our consciousness with others, so that we can all live in cities with some collective understanding. We sit in an amphitheatre where everyone can see everyone else. And the wrap-around energy of the audience fuels the actors to vocal depths and heights, triggering – through sounds – the common chords of grief and joy. We're all sitting *together* and this history is *our* history. And if we're going to fight for our country, it'll be a collective effort – with the gods blessing us and the wind blowing in the right direction. And if we marry a foreigner, we won't betray her but rather welcome her into our midst. And we'll try to be conscious of our desire to kill our fathers and marry our mothers, and not sacrifice our children without due consultation with the spouse! Even if he's married to someone else now!

Gradually Rome took over Greece. And although the Greeks were considered the intellectuals of Rome, Rome's love affairs with their armies, their laws and their acquisition of foreign territories resulted in a less interesting theatre. Rome – as a generalization (and what else am I doing here but making generalizations about great swathes of history and cultural endeavor in order to tell my story?) – understood human behavior well enough to realize that, to control the masses of their vast territories, they needed to divide entertainment into three parts: the theatre, the amphitheatre and the circus. And everywhere they went, they entertained and 'civilized' their great empire with these three activities.

The Roman *amphitheatre* (usually completely round like the Coliseum) was where the real bloodletting took place. Rock-star gladiators fought every sort of wild animal – brought in from every part of the empire – resulting in their own death or that of the animal. They also fought each other, which again resulted in a death. Since gladiators came from the slave class, 'kill or be killed' was one of their few paths to freedom, because there was the slight chance that if you killed enough humans and animals, freedom ('manumission') would be granted – and maybe even the bed of an aristocratic Roman lady. For a short while the Romans also put to death pacifist Christians and other people they despised. And it was here in the amphitheatre that the bloodlust and (hopefully) catharsis would take place, so that the citizens would be too exhausted with the horrors of the bloodletting to turn on their Roman bosses.

The *circus* is where the chariot races took place. The whole empire divided into teams. You belonged to the blue team or the green team or some other color, and you screamed your heart out for your team. It was here in the circus that all the competitive urges could be developed:

> My team wins! Me and my fellow blues are the best team on the gods' earth! We're not a piece of rubbish in the great Roman Empire! We're the blues and we're the best – even though we're just sitting in the stands emotionally connecting with our (invented) tribe.

(This holds good with the Red Sox or Manchester United today)

The *theatre* was a bit of a poor relation in this triumvirate – which may be why tragic Roman plays never reached the popularity of Greek plays. (Though it was the plays of Terence and Seneca that Shakespeare learned at school.) Roman comedy was strong, with masks of grotesques, large phalluses and lots of low humor. There was a short period where they would actually put to death on stage the actors playing various parts. (Can you imagine getting that news from your agent? 'You've got the lead, but you have to die authentically ...!')[3] In any case, as the Roman Empire fell (and it took quite a long time to fall), theatre fell, too, and the last recorded performance seems to be 533 AD.

As an important sidebar ... Once the Barbarians had taken over Rome, Constantinople became the headquarters of the Catholic Church. And it was to here that many of the precious manuscripts and treasures that had been held in Rome (including the Greek and Roman plays) were transferred, as well as to the monasteries around Europe. Because, in the later days of the Empire, Christianity had become the universal religion, there were Christian churches and religious houses stretched all over Europe as far as the northern part of England and across North Africa, as well as Orthodox churches in Turkey, Russia and the Eastern Mediterranean. And here the manuscripts were locked up for hundreds of years. Then, when centuries later, Constantinople fell in 1453, these precious manuscripts were distributed (as far as possible) to the centers of learning throughout Europe, typically the monasteries. They were translated by Christian, Jewish and Arab scholars, all working side by side in many languages to understand the cultural and spiritual history of the world. This information was then distributed across Europe thanks to the printing press, which had been invented in 1440.

However, to wind back the clocks and cross space and time ... For a long time, after the Roman Empire fell, the Catholic Church and its liturgy was the nearest thing to a universal theatrical event, with the Greek and Roman plays locked up in the monasteries. The Bible became the common language. Belief in God and His son Jesus Christ – with the Holy Spirit making up the Trinity – was the common belief system in the great centers of learning including Toledo and Constantinople. And it was really only a tiny group of people who kept alive the idea that humankind was capable of many kinds of artistic endeavor.

72 History and roots

Meanwhile, the common population of Europe was united under the idea that life in this world was a journey between Heaven and Hell. Each person's deeds would be evaluated on Judgment Day, and then they would pay for the sins they had committed.

The common endeavor, therefore, was to build large cathedrals across the lands: beautiful monuments in stone, employing thousands of skilled and unskilled workmen during the hundreds of years in their construction. And the Church held sway. The Church tithed the people. The law was Church law. The nobles and the Church owned the land, and the nobles and the Church learned to collaborate. Tales from the Bible were the official stories told, though very few people were literate. Communication was between villages, not countries. So across Britain the priest would teach a few boys to read, write and speak Latin, providing enough of an elite to carry on the ideas propagated by the Church. Yet the old tales – the stories of goblins, fairies and giants – were the stories that the ordinary people shared. The Celtic stories were never Christianized and lived alongside the imposed Christian hegemony, so those tales found their way back into the people's lives (or perhaps they never left). And thus it was for hundreds of years.

Then (from the tenth century onwards) it was discovered that it worked better in the Easter liturgy if the *Quem Quaeritis?* ('Whom do you seek?') between the Angels and the three Marys at Christ's tomb was a dialog between *two* voices rather than the words of a solo priest. So now the congregation understood the drama of the moment better. Of course, the rites and rituals of the Church – converting the wine into Christ's blood and the biscuit into Christ's flesh, offered by the lead actors (the priests) and then devoured by the audience (the supplicants) – were indelibly marked as a piece of theatre upon the minds of the flock. After all, this ritual was repeated each week. The body knew the movements. The ear absorbed the tone. The nose smelled the incense. The mind experienced psychological relief. And although it might not be quite the same as catharsis – or pondering upon your desire to challenge your father – it nonetheless drew you into relationship with the spiritual story. And, in a cruel, hardworking, disease-ridden, medieval world, it had a certain safety about it.

At the same time, the Church tolerated the people's festivals: the mysterious May rites and the bringing-in of the October harvest. And Christmas, of course, joined together the country rituals of gathering around the yew tree with the birth of Christ. And thus it was that pagan and Christian stories could be merged into one. But the desire for drama was not fully satisfied ...

Then one day the brotherhood of shipbuilders got an idea. They knew more about shipbuilding than anyone. (Or perhaps it was the shepherds, talking one cold night about their ability to star-watch ... I don't really know.) Anyway, the shipbuilders knew they could enact the story of Noah more powerfully than anyone else. They knew how to build ships that could withstand floods and high tides and storms. And they had wives who got pretty

Talk #1: Function of the Theatre **73**

contentious about their way of life. And one had a cousin who ran a dairy: he'd be willing to herd in a couple of cows. And then those shepherds, they'd bring their sheep if they weren't too busy watching their flocks by night …

And now suddenly all the guilds in the town want to take on a Bible story. And there are certainly more than enough to go around. The fishermen, the bakers with their loaves, even the poor and the sick can take part. And before you know where you are, theatre has re-emerged. The story is being *enacted*. People are understanding Jesus's parables in a *visceral* way. The community is watching: everyone is laughing and crying. Life isn't just a long suffering for your sins: it's funny and it's playful. And the shepherds are really taking off on some riotous subplots about sheep stealing and stuffing a stolen lamb under the shepherd's wife's skirts as a fake pregnancy! People are rushing to church and laughing. And some people are really good actors, especially the guy playing Herod. And now we're going to tell the story of how Mary Magdalene was a whore – and now sex is in the picture and we're all having way too much fun … And so the miracle and mystery plays (as they're now called) are thrown out of the church and into the town square …

Actually, this is much better, being in the town square – because now we can build Hell's mouth. And the blacksmiths can stoke the flames. And the carpenters and rope-riggers have even thought of a way to hang Christ on the cross, so that the fellow playing Christ won't actually get hurt: he'll just take on Christ's suffering. And everyone (the whole community) can be there and experience how Christ died for our sins. Potent stuff!

And so you see that the sudden appearance in the Renaissance of Shakespeare, Marlowe, Jonson, Marston, Fletcher, Dekker, Kydd, *et al.,* and the revival of theatre as the place of gathering for ideas – for the community to come together – was a phenomenon with very traceable roots. We go from wandering minstrels, miracle and mystery plays, and the rites and rituals of country folk (Harvest Festival, Christmas, May Day rites and so on) for many hundreds of years to a vibrant theatre scene in London around 1585. Some 17 playhouses (each housing between 1,000 to 3,000 spectators) grew up over a 30-year period. And this is in a city with a population of 150,000. It was an explosion of people's desire to understand the world in a whole different framework from the medieval world of, 'We all suffer in this world to be judged by God when we die – and then we go to either Heaven or Hell.' And this appetite for understanding came about because the new education system, the many new inventions, explorations of the world, language skills, spiritual practices – all coincided and coalesced within a short period of time.

So what precisely happened? Basically explorers built boats that could circumnavigate the world and the perception of the world we live in changed completely …

Suddenly the earth is a part of a solar system, not just a holding place for Heaven and Hell. It's round, not flat. Water is a greater part of Earth than land

74 History and roots

is. There are other people, other languages, other religions, other knowledge systems.

Around the same time in England the Catholic Church is given its marching orders by Henry VIII. Although he's still a Catholic, he's made himself head of the Church and has taken education away from the Church's sole authority and handed it over to the civil authorities. However, it's under the aegis of his Protestant son Edward that the number of civil schools grows exponentially (though of course religion still influences every aspect of life). Elizabeth I in turn is an avid supporter of the emerging school system: she loves her own education and the power it gives her. And all the Tudors want a literate middle class, who can help them rule and *not* have allegiance to the Church or be dependent on the nobles.

Now all children are taught at 'petty school' (as in *petit*) from the ages of 5 to 7. Girls are taught their letters and numbers, so that they can run the households. Then every self-respecting town in Britain builds grammar schools to educate the boys from ages 7 to 15. The new grammar schools teach Latin (the universal language of Europe, as the Bible is still officially in Latin), along with some Greek, and a few very high-class schools teach Hebrew (to read The Old Testament in its original language). Classes are also conducted in English, thus giving the native tongue of the green-and-pleasant land a stature it hasn't previously possessed. Learning is still mostly oral, but the printing press has now found its way into making books for the general population and not just the wealthy few. And the book trade in Europe is exploding. And these printing presses are turning out copies of Greek and Roman manuscripts available for study in the grammar schools. Which means the Bible is no longer the only authority: now Cicero, Caesar, Plutarch, Roman plays, Ovid, Aurelius, are all part of the curriculum.

The grammar schools are teaching through the *Art of Rhetoric* (which is the art of persuading somebody of something they're not convinced of or that they don't know) as opposed to the Church who taught through the *Art of Logic* (which is all about proving what is already known). So all the ideas that have been disseminated for centuries by the Church are now being questioned. And the Art of Rhetoric – a 2,000-year-old language art – is studied, learned, practiced for many, many hours out of the schoolboys' ten-hour school day. There's endless 'memorization' (which is one of the five formal parts of *Rhetoric*, as we'll see in Chapter 7), exercises in style, figures of speech, arrangement of an argument and delivery. So the Art of Rhetoric is naturally Shakespeare's style of writing. Nearly all the sources of his plays come from his school days, and he, like all other actors at the time, is able to memorize a play in a day (more or less) because they've been exercising their memories since they were 7 years old. They know how to write plays because in school they performed plays including those by Terence and Seneca, who used the Roman five-act structure. And many plays are now available because of the old manuscripts that were smuggled out of Constantinople when it fell in 1453. Then when the Jews and

Talk #1: Function of the Theatre **75**

Muslims were expelled from Spain in 1492 (the same year Christopher Columbus 'discovered' America), they traveled across Europe bringing with them their learning, their physician's skills, their banking skills and their constant desire to debate.

Think about it. Align all these currents with: the ability to read and debate the Bible (the only book most people know) in your own language (instead of needing the priest to read and interpret it for you); a curiosity to examine the natural world (as promulgated by Aristotle) versus thinking that it was just made by God; the introduction of knowledge about different religions from different parts of the world. And now it becomes obvious why playhouses (with plays being performed on a daily basis, except Sundays) become the space to think about all these things. The place to listen to new ideas and entertain other 'states of being' – about family, government and spirituality – in ways that haven't been articulated before. And, as an Elizabethan, you go to the playhouse to 'hear' a play. The fights, the dances, the music are all essential to the whole – but at the very center are the new ideas wrapped around with excitement, joy, consequences, tragedy and, above all, great poetic language. And the poetry is important: the density of ideas, the depth of experience, the ability of the rhythm to lodge feelings in the body and mind.

Again, the architecture plays a crucial part. The playhouse is an acoustical chamber, built to amplify the voices – just as the Greek theatre was. The stage thrusts into the audience and, though the tiers may rise above the stage, no one is more than 30 feet away from the actors. The rich may be in the 'Lords' Rooms' or even (at a slightly later date) on stage with the actors themselves. And the poor may be in the pit standing at chest-level with the stage. And the middle classes may have paid sixpence extra to get a seat on the first or second tier. But everyone can see and feel everyone else. And the actors are talking to them all: sometimes in direct address, as in the soliloquies and comic asides. Sometimes absorbing the audience's energy, as actors struggle with their fellow actors in a debate about questions such as: How should they be ruled? What kind of government should they have? Why are they going to war? What does defeat mean? Is poverty the greatest curse – or the lack of a sense of God's goodness? And so on. And so forth. And *love*. Love. Every kind of love.

These plays – and especially Shakespeare's plays – created not just a theatre industry, but a sense of the role theatre plays in our lives (in a way that the Church could never do). For it's all about debate and beauty. Beauty in the language; in performance; in the juxtaposing of song, sound and meaning. And again – just as with the re-enactment of the Woolly Mammoth Hunt or the telling of Oedipus's story – it's for the community to take on, use, be elevated by, question, be united or divided in their common struggle.

This expansive new thinking ultimately led to civil war in England and to the execution of the King – because he wouldn't give up the idea that he was divinely appointed by God and, therefore, had ultimate power. Civil war led to a Republican government of devout Puritans known as the Roundheads. And the playhouses were closed because they were thought of as sinful. When eventually the Roundheads had to admit they weren't any better at ruling than the executed king, they brought his son back from exile and England returned to being a monarchy. With one important distinction. The king (or queen) would no longer serve as a divine appointment from God but rather as a servant of the people.

This great shift in the way the country was governed was, of course, defined by *language* – just as it would be language that defined how America was founded, written in the best rhetoric since William Shakespeare. People to this day struggle with the same dilemma of governance all over the world, both personally and collectively. And arguably one of the best ways to expose and review these ideas is through *theatre*, since an artistic work (if it's good) will put the situation before us and we can understand it together: it will frame the debate. We'll see the different perspectives and arguments *in action* and *in eloquence*. (See Figure 3.2.)

If you know Shakespeare's plays, the three big questions underneath all the dramatic action are: 'What does it mean to be a human being? How shall we act? What must I do?'[4] However, when theatre did come back into English life with Charles II in 1660, it had changed in many fundamental ways. It no longer asked those three questions. It ceased to be an activity for the whole community. First of all, the actors and the audience were no longer in the same space: the actors were 'on stage' with a curtain to be drawn; the audience 'watched' the play rather than 'hearing' it (so the *visual* was dominant over the *aural*). Then the plays were about manners and personal intrigue, with very little serious stuff discussed. In fact, theatre was a great escape from all the serious stuff.

FIGURE 3.2 Rehearsal of *The Merchant of Venice*, dir. Tina Packer, 2016: John Hadden (Antonio), Jonathan Epstein (Shylock) and Tamara Hickey (Portia)

Photo: John Dolan

Civil War – family pitted against family – was too painful to relive. So, let's drop a hanky, kiss another man's wife, play word games and hide behind our fans. Let's watch each other's style – as our clothes are all important, as is the allure of the body and the make-up on the skin. And so for 200 years there were no particularly enlightening plays.

By the nineteenth century, the industrial revolution in Britain kicked in as people moved from the country to the slums. With the hardships of working in mines, foundries, factories and mills or in service, the last thing anyone felt like doing at the end of the working week was asking the big questions. And theatre – what there was of it – became divided. Music halls or working men's clubs for the lower classes; something with glitter for the upper; and maybe a bit of intellectual stimulation for the middle classes.

Theatre in the West has striven to recover ever since. The role of the director has been introduced and the actors all obey the director and follow the 'concept.' The relationship between the actor and audience has lost its primacy. And as we've become more technologically evolved, we've taken the inventions of film and digital media, and separated actors and audience completely, as I touched on earlier. A movie audience has no direct influence over the way a scene gets played, so there's no tacit understanding that we're all in this together; and the audience is in the dark so we're not seeing each other anyway. Television takes place in our own homes, so there's no ritual space of the community gathering together: let alone when we're streaming on our own devices, a solitary audience member mesmerized by pictures. And as we know from our screens and iPhones, the visual inevitably holds even more sway. And the thinking function of our brains isn't activated by the visual in the same way as the listening-and-responding function is. Hearing and speaking are part of a cycle, an interaction. Listening to ideas generates new thoughts, agreement, disagreement, counter-arguments, refinement of ideas. Listening to ideas generates language and exchange. But the visual has no responding activity. We're mesmerized by the visual. And it's starving us, while we surfeit with images.

And not just images, but stories. There are so many stories, we can't keep up with them all. They're beamed out '24/7' from the television news channels, and – if by chance we're not near a television – we can download, stream, Snapchat, Instagram, Facebook, Twitter them. The stories come so fast and furious that there's little time to absorb – let alone ponder, seek information about, have some insight into – the psychological, economic, social roots to people's actions. Nor do we feel we're getting this information *as a community*. We're being mesmerized by what's going on in our *brains*, but the disconnect from our *bodies* – and each other's bodies – is almost universal.

But all is not lost …

Just as more and more people are wanting to know where their food comes from and what the local produce is – and are willing to pay more for non-factory-produced vegetables – so, I think, will the hunger grow to understand what it means to be a human being. And how we should act. And what I must

78 History and roots

do. Looking at the social structures we set up, these questions become more and more urgent. And, although we can read about it all we want, that doesn't give us the same, collective experience of these dilemmas.

So I'd even suggest a new direction for live theatre. If you, the actor, have spent ten years in New York or Los Angeles or London – waiting tables, driving cabs, getting the odd day's television work or commercial – then maybe it's time to reconsider the function of your own artistry. Of course there's nothing wrong with Broadway and the West End and television and films. It's just that too many artists waste their lives hanging around for them, and our profession becomes more and more fractured. So maybe it's time to go home – or live in some town that no one has ever heard of – and set up your own theatre company. Wherever theatre is played – found space or permanent structure – the *ritual* of theatre can be set up. By ritual, I mean the meeting and greeting; the coffee shops and bookstores; the symposia and cross-fertilization with schools, colleges, reading groups, union organizations, businesses, churches, synagogues, temples, mosques. Because actors, by nature, understand 'the other' – they spend their lives walking in the shoes of others – they're born leaders to understand the problems of others. So perhaps they can bring these disparate groups together. After all, *empathy* is the raw material of the Actor's Art. Through empathy the actor touches the audience, awakening in him, her or them compassion and understanding of others. And compassion and understanding are the bedrock of a democratic system of government. The ability to debate and live tolerantly is the attribute for leading the world to a better common understanding.

So in my world, every town, village and hamlet would have its own theatre company. Playwrights called upon to write the history of that community; to understand the tensions and address them; and to tackle the big questions. Poets called upon to train playwrights in their gifts or become playwrights themselves. The collective psyche needs the focus of many plays, many stories, in many places, before many people. And theatre's job is to go as deeply as it can into ideas that not only analyze the world but also offer ways of understanding. And language defines and leads the creative forces in our lives. Since Mother Nature has supplied us with enough actors to work in thousands of places – we could have 90% employment, instead of 90% unemployment!

So, as I suggest, go back to your home or live in a new town. Write about that town. What's its history? What are the tensions? What's unconscious in that community that needs to be brought to consciousness? What's unspoken that needs to be spoken? As you put these insights together, you may ask: what is the play I should be writing? What will it bring to life? What will bring community? Then perhaps we can shift the conversation away from the superficial chatter that our entertainment offers us into thought that can help us save our planet. This needs multiple thinking in multiple ways. And, as we share and express our multiple points of view, perhaps then we'll be collectively manifesting the true function of the theatre.

Notes

1 See Chapter 1, n. 48.
2 Shakespeare, W. (1595), *A Midsummer Night's Dream*, Act V, Scene i, line 17, Theseus.
3 It's not clear that actors actually *were* killed – though it makes for a good story. What does seem to be true is that actors were often replaced in the final scenes of a play by known criminals, who *were* then put to death. Nero and Titus were renowned for enjoying the enactment of myths using criminals, who were then killed on stage.
   Cf. https://godawa.com/wp/wp-content/uploads/2015/12/Coleman-Fatal-Charades-Roman-Executions-Staged-as-Mythological-Enactments.pdf (accessed 15 September 2019).
4 These three questions – as we see throughout this book – are how Shakespeare & Company frame many of their explorations.

ACT II
Training

4
EVOLUTION AND INFLUENCES OF THE MONTH-LONG INTENSIVE

We now scale the first of the three pillars on which Shakespeare & Company is built: *Training*. Housed under the 'Center for Actor Training,' the programs take a number of forms, including weekend and weeklong workshops, the Summer Training Institute (STI)[1] for undergraduates and young actors, and the Month-Long Intensive for mid-career professionals. Acclaimed internationally, the Month-Long Intensive is athletic. It unabashedly combines the visceral and the spiritual. It unites body and mind. It accesses the personal and the communal. It synchronizes the Elizabethan 'then' with the contemporary 'now,' And it forms the focus of this section. For over 40 years, faculty members have been aligning their disciplines to create its comprehensive curriculum, broadly divided (in this book) into *Voice Work*, *Body Work* and *Text Work*. As Director of Training Dennis Krausnick describes, it offers 'the transformation of the whole person [...] we challenge participants from every angle with *Voice, Movement, Fight, Clown, Text* and *Personal Connection* until they have a series of personally meaningful experiences with Shakespeare to take away with them.'[2] This kind of challenge may not be everybody's cup of tea and it's certainly not for the faint-hearted (Keanu Reeves called it 'Shakespeare boot camp'). That said it's very playful. And it's both *specific* and *mercurial*. Specific, in that its structure has been carefully evolved over the decades. Mercurial, in that it's all about the people in the room, so the faculty are constantly adapting their pedagogy to whatever's happening in society at large and within each individual, thus balancing the macrocosm and the microcosm. Adding to the mercur-reality is this particular writer and, because I've participated in the Month-Long Intensive, my own subjectivity will inevitably lend a certain perspective.

Of course S&Co.'s *Training* is only one of myriad acting methodologies. Yet its uniqueness lies in the way in which they harness the key principles of

84 Training

Elizabethan theatre to render *language as experience*, rather than cerebral assessment. As Tina Packer puts it: 'The principal rule of Shakespeare is that emotion [and thought] goes *through* the language, not *around* it. Emotion is rooted in language. Language is rooted in the human psyche.'[3] So the underlying questions during the Intensive are: What happens when we *feel* words – physically in our mouths? Vibrationally in our bones? Viscerally in our emotions? And energetically in our relationships with other actors and the audience? And because these are also fundamental questions about human behavior, the training combines effectively with other acting methods you may already use: for example, my own background in Stanislavsky was deepened by – and, in turn, deepened – my practical application of the Intensive's content.

So, let's get going. We start by looking at the history and pedagogy of the Month-Long Intensive in this chapter, before we turn to the nuts-and-bolts of each discipline in Chapters 6–8. This is by no means a 'How-to ...' manual (obviously you can't really learn acting from a book). Rather it's an invitation to find out more (if you desire) – because, ultimately, the *Training* is a series of curiosity-arousing provocations to bring what Peter Brook might call 'deadly'[4] Shakespeare back to playful life ...

'A rejuvenation of the youthful spirit':[5] how it all began

From the very beginning of Shakespeare & Company, Tina Packer and Kristin Linklater were driven by a desire to impact the way in which Shakespeare was acted, trained and taught. It wasn't enough to put on productions with a posse of performers every summer. They wanted to engage the academic world and the theatre industry in a deep-rooted dialog. That meant drawing into the Company more socially conscious actors and sending out into the academies more teachers with experience of their practices. So how did it all begin?

The first winter workshop

The idea of a winter Intensive was raised in 1978 at the close of the first summer season, when the nascent theatre company was looking for ways to maintain itself financially throughout the year. Kristin Linklater was already widely famed, so it made sense that the first workshop focus on her *Voice Work* to attract international participants. And though it was called a 'Linklater Workshop', master-teachers Broome, Barry, Arnold and Conway would be key faculty. The daily structure would follow that created by Linklater for her previous workshops: *Voice* and *Movement* in the morning; *Text* in the afternoon; and evening sessions with rehearsals and talks. One of her strongest goals for the workshop was 'that people who teach in drama departments undergo this training experientially for a deeper understanding of the creative process, as academic theatre is often cut off from the realities of the profession'[6] (Linklater). So, to fit

Evolution and influences of the Month-Long Intensive **85**

in with the university calendar, the best time of year was deemed late December into mid-January.

True to S&Co. form, their financial pragmatism was balanced by their aesthetic ideals. On the one hand, the Linklater Workshop would be an important means of making money and employing the core Company during the winter. And on the other (equally important) hand, it would achieve a longer-term goal of maintaining 'a permanent professional classical theatre company whose performances are heightened and transformed by a particular training experience so that the actors' and the audience's awareness of their own humanity is awakened and regenerated.'[7] So, this wouldn't be your typical training forum wherein you might learn a few new skills:

> The work we do [at Shakespeare & Company] is based on the belief that the word and the actors are the creative source of theater. We need to restore that power to the theater. You find where your voice is in your body and that connects with the emotions. What we are working for is a balance of voice, body, intellect, emotions.
>
> *(Linklater cited in Borak, J., 'Dreams come alive at Shakespeare & Company,'* The Berkshire Eagle*, 3 July 1987)*

And so it was that, on 28 December 1978, the first month-long workshop was launched with around 25 actor-participants. Within the schedule Packer undertook a unique, three-hour laboratory, in which she set to work galvanizing her own understanding of connecting actor and audience, drawing on all her experiences including est. As those unfamiliar with Packer's work have sometimes been wary of how est fitted into S&Co.'s training, it's worth unpacking a little here …

Speaking from the heart

Est founder, Werner Erhard wanted to understand how we can change our restrictive perceptions of ourselves as human beings. So he combined the techniques of psychologists Abraham Maslow (1908–1970) and Carl R. Rogers (1902–1987) with those of doctor Maxwell Maltz (1899–1975).[8] He wanted to find ways of tuning into the deep-rooted behavior patterns that stop us living joyfully and authentically:

> As you break up these patterns, you begin to get in touch with your natural integrity. And as you get in touch with your natural integrity, you break up the patterns more and more. Thus a beneficent cycle or spiral begins.
>
> *(Erhard cited in Bartley, 1978: 105–106)*

Erhard Seminars Training (the name for est's two-weekend workshops, referring to 'it is' in Latin) was described as 'a new form of participatory theatre that

86 Training

[like] most drama [...] has *catharsis* as one of its aims. Unlike most drama, it also aims to bring the participant to an experience of him or herself that is tantamount to transformation.'[9] Basically, it provided ways for participants to flourish in the present moment – which echoes what many acting processes seek: i.e., how to be '*in the moment.*'[10] And Packer immediately saw the crossovers. How can the unconscious baggage that we carry with us, as both human beings and actors, be either the source of our creativity or its obstacle? She intuited how she might use her three-hour lab in the first S&Co. workshop to adapt her particular experience of est and explore that all-important aspect of Elizabethan theatre: *the actor/audience relationship.* As she details in Chapter 5, she saw how she might encourage people to use the structure of Shakespeare's verse to harness all the chaotic emotions bubbling inside them when they're on stage, and then inject those feelings back into Shakespeare's language to speak 'from their hearts.'[11] She had a hunch that this kind of truth speaking could create an electric actor/audience experience.

And she was right. The exercise she created during the first winter workshop demonstrated how powerful the *collective* impact of theatre can be when revelations are sincerely made. And it informed what has now become the strand of the month-long *Training* known as '*Actor/Audience*' (again, see Chapter 5). 'Words, as the Elizabethans knew, have a power of their own,' said Packer. And by exposing that power in the actors' bodies and psyches

> it is possible to discover levels of creativity and communication beyond our normal [contemporary] understanding. So, the first requisite for any actors performing with us [at Shakespeare & Company] is not only the freeing of the natural voice (which in itself takes several years) but also a willingness to go through a series of exercises which tap the atavistic roots of words and expand the consciousness of the actor. [...] Other actor training elements [such as *Fight, Text, Clown* and *Dance*] support and expand this process, creating a synergy which is greater than any individual component.
>
> (*'Artistic Director's Statement – Ensemble Grant,' c.1984, S&Co. archive*)

The birth of the Month-Long Intensive

By the end of that first workshop in January 1979, the founders of Shakespeare & Company sensed they were on to something. To create theatre that really touches an audience – that reveals truths – you can't just rehearse a play. You need ongoing training (in *Voice, Text* and *Movement*) to ensure that words and actions 'fly' from '"primitive subverbal connections" inside the body, and not from the mind alone'[12] (Linklater). After all, that seemed to be how language was used in Shakespeare's theatre, and therefore, actors so trained might 'express their feelings and thoughts more naturally and with better results from the audience.'[13] In fact, the results of that first Intensive were so fulsome that it

Evolution and influences of the Month-Long Intensive   **87**

made sense to configure it in future years as a collective Shakespeare & Company training, rather than solely 'Linklater Workshop.' And thus the Month-Long Intensive was born.

So how has its pedagogy become so enduring?

The principles of pedagogy

It starts with the faculty, who strive to work as an integrated unit. When Linklater left in 1992, Dennis Krausnick became a designated Linklater teacher and Director of Training (a position he held until 2018). And currently at the organizational helm is Administrative Director MaConnia Chesser (herself a 2016 Intensive alumna and an actor with the Company). Meanwhile, senior faculty consolidates the schedule with a flexible roster of teachers drawn from a panoply of Company members (see Appendix 2). And faculty members return year after year in order to work with each other. As original master-teacher Trish Arnold once described, 'When you have a core of teachers who have worked with each other for as long as we have, teaching becomes an entirely different experience.'[14] And the focused environment of the Month-Long Intensive (along with the STI) 'creates a forum where we can discuss actor training on a serious level'[15] (Packer). 'We share what we teach, and we're not separating the journey of our lives from our journey as teachers'[16] (Borthwick-Leslie). Which takes us to a number of core, pedagogical principles that seem (from this writer's perspective) to underlie the *Training*, starting with *participation*.

The pedagogy of participation

Like any dynamic pedagogy, that of the Intensive remains ever evolving. Not least because all the teachers take the Month-Long themselves at some point. Which means they experience its trajectory from the inside out, rather than assessing it cerebrally from the outside in. To which end, Dennis Krausnick (re)-participated in 2012 to experience afresh what he had helped co-create nearly 40 years earlier and had been teaching ever since. Meanwhile, in the mid-1990s, Dave Demke (at the time, Artistic Director of a theatre company in Portland, Oregon) arrived as a green participant, 'experiencing each moment within the giant month-long arc of experiences without necessarily being cognizant of how they added up to a unified aesthetic and skillset.'[17] Then, when he returned the following year as a teacher-trainee, he gained 'a new kind of knowledge, seeing the *intelligence* behind the exercises and appreciating how each exercise leads to the next to the next, building an aesthetic foundation layer by layer.'[18] Later he became S&Co.'s Associate Director of Training for several years and, as a designated Linklater *Voice* teacher, he's a longtime senior faculty member. And it's worth remembering that this immersive experience of each other's disciplines

88 Training

gave rise to the curriculum in the first place. Which takes us to our second pedagogical principle: *the sharing of practice-based research.*

The pedagogy of practice-based research

As we saw in Chapter 1, the original master-teachers – all experts in their fields – took part in each other's workshops during the 1973 Ford Foundation experiment. So they were able to create new, embodied knowledge from their *experience of* and *synergy with* one another's disciplines. And from this they collectively evolved the core of integrated exercises, which became the spine of the Month-Long Intensive (noted above by Demke). At the same time, they quickly developed the habit of passing the teaching-baton from one generation of faculty to the next, while also acknowledging that each new faculty member will introduce their own nuances. So deep in the DNA of the *Training*, there's a dynamic tension between basic structure and fluid change. There are about 13 faculty members who lead each Month-Long Intensive, supported by about nine teacher-trainees. And, like the original master-teachers, they're all working practitioners, so whatever research they're exploring in their own practices may be channeled into the Intensive's pedagogy. Likewise, as the student-body generationally shifts, the *Training* subtly adapts. So, for example, social movements such as Black Lives Matter and #metoo have impacted on the teaching of violence and intimacy, as well as pertinent conversations around diversity, gender and inclusion, and how everyone has the right to free their own natural voice. Which turns our focus here from the faculty to the participants, and the pedagogy of personal and creative *transformation*.

The pedagogy of transformation

'I would say quite unabashedly that *transformation* is what we're all about,'[19] says Dennis Krausnick. 'By pushing the envelope of the mind, body, voice and emotions at the same time' the Intensive creates something of a 'useful' and 'artistic' crisis in individuals 'that actually allows people to reach out and take something they might not otherwise dare to.'[20] In other words, your transformative courage arises basically because you're bombarded with so much information (with so many classes in so few days) that your body and mind shift from their usual state of dislocation from each other into a kind of union. Indeed, a sizable time is spent during the Intensive 'becoming observant of *your body's mind* and your "bodymindfulness"'[21] as opposed to your intellectual mind trying to figure everything out all the time:

> If as an actor I can begin to trust my tiniest impulses – and have the courage to follow them before I've surrounded them with a concept or I've protected myself against them – then who knows what I might learn about the person I am?
>
> *(Krausnick interview, August 2016)*

Evolution and influences of the Month-Long Intensive **89**

Taking these transformative, liberating leaps isn't so difficult (in Krausnick's view) thanks to Packer's questions: 'What's the function of theatre? Why are we doing this? And why would anyone *want* to do this?' (see Chapter 3). Because, the minute someone starts asking questions about why do theatre in the first place, you have 'the opportunity to start questioning yourself about the "whys" in your own life – without feeling judgmental or guilty or blaming. And that kind of non-judgmental self-questioning isn't very common in our culture.'[22] So, in a nutshell, transformation is all about *curiosity*.

The pedagogy of curiosity

Throughout the Intensive you're encouraged to believe that you're your own trustiest teacher. And that in itself can take some convincing. So how do you go about it? Actually, the strategies are very accessible – and (as Krausnick just touched on) they're basically drawn from traditional, mindfulness practices: namely, curiosity, kindness and non-judgment.[23] Because the faculty comprises performers, they understand only too well how self-critical we can be as actors and, therefore, how easily we can censor our own creativity. So, they invite you almost from the get-go just to 'note' the blocks in your own acting, and then be curious and kind (rather than critical and judgmental) about why a particular block or habit may have arisen. After all, most of us have acquired some restrictive habits along the way, habits 'that provide us with a modicum of safety and comfort' in an increasingly challenging world[24] (Demke). And those habits may be technical or personal, and they may have become so deep-rooted that we're oblivious to them. Yet one of Shakespeare & Company's guiding strategies is to 'make conscious the unconscious.' And becoming conscious of our unconscious habits is exactly what kick-starts the transformative process. Sure, it's not necessarily comfortable at first, because our habits have usually developed precisely so that we can *avoid* discomfort, rather than embrace it. But embracing discomfort (suggests Demke) is really what being an artist is all about: 'Art exists (and Shakespeare does this brilliantly) to articulate the conflict between harmony and discord.'[25] So, if we're working as creative artists, it behooves us to replace all our protective, risk-averse habits with creative, artistic habits. Or to put it another way: 'good acting requires good acting habits.'[26] And we can develop those habits by 'being curious' about our acting processes – both *from within* and *from without*.

Curiosity from within is really about noticing, 'How do I *feel* when I let go of the habit? What's happening to me physically and emotionally? And where is my imagination now taking me?'[27] And usually letting go of a restrictive habit simply feels better. The new experiences are 'more desirable – maybe even more pleasurable – because they're more artistically compelling!'[28] So by being curious about your habits in this way, you can start to transform your acting processes *from within*.

90 Training

Curiosity from without involves *the actor/audience relationship*, explained here by senior faculty, Andrew Borthwick-Leslie: 'If you ask the questions, 'How does the room respond when I shift my old habit? And does that audience response excite me?' then 'nine times out of ten – because the participants are artists and they want to grow and entertain and move people – when they shift the habit, the room becomes thrilled.'[29] So by turning your attention away from your self and your habit, and becoming more interested in the audience's experience, you can 'get out of the toxic cycle of self-judgment no matter what comes up.'[30] And thus you start to transform your acting processes *from without*.

As a participant myself in the 2016 Intensive, this two-way, 'within–without' pedagogy of curiosity seemed to operate around a pedagogy of *invitations*.

A pedagogy of invitations

The key invitations that struck me included: *Immerse yourself in the work. Bring your whole self to your acting.* And *be the author of your own experience*. Let's unpack these a little.

Immerse yourself in the work

Granted, most actor training requires you to immerse yourself in the process to some extent, but here the invitation is almost inescapable. In the depths of winter – when the snow may lie knee-deep – between 45 and 60 participants from around the globe descend upon Kemble Street. They're going to spend 14 hours a day for six days a week for the next four weeks with a curriculum mischievously, but meticulously, designed to 'challenge,' 'discombobulate' and 'illuminate' you with new insights into yourself – as well as into the world of Shakespeare and the world at large.[31] Far from the madding crowd – with intermittent internet, and shared living quarters – there's little time for outside activities. And this inevitable isolation, combined with immersion in the actor's art,

> affords actors the opportunity to work on themselves without industry or public conceptions of what their limitations are. [...] Actors who work primarily in film and TV can do incredible things in a short amount of time – touch[ing] an emotional availability that's staggering [...] – but they can't [always] sustain it or repeat it.
>
> *(Krausnick cited in Nassour, E., 'The Shakespeare Complex,' In Theater,*
> *5 December 1997)*

So this immersive training offers you – novice and old-timer alike – reconfigured tools (and a 'pressure-off-from-the-profession' environment) to reignite your capacity for that sustaining and repeating. As well as time to trust your own instincts, 'rather than fulfill someone else's expectations' of how you should look and sound.[32] And there's always the reminder that you're not immersing

Evolution and influences of the Month-Long Intensive **91**

yourself in the work for your own gratification: the outcome ultimately has to be relevant for the audience. S&Co.'s intent is to train actors who 'not only feel deeply but convey that feeling in every moment – [...] conscious that they are offering it *to the audience so the audience will get it – [rather than] close off against it.*'[33] This interactive, immersive training 'moves swiftly and in depth.' And the disciplines combine to 'accelerate the *physical* release of [your] voice and body [and] the *psychic* release of [your] spirit and soul.'[34] Which leads us to the second, almost unavoidable invitation: *bring your whole self* to your creative experience.

Bring your whole self into the room

'But I always bring my whole self to my acting!' That's what many of us may think. Yet, when we're given the opportunity to 'turn our eyes into our very soul,'[35] it's surprising how much 'stuff' – be it joyous and childlike, as much as 'black and grained' – is hiding in the corners that we're just not using. So during the Intensive you're invited to allow

> the person who is speaking – You – [to be] alive spiritually, physically, emotionally, and that you are intimately connected to [Shakespeare's] sublime text.
>
> As we spend more and more time in front of our computers, [on our phones,] in lecture halls, on the subway, in our cars, in front of the television, we lose the connection with ourselves.
>
> And if we are not connected to ourselves, how can we hope to be connected to Shakespeare's characters?
>
> For one month we create a community where we go further than you thought possible: where we have permission to speak and to listen intently, to fight and to dance, to interact passionately, all through the joy of Shakespeare's words.
>
> *(Packer cited in 'Month-Long Acting Intensive accepting applications,' S&Co.*
> *press release, Berkshire Record, 31 December 2004)*

Though Shakespeare isn't the only author in the Intensive ... Which takes us to the third invitation ...

Be the author of your own journey

For 'obedient' actors (like myself), this is one of the hardest invitations to *hear*, let alone *accept*. With the faculty's insightfulness, it's all too easy to expect them to have the solutions to your creative obstacles. Yet the mirror is constantly turned back on the participants: What do *you* want from this rendition of the scene? What good practices do *you* want to reinforce at the end of this class? What is *your* body, autobiography, breathing pattern telling you? And for

92 Training

participants looking to 'get it right' – to 'do good' by the authority figure in the room and not be called out for 'getting it wrong' – this is perhaps one of the most solipsistic invitations of the *Training*. As we've already noted, the trustiest teachers are ultimately with*in*, not with*out*. And the faculty has no expectations of you beyond whatever you want to explore. They might be the night-stars by which to navigate your journey, but you're the Helmsman and the Captain and the Ship. Yet like any good captain before any long voyage, there are certain things to prepare as you accept the invitations.

Preparation

In advance of the Month-Long Intensive, you're asked to learn any 15–25 lines of a Shakespeare monologue in verse:

> Age & gender need not match your own but it should not be from a non-human character (e.g. fairies, spirits, or ghosts). What's most important is that you have a strong *personal connection* to the piece, even if you can't quite articulate what that connection is. [...] No advanced work is needed other than learning it by heart.
>
> *(Month-Long Intensive 2016 Information Pack: 7)*

(I chose Constance's speech from *King John* beginning, 'Death, death; o amiable lovely death.'[36] Having recently sat by my dying grandmother's bedside, I was intrigued by 'Death' being personified as someone you might actually welcome ...)

You're also asked to learn a Shakespeare sonnet that touches you personally. (As a self-confessed 'love junkie,' I chose Sonnet 40: 'Take all my loves, my love, yea take them all.') And 'touch' is a poignant word. It alludes to feelings *and* to bodies. As human beings, touch is one of our most reassuring means of communication, from a baby being cradled to a griever being consoled. Yet in our increasingly anxious society, the benefits of physical contact are all too easily eroded by those who abuse it. But it's hard to be a fully-fledged actor without being prepared for touch. And the faculty at Shakespeare & Company navigates this pedagogical issue sensitively. Always asking your consent first, they may touch your brow if you're inadvertently frowning during your monologue or sonnet. Or place a finger on your belly to remind you to breathe deeply. Or stroke your jaw to help you release your tension. And, like the subtle shifts of a chiropractor, the nuances of an experienced trainer's touch can help you shift your breath or deepen your experience on the level of fine-tuning. As with all their pedagogical principles, the S&Co. faculty takes this responsibility very seriously, and participants are invited to be prepared for physical contact – not least, of course, with each other (as is the case in most acting processes).

So those may be some of the underlying pedagogies of the Month-Long Intensive. What are the actual logistics?

The structure of the Intensive

It took about ten years for the structure of the four-week Intensive to galvanize, based on Linklater's original schedule. And although – as we've said – it's ever evolving, there are certain *stable principles* by which the Month-Long operates.

Stable principles

Classes run for six consecutive days typically from 8.15 am to 10.15 pm in 90-minute sessions, which, like similar actor-training environments, is consciously full-on:

> Patterns are really difficult to shift. [...] Going at it intensively from eight in the morning until 10 at night means that the amount of information you receive without downtime to process it creates a literal 'body' of knowledge – *within* the human body – without the intrusion of intellect. And that instinctual knowledge is where I would say the actor operates, where the mind-body gestalt is making decisions and evaluating and responding.
>
> *(Krausnick cited in Nesbitt, 1999)*

There are two 90-minute meal breaks, during which the participants eat together in the Lawrence Hall refectory, while down in the basement the faculty assembles to discuss the events of the previous session in what's known as 'Clare's Place'[37] Lining the walls are photographs of the participants. And daily, detailed attention is given to their individual progress, as the faculty endeavors to find the right, creative challenges for everyone to get the most out of their month. During the four-week schedule there are particular anchor-points that have proven over the years to facilitate exciting breakthroughs for the group as a whole and for each individual (detailed in Chapters 6–8). At the same time there's *flexibility*.

Flexible principles

For each participant to get the most of themselves, the Intensive operates with some mystery, in that the daily schedule is only announced from one meal break to the next:

> We used to announce the whole week's schedule, but that practice has shifted in the last ten to fifteen years. What happened was that, if we had to change the schedule for some practical reason [such as a tutor's unavailability] – or if something hadn't worked on the level that we needed it to work and so we wanted to go back – the participants would get really upset. Or if there were certain classes they didn't like, they'd start bracing

94 Training

themselves against those things. So this way we can alter the schedule without disrupting anyone. Mostly, the changes are to do with how far along we've brought the whole cohort. Do we need more articulation work in Week 3 because people aren't using their consonants yet? Or maybe they haven't really plugged into their emotions yet and we need to shift gears. This way we can start doing remedial teaching of our own training without any disruption.

(Packer interview, August 2016)

And so it was, for example, that during the 2016 Intensive the faculty could see in Week 3 that we participants had all become so weighty with Shakespeare's language – so reverent with the Bard – we were bashing each other over the head with words. A lightness of touch was called for, so Kevin Coleman came to our aid with a workshop on Wit, elucidating Shakespeare's nimble turns of phrase and injecting a healthy dose of *irr*everence. This kind of flexibility with the timetable – keeping you on your creative toes – is vital, given the workshop's overall goal of transformation. And although Packer's idealism (outlined in Chapter 1) of transforming and healing the world through Shakespeare might sound inflated or overly ambitious, the *Training* is indeed making an impact on all kinds of fronts ...

A global example

For some years now, Shakespeare & Company has been connected to the Youth Bridge Global Project, which uses 'drama and art to bridge cultural divides, connect youth across cultures, and provide educational opportunities to under-resourced regions of the world.'[38] And so between 2013 and 2019, young participants from Bosnia, Rwanda and the Marshall Islands have been funded to take the STI. For actor Ilija Pujic:

[b]eing a war child in Bosnia and Herzegovina, I had difficulties expressing my emotions, because the world I grew up in taught me to hide things rather than express [...]. Masking emotions was a skill [or habit] that I carefully crafted to protect me from my surroundings. At Shakespeare & Company, I learned how to show my emotions, and I learned not to be afraid of them [...]. For the first time I was breathing and feeling life and I could sense deeply what I had been missing.

(Pujic cited at www.ybglobal.org, accessed 15 September 2019)

Pujic credited his creative and personal transformation to the entire faculty and their ability to make Shakespeare personally relevant: 'They don't teach Shakespeare as something remote from you and hard to understand. They make you feel comfortable with his words, and they introduce you to the plot as if it is happening right now in the world you perceive.'[39]

Evolution and influences of the Month-Long Intensive **95**

Perceiving the world and allowing those perceptions to fuel your creativity is at the heart of S&Co.'s intent. And adding to their multi-disciplinary actor training are four other influential people, whom we'll briefly meet before we head into the studio. Although they're outside the regular teaching faculty, they've contributed practically and philosophically to the *Training* over the years, and are part of the fabric of its unique methodology.

Neil Freeman and the First Folio

Neil Freeman was an actor-director and emeritus faculty at the University of British Columbia, first joining S&Co. in 1980 for *The Tempest*. Three years earlier, he had begun looking at all of Shakespeare's plays in chronological order. And this raised questions for him as to what the different editors had done over the centuries to correct the grammatical issues. In fact, was grammar ever really Shakespeare's concern? After all, he was an actor-director in a working theatre: he 'wrote with *sound* in mind': the orthography he used (i.e., the art of spelling words according to their accepted usage) reflected 'the human way of *speaking*.'[40] This led Freeman back to the First Folio. 'F1' was the brainchild of Shakespeare's actors John Heminge, Henry Condell and Richard Burbage.[41] Collectively – between 1621 and 1622 – they decided to publish all the available plays (written in whole or in part) by Shakespeare (who had died a few years earlier in 1616) and with whom they had all been actors, business partners, colleagues and friends, for more than 20 years.[42] Their project was completed by the end of 1623 when F1 was published as a single volume, largely assembled from the scripts of the original stage managers and actors.

As Freeman went back to the First Folio, he wondered whether the anomalies in spelling, punctuation and rhythmic structure might actually be clues from Shakespeare as to how the actors should perform and what their characters' motivations might be: 'Writing in Shakespeare's time was not grammatical but rhetorical, that is, reflecting the stepping stones of debate and argument, as well as the volcano of underlying human emotions.'[43] So maybe the wide-ranging styles in Shakespeare's writing was completely deliberate, revealing the emotional state of each character. In other words, 'an in-control-character would appear highly grammatical, whereas [...] a character in the throes of uncontrollable emotion or intellectual passion would come across as a grammatical and syntactical nightmare.'[44] As Freeman studied the First Folio, he realized that (aside from the obvious shifts into prose) 40% of Shakespeare's texts aren't in strict iambic pentameter. And, as with John Barton's *Text Work* (of which there's more in Chapter 7), he intuited that when the iambic pentameter is broken, the character must be experiencing some kind of psychological turbulence. So, 'the uneven lines, tidied in later editions, suggested where a breath ends,' whereas 'the apparent misspellings – "mee" for "me" – and eccentric capitalizations were reminders of emphasis.'[45] It was as if Shakespeare the director was reaching across the centuries to enter our contemporary rehearsal rooms.

96 Training

And Freeman knew it was time to allow all those 'abominable errors' to become vital parts of the script: 'I am, in a sense, putting the mistakes back into the text to have it make more sense for the actor. [...] We are using the *text* to liberate the *actor* and as a result both get liberated.'[46]

This was Freeman's mammoth labor when he joined Shakespeare & Company. Thanks to a generous donation from Jane Nichols, he set about programming the entire First Folio into a computer to determine the frequency and patterns of words. And in 1983, S&Co. received a Major Artist grant from the NEA for Freeman to work with them for 38 weeks.[47] As far as he was aware, Shakespeare & Company was the only company in the world using F1 at that time, and he gave them a unique education in Shakespeare's acting traditions. A workshop called 'First Folio: Unlocking the Actor's Toolbox' (including the art of rhetoric, logic, argument, structure of the verse and rhythm) soon became a regular offering in the Center for Actor Training's schedule. And when Paul Sugarman from Applause Books participated in the First Folio Workshop in 1986, an alliance began, which led to the publication of *The Applause First Folio of Shakespeare* (2001). As with all S&Co.'s *Training*, Freeman's research was geared toward developing *the actor/audience relationship*: 'It is for that one magic moment between the actor and the audience and if that doesn't work, then the research doesn't matter.'[48]

Our other three influential people are equally 'magical' – if a little different. None of them is a theatre practitioner. All have worked in mental health. All have been close friends of Shakespeare & Company for many years. All have published seminal texts, which feature regularly on S&Co.'s reading lists. All have taken the Month-Long Intensive – and their experience there has influenced their own professional specialties. In turn, their research into human behavior has influenced the ways the Company handles narrative moments of intimacy and violence. And these three influential people analyze, through their respective disciplines, how we relate to our voices, bodies and emotions. It's hard to separate voice, body and emotion, as they're so wholly interconnected in our human instruments. Yet for a moment we're going to do just that, as we briefly look at how these individuals have impacted S&Co.'s *Training*.

Carol Gilligan and the psychology of the voice

Psychologist, NYU professor and former dancer, Dr. Carol Gilligan has been involved with Shakespeare & Company from the early years. She is globally renowned for her pioneering research into how genders respond, explored in her seminal book *In a Different Voice: Psychological Theory and Women's Development* (1982). And though much of the book refers to males and females, its contents arguably resonate for non-traditional identities and relationships, not least in terms of how we all relate to our voices. In fact, it was while observing Tina Packer's *dropping in* exercise (see Chapter 7) that Gilligan fathomed just how physical, psychological and cultural our voices are. She then took the Month-

Evolution and influences of the Month-Long Intensive **97**

Long Intensive in 1989 and began working with Kristin Linklater, whose training gave her 'a physics' for her psychology: 'a way of understanding how the voice works in the body, in language, and also physiologically.'[49] Through her work Gilligan studied how our voice intimately changes *in relation to ourselves* and *in relation to other people*, both of which resound in actor training.

The intimate relationship of voice to self

Shakespeare & Company's *Training* is all about finding your 'authentic' voice, in terms of where it sits in your body and in terms of what you say. And Gilligan's research quietly percolates throughout the *Voice* classes. In fact, many of us (actors and otherwise) have hang-ups about our vocal instrument. The voice is intensely personal: it's 'what people mean when they speak of the *core of the self*'[50] (Gilligan). So issues with our voice often belie deep-rooted issues surrounding our identity. And because the voice is such 'a powerful psychological instrument and channel, connecting inner and outer worlds,'[51] we share something very intimate about ourselves when we speak. Not least because the act of *speaking* is closely allied to the act of *listening*. Or the 'relational potentiality' of *being heard*. After all, there's no point 'honoring mine own truth'[52] unless someone is willing to listen. And, if we feel our words and voices are received sincerely by our listeners, we're quite open in how we speak. But if our words are *misunderstood* by whoever is in this relational act with us, we start (albeit inadvertently) adjusting our vocal expression. As the passages in our body that connect breath to sound constrict, our voice rises in pitch or thins in timbre, so that it doesn't carry 'the depths' of our feelings. We may even dissociate from what we're saying, which makes our voice sound even less like 'our own' as we shift 'to a more guarded or impersonal register or key.'[53] In other words, how we *speak* is directly connected to how we're *heard*, and *vice versa*. And here Gilligan's research connects S&Co.'s actor training directly to theatre's heart: *the actor/audience relationship*.

The intimate relationship between speaker and listener

The Month-Long's emphasis on *the actor/audience relationship* is unusual (see Chapter 5). Few programs focus on it specifically, let alone train for it, yet Gilligan's research reminds us why we *should* train for the speaker–listener dynamic, particularly when it comes to navigating gender identities. As she listened to people speaking, she noticed how female psychology tends to veer toward connection, relationship and nurturing, whereas male psychology tends to veer toward assertion, boundaries and aggression. The 'different voice' she heard with women operated round an 'ethic of care' that tied *relationship* to *responsibility*: i.e., how much we consider the effect of our words on other people. In comparison, the origins of aggression lay 'in the failure of connection'[54]– i.e., we potentially care less about how our words affect other people, maybe even deliberately hurting them. These relational nuances of speaking and listening are highly relevant to actor training and finding your authentic voice (technically, musically, psychologically). They're also relevant to the study of Shakespeare's texts, where you're navigating the complex relationships between the male, female and gender-fluid characters (such as Ariel and Puck). And Gilligan calls this relational approach to speaking and listening 'a form of psychic breathing':[55] a pithy phrase, given that breath (as we see throughout this book) is the very basis of S&Co.'s *Training* and work. And breath essentially brings us right back to ourselves …

Our intimate relationship with intimacy

It's hard to do any kind of actor training without incorporating some degree of intimacy. How could it be otherwise, when 'Intimacy goes along with identity'?[56] So, if we want to bring our whole selves – our 'essence' or identity – to the acting experience, it behooves us to be willing to have an intimate connection to ourselves. As we'll see in the rest of 'Act II,' the *Training* at S&Co. invites that *personal connection*. And as we re-establish our own connections to our self, we also open our connections to other people, notably our scene partners. After all, 'intimacy becomes the critical experience that brings the self back into connection with others, making it possible to see both sides – to discover the effects of actions on others as well as their cost to the self'[57] (Gilligan). Ultimately this process is all about developing *empathy*. (More on this anon.) And being a potent actor has much to do with eliciting empathy for the character you're playing, be it Iago or Iachimo, Viola or Volumnia, Titania or Tamora. So Gilligan's propositions offer some valuable perspectives on Shakespeare & Company's *Training*, including seeing both sides of a situation; taking responsibility for your words and actions; and understanding the cost of voicing something both to yourself and to others. And, because the voice is so *physical*, you also have to invite your body to the party. Which takes us to our next influential person.

Bessel van der Kolk and the psychology of the body

Professor of Psychiatry at Boston University, Bessel van der Kolk, M.D., has been connected with Shakespeare & Company for some years. He's the founding medical director of the Trauma Center in Brookline, Massachusetts, and author of *The Body Keeps the Score: Brain, Mind and Body in the Healing of Trauma* (2014). In it he reveals neuroscientifically that, whether we like it or not, our body holds on to distressing experiences, and often in ways we don't really notice. Our brain might try to deny the trauma, but the physiological changes that the experience imprints on our bodies can't be denied. So if we don't deal with our traumas, we're destined to be their prisoners. But how does all this fit into Shakespeare & Company's Month-Long Intensive?

Curiously van der Kolk's medical background supports and informs many of the strategies in the *Training*, including *being healthy artists*; *listening to the narratives hidden in our body*; *having the language to express those narratives*; and *understanding the reciprocal power of the actor/audience relationship*. Let's take a look at these.

Being healthy storytellers

Shakespeare & Company has always been committed to exploring the complexities of being human, and that includes violence. So they're attentive to the fact that when you really work with your body and imagination, some disciplines (obviously *Fight* – frequently now called 'Stage or Staged Violence' – but also the simple acts of breathing in a *Voice* class) might unexpectedly access long-forgotten memories. Many of us have some sort of residue of 'trauma' hidden somewhere in our bodies: a sporting accident; a car crash; a less than healthy relationship; for some people, the very act of being born was quite an experience. Yet, the function of the theatre (as we saw in Chapter 3) involves taking the audience through a process of catharsis, letting go, even healing. In fact, Greek drama may actually have served as 'a ritual reintegration for combat veterans,' since every adult citizen of Athens had to do military service: 'so audiences were undoubtedly composed of combat veterans and active-duty soldiers on leave. The performers themselves must have been citizen-soldiers'[58] (van der Kolk). If our task as actors is to bring our whole self to a role and at the same time, we're entrusted with the task of healing society … Physician, heal thyself! It behooves us to be mindful of the score that our own body might be keeping. And we can tackle that by going back to *being curious*.

Being curious about the body

Often as human beings, we're in a state of *alexithymia* – which means we're not able to identify what's actually happening inside ourselves. Yet there are certain, simple activities that help us listen to our bodies and understand what's going on: 'we have the ability to regulate our own physiology, including some of the so-called involuntary functions of the body and brain, through such basic activities of breathing, moving, and touching.'[59] And this is where the Month-Long Intensive starts: from Day #1, the *Training* engages the basic elements of breath, movement and physical contact. It then encourages us to awaken from our *alexithymia* by inviting us to be curious – about our bodies, our blocks, our feelings: 'Once you start approaching your body with curiosity rather than with fear, everything shifts.'[60] Then, of course, as we embark on this awakening process, we have to find *language* to deal with any shifts and transformations …

100 Training

Using the healing potential of Shakespeare's language

What do we do if we don't know how to express the experiences we're having? The invitation to bring our whole self into the room involves some earnest self-reflection, and our rational brain might not be equipped to reflect so deeply. As van der Kolk's medical research shows, 'Trauma by nature drives us to the edge of comprehension, cutting us off from language based on common experience or an imaginable past.'[61] So the distressing experience itself might have shut us off from the very words that could otherwise help us articulate it. Fortunately Shakespeare's plays give us that language. In fact, military veteran and Month-Long Intensive alumnus Stephan Wolfert shares that Lady Percy's description of Hotspur's nightmares about war sums up in vivid detail the psychophysical manifestations of post-traumatic stress.[62] And when we have the right words to express ourselves, we have 'the power to change ourselves and others by communicating our experiences, helping us to define what we know, and finding a common sense of meaning'[63] (van der Kolk). This in turn helps us answer the bigger-picture questions that underpin S&Co.'s ethos: 'What must we do? How should I act?' Ergo, what can theatre do for society?

Applying our artistry to actor/audience

Indeed, both Carol Gilligan and Bessel van der Kolk have seen in their respective disciplines the transformative power of speaking and being heard – in all its 'relational potentiality.' For any kind of healing to occur, we need '*reciprocity*: being truly heard and seen by the people around us, feeling that we are held in someone else's mind and heart. For our physiology to calm down, heal, and grow we need a visceral feeling of safety'[64] (van der Kolk). Since *the actor/audience relationship* is so significant in Shakespeare & Company's work, the Month-Long Intensive provides just such a space. It takes you right to the visceral catharsis of ancient Greek theatre, where 'being able to share your deepest pain and deepest feelings with another human being […] is one of the most profound experiences we can have.'[65] There, within the structure of the *Training* and using the fundamental tools of actor/audience reciprocity, you're given the opportunity to become better equipped in the acting industry for serving a deeper function of storytelling. After all: 'Trauma stories lessen the isolation of trauma, and they provide an *explanation* for why people suffer the way they do.'[66] Take Lindsey Ferrentino's *Ugly Lies the Bone* or Suzan-Lori Park's *TopDog/UnderDog*, two stories surrounding violence, both performed at S&Co. to heartfelt audience reception in 2016 and 2019, respectively. Which actually takes us to our fourth influential person.

James Gilligan and the psychology of violence

We've considered the voice with Carol Gilligan and the body with Bessel van der Kolk. Now we turn to the emotions. James Gilligan M.D. has spent his career examining the causes of violence with some of the most dangerous prisoners in Massachusetts. And as a psychiatrist (a 'physician of the soul' as he calls it),[67] his acclaimed series of books entitled *Violence* demonstrates that if anyone has looked the dark soul in the eye, it's James Gilligan. He's also a lover of Shakespeare and, like his wife Carol, has been involved with Shakespeare & Company for over 30 years. Added to which, his professional perspective as a psychiatrist endorses many of the Month-Long Intensive's dramaturgical components, including *storytelling*, *empathy* and *insight into the genders*.

Stories of violence need to be heard collectively

Just as Packer suggests with the Rain Dance and the Woolly Mammoth Hunt (see Chapter 3), Gilligan upholds that it's 'in telling stories that we originally acquired our humanness.'[68] And our need to tell stories is directly linked to our need to understand violence. It's arguably no coincidence, then, that Shakespeare (not to mention the Greeks) wrote such powerful tragedies:

> tragic dramas are all about violence; that violence is what [humans] have been re-enacting and embodying, meditating and pondering on, and eliciting grief and compassion about, from the time they first evolved from religious rituals two and a half millennia ago.
>
> *(Gilligan, 1997: 7)*

But it's too unsettling to deal with these tragically violent stories on our own. We need community. We need to share. And for Gilligan, we can't just share the stories of the *victims*: 'The whole story of violence includes, inescapably, the lives of the *victimizers*, and the moment we realize that, we are in the territory of tragedy.'[69] Indeed, you only have to look at the Macbeths plotting regicide, Queen Margaret goading York, or Richard III wooing Anne to see that collectively we're as fascinated by the victimizers as we are by the victims. And this is where Gilligan's work shifts us into a slightly different gear.

Violence needs to be understood collectively

We've seen how the Month-Long training involves the work on the self. Yet it's important to remember that this self-work specifically involves embodying Shakespeare's characters. Not only because these characters provide juicy acting material, but also because they radically expand our collective understanding of extreme human behavior: What motivates people to do what they do? What leads them to hurt, to maim, to murder? To help answer these questions, where else to turn but to Gilligan? 'The first lesson that tragedy teaches [...] is that *all violence is an attempt to achieve justice*.'[70] The violent person executes the violent act in order to 'receive whatever retribution or compensation the violent person feels is "due" to him or "owed" to him, or to those on whose behalf he is

102 Training

acting.'[71] And if they *don't* commit the violent act, then they know that they (or whomever they're acting for) will be 'subjected to *in*justice. Thus, *the attempt to achieve and maintain justice or undo or prevent injustice, is the one and only universal cause of violence.*'[72] Let's just think about that for a moment: Violence is all about justice. The minute we really take on board Gilligan's analysis, we start to understand that violence is a desire either to right what someone sees as a wrong or to protect someone else from being wronged. When we look at it like this, a chink of *empathy* starts to open up, as we glimpse into this destructive mystery of humanity. And it doesn't need to be Crips and Bloods, or Capulets and Montagues, or Romans and Volscians. We're facing perplexing violence in our times between the *genders* as much between tribes or nations. And this is where Gilligan's work – along with that of his wife Carol – pendulum-swings our actor training between the epic canvas of Shakespeare's roles and the details of our own social narratives.

The genders need to be reconstituted collectively

There's a synergy in the research of the Gilligans and their fathoming of human behavior. While Carol has investigated the nurturing voice, James has analyzed the destructive force: 'Violence is primarily men's work; it is carried out more frequently against men; and it is about the maintenance of "manhood."'[73] Many civilizations emphasize 'the importance of understanding that it is men who are expected to be violent, and who are honored for doing so and dishonored for being unwilling to be violent.'[74] On the other hand: 'A woman's worthiness to be honored or shamed is judged by how well she fills her roles in sexually related activities, especially the roles of actual or potential wife and mother.'[75] Gilligan wrote this 20 years ago, though it's sadly no less relevant today. In fact, one of the most pressing issues at the center of our current (global) society is the divide between the genders. Male-kind seems to be growing more belligerent in our 'civilized' societies. And female-kind is battling to make herself heard. Gender-fluidity seems to have caused a stir every-which-way. And all sides seem to be taking up arms. Poor Mother Earth is at the center of this battlefield. So Gilligan's incitement is timely and potent:

> If humanity is to evolve beyond the propensity toward violence that now threatens our very survival as a species, then it can only do so by recognizing the extent to which the patriarchal code of honor and shame generates and obligates male violence. If we wish to bring this violence under control, we need to begin by reconstituting what we mean by both masculinity and femininity.
>
> *(Gilligan, 1997: 267)*

'Masculinity' and 'femininity' doesn't necessarily mean 'men' and 'women' *per se*: it could refer to the male tendencies in the female psyche and the female

Evolution and influences of the Month-Long Intensive **103**

tendencies in the male psyche – along with the myriad combinations within non-binary identities. And all these gendered qualities are warring *in our own hearts* as much as in our communities. Again, you may ask, how does all this fit into Shakespeare & Company's Month-Long Intensive?

Completing the circle of respect

Well, bringing our whole self into the room – ergo, into our acting work – really is no small task. It entails not just facing and embracing the myriad experiences we might've had, but also acknowledging the violence innate in our own natures. It entails recognizing 'just how vulnerable we all are; how much our needs for love and care and respect are not just luxuries or negotiable options, but absolute life-and-death necessities'[76] (Gilligan). It entails the curiosity, kindness and non-judgmental mindfulness to 'Speak what we feel, not what we ought to say'[77]– to ourselves as much as to each other. And so, for four weeks in the depths of winter for the January Intensive (or the height of June for the STI), a disparate group of participants comes together with a team of dedicated actor trainers all striving to become more thoughtful storytellers. And collectively they try unabashedly to tackle humanity's messiness: 'What does it mean to be alive? How should we act? What must I do?' They navigate the macro-mysteries of the universe and the micro-mysteries within each individual, since a healing, healthy society starts with a healing, healthy love for one's self: 'Without feelings of love, the self feels numb, empty, and dead.'[78] As James Gilligan has found in his years studying violence, holding respect is a hothouse for love while losing respect is a hot-rod to violence. The faculty's commitment to this complicated journey combines with their collective passion to plumb the depths of Shakespeare's extraordinary imagination and manifest his language as *experience*, rather than *reportage*. In the midst of all this there's also much laughter, merriment and utter irreverence. And the workshop certainly strives for a rejuvenation of the youthful spirit … At its heart lies the irrepressible *actor/audience relationship*.

Notes

1 As of 2019, the name for this workshop was changed to 'Summer Shakespeare Intensive' (SSI).
2 Krausnick, Press Release, 2005. S&Co. archive.
3 Packer cited in Dudar, H. (1983), 'A Troupe Tries to Plumb the Heart of the Bard's Words,' *The New York Times*, 28 August 1983 (my emphasis) (Packer edit, April 2019).
4 See Brook, P. (1968, 2008), *The Empty Space: A Book About the Theatre: Deadly, Holy, Rough, Immediate*, London: Penguin.
5 Krausnick cited in Hennessy-Fiske, M. (1997), 'Celebrating 20 years of Shakespeare,' *Boston Globe*, 4 July 1997.
6 Linklater cited in 'A Catalogve [sic] of the several Comedies, Histories, and Tragedies presented by Shakespeare & Company,' Autumn 1989. S&Co. archive.

104 Training

7 'Shakespeare & Company presents THE 1983 WINTER WORKSHOP' pamphlet. S&Co. archive.
8 Maltz was a reconstructive surgeon and author of the classic, self-development book, *Psycho-Cybernetics: Get More Living Out of Life* (1960). Cybernetics comes from the Greek *cybernitos* meaning 'helmsman,' relating to how we keep the 'ship' of our own temperaments on an even keel. c.f. Bartley III, W. W. (1978), *Werner Erhard: The Transformation of Man, The Founding of est*, New York: Clarkson N. Potter Publishers, p. 70.
9 Bartley (1978), p. 198 (my emphasis).
10 est typically entailed two weekend courses. The first weekend, known as est's 'Standard' training, included exercises or 'processes' such as 'The Truth Process' ('a powerful exercise during which [participants] experience the disappearance of the problems on which they chose to work') and 'The Danger Process' ('the aim of which is two-fold: to experience one's own position, and to experience the fear arising from relationships with others that drives one to retains [the fear]'). Bartley (1978), p. 209.
11 This is where Packer's exercise (detailed in Chapter 5) differs from est's exercise, in which no one spoke out loud.
12 Linklater cited in Faber, H. (1979), 'Shakespeareans Thrive at Old Berkshire Estate,' *The New York Times*, 18 February 1979.
13 Faber (1979).
14 Arnold cited in Epstein, H. (1985), *The Companies She Keeps: Tina Packer Builds A Theater*, Cambridge: Plunkett Lake Press, p. 91.
15 Tina Packer interview with Bella Merlin, August 2016.
16 Andrew Borthwick-Leslie interview with Bella Merlin, June 2016.
17 Dave Demke interview with Bella Merlin, June 2016.
18 ibid.
19 Krausnick cited in Nesbitt, C. (1999), 'Into the Woods with Shakespeare & Company: An Actor takes Tina Packer up on the Total-Immersion Challenge, and Survives,' *American Theatre*, January 1999 (my emphasis).
20 ibid.
21 Dennis Krausnick interview with Bella Merlin, August 2016.
22 ibid.
23 Cf. Boys, K. (2018), *The Blind Spot Effect: How to Stop Missing What's Right in Front of You*, Boulder, CO: Sounds True, p. 18.
24 Demke interview, June 2016; amended in email July 2019.
25 ibid.
26 ibid.
27 ibid.
28 ibid.
29 Borthwick-Leslie interview, June 2016.
30 ibid.
31 www.shakespeare.org/actor-training/month-long-intensive (accessed 17 September 2019).
32 Krausnick cited in Nassour, E. (1997), 'The Shakespeare Complex,' *In Theater*, 5 December 1997.
33 Tina Packer in 'Training Shakespeare Actors in a Modern World: Tina Packer talks to Helen Epstein,' p. 11. S& Co. archive.
34 Packer cited in 'Where there's a Will: Comprehensive Studies Ground Actors in Shakespeare,' *Backstage*, 13 March 1998. Unnamed author.
35 Shakespeare, W. (1599–1601), *Hamlet*, Act III, Scene iv, line 89, 'Thou turn'st mine eyes into my very soul,' Gertrude.
36 Shakespeare, W. (c. 1597), *The Life and Death of King John*, Act III, Scene iv, lines 25–60, Constance.

Evolution and influences of the Month-Long Intensive **105**

37 Named after Clare Reidy, longtime S&Co. faculty member and 'chief witch' in her ability to draw support for the Company.
38 www.ybglobal.org (accessed 14 September 2019). The project was founded in 2006 by Andrew Garrod, Professor Emeritus at Dartmouth College and his graduate David Yorio, and it initially focused on bringing Shakespeare to the post-nuclear Marshall Islands, and later to the Balkans and Rwanda, using texts such as *Romeo and Juliet* to bridge cultural, ethnic and linguistic divides. YGP is also committed to enabling leading actors in Bosnia and Herzegovina and Rwanda to receive further theatre training, which has manifested in a relationship with Shakespeare & Company. In 2018 the Dennis Krausnick Fellowship Fund (DKFF) was created to increase diversity in the Actor Training Programs and enable young artists from war-torn territories to come to Lenox and take the *Training*.
39 Pujic cited at www.ybglobal.org (accessed 14 September 2019).
40 Freeman cited in Barrett, P. (1983), 'Finding Shakespeare's Heartbeat: A Scholar "Puts The Mistakes" Back Into Shakespeare's Plays For The Actor's Sake,' *The Berkshire Courier*, 11 August 1983 (my emphasis).
41 Burbage died before the project was completed.
42 Freeman, N. (2001), *The Applause First Folio of Shakespeare: Comedies, Histories & Tragedies*, London and New York: Applause, p. iii.
43 ibid., p. i.
44 ibid.
45 Dudar, H. (1983), 'A Troupe Tries to Plumb the Heart of the Bard's Words,' *The New York Times*, 28 August 1983.
46 Freeman cited in Barrett (1983) (my emphasis).
47 Twenty of those weeks were spent studying four history plays, including Freeman's analysis of the original scripts and the computer inputting. And the remaining 18 weeks were spent in rehearsals and workshops, where he tested his ideas with the actors.
48 Freeman cited in Barrett (1983).
49 Gilligan, C. (1982, 1993), *In A Different Voice: Psychological Theory and Women's Development*, Cambridge: Harvard University Press, p. xv. In the 1990s, she and Linklater co-created two, all-female, Shakespeare companies: The Company of Women and The Company of Girls. And for several years she worked with Company member Normi Noel and graduate student Annie Rogers in the Boston schools system, before collaborating with other female artists at S&Co. – including Daniela Varon, Elizabeth Ingram, Frances West, Paula Langton, Tina Packer and Victoria Rhoades. She was supervisor on Rhoades' PhD. thesis, which integrates Gilligan's work with S&Co.'s training.
50 Gilligan (1982, 1993), p. xvi.
51 ibid.
52 Shakespeare, W. (c.1609), *Coriolanus*, Act III, Scene ii, line 121, 'Lest I surcease to honour mine own truth,' Coriolanus.
53 Gilligan (1982, 1993), p. x.
54 ibid., p. 173.
55 ibid., p. xvi.
56 ibid., p. 12.
57 ibid., p. 163.
58 van der Kolk, B. (2014), *The Body Keeps the Score: Brain, Mind and Body in the Healing of Trauma*, London and New York: Penguin, p. 334.
59 ibid., p. 38.
60 ibid., p. 275.
61 ibid., p. 43.
62 Shakespeare, W. (c. 1596), *Henry IV, Part 1*, Act II, Scene iii, lines 42–69, Lady Percy. Wolfert models with his extraordinary, award-winning piece *Cry Havoc!*

106 Training

(developed in part through Shakespeare & Company, and combining autobiographical stories of his tours of duty as a soldier with Shakespeare monologues) how Shakespeare's language provides a robust container for chaotic emotions. In many respects, he also models the transition of S&Co.'s *Training* into *Performance*. See www.decruit.org/shows/(accessed 20 September 2019).

63 van der Kolk (2014), p. 38.
64 ibid., p. 81.
65 ibid., p. 237.
66 ibid., p. 239.
67 Gilligan, J. (1997), *Violence: Reflections on a National Epidemic*, New York: Vintage, p. 257.
68 ibid., p. 4.
69 ibid. (my emphasis).
70 ibid., p. 11.
71 ibid.
72 ibid., p. 12.
73 ibid., pp. 16–17.
74 ibid., p. 231.
75 ibid.
76 ibid., p. 261.
77 Shakespeare, W. (1606), *King Lear*, Act V, Scene iii, line 326, Edgar.
78 Gilligan (1997), p. 47.

5

TALK #2

Actor/Audience Relationship

There's one facet of theatre we don't train for in the academies – and yet it's a facet that obsesses every performer. We talk about it all the time. It's almost the first thing the first actor speaks about as they come off stage. 'It's a great house' or 'God, they're quiet, can't tell what's going on,' or 'There's a cougher "House Right," don't let him throw you.' Many of the famous theatre stories, passed down through the generations, are to do with the audience.

I remember in one of the *Hamlet* productions I was in, a woman in the audience leaped to her feet when Gertrude was about to drink from the poisoned chalice and screamed, 'Don't do it!' thereby putting every single actor, but especially Gertrude, in a terrible position, because we couldn't deny the reality of what we had just heard and yet the plot demanded that Gertrude drink. Which of course she did – but nobody could say she hadn't been warned and we hadn't all willfully ignored that warning.

The theatrical event doesn't happen without the audience. Sometimes it's direct interaction. But mostly it's the energy of the room, created by the hundreds (or thousands) of people who are listening to the same story at the same time, and the people who are telling the story as shamans or priests. There are many levels of intensity – which we'll explore a little later in this chapter.

Rehearsal is a process of practicing the truth and the storyline until the audience is brought in. And then, once the audience arrives, the play comes into focus on a collective level and the alchemy begins. Perhaps because it is alchemy, we don't want to question the mystery – and therefore we don't discuss it, train for it, build our courage around it, dissect what the ingredients are or decide how we can better harness the enormous force of the energy in the room.

108 Training

Actually, I shouldn't say *no one* practices it. Clowns do. In classical *clown* training, the relationship with the audience is always paramount and always present. But that's the only discipline in which the response of the audience is built into the techniques of the training. In *Voice*, we're reminded again and again to speak to the back row or up to the highest gallery. In *Fight*, the sounds of the fighters build the impact of the violence, especially for those sitting far away from the stage. And yet for actors delivering soliloquies – that most intimate, revealing exchange between actor and audience – there is no training. Or at best it's, 'Think of them as another character in the scene.'

And yet the whole theatre magic – the sole power, the soul power – the very essence of theatre lies in *the actor/audience relationship*: that energy, with many different levels and colors, intensity and vibrations, created collectively by audience and actors. It's why theatre survives despite films and television outstripping distribution a million-fold (along with the opportunity for profit and fame that goes with it). But performing in the visual media (essentially film and television) gives the actor no access to the present-moment exchange between those who are watching and those who are performing (as we discussed in Chapter 3). Therefore, there's no opportunity to adjust a performance in response to the audience's palpable reaction, whether silent or vocal. There's no symbiosis of speaker and listener, no joint understanding of what this story reveals. And that symbiosis is very important for many reasons: it sensitizes our knowledge of other people; it allows us to contemplate the unspoken exchange between people; it brings deeper knowledge of the other; it taps into the essence of being human: it builds *empathy* and, as we now know, humanity has evolved through the ability to be empathetic.

Placing the actors and the audience in the same room is where the deepest creative impulse can be found and mined. We understand things about ourselves we never knew previously, when the audience is with us, magnifying, reflecting and reacting to our energy. The audience – that collection of people, perhaps 30, perhaps 3,000 (or in Greek and Roman times, perhaps 30,000) – are breathing and responding to the events on stage, as we are enacting them as if in life. Together we transmute the story so that our psyches can encompass the events; our bodies can feel the visceral impact; our thoughts, feelings and emotions can be large enough and focused enough that the whole town can know that we're experiencing this together. It builds community and common knowledge.

In Shakespeare – and with the Greek and Roman playwrights, and even some modern playwrights – the defining mode of communication is *language*. The audience listens to the language, which is made more powerful by the full-bodied response of the actors. The language *is* the story. And we need to go deeply into that language. It's not that Shakespeare doesn't give us visual pictures – the gouging out of Gloucester's eyes, for instance. But the whole story is told through language, with some powerful visuals to support that story. So, first and foremost, the audience is there to *hear* the play. Then the words, the atavistic depths of the words, the syntax, the vibrations, create a response in the audience. They'll make sounds, laugh and gasp – though, in our day and age, they probably won't *speak* their response in that moment. Nonetheless, internally what's being said is working on them, so that they'll become more articulate about who they are, and what they think and feel. Language is the bedrock of democracy. So when it's difficult to say what's going on, either personally or collectively, it's hard to know what the problem is or how to deal with it. Language allows the unknowable to be known. And trauma demands that suffering be put into words.

> Give sorrow words; the grief that does not speak
> Whispers the o'er-fraught heart and bids it break.
>
> (Macbeth, *Act IV, Scene iii, lines 210–211, Malcolm*)

In other words, language has a social function, which the visual does not. To speak the unspeakable, to bring what is unconscious to consciousness in a public place, *is* the function of theatre (see Chapter 3). And yet we don't train to absorb and examine *the actor/audience relationship*, even though it brings the very function of theatre into focus. It's the collective energy – the exchange between actors and audience – that allows the transcendence, the awakening, to happen.

These thoughts came to me in bits and pieces over many years. I was always fascinated by those moments in performance when the world seemed to stop and everyone who was witnessing the moment, on stage and off, took a collective breath and recognized a truth that wasn't present before. One of these moments was in Ariane Mnouchkine's promenade production of *1789* at the Roundhouse in Chalk Farm, London, in 1974 – which was a brilliant production on a multitude of levels. But for me a revelation occurred after the storming of the Bastille when the whole of the Roundhouse went completely dark and silent. Seconds passed. And then someone close by whispered, '*Viens ici*! Come here!' And a group of us gathered secretly around the actor. The actor said, again in a whisper, 'I am going to tell you what really happened that night …' and proceeded to give us an account of the burning of the Bastille. And this was happening in groups of 10 to 20 audience members all over the darkened theatre space. It made us complicit in the rebellion, gave us a role in the uprising, and we felt we had secret knowledge that enriched our understanding and we were being asked to make a judgment about what should happen next! It wasn't entertainment: it was a moment of reckoning. Seconds later we were flooded in light and the public events of the Revolution resumed.

I remember decades ago, before I was even in theatre, I was living in Paris and Joan Littlewood's production of Brendan Behan's *The Hostage* was coming to town. I took myself off to the *Théâtre des Nations*, sitting way up in the gods. The sheer energy of the production knocked me sideways. Not just the storyline (which felt very personal, being English myself and aware of what the English had done to the Irish), but the laughter, the songs, the tragedy as death took over and then the refusal to die in the refrain, 'Oh, death, where is thy sting-

110 Training

a-ling-a-ling?' The energy tumbled off the stage and filled this huge auditorium. It was Bacchanalian. I left the theatre full of exhilaration and contrition, and went to meet my lover at the *Deux Magots* in Saint-Germain. As a small group of us settled in for our usual late-night discussion, there was suddenly a conflagration of laughter and dancing in the square. Brendan Behan and some of the actors were whooping it up, so full of joy about the reception they had received at the theatre, they were spreading their exultation to the people in the streets and cafés. It was an extension of the play itself. And although I was probably the only one who had attended the performance that night, the whole square now lit up with energy and verbal wit as Brendan and his cast capered in the square. 'That theatre can do this!' I thought.

> That the energy of Brendan Behan can spread from the stage to the audience right out into the Paris air! That I'm now explaining to my circle of friends what the experience and message of the play was and why the dancing in the streets is a natural extension of the dancing on the stage!

It was exuberant and effortless. And the following night all of us went to see the performance.

I've thought much over the years about the Bacchanalian function of theatre. The Romans knew about Bacchus (aka Dionysus) and the collective letting-off of steam (as we saw in Chapter 3). Bacchus is our God – yet we don't pay much attention to him now. So he has gone to political rallies, soccer games, gang wars. The only place I know where modern Bacchanalian rites are consciously built into the experience is Kevin Coleman's *Education* program here at Shakespeare & Company (as you'll discover in 'Act III' of this book). And that letting-off of steam is wonderfully positive in creating a learning atmosphere!

Another seminal 'actor/audience' moment for me was not at a theatre performance at all – although it was again in the Roundhouse in Chalk Farm. Stokely Carmichael was coming to speak at the Congress on the Dialectics of Liberation in 1967. I was very interested in the Black Power movement, so I took myself off to hear him. He was an impassioned speaker and he was talking about how the evils of slavery, Jim Crow, and all the other iniquities visited upon the African American population was going to, '*Come on home!*' He repeated this phrase throughout his speech: 'It's going to *come on home!*' And we the audience started chanting it with him, exulting in a sense of rightness and power. He was in the midst of his tirade about what the white man had done, and the energy was growing and growing, when suddenly I realized what was happening! There weren't many whites in the audience but Stokely was very clear that the revolution was coming and it was going to be bloody and a lot of white people would meet their demise. I was chanting for my own destruction! In the emotion about the horrible things that had happened (many of which, not living in America, I hadn't registered before, but about which I now felt morally outraged), he was inciting us to turn our violence on to others. And

Talk #2: Actor/Audience Relationship **111**

I was part of those 'others.' I decided it was time for me to leave ... In later years, I realized that the energy and message Stokely Carmichael used was the same energy Henry V uses in 'Once more unto the breach'[1] and Mark Antony uses in 'Cry havoc and let slip the dogs of war.'[2] And both speeches are more effective if the actor uses the audience as well as his six non-Equity soldiers!

On another note, I've always loved stand-up comics: they're so brave, out there by themselves, telling stories (almost always about themselves in some humiliating situation), wanting the audience to laugh about our common stupidity, or some political situation we've allowed to happen that's going to come and bite us in the ass. The laughter allows us to join together – it might even give us the courage to act – but no one can say that the unspeakable wasn't spoken. I'd often note the vulnerability of stand-up comics and note the difference between the actors who really reveal themselves to the audience in a soliloquy and those who pretend they're talking to their feet or to Noo-Noo Land, never looking at the audience. That's what Alec Guinness did when he was playing *Macbeth* at the Royal Court Theatre (1966) those many years ago, in contrast to someone like Mark Rylance who is the very opposite. He not only talks directly to the audience, but it's as if the audience drags the truth out of him. When he was playing Hamlet at A.R.T. (1991), he was in the scene with Rosencrantz and Guildenstern when the audience giggled at one point. He turned directly to them with the accusing question, 'Why do you laugh?' At which, they – along with Rosencrantz and Guildenstern – were all very shame-faced.

It was actually the 'Danger Process' exercise in est training (now called The Landmark Forum; I'm not sure they still do this exercise) that gave me the framework for fashioning my own training of *Actor/Audience*. In the est exercise, a room of some 200 people was divided into groups of 20 apiece. Each group would come onto the platform and look in silence at the audience. We stood in front of the audience for about ten minutes, which was excruciatingly difficult for most people. And sometimes a staff member stood directly in front of us and gazed into our eyes (which I found very sexy but some people almost collapsed in fear at having to maintain eye contact for so long). Then we sat down again. And then the next row stood in front of the audience. It was all done in silence, except for the occasional observation from the trainer.

I immediately associated this exercise with actors on stage and that we never pause long enough to register what we're feeling when we stand in front of an audience. And I realized that if, as actors, we do recognize what is there and, if we can allow it to be there – acknowledging (instead of resisting) the fear or the shame – then the truth can change or reveal itself on deeper levels. Breath (as always) is the key. Be at one with the fear and then it can change to sorrow, aggression, laughter or love. Resist it and it stays stuck. The emotion of fear is fueled by the adrenaline pumping round our body, the 'fight-freeze-or-flight' button being pushed to the furthest, our skin alive to every message in the air-waves. And this state of heightened awareness is actually the optimum state for

112 Training

actors: our brain is ready to translate every piece of stimulus to an appropriate response, working so fast it bypasses thought and becomes intuition. And that intuition is gold.

Two years later I had the opportunity to put together my first *Actor/Audience* exercise, when we were doing our very first Intensive at Shakespeare & Company in winter 1978–1979. The season had closed at the end of the summer, and Kristin Linklater and I both had sons to bring up so we had no intention of going back to New York. 'Well, let's do an Intensive of all our work in January,' said Kristin. 'And we'll try and get it in before teachers of theatre have to return for their Spring Semester.' It was called a 'Linklater Workshop': Kristin was the best known of us, so participants would apply because of her and the *Voice Work* would underpin the four weeks. And as Director of Training, Kristin structured and led the workshop. However, she wouldn't let me teach something we now call *Basics* (detailed in Chapter 6). It's the text class we do in the first week, where actors find the personal connection between themselves and Shakespeare's words. It's profound work, based on the Stanislavsky method and the work that Peter Kass and Olympia Dukakis had done at NYU – and Kristin felt that, because I hadn't been on the faculty at NYU, I shouldn't teach it. I'd directed there, but she said it wasn't the same thing. And I was indignant, because I thought *all* my work was about owning the words. So when she said, 'Well, we've got a three-hour gap in the timetable, why don't you do something with that?,' I shut up complaining and grabbed the opportunity. I would invent my first *Actor/Audience relationship* exercise.

We had a small but gracious turn-of-the-century ballroom in the private Vanderbilt Westinghouse Mansion to conduct the exercise. There were staircases curving round two sides of the room with a balcony above joining them. So I used the stairs and the balcony as the stage, and the ballroom for the audience. Some people sat in chairs, others on the floor. I numbered off everyone in the room, and they would go up in order, two people at a time. And I emphasized that this was an exercise in self-observation: What does it feel like to be an audience member? What does it feel like to be an actor, getting closer and closer to going on stage? What happens to you when you come off stage? What do you notice about your fear mechanism? Is it excitement? Shame? What happens to your voice, your body? But the real breakthrough happened with the words I got them to say.

As *a director*, what I wanted from my actors was 'revelation.' And yet as *an actor*, what I feared about myself was 'being revealed.' I thought people would think I was rubbish. That I wasn't beautiful enough. That my bum was too big to be accounted sexy. I also thought that the various duplicitous things I'd done in my life would be apparent to all and I was terrified they'd find out I was a fraud. But, of course, those are the very things Hamlet and Macbeth think (well, maybe not the bum bit – but certainly Ophelia might have that going on). And *that*, as a director, was exactly what I wanted to see.

Talk #2: Actor/Audience Relationship **113**

So I asked the actors to speak, as personally and as truthfully as they could, a sentence or two about the following:

'What I want you to know about me is …'
'What I don't want you to know about me is …'
'This is my …' (pointing to a part of the body)
Then two lines of Shakespeare text.
Then finally, 'My name is …'

When it came to a part of the body, it could be something they were ashamed of or thought was the most attractive thing going, or anything in between. And saying their name was simply owning everything that had just happened. Two actors went up at a time. After the first actor spoke they stayed looking at the audience as their fellow actor spoke, and they noticed the difference between having all eyes on them and – when people were watching the other person – what comes up then?

That first time, I modeled the exercise so that everyone would know I wasn't asking them to do something I wouldn't subject myself to. Then I added one more rule. As they got up, two by two, I stood by them as they spoke and gave them the timing. It seemed important to do this, because if the actor was truly fearful, it was important to acknowledge that fear – and not use the words to dodge or cover up the feeling. Also, I could remind the actor to breathe and keep looking at the audience. The Shakespeare lines were stunning – filled with meaning, delicacy and nuance. And something also happened to me as I stood alongside them: I could often pick up on what they were going to say before they said it. I learned that if we listen deeply enough, the messages are there in the thought and the breath, and the words are the manifestation of what's going on – the thing that allows you to *know* that you know.

The self-observation component is very important, too. The actor will be immersed in this 'feeling state' – but the tiny part that *notices* what's happening as they tell their truth is also important. I think the Buddhists call it 'the 5%' in meditation. The actor develops the ability to be totally in the moment and to observe it, too – without self-consciousness.

After everyone had been on stage and we were all sitting down again, we talked about the discoveries for about 40 minutes.

This exercise has become the bedrock of Shakespeare & Company's work to include the audience. Not only does the actor see what barriers he/she/they put up to hide from the audience; they also find out, as audience members, that the actor's struggle to be honest and articulate unbearable truths, draws the audience to them. It aligns the actor and the audience member in empathy and compassion, cutting across age, gender, ethnicity and cultural difference. And the more the actor can 'let it be the way it is' (again, breath is key), the more the audience member can look at their own life, without needing to fix or console the actor. The exercise has stayed more or less the same, although over the years

114 Training

we've brought much more ritual into it. The room is set up like a theatre, with backstage seating (i.e., rows of chairs facing upstage) where participants wait to go on, formal rows for the audience, three acts with two intermissions, and a time for detailed feedback, both immediately afterwards and the next day. Everyone in the room undertakes the exercise, workshop participants and faculty, stage management, even the kitchen staff if they want. This inclusion is important so that we know we're all in the same boat: 'this is humanity' – no one is outside the experience. And of course all the preconceived ideas about others are dissolved. Stories are told. Connections are made. Common ground is found. And even if you've never had the experience the speaker is sharing, you feel it with them. It awakens your empathy. And empathy is key to connection. And connection is the only thing that's going to save the world! The exercise, thus, reveals the true experience of *catharsis* – that word bandied about in History of Theatre lectures when talking about Greek theatre – because the audience does weep with the actors, and laugh, and despair, and grow bored and become angry. It's the knowledge of human behavior, which comes as the result of experiencing the present moment; it's knowledge on a deep level involving the full body, not simply talking *about* it.[3]

This exercise shouldn't be messed with casually in an acting class: in fact, it shouldn't be undertaken without expert facilitation. Over the years we've learned many of the pitfalls and fallouts, and so we have the support systems in place. For instance, the participants are given permission to lie and it's okay if they don't want to reveal, and then they can observe how that shielding feels. However, the faculty mustn't lie. We learned that, if we lied, it absolutely broke the trust of the workshop – so we always tell the truth. If we're weary, it may not be the deepest truth, but it will be the truth. Usually, however, we try to challenge ourselves. (Having done the exercise over so many years, we sometimes have to repeat what we've said before, but that's the actor's job, after all: to repeat something and make it feel as if it's never been said before.)

The essence of the *Actor/Audience* exercise is to experience the very act of being aware of the audience. The enormous power that we get from it is essential to the very act of theatre. In every scene – mob scenes, court scenes, intimate balcony scenes, plotting scenes – the audience is part of the action. How much the actor acknowledges them will vary at different times in the play – *but there is no fourth wall in Shakespeare*. The whole point is that the audience is traveling this terrifying journey with us: we must acknowledge that, draw strength from it, and know it is our shared humanity. Otherwise there's no point doing it!

Notes

1 Shakespeare, W. (1599), *Henry V*, Act III, Scene i, line 1, Henry.
2 Shakespeare, W. (1599), *Julius Caesar*, Act III, Scene i, line 273, Mark Antony.

3 Merlin: 'The movement from "Backstage" to "Onstage" to "Audience" that comprises the three stages of *Actor/Audience* is unique, insightful and (from my experience of the 2016 Intensive) quite inspired. It created (for me) real embodied understanding of the transition from *personalization* to *revelation* to *catharsis* to deep *actor/audience relationship*. Both as actor and audience member, the shared "revealing" and "witnessing" allowed a "letting go," which not only shifted my consciousness of social interactions (as I heard others' revelations) but also ignited me to want to be an advocate for social change. Just as Tina talks about herein and in later chapters, I found myself asking "How can I be sure that as a human being I don't enable human bad behavior in my own interactions in society?" At the same time, it was cracking good actor training in terms of integrating breath/thought, text and feeling: being the instrument and the music at one and the same time.'

6

VOICE WORK AND BASICS

In many ways, the essence of S&Co.'s work – ergo, the point of the Month-Long Intensive – is to own Shakespeare's language to the extent that you barely know where *you* stop and the character begins. On the one hand, the *Training* helps you undo the patterns and habits that normally bind you as an actor into one way of doing things, so that 'you can talk and feel in any way you want'[1] (Linklater). On the other hand, you don't have to think, 'I have to do something different. I have to […] assume this character that is something *outside* me'; but rather 'you begin releasing the character who is somewhere *inside* you.'[2] 'It's like alchemy,' as you transform the 'lead' of your life into the gold of Shakespeare's poetry.[3] And through this alchemy, you ignite *language as experience* rather than *reportage*, so the audience can have a hot-blooded experience rather than a cool-blooded musing. The key to this 'alchemical' transformation is the Intensive's *structure*, which (as we touched on in Chapter 4) has been meticulously forged over 40 years. It's the structure that allows you 'to go right to the heart of Shakespeare's powerful words, in the knowledge that you've got the pathways out of any turmoil, which might be stirred up' when you really do experience the language[4] (Packer). So to guide you through this structure, the core curriculum is packaged here into six major chunks. In this chapter, we begin with the *Rituals* (which bookend many of the classes); we then turn to Linklater's *Voice Work* (which forms the underpinning), which leads us into *Basics* (a series of classes that 'basically' address 'What is acting?'). In Chapter 7, we look at *Text Work* (including sonnets, scenes and Packer's *dropping in*). And in Chapter 8 we explore *Body Work* (including *Movement/Dance*, *Clown* and *Fight*) and *Bringing it all together* (with the *Elizabethan World Picture Day* and the final *Actor/Audience* sessions). It's important to remember that these disciplines run in parallel throughout the four weeks. And each discipline has its own micro-progression within the over-arching structure. The alchemy begins – as all alchemy does – with simple *rituals* …

The 'rituals'

The 'rituals' open the very first day, as a way of pragmatically encouraging you to set intentions for your work and create some new habits …

The opening circle

From time immemorial the circle has served across cultures as a container for shared storytelling, in which everyone's voice is equally valued. And so the Month-Long Intensive starts with the whole group (maybe 60 people) sitting in a circle and answering simple prompts such as: 'What's your name?' (which brings you into the space. 'Bella Merlin' is actually my stage name so immediately my authenticity felt tremulous). 'What's your heart's desire for this workshop?' (which sets an intention for the month as the author of your own journey. My particular heart's desire was 'To get out of my head as an actor and into my body'). And 'Share something that you wouldn't normally tell a group of strangers' (which ignites that spark of speaking from your heart in front of an unknown audience. My public 'secret' was 'My body's getting older and my head doesn't like it'). And then to the 'Ground Rules' …

The Ground Rules

Created over the years in response to the Company's management training and as a result of the faculty's own learning experiences, the Ground Rules are very useful:

1. *This is embodied training* (as athletic as sport). You're invited to take Shakespeare's narratives into your body and not just your head, to understand why physically, politically, psychologically, dramaturgically he has written a particular moment. So, teachers will likely make physical contact with you in class to help you with that embodied learning. If you need them to stop, it's your right and responsibility to say so; they'll then find another way to teach you.
2. *You're the author of your own journey.* During the month, the teachers invite you (as we saw in Chapter 4) to fathom any blocks that prevent you fulfilling your potential as an actor. These blocks could be physical. (I discovered I had a habit of holding tension in my tongue.) Or psychological. (For some reason, I was being very cerebral with the word 'death.') And it's entirely up to you whether or not you want to go on the journey. That said Shakespeare examines extreme situations (be it love or revenge,

118 Training

    scheming or dreaming) and our job as actors is to get to the core of those situations, which may entail being curious about our own extremes.

3. *Stay in the room.* Each class is only 90 minutes, but if you find you need a bathroom break, the whole group will break. This is part of strengthening *the actor/audience relationship,* so that everyone understands that, whether observing other people or actively engaged in an exercise, we're all working all the time.

4. *Don't hurt yourself, others, the furniture or the space.* (Particularly in scenes of confrontation. This is a no-brainer 'directive' given in many acting methodologies, particularly when you're training impulse.)

5. *What's said in the room stays in the room.* Often in the course of the work, actors may reveal aspects of their personal lives. You can ask permission of a participant to address something arising from their experience, and it's up to them whether they say yes or no.

6. *Be on time!* (Another no-brainer.)

Everyone is asked to observe these Ground Rules (which are common sense really), so that a creative environment can be forged effectively.

    This opening circle is an extended version of a practice used right across S&Co.'s programs called *checking in* – and it partners with another 'ritual,' *reinforcing.*

Checking in and reinforcing

Checking in at the beginning of a session involves each person flagging up anything that might be resonating for them that day (e.g., 'I'm worried about my husband in Zimbabwe at the moment'). And at the end of the session, *reinforcing* something positive that has arisen (e.g., 'I've suddenly realized I'm always holding tension in my tongue'). These practices (often used in non-violent communication and mindfulness forums) were actually introduced to Shakespeare & Company by Bruce and Rachel Rogal (two of the corporate advisors they've consulted over the years).[5] And they originate from the management pioneer Ichak Kalderon Adizes.[6] The Adizes® Methodology (which includes *checking in* and *reinforcing*) enables 'complex organizations to achieve exceptional results and manage accelerated change without destructive conflicts.'[7] Over time, S&Co. has adapted these practices to their three strands of *Training, Education* and *Performance.* So the daily 'check in' builds the whole group's cooperative and creative state. And, as a bookend to *checking in,* *reinforcing* puts a positive button on a class or rehearsal, which in turn accelerates the learning process. As *Voice* teacher Dave Demke explains, 'if I "reinforce" a new discovery, it means I *want* to carry it forward. And that act of reinforcement is how fundamental change happens.'[8] Reinforcing new discoveries also reminds you that you're the author of your own transformation throughout the Intensive.

So, that's a very brief glimpse at some of the pragmatic rituals that galvanize the Month-Long Intensive. Now let's turn to where it all began: Kristin Linklater's *Voice Work*. And although Linklater left the Company in 1992, her influence remains fundamental.

Voice Work

Linklater's *Voice Work* explores 'the complexity, resilience and mystery of the human experience and its reflection in voice.'[9] And it does so through 'a very clear logical progression of exercises' carefully designed 'to undo [people's] inhibitions and defenses, and allow the freedom of the natural human being who is limitless in [their] expression.'[10] Beginning with *Physical Awareness* (a series of simple exercises to relax your body and release your spine), the progression aims to liberate your whole, anatomical instrument, before bringing in language and text. Since Linklater's seminal *Freeing the Natural Voice*[11] vividly details the work, we'll briefly look here at some whats, whys and hows of the *Voice* strand, starting with the schedule.

Schedule

The schedule is fairly straightforward. Typically the whole *Voice* progression (outlined anon) is introduced on Day #1. Then, most mornings begin with a collective *Physical Awareness* 'warm up' (incorporating elements of Trish Arnold's and Merry Conway's work (see Chapter 1), stretches, squats and imaginative prompts – e.g., 'Imagine you're a bear coming out of hibernation' – all designed to connect your body, voice and playfulness). The *Physical Awareness* warm up is followed by small-group *Voice* classes, which journey step by step through Linklater's progression. And these classes retune your psychophysical acting instrument, through a series of 'forms' (including breath, vibration, touches of sound, resonance, vocal improvisations and text). (More anon.) At the beginning of each week, everyone comes together to revisit the entire progression. And this mix of individually learning the details of every form (maybe tongue stretches or chest resonance) and collectively experiencing the entire progression ensures your work is cumulative as well as consolidating. Although the four-week journey can really only provide an introduction to your lifelong process, it's still remarkably transformative, not least because of the *vocabulary*.

Vocabulary

As we saw in Chapter 4, the *Training* is based on non-judgmental curiosity about human activities. So the *Voice* teachers (all Linklater-designated) use non-coercive vocabulary, *inviting* you to have new experiences rather than *telling* you to adopt new techniques. This isn't just a question of semantics: it's part of the process of 'dissolving protective habits in the mind and the body' and

120   Training

strengthening your creative freedom[12] (Linklater). And there's no better way to do that than hooking the imagination:

> Imagery is the language of the body. Imagination is the language of acting. When you regularly employ imagery to exercise the experience of voice, you program a mind/body connection that brings imagination out of the head and into the realm of the body.
>
> *(Linklater, 2006: 66)*

To which end, Linklater likens the movement of your diaphragm to the billowing of a parachute silk, and the breathing musculature around your ribcage to a tapestry, while the construction of your pelvic floor is pictured as the weaving of webbing.[13] By playfully merging imagery with anatomy and sound like this, 'human truth' can be expressed through voice.[14] And if you find you can't do a particular exercise, the teachers simply ask you to be curious about why your body is resistant at this moment: 'Celebrate whatever you experienced in the exercise that was of fresh interest instead of flagellating yourself with [...] unsuccessful things'[15] (Linklater).

And yet *why* do we find it so hard to be playfully expressive? Linklater's understanding of human communication offers an answer ...

The fundamental rationale

Once upon a time as human beings, we connected thought to word – and feeling to need – instinctively and organically. And that 'once upon a time' wasn't back in the cave. Or even back in Elizabethan times. For most of us (reminds Linklater) it was as recently as our own childhood. As babies, we expressed ourselves freely and naturally without censoring ourselves, running out of breath or growing hoarse. But then something happened. 'Deep in the unconscious mind, the animal instinct to respond emotionally to stimulus is largely conditioned out of us as children.'[16] As we learn to speak, we become 'unconsciously controlled by habits conditioned in childhood by arbitrary influences such as parents (or lack of them), teachers, peers, fellow gang members, movie stars, or popstars.'[17] And as we're growing up, we're 'stuck with these muscles that have gone mushy on us,'[18] and our connection to expression is 'fragmented and weakened, even false.'[19] It's as if the more socialized we become, the less we listen to what we feel. And as we detach from our feelings, our words become *disembodied* and the pleasure of expressing ourselves vanishes. In fact, the fundamental rationale of Linklater's *Voice Work* (ergo, much of the Company's Intensive) is to bring language back into its '*rightful place in the body.*'[20] To reintegrate our feelings, thoughts, sounds and words, 'so that the body and the voice are saying the same thing.'[21] And that's the path toward language becoming *experience*, rather than *reportage*. (For me, that meant exploring why I was being so detachedly cerebral

about the word, 'death' …) But before we tackle language, let's get back to
breath – which is where Linklater's *Voice Work* begins …

Breathing and sighing

Research into breath has occupied Linklater for over 50 years:

> Breath is the key to restoring the deepest connections with impulse, with
> emotion, with imagination and thereby with language. […] If I am inter-
> ested in rediscovering the authenticity of my voice and thereby a deeper
> authentic self, I must start with an awareness of my breathing habits.
>
> *(Linklater in Boston and Cook, 2009: 102, 103)*

Becoming aware of your breathing habits means nothing less than becoming
aware of your body's activities. And Linklater's particular interest in breath is
'the way in which it creates voice as it passes through the vocal folds and how it
helps us either to reveal or hide the truth as we speak.'[22] For her, the '*prima
materia*' for the 'alchemy of inspired communication' is breath.[23] In fact, you
could say that breath is the '*prima materia*' for the whole of Shakespeare & Company's work, as Kevin Coleman suggests:

> It's a release of breath that allows your body to be more responsive. It's
> a release of breath that allows for a deeper, riskier vulnerability to the lan-
> guage. So, I would say the heart and core of the work [here at S&Co.] is
> profound awareness and appreciation of the essential nature of your
> breath.
>
> *(Coleman interview, August 2016)*

To which end, the early stages of the Intensive's daily *Voice* classes focus on
your body's experience of breath. You begin by simply allowing your breath its
natural in–out rhythm. And before long you're encouraged to turn your breath
into (voiceless) *sighs*. The simple act of sighing on breath is surprisingly evocative, provoking a range of emotions: from relief, appreciation, exhaustion and
satisfaction to profound sorrow and more:

> Sometimes when someone relaxes and the breath drops deeper in the
> body tears will flow. There may be no apparent reason for the tears, no
> story to tell, it's just a relief for the body to let go of its habitual protec-
> tion and allow emotion and breath to reconnect as they are designed to
> do.
>
> *(Linklater in Boston & Cook, 2009: 105)*

A daily schedule of *Physical Awareness* and relaxation. Curiosity. Imaginative
vocabulary. The fundamental rationale of bringing language back into the body.

122 Training

Breathing, and sighing on breath. These are a few of the whats, whys and hows of Linklater *Voice Work*. Time now to introduce *sound*. Since *Freeing the Natural Voice* is the ultimate guide to her *Voice* progression, this is but the swiftest canter through …

Linklater's Voice progression

Stemming back to their interest in the ancient Greeks, both Linklater and Packer were fascinated by vibration. So Linklater's *Voice* progression moves from relaxation, breathing and sighing to a sequence that starts with *a touch of sound* (in which you allow your outgoing breath to play on pure vibration with a 'huh' sound). Always in the progression your imagination is involved and, for this particular 'form,' the imagery used includes 'pools of water' deep inside your body (*FTNV*: 29–86).

The touch of sound evolves into exploring *vibrations throughout your body*, including fluttering your lips, humming, feeling the vibrations in the bones of your skull, shoulder blades, pelvic cradle, even your knees, and then amplifying those vibrations. Here, the imagery used includes 'rivers of sound' flowing through your body (*FTNV*: 87–127).

After you've enjoyed the feeling and release of vibration, the progression then turns to the parts of your body that create speech: i.e., your jaw, tongue and soft palate. And because they *create* speech, they can also *obstruct* you from speaking freely, forming either an 'open door' or a 'prison gate.' (*FTNV*: 129–184). In fact, it's curious how many colloquialisms we have for silencing ourselves: 'I clenched my teeth'; 'I bit my lip'; 'I had a lump in my throat'; 'I held my breath.' (With my own tongue-tension, I wondered if I'd been metaphorically 'holding my tongue' for years – in order to be a good person, obedient and well-liked.) Therefore, several classes are spent noting these inadvertent tensions and inviting you to release them. (Which may in turn release the correlating psychologies.)

The progression then turns to the body's echo chambers – or *resonators*. Sessions focus on relishing the major resonators of your chest, mouth and teeth (*FTNV*: 185–205) and 'the breathing gym' of your ribcage (*FTNV*: 213–244). Then, before moving into the upper resonators of your head, you're introduced to an energizing exercise called '*vacuuming your lungs*' (*FTNV*: 225–227). This allows even more space and breath to explore the head resonators in your sinuses ('the road out'), your nasal area ('the mountain peak') and your skull ('the dome') (*FTNV*: 245–284).

By now, your whole instrument feels awake and attuned – through relaxation, breath, sound, vibration, an open channel through your jaw and throat, and the resonators throughout your body. So, it's time to bring everything together with *articulation* (*FTNV*: 295–319). There are many playful tongue-twisters in the Linklater canon, all designed to excite your spirit with open vowels and a teasingly textured clatter of consonants. Favorites include

Voice Work and Basics **123**

'Dastardly Donald died the death of a desperate drunken dog' and 'Naughty Nelly nibbled the knees of nineteen nautical nerds.'

The *Voice Work* is intensive – and can be challenging. If (like me) you're a mid-career professional, you may find you have some outdated vocal techniques to be decommissioned first. (I'd had a similar British training to Packer: rib reserve, 'two-finger' jaw drop and counting to 30 on one breath, the complete antithesis of freeing the natural voice.) Added to which, there may be physical habits to undo and personal blocks to be released. So your entire body is being invited to a new experience of expressing yourself – and that's no casual invitation!

Voice into Text

If, however, you accept the invitation, your instrument is by now raring to explore some Shakespeare – though text is only brought into the *Voice* sessions very lightly at first. It may be sections of sonnets, morsels of monologues, snippets of scenes, or just the vowels and consonants of a single line (e.g., 'Death, death, o aimiable lovely Death!' or 'Dth-dth-mbl-lvl-dth' – no breath for life in those consonants ...).[24] And because the progression is so attentive, its pay-offs creep up on you in subtle ways. Normally as actors, we start a speech and, when we need more air to get through the next line, we take a breath. With the Linklater *Voice Work* (in synergy with Barton/Packer's *Text Work*: see Chapters 1 and 7), something potentially more mysterious happens. As your voice becomes physically freer, your *imagination* opens up. And your opened imagination builds your capacity for Shakespeare's powerful *thoughts* – as well as your ability to express his big *emotions*. Your new ability to express big thoughts and powerful emotions demands more *breath* of you, so your lung capacity increases. And then, in a kind of metaphorical infinity sign, your increased capacity for breath expands your receptivity to Shakespeare's language! So now, you don't just take a breath because you're supposed to speak your lines: you allow a breath into your body and – *because of that breath* – a new insight suddenly dawns on you. And it's as if that new insight spawns your next (scripted) line. So, in a way, your breath *becomes* your thought. Or rather your breath *changes* your thought. Thus, breath, thoughts and feelings become inextricably interwoven – just as they are in real life – to the extent that

> you might not know what particular color will come out *until* you speak. But whatever comes out is fine: it might be funny, sexual, playful, dark, whatever. So there's a sort of a controlled chaos that happens, whereby the language rides on top of the breath to bring out the character's given circumstances.
>
> *(Rory Hammond interview, August 2016)*

Many of us in the twenty-first century don't necessarily realize how deeply language affects us, maybe 'because we don't love language as much as the

124 Training

Elizabethans might?'[25] (Hammond). Which loops us back to the idea of theatre as 'debating chamber': playgoers in Shakespeare's times were *audiences* (who went to hear a play) rather than *spectators* (watching visuals). And because the voice is vibration, 'when you marry a concrete text with vibration, you're [physically] putting a thought into space'[26] (Demke). And that vibration-thought can provoke deeply empathic experiences in your audience as your voice starts vibrating in *their* bones. So, essentially, the *Voice Work* at the Intensive is recreating that vibrational connection embedded in the Elizabethan playhouse experience.

Putting a thought physically into space is linked to putting your physical body in the space. Which takes us to the series of classes created in the early years by Linklater and Arnold: *Sound and Movement* (introduced in Chapter 1).

Sound and Movement

Sound and Movement classes are held several times a week, bringing breath and vibration into the moving body in 'the physical version of the Linklater approach'[27] (Krausnick). The first sessions of *Sound and Movement* heavily feature Arnold's swinging exercises (see Chapter 1). And as you give your body the pleasure of giving into gravity, with swings from your hips, your shoulders, your spine, as well as loosening your pelvic joints and freeing up your sacrum, you release your voice as well. (The exercises are adaptable to different bodily challenges.) There are also elements of Alexander Technique (drawn from Judith Leibowitz, Linklater's teacher in the 1960s): 'The Alexander technique marries perfectly with voice work. [...] Maximum effect with minimum effort is the criterion [in forging] a simple personal connection between the words and self'[28] (Linklater). And over the years other *Sound and Movement* instructors have incorporated Feldenkrais technique, T'ai Chi, Yoga and Body Mind Centering. There are also echoes of Michael Chekhov in some of the more image-based improvisations, such as imagining you're painting the room with different vocal colors or releasing sound through imaginary mouths in your butt, back, elbows or feet. Thus, *Sound and Movement* contributes to the subtle process of reuniting your body with your mind, 'free[ing] the emotional and psychological self by ridding the body of habitual tensions'[29] (Linklater). The more physically available your body can be to you, the more easily you can express the 'full throated ecstasy' of, say, Imogen for her horse with wings, or the 'full throated agony' of Lear over his dead Cordelia, 'in the confidence that those emotional extremes are not going to strain your vocal instrument at all'[30] (Krausnick).

Breath to thought (or thought to breath) to image to sound to body to word to emotion to human connection. It sounds so sequential and easy. Yet all too often we inadvertently block that natural path, and the process of undoing our self-imposed censors can be tricky. In many respects it takes us right back to *Basics* ...

Basics

The entry point into Shakespeare & Company's *Training* is essentially 'being honest. Everything that has ever happened to you is in your body'; so what happens 'if people can get in touch with themselves, and in time with their audiences'?[31] (Packer). This is the process of *Basics*: 'It illuminates how *your story* meeting the *text* can expand to the heightened level of Shakespeare'[32] (Krausnick). And *Basics* is the major acting component of Week 1 of the Intensive. The cohort is divided into groups of 8–10 under the auspices of two faculty members for a 12-hour series of classes. And during this time each participant works on their self-selected monologue in front of their group. In many respects, *Basics* is a wholesale recalibration of 'true-feeling' acting, as you're asked to dive into what it feels like to speak Shakespeare's words using the material of your own life. And certainly whatever you experience in *Basics* can resonate for you throughout the rest of the month. But before addressing the specifics of *Basics*, let's look briefly at its *origins and intentions*.

The origins of Basics

The origins of *Basics* take us back to Linkater's work at NYU in the early 1970s and the search for 'Stanislavskian truth.' This search for truth has always aligned closely with Packer's passion for *language as experience*, rather than *reportage*:

> for actors to serve their calling, they must first know themselves. They must be vulnerable as artists, must know on some level they can reach what it feels like to bleed and die, and hate and love and fear and connive and laugh. For it is of those things that Shakespeare writes.
>
> *(Packer in Caffery, 1980)*

So if you're going to take on Shakespeare with such whole-hearted investment, you're really taking on yourself.

As the Company headed toward their first Intensive in the winter of 1978–1979, they struggled to find the right name for the class – until they realized that the question really animating them was why, as actors, do we want to get up on stage in the first place? What's so energizing about speaking words in front of other people that we can't talk about on our own? 'That was really the beginning of the Shakespeare & Company *Training* program: regarding theatre as a place to speak the unspeakable. To reveal what has always been hidden. To speak publicly shames that evaporate under the light of the day'[33] (Krausnick) (and there's a whole heap of ashamed characters in Shakespeare).[34] In humble counterbalance to this mighty intent, the class was simply called *Basics*, 'as that was vague enough for no one to get disappointed in what it might achieve!'[35] Though the disappointments are few when you've got Shakespeare's texts to train you.

126 Training

Shakespeare as the best acting teacher

With Shakespeare as the master-teacher, it's hard not to connect personally to some meaty truths:

> Shakespeare's language draws everything from the actor, nothing can be held back. The will power and commitment necessary to speak Shakespeare's text in a way that involves the audience demands that actors draw upon experiences and self-reserves they may never have touched upon before.
>
> *(Krausnick, Press Release, 2004, S&Co. archive)*

But that in itself can be daunting:

> When you have a writer of Shakespeare's caliber, there are so many psychological and philosophical insights that you can feel a bit overwhelmed. For example: You only need to take a question like, 'To whom should I complain? Did I tell *this*, who would believe me?'[36] And if you're really getting someone to connect to themselves, the deepest thing they want to complain about in their *own* life comes up. And that '*this*' comes smack in their face, as it's usually something they've never spoken about before.
>
> *(Packer interview, August 2016)*

Yet because Shakespeare is such a master-teacher, 'he's given you the words that enable you to express your deepest self, so you also feel much safer. In a way, Shakespeare keeps you safe.'[37]

You're also 'kept safe' because your experience is ultimately for the audience in the debating chamber of the theatre. And since *the actor/audience relationship* in Shakespeare's theatre was paramount, so too is *Actor/Audience* paramount at every level of the Intensive, including *Basics*:

> Your job as an actor is to get the information out to the audience in a way that they can 'hear' you. You're owning what's inside you – but you're putting it out there for the audience's collective insight, for us all to look at and consider. And if you're truthful about your experience, emotions start coming up for the audience, too.
>
> *(Packer interview, August 2016)*

And that's when the audience also becomes your master-teacher, as illustrated in the *phases* comprising *Basics*.

The Basics phases

There are the four 'basic' phases in *Basics* as described by Packer (though these phases are so deeply embedded in the process you're hardly aware of them).[38]

Voice Work and Basics **127**

First of all, you take the stage (i.e., the rehearsal-room floor) and deliver your monologue. The two faculty watch what you naturally do the first time round; then they get up there with you. They may start with questions about why you chose the monologue? What do these images inspire? What happens to you as you let these words land in your imagination – and you allow in the breath required to express these thoughts? The two faculty members are exacting and inescapable. They repeat words and phrases over and over. With your permission, they make physical contact, smoothing brows, massaging shoulders, stroking jaws, supporting weight. Their sole aim is to help you access and release whatever feelings are aroused in you when you allow yourself to go to the place where the character's words have the capacity to take you – be it laughter, joy, despair, anger, frustration, lust, fury, vengeance, jealousy, grief, whatever. (For my 'Constance' monologue, I was stuck in my head at first with the word, 'death': 'Mmm, what a strange word! With that flat "e" sound and that weak-feeling "th" at the end ...' Then bit by bit I noticed my body seemed burdened with some unidentified grief ...)

The next phase is to register that that feeling is actually living in you – not least because you may be surprised by what Shakespeare's words provoke in you when you free yourself from being overly reverent with the text. And it's important to experience *the experience of that emotion* and not move too swiftly through this phase. (For me, it was curious: 'This sure is some burdensome grief I'm feeling. But it's not about my grandmother ... Where's this *coming* from? ... Ping ... A regretted action some twenty years ago ... Oh, my ... Oh, no ... Why has *this* suddenly popped up? ... Ohhhh ...')

Third, once you've acknowledged the feeling, you channel it directly back into Shakespeare's words. You then discover that the genuinely sparked emotion can radically expand your original experience of the monologue. And you realize that those words resonate in a far deeper place than you ever anticipated. ('"Ohhh! Amiable, *lovely* death ..." It's welcome. It's a sigh of relief. It's ... "lovely." I never realized ... How wonderful to have the place and framework to plummet this human experience ... It's awful for Constance, but actually for *me* ... it's not so regrettable ...')

In the final phase, you give free rein to the alchemical connection between you and the monologue – which in turn gives you a new understanding of both yourself and the language. You find you connect far more intimately to the extremes of Shakespeare's expressiveness than you thought possible. In other words, it's a two-way street: Shakespeare's words connect you to your autobiography, and (by means of that autobiography) you expand into Shakespeare's words. ('"Death, death..." Bring it on! And I'll show all you church-people and townspeople gathered to gawp at Me/Constance how unafraid of death I am! How unashamed of showing my grief! And no, I'm not *mad* – I'm as articulate as any of you cardinals!')

128 Training

This four-phase process is fast, deep and demanding, as you're asked 'to listen more and more intently and open [yourself] viscerally to the psychic charge the language transmits.'[39] Innate in the process are two important points of attention of which the two guiding faculty remind you: First, your *breathing* is constantly noted (the *Training* always begins with breath); second, you maintain eye contact with the *audience*. And this contact with the audience is the crux of your experience, not least because (as we saw in Chapter 4) your audience is another significant teacher. In fact, the faculty's job in *Basics* is to ensure 'that, when you get up to work, at some point the whole room has a *physiological response* to your work,' says experienced *Basics* teacher Andrew Borthwick-Leslie. 'And I say that because it's very hard for actors to know and name their successes. But when there's an audience to witness you finding the source of your talent, you can't deny what the audience is responding to.'[40] Which takes us right back to vibration. If you truly put your thoughts into space, your energy will literally vibrate for the audience. *Basics* is all about aligning breath to thought to language. Not to mention character.

Aligning with the language

Actually, character is barely mentioned in the Month-Long Intensive. Least of all in *Basics*. In fact, one of the discoveries you make in *Basics* – one that resonates throughout the whole month – is that, by aligning yourself with the language, *you become the character*. When you allow your breath, voice, image, emotion to all land together, 'the language works you, versus you working the language':

> So the language is ravaging me. And now I'm responding authentically and emotionally to what those words are triggering in me, rather than how I'm interpreting those words or emphasizing those words or paying attention to the operative words. Those words are older than me: they're ancient. So what visceral, emotional, imaginative responses to these words are triggered in me? [...] At first, I'm the instrument. And then, as I build my capacity to survive these experiences, I become the player of the instrument as well.
>
> *(Coleman interview, August 2016)*

Basics provides the opportunity to build that capacity and become that player. And it does so by expanding your experience of how language actually shifts you: 'If you don't allow yourself to [align with the language], you'll be stuck pretending instead of acting.'[41] (Packer). And the whole goal of the Intensive is for participants

> to experience that their own life story is a part of the story that's being told. They're not separate from the character. They find the character

within the vibrations of their own experience. *Basics* gives people a visceral experience that their life story matters. And it's an inevitable and inseparable part of their own creativity that somehow must get spoken.

(Krausnick interview, August 2016)

Grotowski might call it the *via negativa*. Stanislavsky might call it the 'state of I am.' For Shakespeare & Company, it's *Basics*: actor and character are one and the same. But you're certainly not playing your everyday self …

Expanding into character: personalization

Nearly every year before *Basics*, the faculty has a discussion about its purpose: 'Because we all teach so differently, it's always an interesting discussion, because the question then is, "What is it that we're all doing that's the *same*?" And the word that comes up is *personalization*'[42] (Borthwick-Leslie). That doesn't mean reducing Shakespeare to the mundaneness of our twenty-first-century lives: it means giving yourself 'the experience of being as large as you really are'[43] (Epstein). In other words, you align yourself with the text to actualize your true capability. And when you do that, something unexpectedly paradoxical happens: 'the more personal it becomes for the actor, the more universal it becomes for the audience.'[44] We're all part of humanity – and humanity is pretty darned big.

Basics is, therefore, very textured. It gives you the chance – if you want to (and don't forget you're the author of your own journey) – to distill and expand; to personalize and universalize; to be more connected to your personal journey and more connected to the audience's experience. To align with the language and hold the binaries of life on the tip of a pin as you tell Shakespeare's epic stories.

Linklater's *Voice* progression plus the 'rituals' and *Basics* form the DNA of Shakespeare & Company's *Training*. Since the flesh–and–blood is Shakespeare's texts, we now turn to *Text Work*, bearing in mind that the *Body Work* (*Movement/Dance*, *Clown* and *Fight*) continually run in parallel throughout the four-week program.

Notes

1 Linklater cited in Mackay, B. (1980), 'Body "Talks" at Voice Workshop,' *The Denver Post*, 13 October 1980 (my emphasis).
2 ibid.
3 Linklater cited in Shreefter, K. (1989), 'Kristin Linklater: Voice to Shakespeare,' *The Berkshire Courier*, 13 July 1989.
4 Tina Packer discussion with Bella Merlin, December 2018.
5 S&Co. tried 11 different management consultant methodologies before encountering the Rogals, who described to them the life cycles of an organization, which typically involves a 'go-go' success state of being, which in time moves into the 'prime' time of financial security. The Rogals had noted that S&Co. had been overwhelmed with

130 Training

the 'go-go' state for over 20 years (even 40, one could argue) without having time to secure finances and fully enjoy their 'prime.'

6 In 1966, Adizes was studying Yugoslavia's 'industrial, democracy-management system,' which he noted 'stood in stark contrast to the top down management approach used in the United States.' And through evaluating the relative strengths and weaknesses of these two approaches, he created his Adizes® Methodology. See adizes.com/history (accessed 17 September 2019) and Adizes, I. and Borgese, E. M. (1975), *Self Management: New Dimensions to Democracy*, ABC-CLIO. Inc.

7 ichakadizes.com.

8 Dave Demke interview with Bella Merlin, June 2016.

9 Linklater, K. (2006), *Freeing the Natural Voice: Imagery and Art in the Practice of Voice and Language*, London: Nick Hern Books, p. 3.

10 Linklater cited in Fuller, B. (1989), 'Actor-centred training,' *The Paper*, 3 August–6 September 1989.

11 Linklater (2006). There are also Linklater's excellent resources at www.linklatervoice.com.

12 Linklater in Boston, J. and Cook, R. (eds.) (2009), *Breath in Action: The Art of Breath in Vocal and Holistic Practice*, London: Jessica Kingsley Publishers, p. 104.

13 Linklater in Boston and Cook (2009), p. 102.

14 Linklater, K. (2006), p. 96.

15 ibid., pp. 62–63.

16 ibid., p. 19.

17 ibid., pp. 19–20.

18 Linklater cited in Meehan, A. (1979), 'Shakeing All Over,' *The Berkshire Eagle*, 18 January 1979.

19 Linklater cited in Jenkins, R. (1983), 'As They Like It: A Devoted Young Theater Group Enhances Shakespeare's Words with Motion and Emotion,' *The Boston Globe*, 31 July 1983.

20 ibid. (my emphasis).

21 Linklater cited in Mackay, B. (1980), 'Body "Talks" at Voice Workshop,' *The Denver Post*, 13 October 1980 (my emphasis).

22 ibid., p. 101.

23 ibid.

24 Shakespeare, W. (c.1597), *The Life and Death of King John*, Act III, Scene iv, line 25, Constance.

25 Rory Hammond interview with Bella Merlin, August 2016.

26 Demke interview, June 2016.

27 Dennis Krausnick interview with Bella Merlin, August 2016.

28 Linklater in Evans, M. (ed.) (2015), *The Actor Training Reader*, Abingdon and New York: Routledge, p. 95.

29 Linklater (2006), p. 2.

30 Krausnick interview, August 2016.

31 Packer in Caffery, B. (1980), 'Tina Packer: A Passionate Woman With Definite Ideas,' *Evening Independent*, 29 November 1980.

32 Dennis Krausnick interview with Bella Merlin, September 2018.

33 ibid.

34 See Fernie, E. (2002), *Shame in Shakespeare*, London and New York: Routledge.

35 Krausnick interview, September 2018.

36 Shakespeare, W. (1604), *Measure for Measure*, Act II, Scene iv, line 184, Isabella.

37 Tina Packer interview with Bella Merlin, August 2016.

38 Packer discussion, December 2018.

39 Sanders, V. (1997), 'The passion of Tina Packer,' *The Boston Globe*, 17 August 1997.

40 Andrew Borthwick-Leslie interview with Bella Merlin, June 2016.

41 Packer cited in Epstein, H. (1985), *The Companies She Keeps: Tina Packer Builds A Theater*, Cambridge: Plunkett Lane Press, p. 118.
42 Borthwick-Leslie interview, June 2016
43 Jonathan Epstein cited in Nesbitt, C. (1999), 'Into the Woods with Shakespeare & Company: An actor takes Tina Packer up on the total-immersion challenge, and survives,' *American Theatre*, January 1999.
44 Jonathan Epstein interview with Bella Merlin, August 2016.

7

TEXT WORK AND DROPPING IN

Now to the meat of acting Shakespeare. The *Text Work* sessions entail 'embodying the language on a deep level and experiencing *the actual feeling of words* as well as *the information in the structure*'[1] (Packer). To which end, your monologues in *Basics* are followed by work on self-selected sonnets and faculty-selected scenes. Concurrent are almost daily self-reflective *Journaling* sessions (in which you're often guided by prompts, drawing on the monologues, sonnets and scenes)[2] and a series of interactive lectures, including 'Function of the Theatre' (see Chapter 3), 'Actor/Audience Relationship' (see Chapter 5), 'The Elizabethan World Picture' and 'Theatre, Therapy and Theology' (see Chapter 14). In this chapter, we look closely at *Structure of the Verse*; *Sonnet*; and *Scene Work*, before turning to Packer's original practice of *dropping in* a role. First to the *Verse* …

Structure of the Verse

Understanding the *Structure of the Verse* is one of the most powerful aspects of the Month-Long Intensive. And it springs from the synergy of Linklater's research into breath and Packer's research with John Barton. Barton was the first person to show Packer that the way Shakespeare wrote – with his line endings, syntax, choice of words – held as much information for interpreting your role as the actual sense of the words: *structure itself gave meaning*.[3] Shakespeare lived

> right on the cusp of the oral and the written [traditions]. Speaking had definite rhythm and emotional power and that was being mixed with the beautiful cadences of written Latin verse. And Shakespeare was steeped in

Text Work and Dropping In   **133**

both – the storytelling of the countryside and the epic poems of Virgil. […] Pauses, nuance, emphasis are all implicit in the structure of the verse.

(Packer in 'Training Shakespeare Actors in A Modern World',
2007: 6. S&Co. archive)

It's toward the end of Week 2 of the Intensive that you really encounter this work, when Packer typically gives her lecture, *Structure of the Verse*. Here she flags up that 'structure makes form out of chaos.'[4] It's clear. It's recognizable. And it provides a 'safe' container for your emotional turbulence in the actual form of the *iambic pentameter*. Intriguingly, iambic pentameters combine the rhythm of your heart with the rhythm of your breath, in that one regular inhal-ation-and-exhalation pretty much covers five heartbeats – i.e., a line of iambic verse. So Shakespeare was consciously writing lines that were easy for actors to remember, because the verse structure was built around the rhythms of the *body*.

But more than that, he also wrote in the rhythms of the *psyche* (as Barton had pointed out to Packer): 'from the thundering rhythms of Marlowe's mighty verse, where you couldn't stop the beat if you tried, Shakespeare started to shift the rhythm to reflect the psychological development of character. It was a revolution in poetry and oratory'[5] (Packer). So, (as we saw with Freeman's First Folio work in Chapter 4), Shakespeare seems to have deliberately broken the iambic pentameter when he wanted to reflect the character's emotional state: 'Like contemporary psychotherapists who listen for their patient's patterns of speech, Shakespeare was interested in thought processes and how the rhythm of a person's speech reflects [their] thought and feeling'[6] (Packer).

But not only did Shakespeare give you the rhythms of the body and the psyche; he also gave you the rhythms of the *mind*, as expressed through *the Art of Rhetoric*. The *Art of Rhetoric* is no dusty-old, grammar-book boredom. It illu-minates a character's personality, their imaginings and emotional connections.[7] As Barton said to Packer, 'Look at the figures of speech your character uses, and ask: "Who is this person, that he/she/they chooses to say it this way? What's the thought behind the structure?"'[8] (Packer). And through the foundations of rhetoric – Repetition, Balance, Expansion and Contraction[9] – the structure of the text will reveal to you how a character is trying to affect their listener, as well as simultaneously affecting you – the speaker, with your own body and breath – as you say those words.

In fact, the *Structure of the Verse* depends on *breath*. If you know what the structure is, you know when to breathe – which is usually at the beginning or the end of a line (or whichever way you want to think of it). And each new breath 'almost always introduces a new thought, or something new into the thought being expressed. So the *Structure of the Verse* itself provides a kind of punctuation that indicates *the process* of the character's thought.'[10] And thus breath and thought always go together in Shakespeare, giving you 'an effective way to engage with the meaning of the line and *always be in the present moment.*'[11]

134 Training

So, you've got the rhythms of the body, the psyche, the thoughts – and it all comes from the breath. And there's more! The actual pace of the scene is written into the structure: 'the length of thought; the lines you share with other characters; the sassiness of the rhyming couplets the silences if there are fewer than ten syllables (where are the silences and what do they mean?).'[12] And these clues will tell you – like a musical score – the tempo of the scene.

Yet for all these invaluable clues, honoring the verse structure can seem constricting at first, as Packer would be the first to acknowledge. So 'you have to practice it like you would scales and arpeggios.'[13] Then, once you've done all the work on the structure, you can almost forget about it. (Just as a pianist forgets about their scales and arpeggios when they're in the full flight of the concert-flow.) And one of the ways in which the Intensive connects all these principles of *the Structure of the Verse* to your full-flow actor's passion is by working on *Sonnets*.

Sonnets

Nowhere is structure more evident than in Shakespeare's sonnets. Each sonnet conjures up a 14-line experience, comprising 3–4-line thoughts (which set up, expand and develop the meat of the argument) followed by a rhyming couplet (which sums up the moral of the tale). The Intensive's series of *Sonnet* workshops begins in Week 2 and culminates in a 'Sonnet Fest' during the *Elizabethan World Picture Day* at the end of Week 3 (see Chapter 8). And the class format is a little like *Basics*, with you working your sonnet in front of a mid-sized group. In the early years, *Sonnet* classes were taught by Kristin Linklater, using the tight verse structure to link breath to voice. Then between 1990 and 2003 Jonathan Epstein evolved the progression, 'connecting the actor's emotional and intellectual experience of each sonnet's dramatic event with the audience's vivid experience'[14] (Epstein). Thereafter, Dennis Krausnick took on the *Sonnet* strand, and much of its current methodology stems from his particular passion for their *form* and *content*:

In terms of *form*, Krausnick notes that, after the 1592 plague-outbreak forced the shutdown of London playhouses, Shakespeare's writing changed significantly. A little detective work suggests he went to stay with the poet Philip Sydney's sister Mary, Countess of Pembroke. And during this visit he probably engaged in the courtly game of sonnet writing, which was a sophisticated exercise in conveying complex thoughts with multiple meanings in strictly condensed form. (At one time in the Intensive, Krausnick used to encourage participants in the *Journaling* sessions to condense their own complex experiences into a strict sonnet-form.) When it was safe to return to London, Shakespeare started writing characters whose thoughts sustained (just like a sonnet) through a full four lines of verse.[15] Which raises the questions:

> What happens to your brain when a thought is sustained through four lines? How do you hold onto that thought? How might you top up the breath during that thought? How do you shift from one extended thought

to the next? And how do you use the *Structure of the Verse* to work your brain and link ideas?

(Packer notes, December 2018)

As for *content*: Krausnick's fascination with sonnets revealed something else in 2015, as he was pondering discoveries made in the previous few Intensives:

I recently had an illumination about why we do *Sonnet* and I found it – not in the sonnets themselves but in the text of *A Midsummer Night's Dream* – when Theseus says, 'The lunatic, the lover and the poet/Are of imagination all compact.'[16] And I suddenly realized very specifically what I'd been trying to say. The structure of a sonnet – with its thesis, antithesis and synthesis – is so strong that you cannot break it. And yet in the final couplet there's an emotional explosion as if the structure can't contain the feelings any longer. In fact, the sonnets are lunacy held almost to the point of an 'explosion by structure.'

(Krausnick interview, August 2016)

The *lunacy* (the medical condition, induced in Shakespeare's day perhaps by gonorrhea or syphilis); the *love* (providing the juice for many of the sonnets); and the *poetic structure* (which acts as a container for the mad love) bring form and content together in total interdependence: 'and that's what gives you the cause to go to such intensity with them: the structure actually frees the lunatic to become a poet.'[17] Thus, the precision of the sonnet-form propels you into a deep experience of *com*pressed emotion *ex*pressed through linking your breath to Shakespeare's structure.

There's a very particular reason why the *Sonnet* progression in the Intensive comes after *Basics* and leading into *Scene Work*: it takes the *personal connection* that you've accessed in *Basics* and weaves it into your direct experience of how *structure gives meaning* and *breath inspires thought*. As always, the instruction in class is exacting: You are repeatedly reminded to 'top up the breath' at the beginning (or end) of each line; 'use the form to contain the feelings'; and 'allow more feelings into the form.' So, what happens if you give your inner Lunatic more permission to be present? Or your inner Lover? Or your inner Poet?[18] At the same time, Krausnick uses the sonnets to flag up where your habits might be impacting your acting in general: for example, 'Where are your thoughts running faster than your breath?' 'What shifts if you let the breath and structure do the acting work for you?' 'Can you let the structural strength of the verse give you power?' And Krausnick's instructions are often playful: 'Cover the final words of the sonnet in glitter.' 'Become the thing you've always wanted to be in a larger-than-life event.' Along with: 'Trust the breath: if you let the breath do the work, it'll be different every time you speak the sonnet.'[19] For years Krausnick mentored Jenna May Cass in his teaching and she now assumes the helm of the *Sonnet* work:

FIGURE 7.1 Dennis Krausnick, *Sonnet* session, STI, 2014
Photo: Enrico Spada

> No longer mourn for me when I am dead
> Than you shall hear the surly sullen bell.
> *(Shakespeare, Sonnet 71)*

Toward the end of the *Sonnet* progression, you're invited to explore your sonnet as your scene character. By transitioning you *from self to character*, the sonnet 'provides absolute *personal connection*. It's Me – You – the World. The words are not abstract: they're a deeply personal expression of *me* being romantically passionate about *you* and exploring what the *world* thinks of that passion'[20] (Packer). And in this way, the lessons from *Sonnet* cross effortlessly into the extended *Scene Work*.

Scene Work

The *Scene Work* galvanizes much of the Intensive after the dialogs are distributed at the end of Week 1.[21] Text sessions are held almost every day (sometimes twice) typically involving two couples, each serving as audience to the other so that *the actor/audience relationship* can be honed throughout. And most faculty work on most scenes at some point over the three weeks, offering different perspectives from their various disciplines to tackle any obstacles. Given the 'tailor-made' nature of this strand, how are the scenes assigned?

Assigning scenes

'Does this scene serve these particular participants?' That's the determining factor. Maybe *he* needs to be in love. *They* need to express their gender fluidity.

She needs to kill someone. And finding the right scene may involve cross-gender casting. For example, non-male participants 'needing to understand their own verbal power' might be assigned the 'tent scene' between Brutus and Cassius in *Julius Caesar* (Act IV, scene iii) which 'contains brilliant rhetoric. And if you go through the scene emphasizing "you" and "thee" and "thou" and "his" and "thine," it suddenly becomes a battle to the death'[22] (Krausnick). On the other hand, 'rolling around with another woman on the floor telling a lot of dirty jokes – as Celia and Rosalind do in *As You Like It* – is exactly how some people need to spend every afternoon for a month!'[23] And the faculty takes seriously the most effective scene distribution, 'going back and forth about the energy of the actors and whether these two people can work together, day after day, through this rigorous *Training* process.'[24] Since all the scenes 'are actually quite magnificent, working on any Shakespeare dialog with such intensity is going to yield incredible results. So it doesn't really matter. Though it's extraordinary how often the work does lead to something serendipitous with the actor's own life.'[25]

Once the scenes are assigned, particular exercises are explored in the first few sessions, including *dropping in, standing the scene up* and *feeding the scene in.*

Dropping In

Dropping in is Tina Packer's most 'original practice.' Simple in its form and nuanced in its results, it's the closest the Company comes to more conventional 'tablework,' accessing a visceral (rather than cerebral) connection to language. We'll return to it in 'Act IV' for how it works in the context of a whole play: here we look at its logistics, beginning with its evolution …

How did dropping in evolve?

Packer has always been driven by a need 'to get this [material] into the body because if it isn't in the body, it doesn't manifest onstage, it's just intellectual [and] the audience won't get it in their gut.'[26] To which end *dropping in* merges an exercise, which came from Gestalt therapy (and was used in the est Communication Workshop, where participants sit opposite one another and look each other directly in the eye) with an exercise she and Linklater co-created during the first Ford Foundation experiment (see Chapter 1). They wanted to tap into 'the greater resonances of the words, to get at their atavistic qualities.'[27] Since language is far older than our own brief existence, how can we viscerally experience its timelessness? And since oral communication came long before literary communication, what were the differences

> between reading words on a page and saying them out loud? [Or] saying them to ourselves and conveying their emotional impact to an audience? We were after more than the description of things being said: we wanted

138 Training

> [...] to find ways of experiencing the [words] directly – here, now [–] outside the context of their being in sentences.
>
> *(Packer in 'Training Shakespeare Actors in A Modern World', 2007: 10)*

So they cut up Shakespeare's sonnets and experimented with individual words.

Out of this experimentation came *dropping in*, a 'kind of associative wordplay used to acquaint actors with the visceral, emotional content of their lines before their mind kicks in to interpret them.'[28] It gives you a chance to be more intelligent than your intellect, because – with *dropping in* – the information that emerges offers something your linear mind might never discover:

> I'm asking *the word* to tell me what it means. It's not 'this is my part; I need to study it.' It's 'what are these words bringing up in me and how does my partner react to what I'm saying?' We're reversing the process of how language is normally dealt with.
>
> *(Packer in 'Training Shakespeare Actors in A Modern World', 2007: 14, (my emphasis))*

How do you set up dropping in?[29]

The *physical set up* is important. You sit opposite your scene partner on sturdy chairs with your bum snug into the back of the seat so that your spine is long and your feet are flat on the floor. You sit closely enough for your knees to interlock (i.e., one person's legs aren't on the outside of the other's, being unintentionally dominant). Your hands rest lightly on your thighs (no 'crotch-clutch'). And the energy exchange between you both remains relaxed, with a 'Let's see what comes up' availability to each other. Your lips remain slightly open (to keep your jaw relaxed) and you breathe through your mouth (so the oxygen goes straight to your belly rather than into your lungs). Once you've both found this position, you're asked by the 'dropper-in' (described anon) to close your eyes gently and note what's going on inside you today. After a few moments, you're given the directive to 'open your eyes and be with each other for a minute.'[30] For the rest of the dropping-in session, you remain in eye contact ('eyeball to eyeball,' as Packer puts it).

What's the process?

Sitting beside each actor is a 'dropper-in' with the script in their hands. During the session, the dropper-in quietly and neutrally feeds the text to you one word at a time, picking active words that have 'some substance or juice'[31] and offering (through a series of free-associating questions) images and suggestions to stir your imagination. All you have to do as the actor is literally and metaphorically allow each particular word to 'drop in': which means drop into your

Text Work and Dropping In **139**

imagination, and drop into your body on the breath. So, let's say the first impactful word in the opening line of a dialog is 'Murder.' The dropper-in says out loud (i.e., 'drops in'): 'Murder.' You repeat that word: 'Murder.' The dropper-in then offers a free-associating question, and ends by repeating the word (e.g., 'Have you ever killed anything? *Murder*'). You breathe in; you allow the word 'Murder' to drop into your body (imaginatively and breath-wise); and on the outbreath you speak the word 'Murder,' infused with whatever resonances are provoked for you by the dropper-in's question.

Here's an example from the dialog between Iago and Othello (*Othello,* Act III, Scene iii) where Iago is going to stir the green-eyed monster of jealousy in Othello that his wife Desdemona might have slept with Michael Cassio. Let's take the second line of Iago's text, 'Did Michael Cassio, when you woo'd my lady,/Know of your love?'[32] (Where 'love' is the juicy word):

> **Dropper-in says**: 'Love.'
> **You/Iago repeat**: Love.
> **Dropper-in**: Do you love this man? 'Love.'
> **You/Iago**: (*Breathe in.*)(*Allow the thought of whether or not you* love *this man to drop into your belly.*) (*On the outbreath, say*) Love (*informed by whatever responses come up spontaneously as provoked by whether or not you* love *this man*).
> **Dropper-in asks another question:** Do you hate this man? 'Love.'
> **You/Iago**: (*Breathe in.*)(*Allow the thought of whether or not you* hate *this man to drop into your belly.*) (*On the outbreath, say*) Love (*informed by whatever responses come up spontaneously as provoked by whether or not you* hate *this man*).

And so it goes for several questions as the dropper-in free-associates, watching how you respond to Iago's text and picking up on your impulses and intonations. Because 'love' is such a resonant word, it might be repeated by the dropper-in six or seven times before moving on. And typically three or four words per line are selected. All the while you remain 'eyeball to eyeball' with your partner as you allow the word to drop in, so that their silent, energetic response is as much a part of your experience of the word as the dropper-in's questions. And your thoughts can come from anywhere: there's no need to censor yourself, as there's no right or wrong response. In fact, the mercurial mix of breath, imagination and autobiography means that 'there's no separation between the life *you* have led and the role: you bring all your history. Let it all be there and use it'[33] (Packer). So your thoughts might be related to Othello and Iago.

Or they might be related to you and your relationship with your own best friend.

Or to some residue of an image seen on the news that morning.

Or to a memory of yourself as an adolescent experiencing the first pangs of romantic jealousy.

Or to a fleeting thought of someone you currently love.

Or to an imagined spying on Othello and Desdemona in love.

Or to a present-tense awareness that the actor sitting in front of you playing Othello is a cast member you really admire.

Whatever. It really doesn't matter. The point of *dropping in* is to stir the deep, ancient resonances of the words (*past tense*), to forge actual in-the-moment connections with your partner (*present tense*), to inspire potential directions in which the scene might go (*future tense*). So you then have a whole heap of possibilities that head-led tablework or solitary investigation might not provoke. And this detailed, attentive process allows you to 'experience the place of the word in the body as well as to allow time for associations that come up' and naturally, without embellishing, to 'transmit the emotional and thinking nuance of those associations' through your voice[34] (Packer). By the end, you're so aligned with the language, it's hard to delineate where you stop and the character begins.[35]

And the whole scene (and ultimately the whole play) is explored in this way, each page of text taking about 20 minutes (see Chapters 13 and 15). After the scene has been dropped in, you close your eyes for a moment; settle into the discoveries just made; open your eyes, push back your chairs and give your body a stretch. You then collectively share whatever arose for you with your partner(s) during the dropping-in session.[36]

That's the process. Now here are some clarifications:

What kind of questions does the dropper-in ask?

As the dropper-in free-associates, they try to ask questions relevant both to the character *and* the actor. So

FIGURE 7.2 *Dropping in*: Allyn Burrows, Tina Packer and Timothy Douglas, 1988

'Do you remember a time when you were playing around Elsinore?' applies only to Hamlet. 'Do you remember a time playing in your backyard in Poughkeepsie?' applies only to the actor. 'Do you remember a time when you were playing when you were five?' can apply either to the actor or to the character.

('Notes on Dropping In,' S&Co. guidelines: 3, S&Co. archive)

The droppers-in riff on whatever occurs to them in response to their sense of the actors with whom they're working (without trawling autobiography). They can stir up the characters' fantasy childhoods or backstories. And if they hit a block (maybe the word in the text is strange or unfamiliar), they can use default questions such as 'Have you ever said this word before?' or 'What does it feel like in your mouth to say this word?' If nonsense words come up, that's fine, too. It's about stirring the unconscious, the intelligence beyond the intellect.

Here are some other examples drawn from the Company over the years:

Example #1: Macbeth: *Macbeth to Lady Macbeth: 'Bring forth **men-children** only'*
Possible dropper-in questions: 'Why men-children, not boys? Do you like being with men better than boys? Do you like being on the battlefield with men?'[37]

Example #2: As You Like It: *Celia to her father the Duke: 'Dear **sovereign**.'*
Possible dropper-in questions: 'Why didn't you call him Father?' 'Why have you remained silent so long while he was throwing out Rosalind?' 'Did Rosalind really get herself done in by Frederick this time?'[38]

Example #3: The Winter's Tale: *Leontes to Hermione: 'Has made thee **swell** thus?'*
Possible dropper-in questions: 'How swollen is she?' 'Did Polixenes do this?' 'Has he always been good with women?' 'Could you feel the baby inside there?'[39]

Example #4: Hamlet: *Packer dropping herself in for Hamlet's line '**there is nothing either good or bad but thinking makes it so**.'*

I allow myself to associate to each word: all the good and bad things in my life might come up, together with the voice that judges them.
There is nothing (I associate to the idea of a void or the whole of the world, or myself as unimportant)
good (I got an image of a lover, feeding people or a puppy)
or bad (murder, shouting at a child, a terrible …)
but thinking (goes up into my head, organizing the material, the voice over)
makes (forces, something stronger than me, being made)
it (what is it?)
so (I live *here, now*)

(Packer in 'Training Shakespeare Actors in A Modern World,' 2007: 14.
Hamlet, Act II, Scene ii, lines 259–260)

142 Training

What should the droppers-in attend to?

The main thing for the droppers-in to notice is what's going on *energetically* in the actors, paying attention to their intuitive reactions and responding to what they're doing. And always without manipulating, because the droppers-in want the actors to respond to the raw word and not to the manipulation. It's all about what the word brings up here and now *between* these two actors in the moment of speaking and breathing, rather than what should, could or might be brought up by the connotations of the word or the history of the play.

Equally important to note is the actor's *physical state*. Are they breathing deeply? Are they tensing up? As a subtle grounding, the dropper-in can briefly place the back of a finger lightly on the actor's belly to remind them to breathe deeply, or cup the back of their neck or stroke their jawbone or touch their brow if they notice tension creeping into the actor's face or throat. They may even massage the actors' shoulders to keep them relaxed, as they may be sitting still for some time.

What's the most important aspect of dropping in?

As always: *Breath*!

> It's not important that the actor actually understands the relevance of *dropping in*. It's important that the breath keeps moving. So *dropping in* is as much about the breath dropping in, as it is about dropping in the individual words or phrases.
>
> *(Krausnick interview, August 2018)*

It's connecting breath and words, and the experience of the words. And that connection is completely psychophysical. It's physical in the sense of, 'What's this particular sound (say, "father") doing to my body?' And it's psychological in the sense of, 'How do I feel about *my* father? How do I feel about being a parent? How do I feel about *not* being a parent?' And because breath is the core of the exercise, the process is curiously active, however static the position may look.

Can the dropper-in get it wrong?

No! It's such a fluid exercise you can't really get it wrong. As a dropper-in, 'you're like the actor's roving imagination'[40] (Hadden). Or, as Elizabeth Aspenlieder (longtime Company member) puts it

> You're riffing off suggestions of relationship and surroundings: 'Where are you at this moment? What's going on politically? Emotionally? Psychologically? Personally?' You're allowing the actors not to think intellectually, but just to look at each other and have the freedom to see what the connections are, finding new possibilities that might not have occurred to them.
>
> *(Aspenlieder interview, August 2016)*

Text Work and Dropping In **143**

Can the actors get dropping in wrong?

No! The idea of *dropping in* is just to see what comes up for you. And to allow whatever comes up to be present and to stay with whatever feelings arise. And because there's no wrong, any response is fine, as something relevant will transpire. 'What happens is that actors, who don't know one another or the script very well, respond to the feeling transmitted, so it works on an unconscious level'[41] (Packer). You're also encouraged to stay 'on voice' and not mumble or whisper, because when we use full voice, the actual vibrations of sound help us connect to deeper feelings.

What do you do with all the discoveries made in dropping in?

You don't have to do anything. Ultimately *dropping in* is research: on yourself, on the language, on the world of the play. So, all sorts of different – maybe conflicting – emotions and images may arise. Yet because it's research, no one expects every layer of feeling and every level of experience to find its way into the final performance of the scene. In fact, they won't. And they probably shouldn't. Nor are you expected to sustain this degree of focus and intensity at every pass. You're simply creating a foundation of backstory, emotional resonance, imaginative treasure, that once you've experienced can't help but be stored somewhere in your body. So: 'By the time the actors bring the words to the play, they have experienced what it means inside their bodies and can speak about it from personal experience'[42] (Aspenlieder). Significantly, the research happens in the scene partner as much as in the speaker. Journalist Ellie Tesher describes being on the receiving end of an actor being 'dropped in' for Hamlet's simple words, 'Now, Mother': 'As my partner said "mother" over and over, I could feel myself responding to the changing feelings reflected in his eyes. I felt a powerful, visceral link to him as well as to the words.'[43] And therefore Tesher's understanding of being 'mother' to this particular actor/Hamlet was also changed and deepened.

What are the benefits of dropping in?

The benefits are manifold. First of all, you establish tangible, sensate relationships right from the start.[44] Second, the way each word – with its sounds, images and poetic content – plays upon your unconscious mind can lead to all kinds of 'unexpected veins of creative response.'[45] Third, you become very relaxed with Shakespeare's language and the words feel natural.[46] Fourth, it's much easier to learn lines because you've already experienced particular images, feelings and relationships:

> Nobody has to discuss or explain them; we're just getting back to the original connection with the word. And when we're done, the actors own

144 Training

the words. Even the unfamiliar word is familiar and has a host of images attached to it.

> *(Packer cited in Dudar, H., 'A Troupe Tries to Plumb the Heart of The*
> *Bard's Words,' The New York Times, 28 August, 1983)*

Fifth, the process allows for *dynamic listening*. You're listening to yourself as the breath drops in and gives each new word and image resonance. You're listening to the energy exchange with your partner(s). You're listening to every word that's being dropped into your partner(s) and how those words affect them. You're listening to the questions posed by the dropper-in, which also unpacks the subtext for your partner(s) as well as the subtext between your partner(s) and yourself. And, finally, it links right back to S&Co.'s mission over the years: 'Truth in acting, truth in emotions. The latter must come first in order to achieve the former.'[47] And your 'truthful feelings' are all *in the service of the play*, as you keep yourself present and available.

Dropping in is a significant part of Shakespeare & Company's history and practice. (We'll look at some working examples in 'Act IV,' with assistant directors doing the *dropping in* and with actors in *Cymbeline* being dropped in.) In terms of the Intensive, once a scene has been dropped in, you then *stand the scene up.*

Standing the scene up

Standing the scene up literally means you stand facing your scene partner, while a teacher stands beside you, prompting you quietly with one iambic line at a time. As simple as it may sound, it's surprisingly beneficial:

> The process takes the immediate response to the individual word that *dropping in* provokes and attaches that immediate response to longer thoughts. But without the responsibility of 'Oh god, I have to do something with this body of mine …' At the same time, we're working with you to make sure your breath keeps dropping deep into your body, so that a new idea or refinement can come to you with that breath.
>
> *(Borthwick-Leslie interview, June 2016)*

In this way, *standing the scene up* allows the text 'to play through you one last time – without you having to make any decisions about spatial relationships, or without using any of your physical habits to cover the emotional information that the text provokes.'[48]

Which leads to the next stage …

Feeding the scene in

Feeding the scene in takes the process further. Now, as you start exploring the spatial dynamics between you and your scene partner, you can move anywhere

Text Work and Dropping In   **145**

you like in the room and an instructor follows closely behind you, quietly (in a 'monotone') feeding you your lines: 'With this technique, the actors are free to look at one another, to focus on relationship, to feel the words in the body, to listen fully, to follow impulses, and begin building the play right away.'[49] This stage is valuable for all actors, but especially for newcomers to Shakespeare:

> *Feeding in* allows the person to remain in relationship with the scene partner, the situation, the story of the play, and not to have to struggle for lines. It's empowering for them to put the enormity of Shakespeare's imagery into their mouths and experience this articulateness and discover what their own personal power might be.
>
> *(Krausnick interview, August 2016)*

All they have to do is just say what's being said into their ear and there's no other responsibility than to see what happens.

Other prompts for *Scene Work*

Once a scene has been *dropped in*, *stood up* and *fed in*, you work on the dialogs during the Intensive in a variety of ways, based on the faculty's ongoing discussions during meal breaks of everyone's individual process. This tailor-made training is backed up by your own independent rehearsal strategies drawn from the lecture playfully named, '100 Ways to Rehearse a Scene.' Those strategies include (1) The Physical Set-Up (exploring the logistics of where you are, what you're wearing, what you need, etc.); (2) 'Who's Dead?' (examining the family structure, relationships and background to the scene); (3) Finding the Physical Score (looking for embedded stage directions; changes in rhythm; shifts in emotional content, etc.); (4) The Scene on the Vowel Sounds (letting all the pre-language sounds carry viscerally to your scene partner); (5) Thrashing About (literally thrashing about on mats to liberate the scene's energy); (6) The Nth Degree (expanding the parameters and sharpening the intentions through deliberately big acting); (7) Different Ages (exploring how the priorities change for your characters if you play them aged 3, 13, 45, 80, whatever); (8) Whispering the Whole Scene; (9) In the Dark; (10) Back to Back; (11) Lying Head to Head; and (12) Lying Down Doing the Whole Scene to the Ceiling. (Simple as these last five may sound you only have to try them to discover what they subtly unlock.) After any scene session (independent or faculty-guided), you and your scene partner offer self-reflections as well as observations to each other along the lines of 'What I experienced was … ' or 'I really heard the words when … ' or 'I stopped listening when … ' Rehearsing with different faculty is deliberately and playfully provocative, so that you remember what proved beneficial for you in one session with one instructor even if another instructor later offers contradictory suggestions.

146 Training

This multi-perspectived process is intrinsically designed to remind you that ultimately you're your own best teacher and always the author of your own journey. And across all the parallel strands of the Intensive this multi-layered exploration of self is pursued: from 'Rituals' to *Voice Work* to *Basics* to *Text Work*, and – now – to *Body Work* ...

Notes

1 Tina Packer discussion with Bella Merlin, December 2018.
2 Prompts may include: 'Words I love in this monologue are ...' 'Words I struggle with in this monologue are ...' 'What excites me about this scene is ...' 'What terrifies me about this scene is ...' (Merlin, B. 'Notes from Month-Long Intensive, January 2016: Krausnick *Journaling* session').
3 Packer in 'Training Shakespeare Actors in A Modern World: Tina Packer Talks to Helen Epstein ...,' 24 January 2007, p. 6. S&Co. archive.
4 Merlin '"Notes from Month-Long Intensive 2016": Packer lecture,' *Structure of the Verse*, 9 January 2016.
5 Packer edit, September 2019.
6 Packer in 'Training Shakespeare Actors in A Modern World,' p. 18.
7 Company members Jonathan Epstein and Rebecca Goodheart have contributed fulsomely to this aspect of the *Training*, not least writing essays and formulating workshops on this 2,000-year-old art.
8 Packer edit, September 2019.
9 These are four of the five foundations of rhetoric, with Memorization being the fifth.
10 Packer in 'Training Shakespeare Actors in A Modern World,' p. 16.
11 ibid.
12 Packer edit, September 2019.
13 Merlin '"Notes from Month-Long Intensive 2016": Packer lecture,' *Structure of the Verse*, 9 January 2016.
14 Jonathan Epstein discussion with Bella Merlin, July 2019.
15 Cf., *Richard III* (1592), *Venus and Adonis* (1593) and *The Rape of Lucrece* (1594). Shakespeare's poetic evolution would eventually lead to him writing 154 sonnets. In fact, any writer with serious aspirations wrote an extended sonnet sequence, as sonnets plummeted 'a deeper truth in sound, rhythm and soul' (Packer). And Shakespeare wanted to prove that he was as good a poet as anyone else and not just a jobbing playwright.
16 Shakespeare, W. (1595), *A Midsummer Night's Dream*, Act V, Scene i, lines 7–17, Theseus.
17 Dennis Krausnick interview with Bella Merlin, August 2016.
18 Merlin 'Notes from Month-Long Intensive January 2016.' Various dates.
19 ibid.
20 Packer discussion with Merlin, December 2018.
21 Your first assignment is to meet with your scene partner and read out loud together the whole play up to and including your scene.
22 Krausnick interview, August 2016.
23 ibid.
24 ibid.
25 ibid.
26 Packer in 'Training Shakespeare Actors in A Modern World,' p. 11.
27 Packer cited in Sanders, V. (1997), 'The passion of Tina Packer,' *The Boston Globe*, 17 August 1997.

Text Work and Dropping In   **147**

28 Sanders (1997).
29 Some of this section is a rewrite of a paper entitled 'Creating the Living Word: An Anglo-Russian-American Perspective on Psychophysical Acting' delivered by Merlin at the Shanghai Theatre Academy's 2nd International Forum on Actor Training, November 2018.
30 Packer cited in Bass, M. R. (1979), '"Dropping in" on "The Winter's Tale,"' *The Berkshire Eagle*, 7 June 1979.
31 Elizabeth Aspenlieder interview with Bella Merlin, August 2016.
32 Shakespeare, W. (1604), *Othello*, Act III, scene iii, lines 94–95, Iago.
33 Packer cited in Merlin notes from 'Dropping in training session with assistant directors of *Cymbeline*,' June 2017.
34 Packer in 'Training Shakespeare Actors in A Modern World', p. 13.
35 Packer cited in Saenger, P. (1979), 'Bringing Shakespeare to the Berkshires,' *The Morning Union*, 29 March 1979.
36 Some people suggest there's no subtext in Shakespeare, and if that's a helpful way for them to approach the texts, fine. But this process reveals that the ancient roots of words can't help but have echoes and meanings way beyond whatever contemporary currency we may now give them – by virtue of the fact they've been around a lot longer than we have. While *dropping in* may certainly touch upon any unspoken (subtextual) dialog that may be going on *energetically* between the characters/actors, more importantly it plummets the *reverberations of the words* below their rational meaning in the twenty-first century.
37 Packer cited in Saenger (1979). *Macbeth* (1606), Act I, scene vii, line 72, Macbeth.
38 Cited in Malkin, L. (1991), 'In Lenox they are "Dropping in" on the Bard of Avon,' *Smithsonian*, November 1991. *As You Like It* (1599), Act I, scene iii, line 69, Celia.
39 Cited in Sanders (1997). *The Winter's Tale* (1611), Act II, scene i, line 61, Leontes.
40 John Hadden interview with Bella Merlin, August 2016.
41 Packer in 'Training Shakespeare Actors in A Modern World,' p. 13.
42 Elizabeth Aspenlieder cited in Monachina, J. (1997), 'Shakespeare & Co. on the road,' *The Advocate*, 26 February 1997.
43 Tesher, E. (1997), 'Time to get Passionate about Art,' *Toronto Star*, 10 August 1997.
44 'The First 10 Years,' 1987. S&Co. archive.
45 ibid.
46 Packer in 'Training Shakespeare Actors in A Modern World,' p. 13.
47 'The First 10 Years,' 1987. S&Co. archive.
48 Andrew Borthwick-Leslie interview with Bella Merlin, June 2016.
49 'Notes on the Hunger for Words: advice on the practice of Feeding In, A Shakespeare & Company Technique.' S&Co. archive.

8

BODY WORK AND BRINGING IT ALL TOGETHER

The *Body Work* in Shakespeare & Company's *Training* basically falls into three disciplines: *Movement/Dance*, *Clown* and *Fight*. And they all involve 'psychophysical coordination,' meaning that 'each of your *physical* actions holds within it a *psychological* resonance, and, conversely, your *psychological* state impacts on your *physical* expression.'[1] And because 'your body is the interface between your inner landscape and the world-at-large, the more expressive your body can be, the more variations of character you can portray.'[2] Each strand has its own take on that inner-outer connectivity. So let's take a look …

Movement/Dance

Release your own body! Then experience the exuberance of dancing together! These are the invitations that the *Movement/Dance* strand offers you. And these joyful invitations stem from master-teacher John Broome, who encouraged his actors at the RSC (including Tina Packer) to work 'from the inside out to express feelings [and] impulses, sometimes pausing to embody a dramatic picture'[3] (Packer). And so inspired were Broome's actors 'that he broke down our preconceptions about what we were capable of doing, and we would find ourselves flying and leaping across the room with joy and some grace'[4] (see Chapter 1). Indeed, there's much flying and leaping across the Elayne Bernstein Studios during the Month-Long Intensive. In their different ways, each of the *Movement/Dance* teachers helps you to contact your own sense of physical grace, with little concern about getting the steps right. As a result you stop judging yourself and you find yourself executing the moves 'better and more beautifully. And then you have a desire to *be* beautiful. And you see each other as beautiful, too'[5] (Krausnick). This recalibrated sense of beauty elicits a lightness of touch and

Body Work and bringing it all together   **149**

playfulness – and (of course) breath: 'Breathe!' incites senior faculty member Kristin Wold. 'Give in to gravity and let the buoyancy of your thoughts and impulses move you.'[6] So with this in mind, what are the basic components of *Movement* and *Dance*?

Movement

The components of the Movement progression adapt (as with all the disciplines) according to each instructor. Typically, the work begins with *releasing your own body*. And that process first invites you to *accept your body* just as it is (with simple exercises exploring when you're off-center and on-center, and celebrating that theatre 'is all about people being thrown off balance')[7] (Wold). Then, you *expand your physical awareness* through exercises connected to *Sound and Movement* (see Chapter 6). These include 'issues of alignment and the ability to stand,' experiencing Trish Arnold's swings, as well as her work on *Pure Movement*, stretching your body in all six Directions Energies (based on Rudolf Laban's 'Box,' namely Forward/Backward, In/Out, and Up/Down), spine work, strengthening, and release impulse[8] (Dibble). This work – steeped in that of Arnold and Conway, and disseminated and honed over the years by Susan Dibble (senior faculty and founding Company member) – constantly connects 'the actor's imagination to the particular exercise at hand' (maybe a feather on the breeze or the pendulum of a clock), so that the activity isn't 'aerobic or mechanical.'[9]

The Movement progression then *extends your awareness out toward the group*. And again, imagination is key: so you might imagine having doors in different parts of your body, such as in your head, heart and hips. Then what happens when you open and close those doors? How does it feel to move around the room, say, with the door in your head open? Or the door in your heart closed? Or the door in your hips opening and closing? And how do these variations affect your *energetic availability* to other people?[10] Indeed, the next step in building energetic availability is through *physical availability* to others – via improvisations in partners and groups, such as mirroring and sculpting. Some of these are standard exercises in movement training; it's simply that they're framed here within the context of a particular actor-training methodology steeped in Elizabethan theatre.

And so, after several sessions spent expanding your availability first to yourself and then to others, the *Movement* progression traverses into *Shakespeare's realm*. You may find yourself exploring figures from the Elizabethan worldview (such as angels, demons and the Seven Deadly Sins). There may be free improvisations with the Elements of earth, water, fire and air (since these influenced the Elizabethan 'humours' and connected people to the natural world). And all the while – be it Sloth or a puddle, Envy or a whirlwind – your body and 'spirit'[11] are subtly experiencing other ways of being.

The exercises then become more specific to *Shakespeare's language*, bringing *rhythm* into your body in response to the drumming of iambs, trochees, anapests and dactyls. You then bring *text* into your body by moving your sonnet through the space. And eventually you morph into your *scene character* to see what then happens to your movement. And all the while – be it 'Take all my loves'[12] or 'coward woman, and soft-hearted wretch'[13] – your body and spirit are subtly experiencing other ways of embodying language. In fact, the *Movement* work parallels the *Basics* work 'in a less literal way, but as a shape – starting with the "me" and moving out into the larger Shakespeare world'[14] (Dibble).

All-important is your sense of structure or *form*. To which end, the *Movement* improvisations are often underscored by music:

> Music is the form – just as Shakespeare is the form. And if we commit to each impulse, word, moment and pause with our partners, the audience will experience the attention of that dialogic form, and they'll emotionally fill in the gaps to become part of that experience.
> *(Victoria Rhoades cited in Merlin, 'Notes from the Month-Long Intensive,'*
> *14 January 2016)*

So here again, *the actor/audience relationship* – as well as your sense of form – is being fine-tuned and filigreed throughout the *Movement* classes, with personal attention to your awareness of own self in your own unique body.

Dance

Building on this sense of form, the *Dance* component of the *Movement/Dance* progression starts with *simple choreographed steps* as the first stage in developing your 'exuberance' toward collective dance. These may simply include crossing

FIGURE 8.1 Karen Beaumont, with participant Ray DuBois, STI, 2017
Photo: John Dolan

the space with a partner in a skip or a turn, or maybe those flying Broome-leaps that Packer mentioned earlier. Hands are clasped. Twirls are whirled. And all with a certain abandon, as Broome 'encouraged listening and breathing the music in' as though it was 'the breath of the dance,' and 'trusting the flow of the music and its structure'[15] (Dibble).

Around Week 2 you're introduced to more *formally choreographed dances* such as the farandole and pavane. Since Elizabethan plays often ended with a dance or jig – to shake the spirit and restore the social order – the joy of dance is highly valued at Shakespeare & Company, again as influenced by Broome. Not only did his dances bring energy to a play and ignite a surge of emotion, but he also accessed 'the ageless humanism of dance, how it levels the heady act of life to simple human innocence and the polarity of existence'[16] (Dibble). Over the years, various faculty members have created their own choreographies which feature during the Intensive. Susan Dibble's 'Sun, Moon and Stars' is shared during the *Elizabethan World Picture Day* (described anon) and her Storm Dance (see Figure 8.2) is performed at the final scene-sharing, along with Victoria Rhoades' celebration of Titania and Oberon with the lovers, mechanicals and fairies. The dances are simple but robust, weaving sensual release with theatrical ceremony.

The constant shifting between free improvisations and semi-formal choreographies in the *Movement/Dance* progression allows your body to explore a range of physical vocabularies. These vocabularies are expanded further with the other two strands of *Body Work* (which in many ways operate at the extremes of human experience): *Clown* and *Fight*.

FIGURE 8.2 Susan Dibble's Storm Dance, Month-Long Intensive, 2018
Photo: John Dolan

152 Training

Clown

Clown is a world where 'something transcendent happens. All things are possible and life is reaffirmed,'[17] says Jane Nichols (senior Company clownmaster). And building from Merry Conway's work in the 1980s, the clownmasters have shaped the progression drawing on their own training (from mask, *commedia*, the schools of Jacques Lecoq, Philippe Gaulier and Keith Johnstone). The *Clown* progression comprises about six classes, typically beginning toward the end of Week 1 with simple playground games, before you don a red nose and find your personal motley from crates of colorful costumes. Later it typically (d)evolves into the grotesque world of *bouffon*. And the whole progression trains: *play*; *being your 'essentialized' self*; *presence*; and *the actor/audience relationship*. Here's how …

Training play

Play 'is an essential entry point into Shakespeare'[18] (Coleman). And *Clown* classes at the Intensive are often scheduled as *Play* to 'undermine the expectations and baggage of the word "clown,"'[19] explains Michael F. Toomey (senior faculty in *Play/Clown* and *Fight*). Yet for all its simplicity, playing games makes serious demands on you as an actor. First of all, 'you have to be willing to be an idiot. You can't be an actor unless you can move your status up and down. So, if you won't play the game, what is it you're hiding?'[20] (Nichols). Which leads to the second demand: giving yourself permission to lose the game and fail. In fact, we're 'not interested in the clown until it fails.'[21] But failure doesn't defeat you: the clown is always 'legislating against gravity,'[22] so they have a buoyancy and lightness of spirit to recover from failure and keep on going. Which means 'giving yourself permission to play freely, openly and in an unguarded way.'[23] And that in turn trains the third demand: *complicité*, or (as Nichols calls it) the 'winkless wink.' Finally, this playfulness demands that you courageously forego your protective ego (with those socially, managed habits that we addressed in Chapter 4) and be what Toomey calls *your 'essentialized' self*.

Training to be your 'essentialized' self

For Toomey, *Clown* training is an 'alchemical process' that takes you back to the little child you once were before you adopted all the managing skills to sustain the 'self' that you thought the world wanted you to be. With *Clown*, you strip away the excess and distill yourself back down to your 'essence.' And, as an actor,

> that distilled, 'essentialized' self is what's useful to me. I can take that distilled self and pour it into the form of clown – and then clown appears. Or into the form of Hamlet – and then Hamlet appears. And there are

elements that are similar in each of those forms, because it's 'me' at the core.

(Toomey interview, June 2017)

Revealing this 'essentialized' self actually demands a huge amount of courage, though the pay-off can be innately delightful. So part of *Clown*'s alchemy is allowing your delightful, unmanaged essence to have validity in your acting. In fact, finding your personal clown is an inherent call to innocence, which in itself leads to *presence*.

Training presence

S&Co.'s *Clown* training works off the premise that your clown only has three brain cells. Therefore, they have no memory and live only in the present. They're like 'puppies. They're like us at our purest, without the sophistication, without cleverness'[24] (Coleman). And this degree of pure, unsophisticated presence unlocks other vital acting tools. First of all, you have to *focus on one thing at a time* 'to the Nth degree': 'you can't think ahead or steer where you're going in *Clown* – or you kill it. All you can do is respond like any actor is supposed to respond – reacting to what you're getting'[25] (Nichols). Next: because you only have three brain cells, you *take everything very literally*. And being absolutely literal allows each moment 'to reveal a delightful treasure-trove of discovery'[26] (Krausnick). These discoveries are even more impactful because *the stakes are very high*: 'Like the epic world in which children live – where everything matters – there's always a matter of life and death in *Clown*'[27] (Nichols). And because you're living in each moment and things are changing so fast, 'you learn *dexterity* in your acting. And you hone your virtuosic instrument to move organically from disaster to epiphany to dread to relief in a space of five seconds.'[28] All these transferable acting tools – focus, discovery, high stakes, dexterity – are trained in *Clown* using deliberately *simple forms* with *very tight structures*. Such as: 'Come out on stage. Look at the audience. Bow. Leave the stage.' With no expectations. Or 'Protect the Cookie,' no matter what, from other marauding clowns (see Figure 8.3). These simple, tight forms allow you 'to explore the work from deep within yourself because it requires you to slow down and *not miss a thing*'[29] (Toomey). And that's training presence – 'whereby you dare to be simple, to not add something extra, but just breathe.'[30] And 'not missing a thing' is as relevant to *Text Work* as to *Clown*:

> When you start training yourself to not miss a thing, it suddenly has this huge impact on your own detail of how you are as an actor and what you can discover from the smallest, unarticulated syllable of a text. Why does this line have 11 syllables, not 10? What excess is there that I can exploit in this line? – And that's a rich discovery.
>
> *(Krausnick interview, August 2016)*

FIGURE 8.3 'Protect the Cookie,' with participants Rebecca Poretsky and Bob Wicks, Month-Long Intensive, 2016
Photo: John Dolan

Attention to the details of being present also refers to the *audience's response*: in fact, you can't train *Clown* without working with the *audience*.

Training the actor/audience relationship

The audience is your 'spiritual acoustics' (says Stanislavsky).[31] And nothing tunes you to that acoustic faster than Clown: 'The *audience* is in charge of what works and what doesn't work. Not *you*. Not the *director*. Not the *writer*. They're either having a collective experience of laughter or tears – or they're not'[32] (Borthwick-Leslie). So, to sharpen your sensitivity to the 'audience-acoustic,' the forms used in *Clown* involve you constantly checking in with them. Take the 'Dying of Thirst' exercise:

> Look at the jug of water on the other side of the stage. Look at the audience. Look in the direction you're going to move. Look at the audience. Keep looking at the audience while you're moving. Stop. Look at the jug. Look back at the audience … etc.
> *(Merlin, 'Notes from Month-Long Intensive,' January 2016:*
> *Toomey Clown class)*

This constant complicity with your audience gives them a chance to read your thoughts and go on the journey with you. After all: 'The clown lives and breathes for and with the audience. It's fed by the audience – negatively or positively'[33] (Nichols).

Body Work and bringing it all together   **155**

Along with these specific acting lessons is an innate development of creative freedom. And nowhere is this more evident than in the second, *Clown*-related progression (one which has evolved in recent years under Toomey's jurisdiction): *bouffon*.

Sacred and profane: the world of bouffon

As the Month-Long Intensive heads toward the *Elizabethan World Picture Day* at the end of Week 3 (more anon), the innocence of *Clown* shifts into the bowels of *bouffon*. Indeed, the point of *bouffon* is 'to explore the lower orders of the Chain of Being, including misshapenness and ugliness. Changing your own experience of what it's like to be in your particular body'[34] (Krausnick). Although elements of *bouffon* had existed in the *Training* during Merry Conway's time, it resumed its significance when Toomey joined the Company in 1997, and by 2006 he had evolved a *Clown/bouffon* progression. S&Co. reintroduced *bouffon* into the Intensive because, with its grotesqueries, 'you can do all kinds of things with buffoon that you can't do elsewhere'[35] (Packer). While crossovers certainly exist between *Clown* and *bouffon* (not least their childlike qualities), Toomey's Lecoq-based training highlights how each world exposes strikingly different aspects of the human psyche – because they have different relationships to *space*. The clown opens very directly outwards to the audience, while the tragic *chorus* opens upwards to the epic space of the gods (as do tragic *clowns* such as Malvolio in *Twelfth Night*, who thinks he's a romantic hero and frequently calls upon Jove). The *bouffon*, on the other hand, opens to the place of hell and madness:

> It's childlike, it's grotesque, it's misshapen. And [...] I find that territory both the most frightening and the most exciting. Because it asks you to inhabit and explore your own madness. And all the taboos that go with that. All the things we're not supposed to make fun of or talk about or play with.
>
> *(Toomey interview, June 2017)*

Which is the very reason that Toomey called the progression: *sacred and profane*. 'First of all, what do we hold sacred? And then how do we play with our taboos? What does it mean to go to those lower, baser elements of the psyche – to eat, consume, procreate and poop?'[36]

This short (but wildly liberating) *bouffon* progression returns you to your most playful years as a child, boisterous and abandoned, making physical contact with other people *sans* censorship or supposition. Building dens. Forging secret clubs with signs of allegiance. Fighting to the death with invisible weapons. Creating swearing circles and letting profanities explode from your body. And all the while – through these simple but provocative exercises – the boundaries

156 Training

between playing and performing are subtly eroded (just as they are throughout the Intensive). Breath links to impulse to imagination to body. And suffice it to say, the progression culminates in *bouffon* appearances before a royal court of faculty on *Elizabethan World Picture Day* … Much hilarity. Much liberation. And much bursting of bubbles of vanity and pride.

From innocence to irreverence and from the sacred to the profane, the *Clown/Play* progression taps into many vocational resonances as part of the grand design of the Intensive (and we'll revisit specifics in the context of *Performance*: Chapter 13). Indeed, Krausnick believes 'you never lose the value of *Clown*, no matter how experienced you are. There's nothing like it to shake you up as an actor.'[37] Though equally multivalent is *Fight*.

Fight

The Elizabethan era – with its bearbaiting, public executions and endless civil wars – was one of the most violent times in English history. And yet it produced the world's most celebrated poet. That piquant paradox has led to *Fight* being a vital part of S&Co.'s *Training* ever since the 1973 Ford Foundation experiment. Not least because Packer and the team wanted to find ways of enacting Shakespeare's violence wholeheartedly, yet healthily. So

> *Fight* became the format for us to explore and understand our own impulse towards violence, and what it does within the actor. Then, in rehearsal, you can be aware of when your own buttons are being pushed and when the character's buttons are being pushed. That way you can stay more in control of the artistic expression of violence and not become a victim of your own unspoken fears [or triggers].
>
> *(Krausnick interview, August 2016)*

In recent years this progression has also been called 'Stage (or Staged) Violence' to reflect the content of all manner of intimate narrative moments. This nomenclature accommodates (as Toomey explains) 'purposeful' violence (including battles and physical fights) and 'accidental' violence (including tripping, falling and the physical slapstick of *Clown* and comedy). And it also helps navigate 'incidental' violence (when, for example, we may jostle a partner in rehearsal without realizing there may be unintended aggression in certain human interactions).[38] Since these are ongoing discussions (reflecting the Intensive's ever-evolving, responsive nature) the rest of this section continues with the name '*Fight*' as part of the legacies of B. H. Barry and Tony Simotes (founding Company member and longtime *Fight* teacher).

At the heart of the *Fight* progression is Barry's mantra: 'Through form there is freedom.'[39] With none of the 'blows to the head' is there direct physical contact and, with every fight form, you're encouraged to respect its precision, because your main intention is to look after your partner. If you're not looking after your partner, you can't fight safely with them: 'There has to be large love first that gives you the permission to get in touch with the violent feelings'[40] (Packer). So that means keeping your partner safe and making your partner look good in the fight – in the knowledge that they're doing the same for you. And, because S&Co.'s *Fight* training is about self-awareness rather than swashbuckling, it's relevant – whether you're a fully-fledged fencer or a basic beginner.

The progression

With about six sessions in the *Fight* progression, the first (like *Play*) is typically introduced toward the end of Week 1 following your intense work in *Basics* and your first *Actor/Audience* session (see Chapter 5). The aim is to ground you in physical work with a partner, as 'one of the most important elements of processing an emotionally impactful experience,' says Claire Warden (faculty member and violence/intimacy director), 'is to bring it back to a place of agency and control. And that involves realigning your connection between mind, emotions, body and breath.[41]

Fight (like *Play*) assists you in that realignment by directly engaging your body in high stakes' situations and energetic release. The *Fight* progression typically begins with simple unarmed forms (such as slaps to the face, punches to the chin, blows to the belly and hair pulling) – always ensuring that you're not inadvertently holding your breath (as we so often do in real-life, conflict situations). Later, the progression may lead to enacting mortal acts of violence, and the final class may end with something 'fun.' Every choreographed maneuver has clear, *physical instructions* that take you on a carefully constructed, *psychological journey* toward understanding the consequences of violence. And the *dramaturgical aim* is to reveal how physical language tells a story as much as verbal language: in that, we sometimes resort to violence when words fail us. Yet to enact truthful violence we need to understand *what we're doing to our bodies* when we put them through violent actions – even the situations are fictional. Not to mention *what we're doing to our audiences*. Which invites the question: why did Shakespeare put violence on stage in the first place?

Why does Shakespeare stage violence?

Shakespeare rarely uses violence gratuitously or sensationally: it's 'always at a point when textual language can no longer carry the story. The story has to be told physically'[42] (Simotes). And S&Co. has been guided in their deep investigations of violence by James Gilligan, M.D. (see Chapter 4). Gilligan suggests that Shakespeare can actually be used to create a healthier, more dignified society by addressing violence dramatically, personally *and* sociologically: 'When people become violent it is because their sense of pride and personal honor, dignity and respect has been so stripped away the only way to get it back is to fight against other people.'[43] So 'the words to look for in Shakespeare for the

158 Training

motivation of violent characters are *shame* and *honor*. Those are words that he uses tremendously often.'[44] Furthermore – and whether it's Lavinia being mutilated, Ophelia drowning herself or Iachimo contemplating rape – Shakespeare addresses these violent behaviors *in a public place*:

> He's not saying it privately in his study, he's not doing it in a church sermon, where 'This is right and that is wrong.' He's out there in the public playhouse, speaking about these things, which is a very, very different context.
>
> *(Packer, transcript of Radcliffe Institute of Advanced Studies: Seminar with*
> *James Gilligan on Good and Evil, 27 September 2000)*

So, clearly Shakespeare wanted society to confront itself (see Figure 3.2, Chapter 3). And by writing such graphic, insightful exposés of the human psyche, he seemingly wants us to do the same as actors when we take on violent roles. Yet, we have to be attentive or it can have consequences …

Taking violence into your body

Taking a violent story into your body as an actor warrants special attention. 'When doing a rape scene or a death scene, or one of great brutality,' says Josh McCabe (*Fight/Violence* teacher in Education and longtime Company member)

> you cannot throw the actor into the deep end of the pool emotionally and say, 'Well, it's just movement,' it isn't. […] When you feel that weapon in your hand, or you're rushing toward somebody or grabbing them, your body still understands it as an action that is actually happening.
>
> *(McCabe cited in Hollenbaugh, 2014)*

So, when your body is exerting itself and your lungs are heaving

> there's a part of you that doesn't realize it's *theatrical*. When you get to that place, you don't want to ever cross the line, [even though] the audience wants you to get as close to it as possible so *their* sense of reality is heightened.
>
> *(Simotes cited in Beck, L. A., 'Dreams and transition: Shakespeare & Co.'s*
> *Tony Simotes,' Berkshires Week, 2–8 August 2001, (my emphasis))*

This can be a delicate operation: simulating violence for the audience without assimilating the reverberations of that violence into your body. Which is why we train to do it. As actors, we 'immerse ourselves in that ugliness so that the audience doesn't have to, but we have to come out of it in a healthy way so that we can tell the story the next day.'[45] And the day after. And the day after that.

This is 'especially significant for women because they don't [often] get to use their bodies that way unless they are professional athletes,'[46] notes Corinna May (senior faculty *Fight* teacher and longtime Company member). Added to which, 'many women in *Fight* classes have more trouble emotionally being the *perpetrator* rather than the *victim* – *because* it's changing the social story or it's re-enacting it on someone else'[47] (Warden). And here the buoyancy of the *Movement* discipline dovetails with the work, as this level of fight demands you have 'a body which is opened up, because our job [as actors] is to *allow the violence to go through us*'[48] (Packer) (just like breath moves through a flute to create music). It's worth noting that, when B. H. Barry and Bill Hobbs were developing stage violence in the 1960s, 'they were using principles of Aikido to keep themselves safe. You went with the flow of energy: you didn't stop it. You let anger flow through you, you never held onto it'[49] (Packer).

So, although the *Fight* training may seem predominantly physical, it's actually highly holistic: you're exercising the body, mind and spirit all at once, so that you can understand 'the most depraved aspects of who we are as human beings,' portray that story to the audience so that they understand it, and 'live through it in a way that's not destructive' to you[50] (Simotes). Obviously the very short *Fight* progression in the Intensive is just a step in that direction. Nevertheless, the intricate interweaving of all the disciplines throughout the month goes a long way toward enabling actors to experience their own bodies in a safe dialog with violence, as well as love, beauty, passion and the gamut of human feelings. We'll revisit the specifics of *Fight* in both *Education* ('Act III') and *Performance* ('Act IV') to clarify how all three pillars of S&Co. support one another.

FIGURE 8.4 Tony Simotes in *Fight* session, STI, 2016. The participant is making the sound of the physical blow with a clap or 'nap'

Photo: John Dolan

160 Training

We've journeyed through *Voice Work*, *Text Work* and all manner of *Body Work*. Time now to see how it all comes together in the final stages of the Month-Long Intensive.

Bringing it all together

As the Intensive drives toward its culmination, a particularly evocative event occurs at the end of Week 3: the *Elizabethan World Picture Day*. Originally a blend of Susan Dibble's vision and Dennis Krausnick's wisdom, the day really needs to be experienced to appreciate it fully. However, here are a few glimpses into its backstory and components ...

Elizabethan World Picture Day

In the mid-1990s Dibble approached Krausnick (as recently appointed Director of Training) with a question: 'What does it mean to have a "world view"?' She wanted to create a sensory experience for the Intensive participants, which would foreground the art of the Middle Ages and Renaissance. She believed that 'seeing light and dark in Shakespeare's world and language was a way to encourage an awareness of nature and the recurring cycle of life and death.'[51] For both Dibble and Krausnick, the Elizabethan Chain of Being resonated deeply in terms of humanity's connection to the universe, as well as the metaphorical light and dark of Heaven and Hell. And they wanted the workshop participants to have a chance to embody that visual and symbolic way of thinking about Life.

For the first *Elizabethan World Picture Day*, Dibble and Krausnick gathered together large, picture-filled art books from their respective family libraries, referencing Africa, Asia, Native America, Europe and myriad cultures of the world. They recognized that, to understand the Elizabethan World Picture, we need to appreciate that *every* culture has its own world picture. Indeed, Krausnick was particularly struck by the Paleolithic paintings on the cave walls in Chauvet:[52]

> These images give you an idea about what I mean by a 'world picture': it's in the cave-people's artistic unconscious. They're holed up in their cave all winter and they start illustrating what they consider the Power of their lives – putting it on the walls and ceilings. Suddenly they see an mammoth's head appear out of the stone. Then they put more color on it. And that's a world picture that is utterly different from the one we have now. They have a different attitude towards life and death, towards the cycle of nature. And then, by juxtaposition, look at the Elizabethan World Picture and how important *status* is for the Elizabethans, and rhythms and speaking and rhyming – and how little of that we actually embody today.
>
> *(Krausnick interview, August 2016)*

Body Work and bringing it all together **161**

In addition to art, Dibble was inspired by Tillyard's description in *The Eliza-bethan World Picture* (1942) of dance being at the heart of civilization. So she created a collective dance for the day entitled 'Sun, Moon and Stars.'[53] Evocatively simple, the choreography pays homage to the Cosmic Design and 'our willingness to be part of the universe and the movement of the stars and planets'[54] (Krausnick). It's set to John Renbourn's *Traveller's Prayer*,[55] which

> gives song to the Roma gypsy people, who travelled by the light of the moon. When they discovered they were being blamed for whatever was going wrong in the village where they'd stopped, they'd often have to move on at night. As actors we're also homeless. If we're not wearing someone's 'colors' (such as the King's Men or the Queen's Men) [or a 'Steppenwolf actor' or a 'Shakespeare & Company member'] – we're sturdy beggars. The moon and stars are how people find their way at night, finding comfort in the darkness as we try to save ourselves and our children and move along to the next place. I think there's something in that which actors instinctively, intuitively, understand and commiserate with. There's a disposability in our existence as actors: we can be disposed of very easily.
>
> *(Krausnick interview, August 2016)*

To which end, we find our own metaphorical sun, moon and stars to guide us on our way.

Indeed, human beings' connection to the cosmos resonates throughout the *Elizabethan World Picture Day*, which now follows a daylong progression instigated by various members of the faculty. It begins in the morning with *Sound and Movement*, as you navigate the lower levels of being human – from primordial sludge, through the four Elements, gradually evolving into *homo sapiens* as part of a collective tribe. Later there's a riotous presentation by the *bouffons* at the Court of Elizabeth I. And gradually through the day you progress to the higher aspects of being human by exploring your scene character. And thus, in some way, the evolution of humanity is expressed through movement, sound, body and partners. And from there into Shakespeare's language …

In the early days of the *Elizabethan World Picture Day*, Krausnick and Dibble had 'thought up the idea of going out into nature and seeing how there is a design of light and dark, symmetry and asymmetry, in nature'[56] (Dibble). And so it is that, in the early afternoon – as the winter light begins to dim and the snow lies glistening on the Kemble Street campus – you head outside to find a place on your own to deliver your sonnet to the cosmos. And maybe because of the earnestly evolved pedagogic progression … Maybe because by the end of Week 3, your creative pores are blasted open … Maybe because Shakespeare is a poetic genius who knows how to mingle microcosm and macrocosm … Whatever the reason, this aspect of the Month-Long Intensive is wholly mysterious, as I discovered in 2016:

162 Training

> The moment I clasped a snow-laden, pine branch with my ungloved hand, and spoke the first line of my sonnet, a strange and unexpected emotion welled up. Then I realized my sonnet was as much about my relationship with 'God' or 'Goddess' or 'Mother Nature' or whatever, as anything else: 'Take all my loves, my love... After all, you (God or Goddess or Mother Nature or whatever) put me on this planet. So "take them all" – and do with me whatever you want me to do with my life ...' And suddenly the sonnet had a relevance that I could never before have imagined.
>
> *(Merlin, 'Notes from Month-Long Intensive,' 17 January 2016)*

Maybe I was drunk on the Lenox-ade ... or maybe I was tasting 'language as experience' rather than reportage ... Either way, it was delicious ...

The day culminates in a kind of 'Celebration' as you return from the outdoor connection to the sonnets to the indoor encounter with the art books. 'For the first *Elizabethan World Picture Day*, the session began with the ritual of marking the participants' hands with a sun, moon or star image based on the Dance'[57] (Dibble). In later years Krausnick added his own, quiet gesture toward each participant's heart with the words, 'This is your heart.' It's a simple reminder of the beating (im)pulse within us all, before you enter the space and absorb the many worldviews. Thereafter follows what Krausnick calls 'Sonnet Fest': you're invited – in any order and without obligation – to share your sonnet and see what happens ... and again it's pretty magical:

> I've spent the entire Intensive demanding that you do the sonnet this way and that way: 'Here you breathe! There you decide the breath isn't coming in deeply enough so you shift the thought!' Then when it comes to the *Elizabethan World Picture Day* ... we've explored Earth/Water/Fire/ Air in the morning's *Movement* class ... and we've brought those Elements into the text of your dialogue with your scene partner in the afternoon's *Text* session ... and we've sent you outside to have an experience of being one with nature – that *your* DNA and the DNA of that *fern* over there are so close that you're letting the air actually breathe you. Then we bring you back inside and there are candles, picture books, music. And the faculty read different pieces of Shakespeare's texts and a teacher-trainee does a sonnet. And then we invite every participant to say their sonnet. But we give no instructions about where you can or can't breathe. And everybody brings *themselves* to and from wherever they are. And there is a truth and a beauty to that, which can't be replicated.
>
> *(Krausnick interview, August 2016)*

And Dennis Krausnick's intuitive understanding of the Elizabethan World Picture – and its truthful beauty in our contemporary psyche – can't be replicated either. 'Look down on us in the darkness below.'[58]

Body Work and bringing it all together **163**

After the celebrations of the *Elizabethan World Picture Day*, Week 4 directs all the components of the Intensive toward the final sharing of the Shakespeare scenes.

Actor/Audience and the final scenes

The final sharing of scenes on the last day of the Intensive has little to do with giving a performance that's boxed, sealed and delivered. Rather, it's a sharing of process, as your main focus is *the energetic exchange between actor and audience*. We've already noted that the audience is the actor's 'spiritual acoustics.'[59] And certainly the auditorium of the Tina Packer Playhouse – packed with partici- pants sharing their fellows' scenes – sets that acoustic vibrating. And it's very much a two-way street: 'One of the things we work on a lot at Shakespeare & Company is how to absorb [that audience] energy and how to let it transform what the actor is doing'[60] (Packer). And we've seen throughout this book that '*the actor–audience relationship* is perhaps the most important of all the relationships in theatre,' as, indeed, S&Co. believes it was for Shakespeare.[61] Which is why '*Actor/Audience* is a discipline in and of itself'[62] (Krausnick).

In fact, the progression of *Actor/Audience* morphs the personal into the public in myriad ways throughout the disciplines during the month: be it the sound vibrations emitted in *Voice*; the sharing of monologues in *Basics*; the first *Actor/ Audience* session (see Chapter 5); *Text* sessions with two couples; collective *Sonnet* in groups; the *Clown* progression; the intensity of *Fight*; and two-minute, on-stage 'dress-rehearsals' of the final scenes on the penultimate day. In other words, the 'actor–audience' acoustic is constantly (and unconsciously) being finely tuned, so that by the time you reach the final sharing, you've been tuned as an audience as much as an actor. You've subtly recalibrated your expectations of what good storytelling can be, because you've experienced how compelling the *Actor/Audience* interaction can be: 'Once you experience that relationship with the audience, it's startling, it's frightening. You're almost unwilling to go there. But once you have the experience, it just makes sense. And it raises the stakes and it raises the authenticity'[63] (Coleman).

And so the final day of the Month-Long Intensive is dedicated to the high- stakes authenticity of sharing scenes. The event is typically compered by Andrew Borthwick-Leslie, who provides just enough context for each scene to make narrative sense to the audience. And then you play! In fact, seasoned the- atre critic Jeffrey Borak offers a succinct summary of the work:

> the underlying drive is toward *taking ownership of the emotions* in a scene; to *make connections between voice and body* that are so integral they become second nature. In that welding, in the insight and understanding that comes from that bonding lies release, *the impulse to take chances*. That's what the final scenes are about.
>
> (Borak, J., 'Completing a circle,' The Berkshire Eagle, *17 February 2002,*
> *(my emphasis))*

FIGURE 8.5 Final scene-sharing with participants Shirong Wu (Kate) and Maeve Hook (Petruchio), Month-Long Intensive, 2019
Photo: Christina Lane

And who knows what'll happen if you do follow the impulse to take chances? This I discovered during the Margaret/Suffolk farewell scene[64] with my acting partner Bob Wicks (now a S&Co. faculty member):

> Just before we went out on stage, I was curious. I couldn't quite tell how I felt. (Was I nervous?) Then we launched into it. And straightaway I knew I was doing too much – my breath was all over the place … But I didn't care …! We just seemed to let the impulse guide us. We had no idea exactly what the other would do next. And the merger of actor and character was bewildering. It was as if two entities emerged – who weren't Bob and I, but rather these two creations (Bob/Suffolk and Bella/Margaret) composed of Shakespeare's language plus two actors' breath and the audience's energy. And these two entities metaphorically, metaphysically, alchemized into a fifteen-minute heartbreak on stage. It was a matter of just 'bringing my whole self into the room.' Trusting my partner. Trusting the audience. Realizing that 'feeling the feelings' doesn't mean bursting into tears every moment: it means playing the scene, backed up with everything that has come into the space from *dropping in* and during rehearsals. Most of all, trust the language and the breath. And play in the moment of performance. And it will all make sense and affect the audience in whichever way it does.
>
> (Merlin, 'Notes from Month-Long Intensive,' 24 January 2016)

Closing circle

The Month-Long Intensive culminates in a closing *reinforcement*. You're each invited to voice aloud the habits you'd like to leave behind and the discoveries you want to take with you. In many ways, 'the training has a real balance of the spiritual, the intellectual, the sensual, and the gut [...] using language as a generative tool'[65] (Packer). And *reinforcing* aloud your intentions for your own acting path is a (re)generative experience in its own right. This simple ritual drives home with clarity that the Month-Long Intensive is transformative and life-affirming, inviting each participant toward a new assessment of 'how to be in the world,' as much as how to stride forth as an actor on 'The Highway of New Beginnings' ...[66]

Notes

1 Merlin, B. (2014), *The Complete Stanislavsky Toolkit* (Revised Edition), London: Nick Hern Books, p. 21.
2 ibid.
3 Packer in 'Training Shakespeare Actors in A Modern World: Tina Packer Talks to Helen Epstein ...,' 24 January 2007, p. 3. S&Co. archive.
4 ibid., p. 3.
5 Dennis Krausnick interview with Bella Merlin, August 2016.
6 Kristin Wold, 'Some Notes From Class,' Shakespeare & Company's 2016 January Workshop.
7 Merlin, 'Notes from the Month-Long Intensive, 2016: Wold's Movement class,' 31 December 2015.
8 Susan Dibble Notes from Merry Conway's reflection, May 2018.
9 ibid.
10 Merlin, 'Notes from Kristin Wold's class, the Month-Long Intensive, 2016.'
11 Shakespeare used the term 'spirit', as indeed does Stanislavsky in his acting methodology, not to mention the methodologies from indigenous cultures. Arguably it's an increasingly common term in acting practice.
12 Shakespeare, W. (1609), Sonnet 40.
13 Shakespeare, W. (c. 1591), *Henry, VI, Part 2*, Act III, Scene ii: the Margaret/Suffolk 'Farewell scene,' assigned to myself and scene partner Bob Wicks in the January 2016 Intensive.
14 Dibble Notes from Conway's reflection, May 2018.
15 Susan Dibble Notes on John Broome, June 2018.
16 ibid., from Adam Broome.
17 Jane Nichols interview with Bella Merlin, June 2016.
18 Coleman cited in Verzi, D. M. (2003), 'Shakespeare Through the Ages,' *The Paper*, 1–13 August 2003.
19 Michael F. Toomey interview with Bella Merlin, June 2017.
20 Nichols interview, June 2016.
21 Nichols cited in Cox, C. (2006), 'Shakespeare Clowns Around,' *The Advocate*, 23 November 2006.
22 Nichols interview, June 2016.
23 Nichols cited in Cox (2006).
24 Coleman cited in Brusie, D. (2004), 'Learning the Actor's Art,' *The Beacon*, 11 March 2004.
25 Nichols interview, June 2016.
26 Krausnick interview, August 2016.

166 Training

27 Nichols interview, June 2016.
28 ibid.
29 Toomey interview, June 2017.
30 ibid.
31 Stanislavski, C. (1980, first published 1936), *An Actor Prepares*, trans. Elizabeth Reynolds Hapgood, London: Methuen, p. 204. ['Stanislavsky' or 'Stanislavski' are equally accepted in scholarship.]
32 Andrew Borthwick-Leslie interview with Bella Merlin, June 2016.
33 Nichols interview, June 2016.
34 Krausnick interview, August 2016.
35 Tina Packer interview with Bella Merlin, August 2016.
36 Toomey interview, June 2017.
37 Krausnick interview, August 2016.
38 Michael F. Toomey interview with Bella Merlin, July 2019.
39 Barry, B. H. (2013), *Fights for Everyone: The Performer's Guide*, Self-published, p. 13.
40 Tina Packer in 'Revolting Shakespeare' transcribed interview with James Gilligan, 1995, p. 14. S&Co. archive.
41 Claire Warden interview with Bella Merlin, August 2016. In 2019, Intimacy Directors International member Warden was the first woman to win a Drama Desk Award for Fight (and intimacy) coordination on Jeremy O. Harris's *Slave Play* at the New York Theatre Workshop.
42 Tony Simotes cited in Hollenbaugh, L. (2014), 'Stage Fighting: Let's Get Physical,' *The Berkshire Eagle*, 11 August 2014.
43 Gilligan in 'Revolting Shakespeare,' p. 7. (1995).
44 ibid., p. 8.
45 Simotes cited in Hollenbaugh (2014).
46 Corinna May cited in Bass, M. (2001), 'Creating the Illusion: Shakespeare & Co.'s [sic] Corinna May Teaches Actors to Fight,' *Berkshires Week*, 26 July – 1 August 2001.
47 Warden interview, August 2017.
48 Packer in 'Revolting Shakespeare' (1995), p. 14, (my emphasis).
49 Packer edit, September 2019.
50 Simotes cited in Hollenbaugh, (2014).
51 Email from Susan Dibble, 23 June 2018.
52 Over 1,000 paintings are thought to be the first figurative images in European culture, dating back over 36,000 years and discovered in 1994 in the Ardeche region of France. It's uncertain whether humans occupied the cave or if the paintings depicting bison, mammoths, wild cat, rhino, bears, aurochs and 'Venus and the Sorcerer' were part of a sacred space used for 'shamanist ritual practice,' www.bradshawfoundation. com (accessed 21 September 2019). In the fullness of time, Krausnick made slides of the Chauvet cave paintings and created a lecture for the Intensive on 'The Elizabethan World Picture,' At the time of Krausnick's death in November 2018, he was writing a book on the subject with Company member Josh Lubarr, with whom Packer is now working to complete it.
53 This dance is based on Dibble's own work with British actor-director Patrick Swanson, who regularly directed the Christmas 'Revels' in Boston, and in which she played the Star in the early 1990s.
54 Krausnick interview, August 2016.
55 www.youtube.com/watch?v=BRxK6tl4-1M. Renbourn, J. (1988) *Traveller's Prayer*, Shanchie Records (accessed 15 September 2019).
56 Email from Dibble, 23 June 2018.
57 Email from Dibble, 23 June 2018.
58 This is the last line of the first verse of Renbourn's *Traveller's Prayer*.
59 Stanislavski (1980, first published 1936), p. 204.
60 Packer cited in 'Training Shakespeare Actors in a Modern World,' p. 3.

61 ibid.
62 Dennis Krausnick interview with Bella Merlin, September 2018.
63 Kevin G. Coleman interview with Bella Merlin, August 2016.
64 Shakespeare, W. (c. 1591), *Henry VI, Part 2*, Act III, Scene ii.
65 Packer cited in Nesbitt, C. (1999), 'Into the Woods with Shakespeare & Company: An Actor takes Tina Packer up on the Total-Immersion Challenge, and Survives,' *American Theatre*, January 1999.
66 This is one of the various 'feeling' destinations on an 'Emotion Map' displayed during the Intensive in the lobby outside the communal dining area in Lawrence Hall. The map was created by Kristin Linklater and a cartoonist friend in the early years to help participants playfully chart with little pin-flags their discombobulating journey throughout the month. Other destinations include the 'The Foothills of Possibility,' 'The Slough of Despond' and even, 'The Bed of Nails of Illicit Love'!

ACT III
Education

9

PRACTICAL PEDAGOGY

'Rouse up thy youthful blood, be valiant and live'[1] is the motto of Shakespeare & Company's second pillar: *Education*. And over the past 40 years – primarily under Director of Education Kevin G. Coleman – the programs have reached thousands of young people and offered workshops to hundreds of teachers. Many, who first encountered S&Co. coming into their schools, are then inspired to go through their own vocational progression: signing up for the on-campus *Education* programs, later taking the professional *Training*, eventually going on to act in *Performances* and/or teacher-train to become education artists and faculty themselves. Thus, the wheel turns full circle, and *Education* in many ways pumps new blood into all three of Shakespeare & Company's arteries. So how did it all begin?

A brief history

In September 1978 – as Shakespeare & Company's first season successfully closed – the creative buzz at The Mount meant that many chose to stay in Lenox and engage with the local community rather than head back home. And where better to forge community engagement than in the Berkshire County schools? Since every school has Shakespeare somewhere on its curriculum, why not bring Shakespeare professionals right into the classroom? But Shakespeare & Company didn't just offer their professional skills: they also had their firm belief that Shakespeare could transform individuals and impact society, inclusively and collaboratively. In fact, Tina Packer's commitment to *Education* was second nature: with mother, brother, uncle and brother-in-law as schoolteachers, a regular topic of family conversation was how people learn. So she laid out – in an early, handwritten document entitled 'Purpose of Schools Program: Classical Training in Thought and Action in the Classroom' – the Company's wide-ranging justifications for teaching Shakespeare to children:

172 Education

1. It develops *creative thinking* within a collaborative process.
2. It develops *an ability to use language,* to express who you are personally [...].
3. It develops *an ability to sustain highly intricate thinking* which culminates in simple poetic truth.
4. It exposes students to *the finest philosophic, psychological and poetic thinking.*
5. It develops *an ability to tell the truth* – no matter how painful – for Shakespeare deals with public offense and private hurt with equal honesty.
6. It creates *an alignment between what you say* and *your actions.*
7. It develops *a great sense of self* within the students, while dealing with material which exposes the political and social context of individual human thought.
8. It exposes students to *their roots*; [as well as] the roots of the English language; the roots of Western philosophic thought which have developed [for better or worse] all our institutions [...] no matter to which ethnic group we belong.
9. It develops *an ability to choose* – not uninformed blind choice – but choice which comes about after immersing yourself in the material, learning the lines, delving into the emotions, interacting with fellow [human beings] in the most stressful and joyful circumstances [...].
10. It develops *lateral thinking and cross referencing* – the merging of many disciplines to create the theatrical moment [...].
11. Theatre makes *a good centre to an education system* [...]. Theatre restores *collaborative creativity* to the centre of a life of learning.
12. Finally there is *the sheer joy,* delight in doing something together, finding communion in the business of being a human being, striving for 'highest truths, universally told,' with healing powers.

> (Packer, T., 'Purpose of Schools Program: Classical Training in
> Thought and Action,' (undated. c.1980). S&Co.
> archive, (my emphasis))

The first iterations

In fall 1978 a diverse team led by John Hadden set off touring 'An Actor at Work,' co-devised by Kristin Linklater and Kenny McBain.[2] Using some of Shakespeare's 'hits,' it introduced students to his language and narratives, as well as to the serious craft of acting. But this was no ordinary show-and-share, as Paul E. Perachi – Principal of Lenox Memorial High School at the time – described:

> An actor stood at the centre and was just getting started when a boy with slicked-back hair and a leather jacket started shouting. He gets out of his chair and walks right down to the front, haranguing the actor. [...] And as he confronted the actor, wham, the actor socked him right to the ground.

Practical pedagogy **173**

We were all amazed. It turned out the boy was a plant from the company. Well, after that they showed how stage fights work and [they] had the kids right in the palm of their hands.

(*Perachi cited in Wapshott, N., 'Poetic Justice,'* The Times, *2 May 2002*)

The success of this performance was pervasive. After the team appeared at Housatonic Valley Regional High, English teacher William Devoti arranged for the school to hand over a week of P.E. classes to eight Company actors. Indeed, Devoti and Perachi (who raved about S&Co. to the Berkshire County Principals' Association) powerfully propagated the future of the *Education* programs. Though they still had a ways to go ...

Out of the classroom and into the body

At the end of 1978, Kevin Coleman joined the Company and quickly entered *Education*. He soon saw, however, that few teachers were as inspired as Perachi and Devoti, and all too often S&Co.'s workshops were assigned to regular classrooms. And of one thing he was clear: you can't teach Shakespeare in a classroom, like you can't teach basketball in a classroom: 'You can *talk* about it, but it's merely a cerebral activity, discussing characters intellectually with no deeper, emotional connection or visceral experience'[3] (Coleman). And when that happens, students find Shakespeare inaccessible and boring, and feel 'his themes have nothing to do with them.'[4] So they leave high school 'with little understanding of Shakespeare's accomplishments or their own capacities to enter into those plays [and] draw meaning and pleasure from them.'[5] But because Coleman (as an adolescent) had been so inspired by Shakespeare (see Chapter 1), he knew the Company's first forays into education should have a truly deep impact. He believed they could bring Shakespeare to the schools 'in a more difference-making, more authentic way,' a way that would excite the students like he'd been excited as a youth.[6] So he started thinking from an adolescent's point of view, asking himself, 'Why would this interest me? What should I care about this? What's here that would excite me?'[7] And more importantly: 'Why should I *need* Shakespeare?' Actually, he saw that adolescence is the *very time* young people need Shakespeare: they need 'deep and dangerous experiences and to encounter *these* characters in *these* plays – because Shakespeare's characters are very passionate, they're in extreme situations, and yet they're expressing their thoughts and feelings eloquently and insightfully.'[8] But school students will only experience this profound relevance if they get Shakespeare 'on his own terms.'[9] Which means *playing* him. Shakespeare & Company had to get the Bard out of the classrooms and into the students' bodies. Only then could they go beyond the superficial, interpretative level of work that happens 'where students are sitting still, where they're not engaging their bodies, where their voices are muted and conversational and all they're having are cerebral encounters and judgmental conversations.'[10]

174 Education

By March 1980 an early iteration of the 'Shakespeare in the Schools' programs had emerged. A five-day residency at Mount Greylock Regional High entailed Company members performing an abridged play, followed by student workshops on 'Scenes from Shakespeare.' Then in May, three Company members – Kevin Coleman, Ariel Bock and Tim Saukiavicus – were invited to Lenox Memorial High for a project they called 'Shakespeare Off the Wall.' Again Principal Perachi saw the impact they were having on the students and hired them to work with grades 9–12 for the entire, ten-week Fall term. They were granted three hours a day of class-time, with a further 5–10 hours a week of evenings, culminating in a full production. As the project unfurled, Perachi became increasingly impressed by the way they navigated complex themes and emotions with the children, enabling them to understand the violence in Shakespeare's plays, as well as the love. He also witnessed the transformative, transferable life-skills the young people were garnering, such as self-confidence, teamwork and public speaking. In fact, Perachi was so impressed with S&Co. that he became a major advocate for the *Education* programs throughout his working life – particularly when he moved from the classroom to the courtroom (as we'll see in Chapter 12).

Key education artists in the early years

The early success of the *Education* programs owed much to the professional standards demanded of the students by the Company actors as they used their own S&Co. *Training* to 'revolutionize the teaching of Shakespeare in schools.'[11] And at the heart of this revolution was dynamic duo Kevin Coleman and Ariel Bock. Bock had joined S&Co. in Summer 1979 from Boston-based Reality Theatre (led by graduates of Kristin Linklater and Peter Kass). With Coleman she co-created 'Shakespeare Off the Wall' (Spring 1980), before they worked together on *As You Like It* (Fall 1980) and *Alice in Wonderland* (Spring 1981). And by 1982 they were the bedrock of *Education*:

> Understanding that verbal self-expression, as well as physical exuberance, are being lost in today's world, we've made a commitment to help nurture students in the love of language, poetry, words and expression. Our skills as teachers, directors, lecturers and actors [can] help students realize the enjoyment of words and a sense of their vital function in anyone's life. […] Being a multi-racial, multi-cultural company means that we personally have to go further than our own individual backgrounds to reach that which is universal in all of us. Guided by Ariel and Kevin these students [have] the opportunity to personally discover and experience how Shakespeare & Company's training methods help one achieve our philosophic goals.
>
> *(Macbeth playbill, (1982). S&Co. archive)*

Practical pedagogy   **175**

Bock and Coleman worked as a kind of double act. If Coleman wanted more from a scene's progress, he would chivvy the students for reducing their lines to 'grocery lists': an analogy 'so graphically accurate – and so often used – that all Kevin needed to do was shout something like "Yeah, yeah – Eggs, butter, milk, cheese …" and the scene would immediately improve.'[12] Bock, on the other hand, would quietly halt a scene if it wasn't working, simply ask, 'What's the problem?' and let the students carry the conversation from there: 'Her approach was to remain as unobtrusive as possible […] speaking only when it was necessary to keep the lines of communication open and the conversation going in the right direction.'[13] With their complementary styles, Coleman and Bock treated the young performers with the respect of creative artists. And, because they were both actors themselves, they knew only too well

> what it costs, and how frightening it is to step out on stage: 'It's not like we're standing on the edge of a pit scolding the students. We're actually down in the pit with them thinking, "I know this is terrifying, because as an actor, I've been there, too."'
>
> *(Coleman cited in Ross, B., 'A Shakespearean Education,' The Paper,*
> *1 September–5 October 1988)*

This blend of high standards and compassionate practices quickly became the hallmark of Shakespeare & Company's *Education*. And, in 1982, a grant from the Cultural Collaborative branch of the Institute for the Arts enabled six actors, including Peter Wittrock, Lisa Wolpe and Jonathan Croy, to create a three-day workshop with Tantasqua Junior High. Croy was to become a significant member of the *Education* programs: after his first, brief bout with S&Co., he returned to his life as a jobbing actor; but, by 1989, he was so dissatisfied that he headed back to Lenox for the Month-Long Intensive. This proved to be 'one of those seminal moments where you shift the course of your life. What swept me up was that, in the Intensive, I dug deeper, went further, experienced more as an artist. I was flabbergasted.'[14] A mere 18 hours later Croy had joined the *Education* department. And he remained with the Company until 2018 as an actor, director, educator and Joint Artistic Director with Ariel Bock (2015–2016). For much of that time, he worked alongside Jenna Ware, who had joined the Company in 1990 and married Croy in 1997.

Ware's own lure toward the *Education* programs had been equally potent: she had been a student at a high school near Boston, where Coleman had directed a production of *Romeo and Juliet* in collaboration with two other schools.[15] Bitten by the S&Co. bug, she wanted to train further. So, after graduating from university, she took the Month-Long Intensive and the (then) Summer Performance Institute (SPI), and stayed on with the *Education* department for the Fall Festival of Shakespeare in 1992 (see Chapter 10). Her intent was to give other young people the experience that she had had at high school with S&Co. To which end in the years that followed, she became founder of Shakespeare &

176 Education

Young Company, originator of the 'Shakespeare in the Courts' Program (in collaboration with Coleman, Mary Hartman and Croy), Youth Programs Director, director/adaptor of numerous Shakespeare plays for the Young Company, Associate Director of Education and mentor to many, young education artists until 2017.

High schools weren't the only institutions to benefit from S&Co.'s *Education*. The elementary schools program was initiated in the 1980s by Jane Nichols, whose work was based on that of British child-development pioneer Peter Slade.[16] At first glance, Shakespeare's realm may seem worlds away from the psyche of a 7-year-old. Yet, just as Coleman understood the adolescent mind, Nichols grasped that of the child. Having founded a Boston-based theatre company for physically challenged children in 1977, she knew only too well that a child's ability to enter an imaginary world and turn on an emotional dime is deeply worthy of nourishment. When her company disbanded in 1983, Nichols headed straight to Shakespeare & Company for the (then) Summer Month-Long Intensive. And once there, her commitment to both Shakespeare and child development proved invaluable for the burgeoning *Education* department, which had yet to reach out to younger children. But Nichols understood that

> children crave drama. Look at the games they play – always to the edge, always filled with passion, loud language, utter abandon to the moment, the goals, the obstacles, the hope for victory, the steadfast commitment to the rules. They crave heroes; they crave adventure; they crave epic feelings running through their bodies. They crave size. And Shakespeare gives them size.
>
> *(Nichols interview, June 2016)*

Another valuable contributor to *Education* was Mary Hartman. Like Croy, Ware and Nichols, Hartman came to the programs after taking the *Training*, in 1988. Later that year she became an education artist leading residencies in both elementary and high schools, as well as directing for the first Fall Festival in 1989. On all fronts, Hartman's contribution to Shakespeare & Company was extensive: designing and promoting workshops for teachers, scholars and students; acting in the summer festivals; crafting copious reports; and serving as Director of Education Programs (1998–2003). She was also heavily involved in the Rose Playhouse project and the proposed setting up of an international scholarly center (discussed in Chapter 2).[17]

Peopled by such ardent education artists, it didn't take long for S&Co.'s *Education* department to garner endorsements from teachers, parents, participants and local media.

Community endorsement

When in November 1980 Bill Devoti invited S&Co. back to Housatonic Valley Regional High on the 'Visiting Artists Program,' journalist Donald Kobler saw

Practical pedagogy **177**

how their training methods 'encourage the students to discover for themselves the meaning of a scene, character and action. [...] Shakespeare & Company, in its schools program, is releasing some of the emotional and intellectual potential in scores of young people.'[18] Similarly enthused was Dr. William Irvin, Director of English curriculum for Grades K-12 for the nearby Pittsfield schools. He saw how the students' oral and verbal literacies expanded exponentially through performing such complex texts. For him, S&Co.'s approach 'allows the children to deal with a great work of literature intimately. It exposes them to more complicated syntax' and, because students are all actively engaged as participants, the 'potential for true learning is there.'[19] Irvin went so far as to create a 'Reading, Writing and Shakespeare Program' in 1988 for fourth and fifth graders, combining social science and writing, and designed to help children work on the figurative language of Elizabethan texts. Shakespeare & Company had reignited the whole region's overhaul of curriculum.

This community endorsement fueled Shakespeare & Company's educational zeal. Just three years into their existence, their *Education* teams had performed and/or offered workshops in almost every Berkshires public school district, private school and college. Ten years in, they had 20 to 30 actors and directors working across the region. And after 17 years, they had expanded further, with their ongoing dedication to training teachers as much as teaching children. The integrity of their practical pedagogy was officially endorsed when they were selected for Harvard University's prestigious *Project Zero*.

Project Zero

Project Zero was founded in 1967 by Nelson Goodman, a philosopher at the Harvard Graduate School of Education to investigate the value of the arts in learning and teaching. Each year researchers examine how various institutions and programs activate young people's artistic expression: 'Our research endeavors are marked by a passion for the big questions, a passion for the conceptual, a passion for the interdisciplinary, a passion for the full range of human development, and a passion for the arts.'[20] And in 1995, Project Zero chose two of Shakespeare & Company's *Education* programs: 'The Fall Festival of Shakespeare' and 'The National Institute on Teaching Shakespeare' (see Chapter 10). Although the Company had been going for less than 20 years, its *Education* program was already deemed 'one of the oldest and most fully developed of the educational theater programs in the country.'[21] Project Zero's primary questions were: Why do these programs work so well? What are participants actually learning? And what's critical to the programs' success?[22] Over two years, the researchers attended workshops and performances, and conducted interviews with students, teachers, administrators and Company members. And in 1998 they completed their report. The most important educational principles to emerge were: valuing 'truthfulness'; encouraging openness to new possibilities; freeing the natural voice; playing Shakespeare; experiencing visceral language; along with presence, permission to fail and generosity.[23]

178 Education

Educationalist Steve Seidel summed up, from Project Zero's findings, the conditions essential to S&Co.'s practical pedagogy. He particularly noted the learning environment they create: It's physically and emotionally safe. Everyone's ideas are considered and valued. Discipline and work ethics are mixed with humor and playfulness. There's 'support and respect for the subjective knowledge of the learner and the individual connection that the learner makes to the text, the play studied, and the work process.'[24] They integrate scholarship into practice of Shakespeare. And they offer ample opportunities for students to 'reflect on one's work, both individually and collectively.'[25] Seidel concluded: 'The programs created by Shakespeare & Company provide examples of excellence in professional development, teaching, and learning to be studied and adapted by other artist-teachers, classroom teachers, and teacher-trainers.'[26] Thus, 20 years into the existence of their *Education*, S&Co.'s practical pedagogy was deemed exemplary.

Tenacity and accolades

A further 20 years on – in 2019 (the time of writing) – the programs remain vibrant and robust, with a strong cadre of dedicated education artists and administrators engaged over the years (see Appendix 2). They've won awards and accolades across the country, as well as being featured by CNN, the BBC, *The New York Times* and *The Wall Street Journal*.[27] In 2006, 'Shakespeare in the Courts' received the 'Coming Up Taller' Award from the President's Committee on the Arts and Humanities presented by First Lady Laura Bush at the White House. In 2011, the *Education* department was awarded the Massachusetts Cultural Council's Gold Star Award for exemplary programming. And among the many other accolades are distinctions for Kevin Coleman himself. In 2009, he was awarded Distinguished Arts Educator in theatre from the Massachusetts Arts Education Collaborative. And in 2016 he was the runner-up in the Carnegie Mellon University and Tony Award for Excellence in Theatre Education. In fact, if you were to ask, 'What's so striking about Shakespeare & Company's *Education*?' many would answer, 'Kevin G. Coleman.'

The heritage of Kevin G. Coleman

Kevin Coleman's ability to inspire springs in part from his passion for the potential of learning: 'Learning should be exciting, dangerous, thrilling and pleasurable, and should remain so for the rest of one's life.'[28] It certainly shouldn't be a process of 'filling the pail' with the essentials of core curriculum, while marginalizing or ignoring the parallel essentials of community, creativity, relationship and self-awareness. Particularly vital for Coleman is self-understanding: 'If I can't distinguish between thoughts and feelings – if I can't *name* my feelings more specifically and insightfully than "good" or "bad" – I have very little deep insight into or honesty with myself.'[29] And without that insight and honesty, how can we really understand and empathize with others?

> At school, we're not learning and practicing the self-awareness and honesty we need to think more deeply and respond with more mindfulness. We need to learn not just to respect other people, but to go further – to plunge below respect and to discover what it is in other people that's admirable, that's the same as myself, that's worthy of compassion.
>
> *(Coleman interview, August 2016)*

If these lessons were taught with the same emphasis as critical thinking, then Coleman believes schools would become 'the most exciting, thrilling and pleasurable places in the country. Here one starts to fully discover one's humanity. If the arena you're playing in is this exciting, you must have material that will be equally exciting.'[30] And the material that *is* equally exciting is Shakespeare: 'Shakespeare explores and expresses the complexity of human nature like no one else.'[31] So, the *Education* department (under Coleman's aegis) has created models that

> give kids a chance to dive into this complexity more deeply. And that in turn creates relationship and community. Which creates a more vibrant sense of the world. And by giving kids a chance to see the pleasure in being *in community* – being *in relationship to other people* that isn't tainted with suspicion or fear or posturing – we can allow the essential art of theatre to be a valuable, exciting and pleasurable experience for almost every student.
>
> *(Coleman interview, August 2016)*

Coleman's ardor is underpinned by his deep *understanding of adolescence.*

Understanding adolescence

Teenage years are 'hot' years:

> Kids are confused. Their brains are firing in new ways. They're filled with hormones and new social rules. They're beginning to want to step into the world in meaningful ways, to be independent, to think their own thoughts, have their own judgments and emotional responses. And they want to be able to give these thoughts and feelings expression.
>
> *(Coleman interview, July 2019)*

Which means that adolescence is also a time of both danger and opportunity: 'It's far too vital a time to be spent solely acquiring prescribed information and rules, without concurrently developing one's ability to respond conscientiously, creatively and courageously.'[32] And since adolescents need to test the

180 Education

boundaries, take some risks (which will inevitably be either beneficial or destructive), Coleman understands how Shakespeare can provide a navigation system for these risks:

> Shakespeare's ideas were profound and startling even for the Renaissance, when it was all about pushing the envelope, re-discovering classical ideas or thinking thoughts humans had never thought before. But Shakespeare went even further. He was writing ideas that we won't revisit until the Existentialists: 'To be or not to be, that is the question.'[33] 'I am not what I am.'[34] 'We know what we are, but not what we may be.'[35] I believe Shakespeare was taking gigantic leaps even beyond the milieu of the forward, dangerous thinking that was the Renaissance. Yet that's the kind of emotionally charged thinking that adolescents are beginning to have, as their minds are waking up and their own thoughts are becoming independent of their parents' thoughts.
> *(Coleman interview, August 2016)*

So, Coleman sees how Shakespeare's risk-taking and leaps of imagination align with the explosions of an adolescent's mind – with one significant difference: 'Shakespeare examines and articulates – where adolescents struggle, fall silent or posture.'[36] Therefore, Shakespeare provides young people with the very language that can free them psychologically, emotionally and intellectually:

> there's no one more accurate in expressing what's going on for a human being. The words [Shakespeare] used are precise, moment by moment. This is especially needed for teenagers, because they're going through a kind of renaissance of their own – expanding in every direction.
> *(Coleman cited in Ross, B., 'A Shakespearean Education,' The Paper,*
> *1 September–5 October 1988; Coleman edit July 2019)*

Yet the expansion-experience doesn't stop there. While Shakespeare gives teenagers the tools for expressing themselves, Coleman also recognizes that there's a very dynamic transaction at play: Shakespeare may give them the most, but he also demands the most from them on *three critical levels.*

Three levels of being

'I think Shakespeare is operating on at least three levels simultaneously – intellectual, emotional and visceral'[37]– which is why sitting at desks is anathema. When students are sitting at desks, the intellect inevitably dominates and all the visceral and emotional experiences are dormant. As a result, they judge they won't be able to understand the language and they won't care about the characters.[38] And while, intellectually, they *can* handle the language, 'they have small desire because they haven't been "hooked" by the emotional or the visceral side – all the love and the fear and the violence and the humanity.'[39] So,

Practical pedagogy **181**

to reconnect to the plays as *Play*, Coleman makes sure that S&Co.'s first action when they go into a school is to access all three levels as directly and immediately as possible: 'Through workshops and exercises, [we] try to [dissolve and relax] the barriers students have put up around themselves'[40] – whether those barriers are the students' own concept of themselves, or crippling social rules, or their preconceptions of Shakespeare. And because S&Co.'s work is all about personalizing and 'owning' the language, pretty soon the students' armor softens a little. They find in Shakespeare every type of character, and every type of thought and feeling. So it doesn't take long for each student to find some point of *personal connection* within the rich range of material. And then they're able to use this connection to expand beyond their familiar selves into complex, new insights: 'The things they discover about Shakespeare, about the plays and about themselves … [are] really thrilling. […] They start coming alive.'[41] By which point, the students are saying, 'Hey, this isn't what I thought Shakespeare was like':[42] he becomes relevant to their lives and personally important. Which leads to one of the most significant, learning tools that Coleman advocates: *empathy*.

Discovering empathy

As with all Shakespeare & Company's work, the practice of *reinforcing* discoveries at the end of a workshop is an integral part of learning. And often this is where the real self-awareness and empathy for others start to emerge. As Coleman puts it, a student may say in a *reinforcement*:

> 'I learned more about Ophelia in twenty minutes today than I learned reading *Hamlet* for four weeks.' And I believe what she's getting at is that something *happened* to her. She had an 'Ophelia experience': intellectually, emotionally, viscerally. The opportunity to speak Ophelia's words with feeling helped her to personally identify with Ophelia. So Ophelia's feelings are now her feelings: and her feelings are being expressed by Ophelia. Then she starts making connections to her own life. She comes out of the experience going, 'I know more about Ophelia now because I'm starting to *think her thoughts* – because I'm *speaking her words*: rather than just looking at her words from the outside and *judging* her. And because I know what her thoughts are, certain feelings come up for me when I speak these words or when Polonius speaks to me. So now I know more authentically *who Ophelia is*, because the part of *me* that is Ophelia is waking up. And now I can speak *for* and *about* Ophelia – because I've had her experience.' Essentially that's the heart of the Education program.
>
> *(Coleman interview, August 2016)*

And for Coleman, this 'heart' – this empathy – comes about because the students 'meet Shakespeare on his own terms at all three levels':

They understand what the character is saying (the *intellectual* level); they have feelings that come up as they speak or hear the text (the *emotional* level) and they have an experience that the words trigger in their bodies (the *visceral* level).

(Coleman edit, July 2019)

And 'most of them catch on fire. They start talking about their own life experiences, so that the text becomes much more personal, more authentic, much more deeply rooted in their own lives.'[43] In fact, Coleman has seen over the years the exponential connection between the students' willingness to be authentic and their forging a stronger *community*.

Community through Shakespeare

'We have a lot of fringe students,' says Coleman. 'At first, there might be some teasing and the shy ones hold back from the others. But as time goes on, the actors begin to feel for each other. They become protective, caring and proud.'[44] And they also start to question their own behavior. The 'Number One' student who has worked so hard academically 'begins to feel that he's valued for other things which he hadn't valued himself.'[45] The student who struggles with attendance in school 'has little problem with attendance when he is wanted and appreciated in rehearsal. And he often begins to pay more attention to his schoolwork and his grades.'[46] And part of this voyage of self-knowledge and community is the students' increased verbal literacy, as Shakespeare bolsters their confidence to speak: students, who would habitually say nothing or only talk in monosyllables, are suddenly offering answers in their classes.[47]

FIGURE 9.1 Kevin G. Coleman in an *Education* workshop, 1997

Practical pedagogy **183**

Through his multi-layered appreciation of adolescence, Kevin Colman has galvanized potent teams in the *Education* department for over 40 years. Collectively they've evolved their instincts and observations into certain principles that underlie their *practical pedagogy*.

The principles of practical pedagogy

The intention: a meaningful experience

First of all, the *Education* faculty's intention is to give every participant a personal and meaningful experience through the art form of theatre, specifically Shakespeare, in 'a kind of rite of passage'[48] (Coleman). Since significant rites of passages are rare in our 'protected and inauthentic world,' the education artists create one

> by eliciting, cajoling, helping to create *fuller human beings*. Every inch of our philosophical bent is a manual for pushing the boundaries of who you are as a person, determining and discovering self. This work is healthy in a real humanistic way. There's hardly anything that we do with the students that isn't about striving to make their world a better place.
>
> *(Jonathan Croy interview, August 2016)*

Part of creating that 'better place' involves counterbalancing the challenges now facing young people – be it technology, social media, 'the enormous pressures high-school kids are under today when they apply to college.'[49] To which end, S&Co. seeks a 'win' for every student: 'How do we take their sense of a particular play and put it towards telling *their* story and expressing *themselves* in poetic language?'[50] (Ware). And expressing themselves through poetic language is actually a major part of the 'win,' because it makes the experience meaningful for them. The science-orientated language which dominates our lives 'tries to pin things down,' whereas poetic language 'is expansive and opens up,' and 'in our over-emphasis on science and math in schools, in our love affair with technology, we have left our imaginations impoverished'[51] (Coleman). Fortunately … Shakespeare's poetic language feeds that famished imagination. With its metaphors and ambiguity, it provides the students (in a playful paradox) with a far more *accurate* reflection of their human experience than the cut-and-dried precision of all that techno-speak and math. And, as the students master the poetic complexity (as Project Zero noted), they gain the courage to learn other new things – not least about themselves.

So how do the education artists actually manifest the meaningful experiences? Through the practical pedagogy of *project-based learning*.

The form: project-based learning

Project-based learning (as defined by Project Zero's researchers) is

184 Education

> an alternative to the desk-bound, transmission-based approach of most traditional classrooms. With projects, students get to work on solving authentic problems, working in groups, using the materials and methods of the professions, and creating products for performance.
>
> *(Seidel, 1999: 84)*

And this is precisely what happens in the S&Co. *Education* programs, where every 'product' is geared toward some kind of performance. Essentially, project-based learning has six key elements: authenticity; academic rigor; applied learning; active exploration; adult relationships; and assessment practices.[52] And on all fronts, S&Co. scores straight 'A's. Not least because the education artists use their own acting *Training* to activate their students' rites of passage: '*Training* is absolutely essential to the *Education* department. Almost everyone has taken the Month-Long Intensive [or the STI]. So we have a common vocabulary and aesthetic, and a shared desire in the way in which we perform Shakespeare'[53] (Ware). And (as we saw in 'Act II') the *Training* ticks all the project-based, learning elements. It addresses *authenticity*. It's *rigorous* in its various progressions. It *applies* actor-training skills to social interaction. It *actively explores* personal connection to the world through Shakespeare's language. It incorporates *adult relationships* through learning with master-teachers. And it *assesses* the work through its effect on the audience. We'll look at specific *Education* programs in Chapters 10–12. Here, let's briefly consider how S&Co.'s *Training* is incorporated into the *Education*'s practical pedagogy.

The practices: incorporating training

Linklater Voice

As with all Shakespeare & Company's work, the starting point is Linklater's *Voice* progression. Although the *Education* programs use a distilled version, they nonetheless

> take the essential ideas of various voice exercises and transform them into a different context. At all times we're continuing the work that Kristin created – trying to free the voice of an individual. It's not dumbed down or simplified, but we try to disseminate the components using vocabulary that the students can succeed in and thrive in.
>
> *(Croy interview, August 2016)*

They do this through warm ups and *Text Work*, giving the young people a meaningful sense of themselves through breath, sound, vibration and language. Not to mention *Play* and *Fight*.

Play and Fight

You can't thrive and succeed without a healthy dose of *Play*, and the education artists are certainly playful: it's hard to be otherwise with Coleman's sagacious irreverence at the helm. He recognizes only too well that we need a little laughter in the classroom: 'Humor helps us to take risks. Humor gives us a little respite. Even in tragedy, there will necessarily be scenes where we laugh [and] take a little breath.'[54] And playfulness is equally celebrated in *Fight* (also called 'Stage Combat' in *Education*).[55] As early as 1979, Dennis Krausnick incorporated into the *Education* workshops B. H. Barry's tumbling and somersaults, developing into fake punches and hair pulling.[56] And over the years Coleman has evolved the work, creating the famously fatal yet invisible 'air broadswords,' not least because (as he notes) when you're fighting with air broadswords, you're immediately brilliant! Grizzly battles with more than a hundred schoolchildren can ensue with not a droplet of blood or a bruising blow (see Figure 10.3: Chapter 10). In fact, staged violence is used in *Education* workshops to *break the ice* and *warm up the body*. So: 'On the count of three,' incites Coleman, 'I'd like you to die a horribly painful death from boredom. 3 ... 2 ... 1 ...' And 'two hundred bodies spen[d] half a minute degenerating from an upright position to a blob of ennui.'[57] Through their bold physicalizations of violent deaths, the students 'can stretch and grow. People won't smirk at them for taking risks. They can exaggerate, they can yell, they can move. And they can die gloriously – several times in one evening'[58] (with the scene-stealing delight of a Pyramus-Bottom!).[59]

Stage Combat is also used to introduce *physical discipline* and *collaborative storytelling*: the students learn that they can't perform a convincing brawl without taking care of each other as physically disciplined storytellers and ensuring nobody gets hurt. This in turn puts them *in relationship*:

> Both partners in a stage fight, Coleman tells the students, have a story to tell. One delivers the best punch she can; the other delivers the best reaction he can. They each have a story, and the stories have to match. Without both there is no stage fight.
>
> *(Burns, 2003)*

From the physical to the psychological, Coleman also uses Stage Combat to sharpen young people's *social responsibility*. And for a generation brought up on the violence of gaming and movies – where there's (typically) very little cost to the perpetrators – this is an important lesson:

> When people leave a violent film, they often want to copy the violence they just saw on the screen. [They leave in a heightened state of titillation.] In Shakespeare you also see the violence, but while the acts are going on the actor is also talking to the audience about his inner rage and fear.
>
> *(Coleman cited in Barrett, 'The Voice Has It: Shakespeare In The Schools,'*
> *The Courier, 7 April 1983)*

186 Education

And this powerful *actor/audience relationship* is important for the students to understand: the actors 'are showing living, breathing human beings affecting each other, and we are taking the audience into the experience'[60] (May). So, when the audience leaves *Macbeth*, 'you don't want to be violent, you want to weep [because you now understand the feelings beneath the violence]'[61] (Coleman). And building this sense of social responsibility toward violence doesn't end in the *Education* workshops: Coleman and his team point out that, once the students have had the privilege of learning stage fights, they have an ongoing, civic responsibility: 'Don't show off your combat skills at the [local supermarket]. We're entrusting you with this; it's not for the hallway at school.'[62]

For all the pleasures of playing and fighting, the practical pedagogy ultimately applies to the details of Shakespeare's *language*.

Text Work

Getting the words into the body – so that language is experience, not reportage – is the *raison d'être* of Shakespeare & Company, though the *Education* team doesn't really need to 'drop in' the words in the way that *Training* and *Performance* do (see Chapters 7, 13 and 15). Typically, younger children are

> already imaginatively free and playful for the most part. They're always *learning* language, so they're already very connected to words and they're encountering new vocabulary on a daily basis. So new and/or unusual words in Shakespeare are just an everyday experience for young students.
>
> *(Ware interview, August 2016)*

Meanwhile, the 16-year-olds are 'already chemically and emotionally awake. There's no way around it: they're in the middle of puberty!'[63] So much of the text prep focuses on *dictionary work* (introduced into the *Education* programs by Ware). *Dictionary work* isn't dull and heady: it's a matter of the students figuring out exactly what they're saying and fathoming their options:

> 'Fiery' could mean 'hot' or it could mean 'spicy.' And they have the opportunity to try out those choices on their feet and see what connects with them. It's not about picking the right answers: it's about finding out what your options are and actually feeling the feelings of what you're saying.
>
> *(Ware interview, August 2016)*

The success of this particular practical pedagogy was flagged by Project Zero. One student stated,

> When I walked out of classes *reading* Shakespeare, I used to be confused as to what it was about. After you walk away from these rehearsals, you can

Practical pedagogy **187**

really understand the scenes because of the many techniques used to go over the various interpretations of the text.

(Student cited in Seidel, 1999: 82)

Another student noted, 'When Shakespeare & Company makes us go through things word by word if we don't understand them, it is weird how much you learn, and what doesn't leave your head.'[64] And much of the 'unforgettableness' of the *Text Work* is S&Co.'s refusal to simplify: they want the students to tackle all the complexities of human communication.

These brief glimpses into the history and practical pedagogy of Shakespeare & Company's *Education* programs suggest that it takes a certain kind of person to become one of their education artists. So, to conclude this chapter, who are they?

Education artists 'from the heart'

'The people we look for [...] to do this are human beings who can come *from within themselves*'[65] (Coleman). While of course they 'have co-workers, co-directors, more experienced practitioners, and master-teachers to learn from and consult with regularly,'[66] the education artists 'have to do it *from the heart*'[67] (Coleman). Take Jennie M. Jadow, the current Education Programs Manager. A native of the Berkshires, Jadow took the Month-Long Intensive in 2001, after which Coleman asked her to work with him as an actor in one of his productions at the Austen Riggs Center (a renowned open-setting psychiatric facility in Stockbridge, Massachusetts). And with a master's degree in Clinical Psychology and Dance and Movement Therapy, Jadow has remained at S&Co. as a senior education artist, actor, director, and one of the directors of 'Shakespeare in the Courts' (as we see in Chapter 12). Like Jadow, the other education artists typically emerge out of the Company. Because they've taken the Month-Long Intensive or the STI, they all have an openhearted willingness to learn. And such has been the case since the early years of the *Education* programs, when everyone trained for a week in *Clown*:

> This opened us up to remembering what it was like to be a child, to be playful and vulnerable, as well as to find a different place to teach from. Not a pedagogic, pedantic place, but one of porous availability and wit, heart and intuition.
>
> *(Nichols interview, June 2016)*

At the core of it all is *kindness*, a quality referenced in *Training* and an educational quality valued by the Project Zero commentators: 'Treating oneself well, and being treated well by others – with kindness and generosity – increases the likelihood and willingness to take risks.'[68] And we can't learn new lessons if we're not willing to take risks.

188 Education

This potent edu-cocktail of collaboration, mentorship, playful risk and kindness percolates the multiplicity of *Education* programs, to which we now turn …

Notes

1 Shakespeare, W. (1595), *Richard II*, Act 1, Scene iii, line 83, John of Gaunt.
2 The cast also included Gregory Uel Cole, Andrea Haring, Kaia Calhoun, Jeff Deutsch and Steven Sylvester.
3 Kevin Coleman interview with Bella Merlin, August 2016.
4 Coleman cited in Leuchs, E. C. (1984), 'Shakespeare Knows No Bounds,' *Only in the Berkshires* (date unspecified).
5 Seidel, S. (1999), '*Stand and Unfold Yourself*: A Monograph on the Shakespeare & Company Research Study*, p. 82. artsedge.kennedy-center.org/champions/pdfs/Shakespe.pdf (accessed 15 September 2019).
6 Coleman interview with Merlin, August 2016.
7 ibid.
8 ibid.
9 ibid.
10 ibid.
11 'The First 10 Years' (1987). S&Co. archive.
12 Cahill, T. (1981), 'The Lenox Rehearsals: Two Adults and 36 Kids Work with Shakespeare After School,' 20 December 1981.
13 ibid.
14 Jonathan Croy interview with Bella Merlin, August 2016.
15 This joint production has continued for years through multiple school-administrative changes, thus becoming a tradition.
16 Peter Slade (1912–2004) advocated the use of athletic movement as cathartic release, and pioneered play and drama in children's education and development. His seminal publications, including *Child Drama* (1954) and *Child Play: Its Importance for Human Development* (1995), were intended for parents, teachers, social workers and police.
17 During her time at S&Co., Hartman took a year off to go to London, partly to help Patrick Spottiswoode create education programs for the new Globe Theatre.
18 Kobler, D. (1980), 'Students' Potential Released In Shakespeare's Production,' *Lakeville Journal*, 20 November 1980.
19 William Irvin cited in Borak, J. (1986), 'Something Creates Something the Shakespearean Way,' *The Berkshire Eagle*, 4 December 1986.
20 www.pz.harvard.edu/who-we-are/about (accessed 15 September 2019).
21 Seidel (1999), p. 84.
22 ibid., p. 80.
23 ibid., p. 88.
24 ibid.
25 ibid.
26 ibid., p. 90.
27 To their delight, the *Education* department was even roasted on *The Colbert Report*!
28 Coleman notes, July 2019.
29 Coleman interview, August 2016.
30 Coleman cited in Borak (1986) (Coleman edit July 2019).
31 Coleman notes, July 2019.
32 Coleman cited in Anderson, M. K. (1997), 'In the Hands of Adolescents,' *The Valley Advocate*, 16–20 November 1997 (Coleman edit July 2019).
33 Shakespeare, W. (1599–1601), *Hamlet*, Act III, Scene i, line 56, Hamlet.
34 Shakespeare, W. (1601), *Twelfth Night*, Act III, Scene i, line 155, Viola.
35 Shakespeare, W. (1599–1601), *Hamlet*, Act IV, Scene v, line 43, Ophelia.

Practical pedagogy **189**

36 Coleman edit July 2019.
37 ibid.
38 Coleman cited in Leuchs (1984) (Coleman edit July 2019).
39 Coleman cited in Dunbar, K. (1981), 'Shakespeare in the Schools: A New Approach to Classical Theatre,' *The Saturday News*, 29 August 1981 (Coleman edit July 2019).
40 ibid.
41 Coleman cited in Leuchs (1984).
42 ibid.
43 Coleman interview, August 2016.
44 Coleman cited in Leuchs (1984) (Coleman edit July 2019).
45 ibid.
46 ibid.
47 Coleman cited in Dunbar (1981) (Coleman edit July 2019).
48 Coleman cited in Borak, J. (1997), 'The Bard Wins Young Hearts and Minds,' *The Berkshire Eagle*, 11 December 1997.
49 Croy interview, August 2016.
50 Jenna Ware interview with Bella Merlin, August 2016.
51 Coleman cited in Seidel (1999), p. 83.
52 Adria Steinberg cited by Seidel (1999), p. 84 from Steinberg, A. (1998), *Real Learning, Real Work: School-to-Work as High School Reform*, New York: Routledge.
53 Ware interview, August 2016.
54 Coleman cited in Brusie, D. (2004), 'Learning the Actor's Art,' *The Beacon*, 11 March 2004 (Coleman edit July 2019).
55 Given S&Co.'s fine-tuning into language, 'Stage Combat' is the term typically used with the young people in the *Education* programs, rather than the potentially 'hotter' vocabulary of 'Fight' or 'Stage(d) Violence.'
56 Michaels, J. (1979), 'Shakespeare is a Knockout,' *The Berkshire Sampler*, 21 January 1979.
57 Anderson, M. K. (2000), 'Students Tackle the Text,' *Dramatics*, April 2000 (Coleman edit July 2019).
58 Burns, D. (2003), 'Fighting the Good Fight,' *The Berkshire Eagle*, 21 November 2003.
59 Shakespeare, W. (1595), *A Midsummer Night's Dream*, Act V, Scene i, lines 302–312 ending 'Now die, die, die, die, die,' Bottom.
60 Corinna May cited in Bass, M. (2001), 'Creating the Illusion: Shakespeare & Co.'s Corinna May Teaches Actors to Fight,' *Berkshires Week*, 26 July–1 August 2001.
61 Coleman cited in Barrett, P. (1983) 'The Voice Has It: Shakespeare In The Schools,' The Courier, 7 April 1983 (Coleman edit July 2019).
62 Coleman cited in Burns (2003).
63 Ware interview, August 2016.
64 Student cited in Seidel (1999), p. 82.
65 Coleman cited in Borak (1986), (my emphasis).
66 Coleman cited in Seidel (1999), p. 89.
67 Coleman cited in Borak (1986), (my emphasis).
68 Coleman cited in Seidel (1999), p. 87.

10

SHAKESPEARE IN THE SCHOOLS

Imagine being a teenager struggling with schoolwork, parents, your own hormonal body. And into your school bursts a posse of passionate actors propelled by the power of Shakespeare to transform your life. That's Shakespeare & Company's 'Shakespeare in the Schools,' of which the key programs are the *Northeast Regional Tours*; the elementary- and middle-school tours of *Shakespeare and the Language that Shaped a World*; the *School Residencies*; and the nationally acclaimed *Fall Festival of Shakespeare*. So let's go to school and take a look …

Northeast Regional Tours of Shakespeare

From Maine to Maryland, six to eight education artists tour 90-minute adaptations of Shakespeare plays to around 50 schools over 15 weeks. The program began in 1982 with a troupe led by John Hadden in *Romeo and Juliet*, and it's now something of training ground for young actors to become more seasoned Company members. Rehearsals begin in December before the troupe hit the road in February. They drive to a school; erect the set; perform the show; run an interactive Post-Show Forum; strike the set; lead a workshop; and (on a two-school day) drive to the next school. Workshops range from 'Shakespeare and the Renaissance: Wild and Whirling Words' (an introduction to Shakespeare's language, his portrayal of women, and the differences between the comedies, tragedies, histories and romances); *Actor/Audience* (with dances, fights and 'Death by a 1000 Directors,' in which the student-audiences offer the actors new directions for demonstrated scenes); to 'Workshops in Performance' (in which students explore mini-performances, discovering Shakespeare is 'accessible, outrageous and immediately engaging').[1] The education artists have 'very focused ways of working with students for a limited period of time, using

FIGURE 10.1 *Love's Labour's Lost*, dir. Kelly Galvin, 2018, at the Dell at The Mount
Photo: Eloy Garcia

creative dramatics, to take them from theatre games and exercises to performance of Shakespeare'[2] (Coleman). And for those schools that can't bring S&Co. to them, student matinees are performed at various venues in the region and at the Tina Packer Playhouse.

Typically in the summer, actors from the Northeast Regional Tours perform on the outdoor stage of The Dell at The Mount. Often they're also instructors in the 'Riotous Youth' program (see Chapter 11), so the summer-camp participants can see their teachers perform (again interweaving the strands of *Training*, *Education* and *Performance*). And the performance style is a robust mix of the lyrical and the ludicrous, with plenty of interaction with the picnicking audience.

Similar lively components feature in the *elementary- and middle-school tours*.

Elementary- and middle-schools tours

Shakespeare and the Language that Shaped a World (SLaW)

At the heart of the elementary- and middle-school tours is *SLaW*, a 45-minute compilation shaped by Coleman in 1992 to demystify Shakespeare and 'unleash an immediate, exciting and personal experience of Shakespeare's language.'[3] Between February and April *SLaW* is performed at local schools by six education artists. And this fun-packed feast is full of frolics, biography, swashbuckling swordfights, famous lines and oodles of insults! All designed to reveal to children as young as seven how Shakespeare's 400-year-old language is actually 'younger, more exciting, more raw and more alive' than the English we speak today, and that Shakespeare's 'language, in a very real, tangible, daily way, has shaped our

192 Education

FIGURE 10.2 *SLaW*, dir. Jenna Ware, 2013: Ryan Winkles, Enrico Spada, Kelly Galvin, EBT

Photo: Kevin Sprague

world."[4] *SLaW* is then followed by a workshop (usually involving the whole audience, including teachers and parents): it starts with physical/vocal warm ups, and ends with two-minute playlets created from eight lines of text. The whole experience defuses the intimidating nature of Shakespeare, rendering it approachable and fun. Likewise with the *Schools Residencies*.

Schools Residencies

The residences comprise individually designed workshops, lasting anything from one day to ten weeks and created in collaboration with teachers to serve the needs of each school.[5] Using scenes, compilation pieces or full productions, there are also teacher-led discussions and writing assignments to support the performance component. And one of the most popular choices is the ten-week *Director-in-Residence*.

For a typical elementary-school Director-in-Residence the first four weeks are spent in an atmosphere of focused fun exploring the chosen play's plot, language and characters. Week 5 shifts gears as those themes and images are then manifested through visual arts projects. It's only in Week 6 that the directors actually cast the play using the entire class. Students who don't want to speak can play attendants or even dead bodies and statues; and those 'who don't want to leave their seats can provide the sound effects, or even help "direct" the scene"[6] (Hartman). Weeks 7–10 are then devoted to rehearsals, with the emphasis always on process rather than production. And this project-based approach (as outlined in Chapter 9) is beneficial on many fronts. First of all, the students are slap-bang at the center of the learning experience, so they have *greater personal responsibility*:

Shakespeare in the Schools

When they are in a scene, they must solve the problems inherent in that scene. Romeo only has a fourteen-line exchange with Juliet in which to pique her interest, and he can't show his face or he would be discovered at his enemy's house.

(Hartman, 'On Playing Shakespeare in the Classroom,' 2003: 2)

Personal responsibility also gives them more *experiential authority*: 'What better way to understand Hamlet's plight than to assume it?'[7] And this experiential authority transcends anything curricular: they're gaining

insights into human behavior that they can apply directly to their lives. […] A sixteen-year-old girl was asked to play Polonius, and her initial response in rehearsals was, 'I can't stand the way this character treats Ophelia. This is the way my dad talks to me.' After a few weeks, her perception shifted. 'Polonius loves Ophelia,' she said one day. 'He's just trying to protect her.' She was quiet for a moment, then said, 'Maybe that's why my dad talks to me this way.'

(Hartman, 'On Playing Shakespeare in the Classroom,' 2003: 3)

For ten particular high schools, the Director-in-Residence manifests in the flagship of the *Education* programs: the annual *Fall Festival of Shakespeare*.

Fall Festival of Shakespeare

Initiated by Coleman in 1988, this celebration of Shakespeare is a four-day culmination of a ten-week process. And it's huge – on every level:

Fall Festival can be as *physically* demanding as any varsity sport, as *intellectually* rigorous as an honors class and as *emotionally* challenging as adolescence itself. For each of the hundreds of students involved – whether they be actors, technicians, costumers or producers – the Fall Festival is a celebration of inclusion, cooperation, non-competition, courage and personal investment. There are no external rewards or trophies. This is not a competition between students, teachers or directors, or even between the 10 schools. The reward in this model is the pride and pleasure students find in themselves and each other, the personal meaning and value they discover in Shakespeare's language and stories, and the self-esteem they earn in challenging themselves in this daunting and demanding task.

(Coleman cited in Murray, L., 'Shakespeare & Company's Fall Festival Underway,' 21 October 2010. S&Co. archive)

The history behind the first festival is powerful and poignant.

194 Education

How the Fall Festival began

Over a hundred years ago in the late 1800s, the small town of Lenox flourished into a fashionable resort for the wealthy of New York City. There they would spend their summers, writing, motoring, hosting their illustrious friends. Meanwhile the artisans who built the grand mansions and the tradespeople providing service and labor lived in the less luxurious town of Lee. And so it was that, over the decades, a social hierarchy subtly formed between these neighboring towns ...

A hundred years later, in the early hours of a July morning in 1981, two rival teams of teenagers from Lee and Lenox set about goading each other round the byways of the Berkshires. The night ended tragically when a white Cadillac occupied by two lads from Lee accelerated off the boat launch at Laurel Lake and plunged into the water. They drowned. Five months later in December 1981 seven Lenox boys were charged with assault and battery and the involuntary manslaughter of the Lee lads. And they were subsequently sentenced to two-and-a-half years in a house of correction. This sentence was immediately appealed. And, although the charges were overturned on 9 March 1983, the communities of Lee and Lenox were deeply scarred by the events.

Shakespeare & Company's home at The Mount placed them geographically between the two communities. And in 1988 Kevin Coleman was directing *The Taming of the Shrew* at Lenox Memorial High while two other Company members were directing *Romeo and Juliet* at Mount Greylock Regional High in Williamstown. As the end of term approached, the students at the two schools voiced how much they wanted to watch each other's performances. Heeding their call, Coleman arranged for a final sharing of the two schools' productions at Boston University's Tanglewood campus in Lenox. From the get-go he knew that the spirit of the event should be one of support, not rivalry. And the students were wholly 'responsive to each other's shows having worked on Shakespeare themselves [so] they knew how difficult it was'[8] (Coleman). Indeed, the night was such a huge success, the cogs began to whirr ... For a while there was thought of a possible co-production between Lee High and Lenox Memorial High, but there was a subtly pervading lack of self-confidence in the Lee students that they could really tackle Shakespeare. Not to be deterred the (then) English teacher at Lee High, Bob Lohbauer, worked with Coleman to bolster their confidence – and then the idea arose: 'What if there was a collaborative festival across more schools in the area – maybe even part of a healing process between neighboring Lee and Lenox?' And thus was born the Fall Festival of Shakespeare. The first was held in 1989 and, with time, the high schools of Lenox and Lee became seminal participants. (And with time Bob Lohbauer became S&Co.'s armorer, a role he holds to this day.) As a result of Coleman and Lohbauer's faith, there were ten schools within a matter of years comprising the Fall Festival. And in 2019 it celebrated its 31st anniversary.

The popularity of the Fall Festival is heralded. When S&Co. suffered financial duress in 2009 and could only budget for six schools, the ten institutions

Shakespeare in the Schools **195**

regularly involved rallied to fundraise. And largely through parent-supported activities – bake sales, dances, program advertising – they found the (then) $13,000 needed for each school to participate. When Harvard's Project Zero witnessed the Fall Festival, they were deeply impressed: 'these performances are not simply school-room exercises: they are authentic acts of communication, culture and community.'[9] They also noted that each individual may well be pushed beyond their sense of personal limits, but in 'this collective effort, each person deserves support and attention from the group, and the ultimate success of the group's effort is dependent on providing that support and attention.'[10]

So what exactly is the Fall Festival that it garners such praise from respected educational researchers and local communities alike?

The logistics

First off, the Fall Festival is an enormous feat, involving 10 schools, 20 directors, 6 technical experts, 6 costumiers, 1 week of staff workshops and 9 weeks of rehearsals. Two directors per team go into a school and rehearse a Shakespeare play, with a production team and costume designer covering two schools each. And a liaison person at each school takes care of them: 'Each school is its own kingdom and no two kingdoms run the same'[11] (Coleman). Any student at a particular school can be involved in some capacity – be it acting or production – and the play is usually selected by the directors only after they've seen the group's auditions and have a sense of who their participants are. All ten productions are performed in the TPP during the November weekend before Thanksgiving.[12] And this extraordinary event brings together almost 500 high-school students with the exuberance of what the *Boston Globe* described as a 'rock concert of Shakespeare.'

The festival model

The festival model is based on the style of direction nurtured by Packer at Shakespeare & Company from the beginning, when she set up the practice of directing actors by asking questions about human behavior (see 'Act IV'). This isn't a traditional way of directing, and Coleman ensures this non-traditional approach permeates the whole Festival, starting with auditions:

> The traditional 'professional model' of 'memorize a monologue, show up, be prepared to sing a song' is inappropriate for the educational environment. It excludes too many kids from the get-go: 'I don't even know what it is to *memorize*. What's a *monologue*? It's too big a hurdle to go from *what I know* to *where you want me to start*.' So rather than set up an initial moment so frighteningly and impossibly high, let's take baby steps into this art form, so that more of them catch fire right from the beginning.
>
> *(Coleman interview, August 2016)*

196 Education

To which end auditions involve group games. As for rehearsals, the traditional 'professional model' with directors blocking a play straightaway is also eschewed:

> The director in most professional theatres says, 'This is my concept and interpretation. These are my set designs. This is my vision.' And professional actors come in and go, 'Oh, I have the skillset to support that vision. I've been trained, so I know how to do that.'
>
> *(Coleman interview, August 2016)*

This isn't how Shakespeare & Company has historically operated, especially in *Education*:

> These kids don't necessarily have the training to realize what the director is telling them. So if I impose the usual professional model on them in an educational setting, all I'm doing is reinforcing that they're obedient students. All they can do is obey my interpretation, move where and when I say, and become the characters I think they should be. They're not able to discover for themselves how they need to speak these words, because they don't own them yet. The usual professional model doesn't make for very rich self-discovery experiences for those kids, so once again they're being infantilized.
>
> *(Coleman interview, August 2016)*

Therefore, the director's job in the Fall Festival is very different. It's

> metaphorically 'to let loose the sled-dogs.' First of all, I'm going to work bit by bit to have them come alive. Once I see they're coming alive, I'm going to align all of these dogs that I've turned loose so that they're running in one direction. Now they're a sled team. But first I have to wake them up: I have to let them run around and discover that they're dogs. Only then can I bring them together into a team that's running in one direction. In the professional model, I'd be saying at the very beginning, 'This is the direction we're going. This is my interpretation and concept. Harness up!' In *this* model, the director's job is much more difficult – but it's much more exciting, pleasurable, risky, wild. And the payoff is huge!
>
> *(Coleman interview, August 2016)*

Because it's difficult, risky, wild, the education artists are well prepared.

Directors' preparation

Just before the process begins in September, Coleman leads a weeklong training. Although most of the 20 directors are returning education artists who have been with the Company several years, all of them come together to prepare (individually and as a group) and tap into 'their own creativity,

Shakespeare in the Schools **197**

inspiration, energy and troubleshooting skills.'[13] The first three days are a mini-Intensive, featuring Linklater's *Voice Work* and Packer's approach to text. They're reacquainted with the Company's aesthetic, as well as how to work with the schoolchildren, using non-judgmental language and strong organizational frameworks. One of the main lessons for the directors is tackling their own fear of failure:

> You are going to fail in big ways. [...] Your rehearsals will sometimes *suck*. You will be confronted with acting problems very similar to your own – and different. And you may have nothing to suggest. Remember, you're asking your students to break the social rules that they're very invested in – rules that they've embodied to survive. You're telling them, 'Reveal yourself. Find your voice. Live in your body. Name your feelings' … We need to be gentle and we need to push.
>
> *(Coleman cited in Anderson, 1998; Coleman edit, July 2019)*

So one of the main rationales behind the training is to reassure the directors of the truly collaborative nature of the work: they're really there for each other as well as for their students. Not least because the learning goals are high, including: enabling each student to make a *personal connection* to Shakespeare's language; sharing a human moment; and creating a rite of passage. For Coleman (as we saw in Chapter 9), rites of passage in contemporary society have lost the power they once had. Therefore, young people often create their own alternative, more destructive rites, which may include experimenting with drugs, breaking the law, sexual activities, or testing themselves in other ways. But the main rite of passage here is experiencing the challenges of theatre, the risk of revealing oneself – an experience no less adrenaline-filled. So, to shape this rite of passage, the directors will foreground the students' ideas and bravery: 'Going out on stage is a huge risk, and the kids are rewarded for their courage'[14] (Coleman).

The directors will also encourage the participants to celebrate each other's performances and other schools' productions – which may be something of a shift in the students' psyches. Education has to go to extreme lengths to resist young people's cynicism, disenfranchisement and (for a tech-addicted 'iGeneration') isolation. As Company education artist Wolfe Coleman describes it, every effort is made to ensure 'the rehearsal environment is always safe and free from any judgment or shame, but really it takes a bold decision from the actor to make that happen.'[15] So the directors' task will be to guide their young casts toward those bold decisions. To which end, the directors' training includes bringing them up to speed on where the schoolchildren may be in terms of their development and which plays have previously been done in each establishment. Then out the directors go into the schools to let the sled-dogs loose …

198 Education

Auditions and play selection

Pleasure, risk and a willingness to say 'yes' have to start at auditions. From the get-go the students are advised that the process will be physically demanding (as huge feelings will course through their bodies) and intellectually rigorous (as they grapple with complex thoughts that they may never have encountered before). Yet the advice comes with a promise that their voices will be heard and they can stand up for what they believe. And with such appetizing expectations, 'auditions' begin. Through the games the directors get to know their group and fathom which play would suit them. And although everyone who auditions can be involved in some way (on or behind the scenes), the cast can't top 30, otherwise costuming is a nightmare! Auditions over, the play is selected. And as Philmot High School senior Darrin French describes, the excitement mounts even higher: 'The directors don't tell us which play we're going to do until the very last moment. The mood is frantic. Many of us flip through Shakespeare anthologies looking for a clue.'[16] And as soon as the play is chosen, there's an equally frantic editing process as directors pare down their storylines to a coherent 90 minutes. The mania continues into rehearsal scheduling, as they work around hockey practice, piano lessons and regional bus timetables. And then they have to consider in which era to set the play so that it makes sense for the narrative, the students and the costuming possibilities! All before rehearsals can begin ...

Rehearsal processes

Once rehearsals do begin, they typically kick off with a brief version of the *Training* 'ritual,' *checking in.* This gives the students an invaluable opportunity to share what's going on for them in terms of tests, accomplishments, extracurricular activities. Sometimes there's a feeling-based prompt from the chosen play such as 'What does the word "love" mean to each of you?':

> Love is unexpected. Love is a game for some people. Love is giddiness. Love is like a present from your grandmother: it looks exciting to open, but no matter what it is I'm pretty sure I don't want it.[17]
> *(Taylor-Williams, C., 'The Fall Festival of Shakespeare & Company: A Labor of Love,'* The Advocate, *20 October 2006)*

And here's the nub of it: the students are given a space to validate their emotions. As Eric C. Williams (longtime contributor to Shakespeare & Company, including production coordinator for the high schools, and former FBI agent) says: 'To deal with Shakespeare, you have to ask about feelings. It is the first time in school that people ask [the students] how they feel.'[18]

'Feeling Shakespeare's texts' can only really happen when you know exactly what you're talking about. So, in comes the *dictionary work* (see Chapter 9). The precision of *dictionary work* allows each student to have a *personal connection* to

Shakespeare's language and, once done, the scene practically directs itself: 'When a specific thought/image is applied to each word in Shakespeare's language and fuelled by the tumultuous undercurrent of adolescent experience, the scene comes alive and requires little more from the director than a container to hold the experience'[19] (Ware). Not that the students have to fix their choices: there's always an atmosphere of discovery and play, as they mentally chew on the language and taste the heartbreak, beauty, violence and jokes. And with plenty of gender-fluid casting everyone has the chance to relish the words of kings, princes, fairies and fools, as well as Shakespeare's sassy women. 'When they start playing with words,' notes teacher Mimi Paquette, 'they begin to realize how much richer their language can be to describe human emotion.'[20] And it's no exaggeration to say that giving young people the words to express their complicated teenage experiences can prevent them from personal melt-down: 'Teenagers, not famous for their communicativeness, here become eloquent, using jeweled language to express and understand unwieldy emotions like love, anger, betrayal, jealousy, regret, and joy.'[21]

So joyous is their experience that, often after rehearsals, the students don't want to leave:

> they're deeply passionate about what they're doing. [...] And they'll go deeply into it. [...] They learn how to help each other be successful. They learn how to speak, they learn how to think clearly and put their thoughts forward. They learn how to differentiate between their thoughts and their feelings. They don't use language any more like 'I feel bad' or 'I feel good.' They can specifically name what they're feeling.
>
> *(Coleman interview with Taylor Cannon, WHDD Robin*
> *Hood Radio, 2013)*

And (as we touched on in Chapter 9), 'that kind of self-knowledge – that kind of [...] insight into yourself about "Who am I? What do I think?" – that's a tremendously powerful education.'[22] Since the focus is on each *individual's* experience, they *collectively* come to know a multitude of perspectives: which in turn expands their humanity and empathy. And this shared experience is enhanced by a series of *common classes*.

Common classes

Four 'common classes' – focused on non-competitive teambuilding, group learning, creativity and fun – bring the students together from all ten schools. And with 200 or 300 students in each common class, disciplines include *Stage Combat*, Elizabethan *Dance/Movement*, *Technical Production* with publicity and marketing, and finally the common class in *Performance*. The Stage Combat common class is a big favorite with its emphasis on physical discipline and 'making your partner look good.' And it often ends with a big battle with air

FIGURE 10.3 'Air broadswords' in *Stage Combat* common class, 2017
Photo: Olivia Winslow

broadswords, and maybe Macduff's line, 'I have no words. My voice is my sword'[23] (see Figure 10.3). The *Dance/Movement* common class takes the intellectual vagueness out of some of the more strange-sounding phrases, such as 'Most bounteous' or 'Wingéd strife,' by adopting one of John Broome's exercises and incarnating those phrases as physical statues. And the final *Performance* common class may involve each school creating 'a sensational, grab-you-by-the-collar' movie trailer for its show, with soundtrack, mandatory car chase, gratuitous violence, romantic interest, and a tagline – 'the quotable quote like, "This fall, Chucky gets lucky"'[24] (Coleman). All these exercises are designed to help the students own Shakespeare through contemporary, tangible experiences – and to make new friends from the other schools.

Directors' powwows

Friendship isn't just for the students. Throughout the rehearsal period the directors meet for weekly powwows to thrash out who needs help with what – from acting challenges to production necessities, from why all the students are suddenly using bad English accents to who knows a Gregorian chant:

> There's no sense of each show living in a vacuum. In any given week, someone will say, 'This scene is driving me crazy. Hey, you're good at romantic scenes: can you come in and take a look? Who's really good at fight? Could you look at this *Hamlet* duel?' Whatever it may be, we're trading skills, so that it's not 'my show,' it's 'The Festival's Shows.'

(Josh McCabe interview, August 2017)

And as the team heads toward the final week, a preemptive powwow airs every anxiety in collaborative camaraderie:

> 'Our comic scenes are going to be pretty tragic,' voices one director, 'and I think we're going to have some pretty funny tragic scenes, too.' 'Well,' Coleman paused for a moment [and with his tongue planted firmly in his cheek, replied] 'Just put a paragraph in the Directors' Notes about a 'concept'!
>
> *(Coleman cited in Anderson, 1998; Coleman edit July 2019)*

The lead-up

In the final week, the schools debut their show at their own institution, before heading to the TPP with its professional resources. Each school is bussed to the Kemble Street campus for a 45-minute dry tech on one day, and a 90-minute full tech on another. And now the camaraderie between the 20 directors kicks into top gear: there's much ado about figuring where sets go, spiking the floor, adjusting light cues and sound levels,

> and the reason it's doable is that it's not just two directors in there – it's you, me and eighteen collaborators. 'Hey, Jennie, I'm going to spike the floor, so that you can listen to the sound cues.' 'Hey, Josh, you might want that light a little brighter, as it's kinda dark over there.' We're all helping each other.
>
> *(McCabe interview, August 2017)*

The festival itself

The Fall Festival itself is logistical lunacy: cooking, parking, front-of-house management, concessions and an intricate bus schedule bringing all the students to campus. And then – the performances …

For four days – in the chill of November – the Tina Packer Playhouse is packed to the rafters. Each day's Festival participants squeeze into the auditorium like sardines in a can, in what might be the closest you get to an Elizabethan audience. Caitlin Partridge (multi-year, student-participant from Taconic High School) describes it as

> a festival of unrestrained enthusiasm. […] We scream, we laugh, we stomp our feet, we hiss at the villains. A chorus of 'awws' greets the frequent bouts of unrequited [or requited] love. And at the end, we fill the little theater with thunderous, deafening, utterly appreciative applause that I'm sure can be heard from the street.
>
> *(Partridge, C., 'Shakespeare gala a passionate affair: Festival provides a lasting memory,'* The Berkshire Eagle, *9 December 2008)*

202 Education

This *actor/audience relationship* is a heart-pounding manifestation of Shakespeare & Company's ethos. 'We just put all our feelings into the show. The audience can feel what we feel,' says Mohamed El Petitui (an Egyptian exchange student at Mount Everett Regional High).[25] And Ava Lindenmaier (a senior playing King Lear at Monument Mountain Regional High) voiced:

> What happens to [Lear] is so heartbreaking – imagine carrying your own daughter, the only one who was loyal to you and you didn't recognize it, and thus caused her death. [...] I really don't have anything else in my life where I can feel and care so much about someone. Giving these feeling to an *audience* – that's real life.
>
> *(Lindenmaier cited in Scribner, D., 'Offering Fighting & Leaping & Flipping & Swordplay. S&Co. brings the Bard to High School,'* Berkshire Record, *12–18 November 2010, (my emphasis))*

And the adult audience feels the young participants' authentic communication:

> I've never seen anything like this mix of extracurricular activity, English lit course, marathon event, excellent adventure, and free pass to 'a Renaissance world of beautiful language, profound thought, and passionate feeling.' [...]
>
> [I] watch the end of another school's production of *A Midsummer Night's Dream*. It is astonishingly good, and when it's over, the place literally explodes in cheers – stomping and shouting, audience and cast grinning at each other across the footlights. I catch my breath and burst into tears.
>
> God, how happy they are. How lucky. How alive. And how beautiful, how meaningful, how human is theater. How worthy of all that time and energy and effort.
>
> This moment of ecstasy (there's no other word for it) [...] is made possible by virtue of the depth and breadth of talent and experience at Shakespeare & Company.
>
> *(Futterman, E., 'Shakespeare & Company Comes to School,'* Ourtown, *12 November 2015)*

For all involved, it's a four-day 'rock concert' of students shouting for Shakespeare – and for each other. And the only prize is the pride and pleasure they take in each other's work.

Bringing it to a close

For all the cheering, the Festival weekend typically closes in silence, with a ritual Reverence. The Reverence 'extends a gesture up to heaven, down into the earth, looks at the past, embraces the future, holds the heart and offers it to everyone in the room'[26] (Packer). It's a

FIGURE 10.4 Fall Festival, 2017: *As You Like It*, dirs. Lezlie Lee and Ellie Bartz with Springfield Central High School

Photo: Olivia Winslow

> shared expression of gratitude by hundreds of adolescents [and their audience], to Shakespeare, to Shakespeare & Company, and to each other, and is the culmination of [ten] weeks of intense work. It may be wordless, but it is redolent with meaning.
>
> *(Futterman, E., 'Shakespeare & Company Comes to School,'*
> Ourtown, *12 November 2015)*

Within that silence, there's also

> undeniable proof that cooperation and inclusion, the supporting of others and the celebration of the common good creates a model more humane and healing, more effective and productive than the more familiar model of competition; of winning and losing. The participants from these 10 different schools have shown us the model that needs to shape our world's future.
>
> *(Coleman cited in Horst, E., 'S&Co.'s Fall Festival of Shakespeare returns to CHS with "Macbeth,"'* Chatham Courier, *10 November 2011)*

And for the directors and creative teams? 'We celebrate with the students. It's as good as we make it together ... And when it's over, it breaks your heart. That's the only model we know [as human beings].'[27] Once the schools have all disappeared into the chilly, Sunday night, the directors, designers and production team clean up the TPP – before descending on one of their houses for their customary 'Margarita-ville'!

204 Education

The impact

The profound impact of the Fall Festival reverberates long after the lights are dimmed and the margaritas are downed. The *students* reveal: 'These experiences have affected and changed my whole lifestyle. They have helped me grow up and express myself.'[28] And: 'The whole project is particularly meaningful because it helped me figure out me.'[29] The *teachers* note that students' test scores 'increase during this time and feel that they become more focused and organized.'[30] The *parents* describe the program as 'a lifeline,' where their children can explore who they are and at the same time learn about literature, theatre and history: 'It's a priceless, lifelong gift, and the directors share [their professionalism, idealism, and love of Shakespeare] with our teenagers with abundant generosity.'[31] For the young *directors* (many of whom were once student-participants themselves):

> It's the most rewarding job I've ever had in my entire life, watching the young people and seeing how this changes their lives. For a lot of them, it's about having a safe place to go [and] it's a huge commitment for them, on top of their school day. But to see them work so hard on something and then go out there and be so celebrated, and then feel so proud: that's the best!
> *(Caroline Calkins interview, July 2016)*

In fact, the impact of the Fall Festival resonates well beyond the local community. Journalist Richard DiMaggio notes that Shakespeare & Company 'has literally revolutionized learning,' describing the Fall Festival as

> second to none – an event that every single educator in American should come and see. Not only do [S&Co.] get students involved in Shakespeare like nothing I have ever seen, but their techniques can be used across the board, in all topics [...] Now we need the rest of the world to follow its example.
> *(DiMaggio, R., 'Short Description Of Learn All About The Shakes, About The Shakes, No Trouble!'* didyouweekend.com, *(undated), hard copy in S&Co. archive)*

And to some extent it is. For several years Coleman and his wife Lezlie Lee (a longtime Company education artist) have been working with Portland Playhouse, Oregon, on their Fall Festival of Shakespeare. And in 1997 Coleman mounted a similar festival in Jackson, Mississippi:

> Generations of people had been working to keep these kids apart, and we brought them together, and what happened was miraculous. [...] When you see a white middle school on their feet cheering for a predominantly black school, your brain explodes. [...] It changes the way students

interact with other schools, and could change the way people interact in the world.

(Coleman cited in Grady, 1997)

To which end in 2019, under Packer's aegis and in collaboration with Noa Egozi and Ryan Winkles, the Fall Festival model was manifested in a town in Israel, bringing Arab and Israeli students together. The revolution continues ...

Having glimpsed some of the ways in which 'Shakespeare in the Schools' teaches students, let's now turn to how S&Co. teach those who teach.

Professional development for teachers

Vertical training down the generations and horizontal training across the departments are modeled throughout Shakespeare & Company. *Training, Education* and *Performance* all hook back into Kristin Linklater's and Tina Packer's original ideas and idealism, of which a huge part has always been professional development for teachers. There's a collective desire that, at every level, teaching Shakespeare should connect breath to word to image to feeling to expression to audience. And it shouldn't be stuck in the classroom or head!

And so it was that in 1988 an experiment entitled 'The Summer Institute on Teaching Shakespeare'[32] was funded to the tune of $150,000 by the National Endowment for the Humanities. In a custom-built 'Month-Long Intensive,' 24 teachers trained from 8 am till 10 pm Monday through Saturday. And their schedule included components of S&Co.'s professional *Training*, as well as rehearsing scenes, discussing those scenes in terms of personal experience and contemporary America, and lectures on pedagogy by Dr. Carol Gilligan (Harvard Professor of Education: see Chapter 4). The Institute was intended as a two-way 'learning-street': It provided a safe space for teachers to examine their own teaching practices (not to mention exploring, through Shakespeare, their own ribaldry and violence). And in return, Coleman and the *Education* team gained insights into what was going on in classrooms across the nation, especially for teachers seeking alternative methods for teaching students with behavioral problems or challenged skills-levels. Coleman's empathy connected to the ongoing battles teachers face and their inevitable burnout:

Often times [in] the environment of a classroom – the 43 minutes – and the way things are done, there's no permission or support for [teachers] to be alive. And there's very little place for their feelings to have expression. [...] So Shakespeare & Company decided it was time to develop something special for that side of the desk.

(Coleman cited in Bass, R., 'Shakespeare comes alive as teachers take stage,'
The Berkshire Eagle, 7 *August 1988)*

206 Education

Two years later in July 1990, a 'Shakespeare Summer Institute for Teachers' was sponsored by the National Endowment for the Arts in collaboration with the University of Massachusetts, Boston. And at the time of writing, Coleman and his team typically run a Summer Institute in August for two weeks, and other (weekend) workshops for teachers throughout the year. These workshops focus on scholarly enquiry, immersive experiential activities, curricular development, and ways to bring Shakespeare to life for students from grades 4 to 12.[33]

In 2002 – at the height of plans for the reconstructed Rose Playhouse (see Chapter 2) – the *Education* department received \$121,256 from the NEA for a month-long program looking at *Henry V* and *Macbeth* as part of the 'Rose Playhouse Institute.' Under the leadership of Mary Hartman, 24 secondary school teachers from across the nation were selected to participate in the Institute, following five lines of 'playful' enquiry: the players; the plays; the playhouses; the aesthetic of playing; and the playgoers. 'Practical classes conducted by theater professionals, the master-teachers of Shakespeare & Company, in the basic performance skills of voice, movement, and textual analysis augment their study'[34] (Hartman). The core faculty included Julian Bowsher (Museum of London Archeological Services); two British-based professors (Janette Dillon, University of Nottingham; and Andrew Gurr, University of Reading) and two American-based professors (Michael Egan, University of Massachusetts, Amherst; and Franklin Hildy, University of Maryland). The teachers then staged their scenes in the context of the Elizabethan playhouse, assessing how its architecture affected *the actor/audience relationship*: 'By working physically and imaginatively as well as intellectually, they experience Shakespeare's language in the most dynamic and engaging ways. They are more able to translate their experience to their classrooms.'[35] In fact, an invaluable discovery made through this Institute was the direct link between the physical limitations of the Elizabethan playhouse and those of the average classroom:

> A small, bare space with minimal technology, in which the audience is very close to the action, forces our attention on the players and the language. These limitations illuminate the essence of the plays. These limitations closely parallel the physical structure of most school classrooms. In this context, Shakespeare's plays and our exploration of them are distilled to their most potent form.
>
> *(Hartman, 'On Playing Shakespeare in the Classroom,' 2003: 6)*

The valuable lessons learned from the pilot Rose Playhouse Institute have resonated across the Education department's teacher development workshops ever since.

So having brought the teachers onto the campus, now let's bring the students ...

Shakespeare in the Schools **207**

Notes

1 www.shakespeare.org/education/northeast-regional-tour-of-shakespeare (accessed 17 September 2019).
2 Coleman cited in 'A Catalogve [*sic*] of the several Comedies, Histories, and Tragedies presented by Shakespeare & Company,' Autumn 1989. S&Co. archive.
3 www.shakespeare.org/education/elementary-middle-school-tour (accessed 17 September 2019).
4 Rohmann, C. (2012), 'The Bard: 400 Years Young: Demystifying Shakespeare's Language with Jokes and hijinks,' *The Valley Advocate*, 12 April 2012.
5 www.shakespeare.org/education/school-residencies (accessed 15 September 2019).
6 Hartman (2003), p. 4.
7 ibid.
8 Coleman cited in Bevan, K. (2010), 'Getting to Know the Bard: Options in Education,' *The Advocate*, 18 November 2010.
9 Seidel, S. (1999), *'Stand and Unfold Yourself': A Monograph on the Shakespeare & Company Research Study*, p. 84, artsedge.kennedy-center.org/champions/pdfs/Shakespe .pdf.
10 ibid., p.86.
11 Coleman cited in Bass, M. (2005), 'Teaching Shakespeare: Actor/Director Kevin Coleman Finds Satisfaction in Front of the Classroom,' *Berkshires Week*, 15 September 2005. In addition to Lee High and Lenox Memorial High, the regional high schools typically include Chatham, Taconic, Taconic Hills, Springfield Central, Berkshire Waldorf, Mount Greylock, Monument Mountain and Mount Everett.
12 Thursday (two shows), Friday (two shows), Saturday (four shows) and Sunday (two shows).
13 Anderson, M. K. (1998), 'The Complete Work of Shakespeare: Shakespeare & Company's Four Steps for Helping Students Achieve Clarity, Voice and Cool Sound Cues,' *The Valley Advocate*, 26 November 1998.
14 Coleman cited in Grady, M. J. (1997), 'Shakespeare Goes to School,' *Berkshire Record*, 14 November 1997.
15 Wolfe Coleman cited in Dupont, N. (2009), 'Rise Up My Youthful Blood,' *The Advocate*, 21 November 2009.
16 Darren French cited in Futterman, E. (2015), 'Shakespeare & Company Comes to School,' *Ourtown*, 12 November 2015.
17 Taylor-Williams was an actor in the Fall Festival when she was a 5th-grader, and in 2006 she directed her first Fall Festival.
18 Eric C. Williams cited in Horst, E. (2011), 'Discovering Shakespeare,' *The Chatham Press*, December 2011.
19 Jenna Ware cited in Taylor-Williams (2006).
20 Mimi Paquette cited in Berg, E. (2003), 'The Age of Elizabeth,' *Humanities Magazine*, July/August 2003.
21 Burns, D. (2003), 'Fighting the Good Fight,' *The Berkshire Eagle*, 21 November 2003.
22 Coleman interview with WHDD Robin Hood Radio's Taylor Cannon, 2013 Fall Festival.
23 Shakespeare, W. (1606), *Macbeth*, Act V, Scene viii, line 7, Macduff.
24 Coleman cited in Anderson (1998).
25 Mohamed El Petitui cited in Smith, J. (2009), 'Saving Shakespeare,' *The Berkshire Eagle*, 19 November 2009.
26 Tina Packer discussion with Bella Merlin, December 2018. As *Movement/Dance* faculty Victoria Rhoades describes, 'The word "reverence" comes from "a gesture of respect" and it is a term used at the end of formal dance classes like Ballet. At the end of all of my ballet classes growing up, we closed with a "reverence" – there were always certain predictable gestures, but it could be anything really that helped

208 Education

to end/close the class. It always had a reflective, more adagio type of feel to it' (Rhoades email correspondence with Merlin, 19 June 2019).

27 Coleman cited in Anderson (1998).

28 'Fall Festival of Shakespeare: Quotations from Students, Educators and Parents': osric: edu\ffs\general\quotes.doc. Hard copy S&Co. archive.

29 Heather Duquette cited in Murray, L. (2010), 'Shakespeare & Company's Fall Festival Underway,' *berkshireonstage.com*, 21 October 2010.

30 Hoffman, T. (2008), 'Letter to the Editor: Shakespeare Program Hones Many Skills,' PTO president for Taconic Hill High School, 28 November 2008.

31 Burns, D. *et al.* (2001), 'Shakespeare a Hit at Greylock' Letter to the Editor, *North Adams Transcript* on 10 November 2001. S&Co. archive.

32 Later known as the National Institute for Teaching Shakespeare.

33 www.shakespeare.org/education/professional-development-workshops (accessed 14 September 2019). Over the years, the workshops have included 'Classroom as Theatre' (led by Coleman and Packer, looking at teaching as an art form and the teacher-actor/student-audience relationship); 'Education in Action: Playing Shakespeare in the Classroom' (helping teachers ignite students with the beauty and power of Shakespeare's language); 'Teachers and Actors: Putting Shakespeare in the Hands of Adolescents'; and Clown workshops (led by Jane Nichols).

34 Hartman, M. (2003), 'On Playing Shakespeare in the Classroom,' *CBE Basic Education Online Edition*, March/April 2003, Vol. 47, No. 3, p. 5.

35 ibid., p. 6.

11

SHAKESPEARE ON THE CAMPUS

Shakespeare & Company's *Education* department has several programs that bring young actors to Kemble Street. So in this chapter we join them on the campus ...

Riotous Youth[1]

It's June 2016 and I'm sitting in the Rose Footprint tent watching a 7-year-old give a searing rendition of a role I'm performing in the main season. When this tiny thespian delivers a particularly bothersome line, I suddenly learn how it should be played! That's the power of Riotous Youth.

Riotous Youth is a Shakespeare summer camp founded in 1999 by education artists Karen Torbjornsen and John Beale. And the program came into its own in 2002, after S&Co. moved to Kemble Street with its multiple rehearsal spaces. It operates in two-week blocks three times throughout the summer on a first-come-first-served application basis, with three groups in each block: 7–9-year-olds; 10–12-year-olds; and 13–15-year-olds. Each group has two team-teachers plus an intern, who adopt a play (typically from the main summer season). And in exploring the play's theme, story, language and characters, they apply modified tasters of the professional *Training* (*Voice*, *Text*, *Movement* and some *Fight* and *Clown*). On the second Friday of each block, the groups share their 45-minute renditions on the Rose Footprint stage, joyfully anticipated by family and friends (not to mention the casts of the main productions, eager – as I was – to gain some innocents' insights). By the end of the summer, over a hundred young actors have filled the rehearsal rooms and fields at S&Co. and trodden the Rose Footprint boards. Given the potential riotousness of these youths, the education artists at the helm have a particular preparation of their own.

210 Education

Preparing the Riotous Youth leaders

As with all the *Education* programs, the Riotous Youth leaders have at some point taken the Month-Long Intensive or the STI. In addition to their own theatre degrees, they've worked with the Company in various capacities, often including extensive mentorship. In turn the Riotous Youth leaders provide mentorship during the program to the college-age apprentices, who are usually graduates or interns from Shakespeare & Young Company (more anon). And these apprentices serve as teaching staff and administrative support, leading warm ups, running games and keeping the daily log. Ultimately all the Riotous Youth leaders and their assistants are guided by the comprehensive Handbook, which foregrounds the *Education* programs' practical pedagogy:

> When young people encounter Shakespeare as *actors*, they experience it in the most engaging, compelling, and personally meaningful way. They meet characters that inspire them. They tell stories that capture their imaginations. And they learn language that helps them make sense of and articulate their own thoughts and feelings, thereby improving their ability to communicate in constructive ways.
>
> *(Riotous Youth Handbook, 2014: 2, (my emphasis))*

Also highlighted are the benefits (touched on in Chapter 9) of teaching Shakespeare to children as young as 7, who

> already possess the passion, curiosity, and feeling required to play Shakespeare. They are uniquely suited to understand and illuminate his stories. By offering a joyful, collaborative experience of playing Shakespeare we empower them to discover the [...] richness of the English language and, through that language, to examine and celebrate our common humanity.
>
> *(Riotous Youth Handbook, 2014: 2)*

In preparing for that common humanity, the leaders and interns convene for a weeklong 'June Prep' just before the program begins. In addition to their own *Training*, they edit the plays and select relevant monologues, character tableaux and images. They update the educational and logistical information. They replenish art supplies. They make scrap-paper journals for the riotous ones to fill in at the end of each day (*Journaling* and reflection are as relevant here as they are in the *Training*). Last but not least they order the annual Riotous Youth tee shirts, which serve as the brightly colored basics for the final-performance costumes. There's certainly much ado about many a deal. And that's just the start of it ...

Running Riotous Youth

From Monday to Friday the three age groups meet for six hours. For every two-week block, the education artists follow a similar schedule, with each day having a very clear goal and suggested activities for achieving that goal. And, as with *Training*, structure is vital:

> The kind of play required when working on Shakespeare can be challenging. In order for the students to respond sincerely and play fully it is essential that a structure be created that allows for safe exploration and failure. The safer each child feels the farther and faster [they] will go to where you are inviting them.
>
> *(Riotous Youth Handbook, 2014: 28)*

And repeated *rituals* are part of that structure ...

The rituals

The 'rituals' stem directly from the *Training*, including *checking in* at the beginning of the day (so that each child has a moment in the spotlight); warming up; and *reinforcing* at the end of each day (so that each child has the opportunity to strengthen something positive from that day).

So, why do people as young as 7 need to *check in*?

Three experienced, Company education artists – Rory Hammond, Caitlin Kraft and Caroline Calkins – shared their insights, explaining that, even if it's as brief as one sentence or ten seconds, *checking in* helps the children start tuning into and appreciating what they're feeling. In a circle (which instantly shifts the teacher–student hierarchy) one person begins talking while the others listen. They speak as long as they need and then they turn to the person on their left or right and say that person's name. That person then speaks for as long as they need before turning to the next person. And so it goes around the circle until everyone – including the education artists – has spoken. This framework for expressing feelings and listening to others helps the children learn to differentiate between their feelings and their thoughts, an important part of Kevin G. Coleman's philosophy (see Chapter 9). After all, 'careful attention to the language we use creates better communication, better learning, and develops emotional intelligence and vocabulary.'[2] For the children this is a huge journey of self-discovery, so the education artists guide them on their way by offering up lists of adjectives such as 'excited, nervous, sad, ecstatic, anxious.' For the younger groups, metaphors can be useful: 'If you were a color right now, what color would you be?' 'Let us know how you are feeling in this moment by using the terms of a weather report (e.g., it's cloudy now but there's a chance of sun later this evening).' 'In this moment, are you feeling more like a bird, a lion or a muffin?'[3] The children 'might not have the tools to name "I'm angry" –

212 Education

but they do know they feel like a lion. So these clues are very telling'[4] (Calkins). If the children default to, 'I'm fine. I'm good. I'm okay' (which are basically thought-based judgments, rather than precisely named feelings), then the team leader might respond, 'That could mean different things for each of us. What does "good" or "fine" mean to you? What's the emotion word that you can use instead to describe how *you* feel?'[5] (Kraft). Thus, for all its simplicity, *checking in* actually develops all manner of complex human skills: such as emotional intelligence, awareness, deep listening and empathy. And because it gives everyone a chance to speak before the work begins (and for the shyer ones it may be the first time that day that they've spoken or been listened to), everyone comes to understand what others are experiencing each day.[6] And it gives the children who aren't so good at listening a chance to practice that skill, too.

So, why do children as young as 7 need to *reinforce*?

Again, the answers are pedagogically multi-faceted. First of all, the ritual of *reinforcing* brings the group together at the end of a working day to reflect for a moment on what they've learned. Some of their experiences can be pretty impactful, so it's important for them to have the opportunity to say something about it, rather than carry on as if it never happened. Second, it ensures that whatever they've experienced that day can be intentionally framed as something positive, rather than self-effacing or ironic (which can otherwise be the case, particularly with the older age groups). Third, it models for the education artists practical pedagogy, as they adjust to the group in front of them:

> With the 7–9-year-olds, I might say, 'What was something that you really enjoyed today? Maybe it's not lunch or recess!' And with the older kids, who may be navigating complicated group dynamics, 'What would you like to reinforce that you saw somebody else do today?'
>
> *(Rory Hammond interview, August 2016)*

Ultimately, *reinforcement* 'helps bond the group in future action, express gratitude, appreciation or thanks. *Reinforcement* is another opportunity to practice empathy, to listen, to speak, to be human.'[7] This kind of positive *reinforcement* is vital with a discipline as vulnerable as acting, not least because the children can 'explore the idea that it is OK to not be perfect or right but to just *play with the story*.'[8]

Playing with the story

'Playing with the story' is no small journey and it starts by choosing a role. Just as the remit of the Month-Long Intensive is 'Be the author of your own journey,' the remit for Riotous Youth is 'Pick your own adventure!' So as early as Day #1 or #2 the children are asked to fill in a form indicating their top choices for the characters they'd like to play or 'I WILL TAKE ANY PART THAT YOU THINK I WILL HAVE FUN PLAYING.' That said – and no matter how painstakingly each play is cast –

Shakespeare on the campus **213**

a few tears may be shed, especially among the younger ones. Ever resourceful, the directors have all kinds of creative responses up their sleeves, such as: 'Mustardseed is an undercover agent for Oberon' and 'Puck is short for "Puckerella," clearly a female character.'[9] And before long everyone is excited about their role.

Once the roles are cast the focus is on freeing the children's personalities, rather than performing the perfect rendition. So directing follows the S&Co. model of being curious and creating experiences, such as 'How might you be feeling *right now?*' Or – with the younger actors – giving them simple tasks such as:

> 'Name three feelings you imagine you might be feeling.' 'Love! Joy! Anger!' they might reply. To which the director might say, 'Okay, here's the backpack of love! The ball of joy! The hoodie of anger! Now go to the extremes of physical expression with these props whenever you say the feeling-words.' And the children get to where it's 'Choose your own adventure.' They get to leap to those experiences themselves.
>
> *(Caitlin Kraft interview, August 2016)*

Because it's all about inviting meaningful experiences, the directors offer feedback in an equally non-judgmental, curious way, with questions such as:

> 'What just happened between you?' 'What feelings came up for you when you said that text?' 'What feelings came up for you when you heard what the other character said to you?' 'Did anything surprise you?' 'What can we do to make the scene even more exciting?'
>
> *(Riotous Youth Handbook, 2014: 36)*

As we saw in Chapter 9, the meaningful experience always outweighs the perfect scene. And that meaningful experience is important for the education artists, too; so throughout the program the *peer mentoring* continues.

Ongoing mentorship

In various ways Riotous Youth is a focused training-ground for young educators. First thing each morning there's a mandatory meeting, which 'is critical to staying connected as a team.'[10] Teaching in and of itself can be something of an acting exercise. So the daily ritual of *checking in* for the education artists gives them the opportunity to express any challenges they might be facing, so that they can hold 'stuff' at arms' length once the young participants arrive. The meetings also provide an invaluable support mechanism, as the leaders and apprentices discuss and evolve their own pedagogical self-reflections: 'It's our responsibility to actively *hold the space* at all times'[11] (Calkins).

214 Education

Holding the space

Holding the space is another practice drawn from mindfulness and non-violent communication as a means of being consciously present to others, and allowing and being protective of what others in the group need.[12] Right across Shakespeare & Company, it's used in *Training* by the teacher-trainees, in *Performance* by the assistant directors, and in *Education* by the team-teachers (education artists and interns). And it's all about: keeping an eye on the whole room while the main teacher (or director) is working; taking the energetic temperature of the room in terms of checking that all the participants are fine; and modeling honesty and integrity in the work. If a participant clearly isn't sure what they're doing or is having an emotionally charged experience, the 'space-holders' (like stabilizers) '*reinforce* something helpful and aim to re-balance the space'[13] (Packer). 'Which is part of the joy of team-teaching. We're all "on" all the time' – for the students and for each other'[14] (Calkins). They continue this reflective process through daily logs, in which each team notes 'What we are doing and How it is working' including the exercises they used and how well the session went. They're then able to share particular successes and challenges in their daily *check-in*. And part of this ongoing practical pedagogy involves them exchanging insights into the ways in which the different age groups learn.

Learning about learning

Each of the three age groups brings various pleasures, as well as revealing aspects of being human in the twenty-first century.

In many respects *the 7–9-year-olds* require least from the teachers. They're naturally playful. Their imaginations are vibrant. And Shakespeare's plays often

> make complete and total sense to them 'Of course I'm the King! Of course I'm the Queen of the Fairies.' The bigness of the worlds is a perfect land for them. And as long as I, as a director, give them one anchor-point to hang on to and walk them through the text so they know what they're saying, I don't have to add anything. I can just say, 'Go and be free to use your wonderful 7-year-old imaginations!'
>
> *(Caroline Calkins interview, August 2016)*

This experience of sharing Shakespeare with such willing imaginations brings its own rewards to the education artists:

> Giving them that language to express themselves – to express the specificity of extreme love, rage, whatever it is – is so important, because it's saying, 'It's okay to have those feelings. And it's okay to express them in this environment.' The way most teachers or parents are 'Authority Figures' doesn't necessarily lend itself to creativity or self-expression. So it's

really delightful to watch these kids express themselves and experience, 'Wow! I just said that out loud in front of everyone!'

(Hammond interview, August 2016)

(There is, indeed, something very delicious about hearing an 8-year-old saying 'pernicious'!) And the children's willingness to express themselves extends to the broader goals of building human community: 'If we could just get *this small group* to be curious about leading with love and compassion and an open mind – then maybe, when they're older, things will be different in the world'[15] (Kraft).

By the time the children reach *10–12 years*, something shifts:

> This is often when their awareness of 'Oh, people are watching me' starts to happen. 'I need to control and monitor what I'm doing. And I may be less willing to be big and bold and playful.' And sometimes it can be heartbreaking to have seen a kid when they're nine, and then they come back and they're ten, and they're having a completely different experience of the world.
>
> *(Calkins interview, August 2016)*

And that different experience has often been compounded by their transition to middle school. Their self-consciousness impacts on their self-expression and can subtly disconnect them from their own authenticity. They may either make their acting very underplayed and self-effacing, or they may exaggerate and play in high-performance mode: 'And I think it's because in their bodies there's a sense of "What the heck is going on?"'[16] (Kraft). And so their acting becomes a kind of inadvertent 'mock of what the moment should be because, "I don't really know what I'm feeling: so I'm going to do this"'[17] (Hammond). To ease them through their self-effacement, the education artists keep moving with compassion: 'One of the things we talk a lot about in our training is "meeting the children where they are." In other words, teaching the *student* as opposed to teaching the *material*'[18] (Calkins). And that means helping the individuals strike a personal win, with 'a feeling of, "Oh, I did it!" And if that means they get four lines of text more to learn, or four lines less, it's fine. It's all part of what the child needs'[19] (Hammond). After all: 'Sometimes just standing up by themselves on stage and saying their monologue is a huge win'[20] (Kraft). Therefore, the educators won't push them to do something they might not want to do for fear their peers will laugh at them: 'At the same time, if I can metaphorically hold their hand and let them step out of that self-consciousness a little bit through the magic of pretending – then great!'[21] (Calkins).

The *13–15-year-olds* are another ballgame entirely. Many of them have participated in Fall Festival, so the education artists can work with them more deeply on the wit and clarity of the texts. Some have participated in Riotous Youth for six or seven sessions, so they can be nudged a little further. Others

216 Education

are old enough to have done quite a bit of theatre at school and have a real notion of what acting means to them – not least some (restrictive) ideas inherited from their teachers about what Shakespeare should be. So

> this can be when we start feeding in new ideas: 'What if you *didn't* decide exactly what you were going to do onstage before performance? What if you didn't use that English-accent voice but allowed your own self to speak? Maybe then you could really engage with your partner and be different each time?'
>
> *(Calkins interview, August 2016)*

Riotous Company

As well as these three colorful age groups, there's a fourth team comprising 15–17-year-olds, who come together for three weeks in August to form Riotous Company. All of them have participated in at least two previous sessions of Riotous Youth or another S&Co. experience such as the Fall Festival of Shakespeare (see Chapter 10). And applicants have to write a letter explaining why they're interested in returning. There's always an overflow of applications and long waiting lists, not least because of the serious-mindedness of the program, which is a mini-version of the professional *Training* (albeit significantly modified). For many there's a stronger focus on acting as a potential choice for college, and scenes are specifically chosen for them by the education artists. Because the participants are that bit older, the educators strive to challenge them a little further; so, there's a greater awareness of articulating word and thought. And there's even a taste of *Basics* (see Chapter 6):

> We might start feeding in the idea of having a real feeling on stage, and that it's okay to feel that feeling. In other words, some of them may actually have the experience of speaking Shakespeare and genuinely connecting with the language. And while some kids won't be ready for that, some kids do it automatically.
>
> *(Calkins interview, August 2016)*

Which takes us to *performance* …

Riotous Youth performances

On the last Friday of each program, the Rose Footprint is packed with family, friends and Company members, all watching the young Shakespeareans in interpretations they may never have seen before. Each participant performs a monologue (c. 7–9 lines for the youngest groups and 10–12 lines for the oldest) and a scene (c. 5–12 lines per actor for the youngest and 12–18 lines per actor for the oldest). Speeches are split between multiple voices. Several actors play the same role in different scenes. Some even deliver the same speech, with ne'er a creak of competition. And with non-traditional casting right across the board, they all have their moment to play with the poetry: 7-year-olds play sages and soothsayers, young girls play rulers of Rome, anyone can play any gender. And 'making it live' is far more important than 'getting it right.' If a tragic scene turns comic, fantastic! If an actor needs a prompt, it's 'business as usual.' And just as Shakespeare's own view of humanity teetered between outrage and compassion, so the Riotous Youth tug *the actor/audience relationship* in myriad, experiential directions. They woo with guileless pleasure. They stamp their feet and insult the 'crook back.' They clatter the consonants of 'couldst' and 'wouldst.' They help each other out when they forget their lines. They run through the audience and out into the meadows with battles and dances and shivering shipwrecks. They're present and unpretentious, as they give themselves permission to pitch for the pounding passions.

Throughout each performance the team leaders serve as narrators, filling in the necessary plot and linking the scenes together to the beat of a bodhrán. At the same time, they're learning from their youthful protégés:

> I see the kids fall into habits that *I* fall into. So watching them opens my brain to think about what I do on stage. And that freedom in their imaginations – coming up with all kinds of wonderfully insane choices – I strive to have that openness in my own imagination.
>
> *(Kraft interview, August 2016)*

'Their sheer playfulness – especially with the younger group – is an inspiration'[22] (Calkins). And:

> The most important thing that I learn, from having grown up here,[23] is to have humility as an actor. And I ask myself all the time, 'If I actually start from zero, what will my performance be like?' What if I actually approach this afresh from, 'I have no idea what's going on. Let's figure it out.' And that's what the Riotous Youth teach you: 'Let's have fun, and see what happens.'
>
> *(Hammond interview, August 2016)*

Performances over, each group reconvenes with their team leaders and interns for a farewell *reinforcement*. Riotous Youth is a big experience for many of the participants and they need a space to give it closure: 'I often say, "This is our final reinforcement. So say whatever you need to say so that we can move on joyfully to the next adventure"'[24] (Calkins).

And for many, the next adventure may be returning to Kemble Street in future years as part of *Shakespeare & Young Company* ...

218 Education

FIGURE 11.1 Riotous Youth rehearsing, 2016
Photo: Ava G. Lindenmaier

Shakespeare & Young Company conservatories

During the summer season a network of young adults weave together the fabric of the campus. Booking tickets in the box office. Selling concessions. Galvanizing the gala. Directing drivers to parking lots. And entertaining audiences in the Rose Footprint. They're the members of Shakespeare & Young Company, Summer Conservatory. The Young Company began in August 1982 when Coleman directed *Comedy of Errors* outdoors at The Mount with a cast of 15 people, whose average age was 20. And at that point, it operated as an Apprentice/Intern program:[25]

> The idea of the apprenticeship is that the hard work and dedication will pay off later in professional recognition. Apprenticeship began in the Middle Ages but the practice has continued through the Elizabethan Age and even into the present. Interestingly enough, William Shakespeare began his career in the theatre as an apprentice actor.
>
> What makes Shakespeare & Company's Apprentice/Intern Program so unique is the priority and careful emphasis we place on our training. The Apprentice/Interns are exposed to and experience daily the philosophy behind Shakespeare & Company.
>
> ('Macbeth *Playbill*,' 1982. S&Co. archive)

So although the participants in 1982 took classes, they were also offered a firsthand experience of the 'artist manager' structure that maintained the Company for years.[26] Today it operates as two Conservatories:

The Spring Conservatory begins with auditions in December shortly after Fall Festival, and draws local applicants from all ten schools who are interested in

Shakespeare on the campus **219**

further training. Typically around 30 participants meet at Kemble Street twice a week between February and April, with classes focusing on ensemble building, *Voice*, *Text*, *Movement/Dance*, *Clown* and *Fight*. And the experience culminates in May with two performances in the TPP.

The Summer Conservatory was formally founded in 1991 to provide nine weeks of *Training* to 12 students, aged 16–20 from around the country. As program director Tom Jaeger describes, it had quickly become evident 'that there were a lot of people in that age range who would like to take more training, especially looking at Shakespeare's texts, and there really wasn't a place for them to do that.'[27] Auditions are held between March and May, and the Mission Statement for the program reads:

> The Young Company [Conservatory] is designed to develop young actors as theater artists who will thrive as contributing members of a company. Shakespeare & Company was founded on the belief that the finest theater is made by actors who have ownership in the creative process of the theatrical event. Our training develops the skills necessary to be open, spontaneous and to effectively communicate thoughts and feelings in an ensemble environment. Alumni of Shakespeare & Young Company are sought after not only for their talent and skills, but also for the collaborative spirit they bring to any studio or rehearsal room.
>
> *('Shakespeare & Young Company, Summer Conservatory: General*
> *Information Pack')*

The Conservatory plunges the participants deep into S&Co.'s methodology, with a taste of all three strands of *Training*, *Education* and *Performance*. And – as the idea of apprenticeship or internship intimates – they're given the chance to contribute to the running of the Company. So half the week (around 20 hours) is spent in classes, lectures, rehearsals, talkbacks and performances. And the other half involves administrative and customer-service roles.

Involvement with the Company

Those roles may involve being part of the Front of House team and facilitating the annual community picnic on 4 July (known as 'We Hold These Truths'), which includes the public reading of the Declaration of Independence. (In recent years this has involved Conservatory participants and Company members reading from authors and orators including W. E. B. Du Bois and Barack Obama.) Often the Conservatory members also serve as interns for Riotous Youth. And through these opportunities the participants experience the rich tapestry of Shakespeare & Company's life: 'they're recognized as members of the Company for the summer – and that's how they perceive themselves. So it's not just their inner journey: it's their professional journey, as they get to understand how the Company has to operate'[28] (Rhoades). Indeed, they're really given a pre-professional experience, providing

220 Education

FIGURE 11.2 Summer Conservatory 2019: *King John*, dirs. Caroline Calkins, Rory Hammond, Tom Jaegar, with participants Ashli Funches (King John) and Eliza Carson (Queen Elinor), Rose Footprint

Photo: Zachary De Silva

them with skills to walk into job interviews or acting auditions with confidence and flair, and sometimes going on to audition for S&Co.'s Northeast Regional Tours. But before that, they have their own performances …

Preparing for performance

The Summer Conservatory culminates in two performances in the Rose Footprint. As with all Shakespeare & Company's *Training* and *Education* programs, the emphasis is less on product and more on process and individual growth. Which is why it's crucial to choose the right material. And the choice of roles usually comes from conversations with the participants: 'What interests you? What have you not worked on that you want to? What scares the hell out of you that you would really prefer to avoid?'[29] (McCabe). Frequently the script is a compilation piece looking at a particular theme from various Shakespeare plays or the subplot of a play turned into the main plot. Sometimes it's the distillation of a whole play. And the point is two-fold: 'to challenge all the students with playing more than one character' and to afford them 'the opportunity to become familiar with more than one script.'[30]

The experience of public performance itself is a very important transition for the Conservatory participants. While of course their tutors want them to have a good show, the real purpose is to try out in front of an audience all the new tools that they've been acquiring for nine weeks and to avoid reverting back to old, safe habits:

It's a real challenge for these young people, because they're at an age where they're coming out of an academic setting where they're rewarded for getting things right and punished for getting things wrong. They're very judgmental of themselves. And they tend to pull their focus inward. If they've finished rehearsing a scene and I say, 'Let's try *this* now,' I can see them go to a place of, 'Oh? I failed! I suck!' So playing in a place where there is no 'right' and 'wrong' is a particular challenge for them.

(Victoria Rhoades interview, July 2016)

Ergo, when they do dare to go beyond 'trying to get it right' in performance the experience is thrilling for everyone. This was certainly the case with the 2019 performance of *King John* directed by Hammond, Calkins and Jaeger, modeling clarity of *Text*, *Fight*, *Clown*, multi-gender and multi-racial casting, and a celebration of heart-rending storytelling.

From King John's court in England to the juvenile courts of New England, for our final *Education* program …

Notes

1 So named after Angelo's reference to Claudio in *Measure for Measure* (1604), Act IV, Scene iv, line 29.
2 Riotous Youth Handbook, 26 May 2014 p. 30.
3 Riotous Youth Handbook, p. 31.
4 Caroline Calkins interview with Bella Merlin, August 2016.
5 Caitlin Kraft interview with Bella Merlin, August 2016.
6 Riotous Youth Handbook., p. 30.
7 ibid., p. 32.
8 ibid., p. 62 (my emphasis).
9 ibid., p. 27.
10 ibid., p. 19.
11 Calkins interview, August 2016.
12 Cf. Brady, A., 'Holding the Space: The Art of Being Present with Others,' chopra.com. articles/holding-the-space-the-art-of-being-present-with-others (accessed 23 September 2019).
13 Packer notes, March 2019.
14 Calkins interview, August 2016.
15 Caitlin Kraft interview with Bella Merlin, August 2016.
16 ibid.
17 Rory Hammond interview with Bella Merlin, August 2016.
18 Calkins interview, August 2016.
19 Hammond interview, August 2016.
20 Kraft interview, August 2016.
21 Calkins interview, August 2016.
22 ibid.
23 Rory Hammond is the daughter of S&Co. actors Diane Prusha and Michael Hammond: she literally grew up at The Mount, along with Riley Hadden (John Hadden and Susan Dibble's son), Hamish Linklater (Kristin Linklater's son), Finn and Dylan Wittrock (Peter Wittrock and Kate Crowley's sons), and Wolfe and Tiger Coleman (Ariel Bock and Kevin Coleman's sons). Collectively they used to perform as Shakespeare & Very Young Company.

222 Education

24 Calkins interview, August 2016.
25 The program ran as an internship for a while, before evolving in 1987 into a training program run by John Hadden, then an iteration for more experienced actors known as the 'Summer Performance Institute' (SPI), and later a 'Performance Internship Program' (PIP).
26 Classes included *Movement* with Susan Dibble, *Voice* with Zoë Alexander, *Clown* with Merry Conway, *Text* with Dennis Krausnick, *Fight* with B. H. Barry and Ellen Salland, and seminars with the Company's then resident psychologist John Werhle.
27 Tom Jaeger interview with Bella Merlin, August 2016.
28 Victoria Rhoades interview with Bella Merlin, July 2016.
29 Josh McCabe interview with Bella Merlin, August 2017.
30 'Why Compilation Pieces?' from Shakespeare & Young, Summer Conservatory performance program, 2016. Over the years, many compilation pieces have been created by directors Ware, Croy, Jaeger and Jadow, including *Sweet Division* (drawn from *Romeo and Juliet* and *A Midsummer Night's Dream*); *Fringed Curtains* (drawn from *Macbeth* and *The Tempest*); *To Be or To Become* (*Hamlet* through Ophelia's eyes); *Marina* (drawn from *Pericles*); *Love Dance* (drawn from various texts about love, with music and movement), *Distract* (exploring madness in *Macbeth*, *Hamlet* and *King John*), *The Journey of Margaret* (drawn from the 'Henry VI' plays) and *In Another Part of the Forest* (adapted from *A Midsummer Night's Dream*).

12

SHAKESPEARE IN THE COURTS

One of the epithets of the *Education* department is: 'Shakespeare belongs in everyone's hands'[1] (Hartman). And perhaps nowhere is that theory more tested than in 'Shakespeare in the Courts'. At the heart of this challenging program for juvenile offenders is a key figure in Shakespeare & Company's evolution, The Honorable Paul E. Perachi.

How it all began

Paul Perachi had been an algebra teacher and athletics coach at Lenox Memorial High School before becoming Principal in 1970. And in this position he found himself liaising with lawyers, be it in disciplinary issues with students or collective bargaining with teachers.[2] So in 1978 he decided to take a law degree at night school and on retiring from education he became a fulltime attorney. In 1997 he was appointed First Justice in the Trial Court of the Commonwealth Juvenile Court Department, Berkshire division. And then his association with S&Co. took a significant turn …

For years he had witnessed the impact made by Shakespeare & Company in Berkshire County schools. He saw how young people flourished under the Company's demand for excellence, and their sense of self soared as they expressed themselves through Shakespeare (not least, through stage fighting): 'Because of Shakespeare, Perachi realized that any role – and any role *change* – is within a person's reach: The fighter can become the healer, the slacker become the scholar. The bad boy become the prince.'[3] So for several years he brainstormed with Kevin Coleman and Mary Hartman to find ways of manifesting a Shakespeare juvenile program, which would be less about great performances and more about personal change. In February 2001 a pilot 'Juvenile Youth Project'

224 Education

was funded by the NEA's 'Creative Links: Positive Alternatives for Youth' along with generous donations from the Bernstein Rubin family. Perachi believed this pilot could give troubled youngsters higher self-esteem, better communication skills and an outlet for aggression. 'Some [kids] have never had the opportunity to do something positive, so they seek attention through negative acts'[4] (Perachi). So the pilot would be a 'cog in the wheel' to provide them with that positive opportunity. And his long-term hope was that by empowering the young offenders in everything from choosing their own costumes to performing in front of an audience 'they'll begin to see being on stage is a lot more fun than getting in trouble.'[5]

The project began with two-hour meetings on Tuesdays and Thursdays for 12 weeks. And for a reduction in community-service hours, 12 young juveniles were given the opportunity to be 'sentenced' to Shakespeare. Jonathan Croy and Jenna Ware led the sessions, beginning with theatre games and ensemble-building exercises, eventually leading to rehearsals of scenes from *Hamlet*.[6] And they soon saw that, far from being frightening delinquents, these were disenchanted teenagers who had constantly experienced failure and were afraid of failing again. So the practical pedagogy of S&Co. – with its emphasis on self-discovery and personal responsibility – was in many ways a perfect 'punishment.' Obviously there were challenges: three participants dropped out (well, Shakespeare can be tough!) and, when several participants reoffended in the first year, there was some circumspection about the project's effectiveness. But when the implicit values were analyzed as much as the explicit ones, the pilot was deemed a success.[7] Nearly 20 years later there are now two six-week programs each spring operating out of Pittsfield and its environs. The teams work on *Text*, *Voice*, *Movement* and *Stage Combat*. And the final performance is a 50-minute montage of scenes from a Shakespeare play. In 2006 'Shakespeare in the Courts' received the White House's 'Coming Up Taller' Award from the President's Committee on the Arts and Humanities:

> Using Shakespeare's text, teacher artists guide the participants through a process of self-discovery, through which students consider their choices as actors in a scene. The teens translate that process to their life choices, and learn about the power they can exert over their futures. As these young people transition from 'acting out' to acting, they develop a sense of accomplishment while gaining respect and recognition from the adults in their lives.
> *(Press Release, 'Shakespeare & Company Celebrates National* Coming Up Taller *Award,' 1 February 2007)*

So, who are the young people whom this experience might transform?

The participants

The eligible juveniles are predominantly 'good kids who just screwed up'[8](Perachi) by committing a petty offense (such as truancy, breaking and entering, or possession of a dangerous weapon). Coming from diverse educational and ethnic backgrounds, they're selected by their probation officers, defense lawyers and district attorneys. And ultimately they're all in need of some help. 'They are also at an age when they are receptive to services.'[9] And if they have a positive experience through a judicial service – in which they complete something, communicate with each other and see the benefit of making better decisions – Perachi upholds that's value enough. Certainly S&Co.'s practical pedagogy offers them gold-dust: learning to articulate their thoughts and feelings; respecting other people's feelings; committing to and collaborating with each other; and bolstering each other's achievement within a group. And perhaps one of the most direct ways in which S&Co.'s education artists can help them is in *making better life-choices* …

Making better choices

Acting is all about making choices: 'What does this character do within these given circumstances? And why?' And when it comes to the juveniles in the Courts Project, Coleman's understanding of adolescence brings even more insight:

> I believe that often they make the best choice they can *in that circumstance* to survive. So – a cop car drives by. The girl on the corner lifts up her shirt and flashes the officer. It was a bad choice – because she's going to be stopped and she's going to be arrested.
>
> *(Coleman interview, August 2016)*

But when this girl talked about the incident in the Courts Project, Coleman saw there was something honest in her choice:

> Her exposing herself was a kind of 'Fuck you for staring at me!' That's what was going on for her. She wasn't thinking of the outcome. But what was going on for the cop was very different. And that miscommunication got the girl into trouble. These young people are making choices with some painful or dangerous consequences – but sometimes the choices that they make speak more truthfully to something healthy about them. Lifting her shirt speaks that this girl was protesting to being objectified. Sometimes these are healthy choices from their point of view given their limited judgment or situational awareness, but you have to *find* the healthiness in it.
>
> *(Coleman interview, August 2016)*

Finding that healthiness – and then expanding the young people's self-knowledge to make better choices for their longer-term survival – is in many ways at the heart of the Courts Project. So how does S&Co. go about it?

226 Education

The logistics

Sessions are held in a church-hall two blocks from the Pittsfield courthouse and across the street from the police station (just in case!). Typically two education artists (directors) lead the sessions (often mixed genders to balance the energies in the room, for example Jennie M. Jadow and Josh McCabe, who team-taught for several years). And they're backed up by a dedicated probation team (including Chief of Probation William Gale), who help with behavioral issues.

The first day

'When the teenagers come in on the first day, they're angry, impatient and in shock that they really have to do Shakespeare – or go back to court for re-sentencing'[10] (Coleman). They don't want to do Shakespeare because it's difficult material. And like most teenagers, they're terrified of public speaking: 'So we walk in. Their arms are crossed. They're scowling at us'[11] (McCabe). And they're doubly angry because they have to render up their cell phones, which are not only the most expensive (maybe the only) things they own, but also their main way of communicating, so here they're going to have to communicate face to face. To quell the adversarial atmosphere the directors cannily begin by telling the teenagers that Shakespeare was a rebel and, if he were around today, he probably would've ended up in juvenile court. Straightaway the young offenders glimpse a *personal connection* to Shakespeare and a potential credibility in performing him. And (for Coleman) they're certainly capable of performing Shakespeare – if they're given the chance in the right *learning environment* ...

The learning environment

The right environment means establishing the right rules. And these rules are strict – because the stakes are high. If the students succeed in this program – by showing up, showing respect and participating in the rehearsals and performance – they could finish their probation early. And if they fail to participate – they could get jail-time. So endorsing the rules needs its own particular use of language: 'We talk to them like adults and we listen to them like adults. Something as simple as that is pretty huge'[12] (McCabe). So they use no-nonsense toughness, humor and support: after all, they're not the authority here, the court is. They're just here to direct a play.[13]

Treating the teenagers like adults also entails forming a 'company agreement,' which includes being punctual and being respectful. The juveniles word it and vote on it. 'We set a goal for the day, for the week and work together,' says 17-year-old Ciara. 'You see that [S&Co.] care about how we feel while at the same time trying to get a show on its feet.'[14] And this caring, student-centered approach is very different from the learning environment that they're used to:

Many of these youngsters are marginalized in the classroom. Mostly they keep to themselves – because they feel shamed or embarrassed that they're not as smart as the other kids. Or they're much smarter and they're impatient with the whole classroom situation, which they judge to be stupid and a waste of time, and they have very little compassion for the other students.

(Coleman interview, August 2016)

And their home environments may be worse:

Many of them are constantly judged and coming up short, as their dysfunctional families may be acting out their own shame and projecting it onto these kids. So learning to care about others in a group is an experience they may not have had for a long time – maybe since kindergarten or first grade. And I'd almost go so far as to say it gives them pleasure. They like what this says about themselves. And they like the other people in the group and they start caring about them.

(Coleman interview, August 2016)

Getting to the pleasure of caring is, however, a delicate process …

The exercises

From the very first exercises, Coleman and his team of directors work on opening up the participants and building trust. And they start by asking them to walk around the room. Simple as that. They then give them simple prompts so that they're not walking aimlessly, and then the exercise becomes more nuanced: 'Just walk on your toes, or on your heels, or walk backwards. Then, when you bump into someone, scream and fall down'[15] (Coleman). Little by little, the juveniles come out of their bubble of self-protection and physically release themselves, until 'after maybe thirty prompts, they're out there waving their arms in the air and we get to a full-body warm up, but it's incremental. If you take too big a jump, you'll see them [metaphorically] hit the wall.'[16] Once the participants are a little more relaxed and the space feels safe enough, Coleman and/or his team shift the juveniles' awareness from themselves to other people. Now the prompt may be:

'Don't make eye contact with anyone – just look at the floor.' Most of them are thinking, 'Great, I'm doing that already,' but then I say 'Now begin to notice people as you go by, but don't let them see you looking.' And next: 'Just make eye contact for a second.' Then: 'no eye contact … now, contact … now, no contact. Now, make eye contact and *hold* it … too long. You'll know when it's too long because you'll either want to start dating that person or to have a fight with them.'

(Coleman cited in van der Kolk, 2014: 338)

228 Education

The teenagers aren't used to holding eye contact with other people, because that other person may be a threat: 'So what you're doing is making it safe for them *not to disappear*' when someone looks at them.[17] But this work is delicate and incremental.

From making silent eye contact (a major act of communication in itself), the exercises evolve into speaking something feeling-based in front of the group. Again the prompt starts very simply, maybe: 'Say your name and your favorite pizza topping.' It may then become more overt: 'Share with us something that makes you angry or sad.' To which they may say, 'I hate school. I hate cops. I hate people.'[18] But at least they're talking publicly and speaking their truths. And these are the first tiny steps toward doing a 50-minute, Shakespeare play. In fact, it's striking how quickly the directors see the participants' use of language change. They go from 'hopeless, often blaming, quickly posturing'[19] in Week 1 to 'less judgmental, more hopeful, taking more delight in each other'[20] by Week 2. And then it's time for Shakespeare …

Bringing in Shakespeare

'What's a dangerous situation?' asks Coleman. 'A robbery. A crackhouse. A crackhead stealing your shoes,' the teenagers reply. 'How about a story where a guy murders his brother to become king, and then marries his wife?' suggests Coleman.[21] And this is the plot of *Hamlet*. When he hears how the passive, 16-year-old Shaina had snapped at school one day and given her peer-tormenter a wound worth nine stitches, he figures she could be 'the perfect Ophelia.'[22] And when he hears about Mike, who stockpiled his emotions about the birth-father he never met, the stepfather who was cruel and the mother who worked all hours till there was 'no option left but to explode,'[23] Coleman figures he could be the perfect Hamlet. And not only do the teenagers' life stories have curious resonances with Shakespeare's characters (which in many ways gives them a sense of validation for their own life stories), but they also have the language to express themselves …

Expanding expression

For many young offenders, reading and speaking are struggles in and of themselves. So if they're relying on four-letter words, 'it's not only to show they're tough but because they have no other language to communicate who they are or what they feel'[24] (van der Kolk). In comes Shakespeare & Company's process of *feeding in* the text line-by-line (see Chapter 7). By *feeding in* the wealth of Shakespeare's words, the young actors don't have to worry about reading or memorizing, and they quickly start to connect to their own experiences. And as they understand the meaning of the words, they begin to share the ideas that these characters are expressing. And that excites them – because they've never had those big ideas before. And we'll hear them say, 'I didn't know you could say something like that.' Or: 'Oh, there are different kinds of love! I'd never thought of that before.'

(Coleman interview, August 2016)

And because *feeding in* happens on their feet, they're making these discoveries through their bodies and voices and, pretty quickly, *feelings* start coming up, too.

Naming their feelings

As the teenagers realize they actually have an aptitude for language, they also discover 'their emotional life is richer and more complex than they ever imagined'[25] (Coleman). And this can be an immense relief to them. Over time they've suppressed their capacity for feeling anything other than anger, least of all tenderness and love, because they're afraid 'their friends will call them out on it and shame them. It's too scary to have feelings of friendship and affection. And it's too risky to express fear or caution or patience.'[26] And it's hard to learn emotional expressiveness in a traditional classroom, where 'you can only have cerebral thoughts, speak in a soft voice, sit still and be quiet. The environment is usually far too hostile to express personal uncertainty or vulnerability.'[27] So their articulation of themselves has gradually become riddled with the phrase, 'I feel *like* …' – which (as we've seen in earlier chapters) isn't an expression of feelings: it's a judgment. And confusing emotional experiences with thought-based judgments leads to vagueness not only in your acting, but also (more importantly) in your self-knowledge. So (again, as with all S&Co.s *Training* and *Education* strategies), the directors rehearse by means of questions, such as 'How did that *feel*?' 'Did you notice any specific feelings that came up for you doing that scene?' Then the teenagers start learning to name their emotional experiences: 'I felt angry when he said that.' 'I felt scared when he looked at me.'[28] And learning to name their emotional experiences is a major step on the journey toward them increasing their self-knowledge.

From naming a favorite pizza topping to using Shakespeare's words to naming their own feelings: it's all part of the delicate process of helping them make better life-choices. It may come as no surprise that one area, through which the juveniles find particular self-expression, is the 'Combat' or *Fight Work*.

Fight Work

'There's something about all the violence […] in Shakespeare,' says Paul Perachi. 'For some reason or other, when [these teenagers] get involved in acting it out, it helps with their ability to manage anger, I think.'[29] In the early days of 'Shakespeare in the Schools' he had had been struck by Shakespeare &

230 Education

Company's fearless approach to violence, and he saw that this could be a healthy channel in the Courts Project for the juveniles to express their own pent-up emotions within a disciplined form. 'Actually,' says Josh McCabe (Courts Project director and *Fight* teacher), 'the *Fight Work* is one of the greatest things about the Courts Project, in that it requires something different from them that can be both remarkable and terrifying.'[30] And he has a great story to illustrate his point:

> One year we were working on *Macbeth* and I brought in this bag of broadswords and daggers, and I said, 'Okay, guys, we're going to do the Banquo death scene.' I open the bag. And this one young man says, 'Are those real swords?' I say, 'Yes, they are.' They look at each other. They look at the bag. They look at me. And this young man has a half-grin on his face and he says, 'You know who we are, right?' And I say, 'Yeah. I know who you are.' And he's not menacing, just amused. And he says, 'You know we outnumber you?' And I say, 'Yeah, I do. So, here's what's going to happen. You guys are going to take beautiful care of each other with these weapons – because if you don't, you're going to surrender them. And you're going to look really childish doing the fight scene with imaginary swords. The choice will be yours. It'll either be a really cool fight – or you're going to look really silly.'
>
> That fight was so touching to watch – because staged violence requires eye contact. And eye contact is not a place these guys will go. But you have to stay eye-to-eye and take great care, so that whatever's going on with *you* doesn't come out through the weapon. And this group really took that to heart. They genuinely didn't want to hurt each other – which means, on a subconscious level, they were *taking care of each other*. They're really good at fight work because they're used to having weapons. But they're not used to taking care of each other. And seeing that they could care was wonderful.
>
> (McCabe interview, August 2017)

And, as Coleman suggests, taking care of each other gives them pleasure.

So, there's the *Fight Work*; understanding the language; gaining deeper self-knowledge to express real feelings. And there's caring about each other. Then there's the directors in the room caring about these young offenders ...

Who are the Courts Project directors?

As you can imagine, it takes 'some pretty developed, evolved, experienced people' to work in the Courts Project:

> You have to be really authentic with the participants. And the environment in the Courts Project has to be genuinely warm. You have to be very patient with their posturing and their fearfulness, which arises from

Shakespeare in the Courts 231

very poor self-image and manifests as hostility. But if you can let their fearfulness blow right through you, their fearfulness will start to go away. And their self-image will start to shift, as they perceive themselves as worthy, valuable and something different than what [their authority figures] have been telling them they are.

(Coleman interview, August 2016)

After all, their experience of themselves is 'like a desert':

And the little oasis of the Best of Themselves is just withering. This project is rain on that oasis. It's a tremendous opportunity for them to gain new self-knowledge, new insight, new valuing of themselves. Then the Best of Themselves starts to blossom again. A little bit … a little bit …

(Coleman interview, August 2016)

Providing the rain on the oasis of the juveniles' self-knowledge is as delicate as all the other processes, because it's not just about forgiveness and patience:

It's about speaking the truth to them and really calling them to task. Letting them see that there are consequences to their actions without the additional layer of *shaming* them for those actions. Because if they feel shamed by you, you've just exacerbated the problem, instead of giving them the learning experience of, 'See what the consequences are.'

(Coleman interview, August 2016)

So you need patience, you need experience, you need balanced judgment, you need wisdom. And you need to want to do the work. Jennie M. Jadow started off teaching 'Shakespeare in the Schools' and slowly discovered she had a particular affinity with the children struggling to find their way:

At its core, 'Shakespeare in the Courts' is emblematic of what we say 'the work' at Shakespeare & Company is. We're really investigating ideas of 'What does it mean to be alive? Who am I? What's my place is this world?' And for these kids who are so disempowered, this sense of enquiry and discovery is what we're seeking to give them. For a young person who has continually been left behind (in the way that many of the court youth have), experiencing the opportunity to investigate those ideas is a real gift. And I actually believe the Company was founded to do this kind of work.

(Jadow interview, July 2017)

And this kind of work is ultimately all about *performance* …

232 Education

Performance

As the performance draws closer, the 'anxiety is going to be in the red zone. They've never been in a theater'[31] (Coleman). And to stand up, put on a play, and reveal yourself in front of your parents, friends and members of the court is personally very demanding: 'It takes a particular kind of courage to stay open, to listen, to not shut down and, using Shakespeare's words, to speak from a deeper part of yourself'[32] (Ware). That's how high the bar is held for them. And yet, when the bar *is* that high, 'they'll absolutely get there. They will soar'[33] (Jadow). Even if it comes with some hairy moments along the way, like the time McCabe's whole cast was put in lockup on the day of the performance ...

> I'd walked into the tech rehearsal and a young guy was screaming: he'd just punched a wall and broken his arm. Someone had apparently peed in his shoe and his water bottle, and he'd flipped (understandably) and punched a wall. We called everyone into the room and asked who'd done it. No one would speak. So we talked to the probation officer, who then contacted the judge. And we all had to show up in court at 3pm. (The show was at 7pm.) [...]
>
> We arrive. They escort Jennie [Jadow] and me into a side room and they take the juveniles to the courtroom. There the judge said to each of them, 'I want your name, how old you are, and what role you're playing.' But they all pleaded the Fifth Amendment. So the judge ordered their belts and shoelaces to be taken away, and they were put in lockup. (I didn't know if we'd have to cancel the show or not ...)
>
> The judge kept them in lockup for a while to let them think. Then she brought them back into court where Jennie, Kevin [Coleman] and I were to join them. And the kids were all in tears. The judge said, 'I owe you an apology. I treated you like adults when I appreciate you're still young people. So we're going to try this one more time. You're going to walk up here and you're going to give me your name, your age, if you go to school what school you go to, what role you play. And you're going to tell me what you're going to do tonight to impress me when I'm at your performance. Who'll go first?' Ten hands shot up. And one by one they were handed their belts and shoelaces and shown out of the courtroom. The judge was nearly in tears as she apologized to Jennie, Kevin and me: 'We let you guys down,' she said. 'Not many people want to take on this population, and you at Shakespeare & Company do.'
>
> *(McCabe interview, August 2017)*

Performing Shakespeare in front of people who might have thought these young offenders incapable of anything positive is ultimately transformative. There, in the EBT, with the full support of S&Co.'s costume and scenic shops, they perform to an invited audience of family, friends, lawyers, representatives

Shakespeare in the Courts **233**

from the juvenile court system and (in recent years) acting students from the STI. So the theatre is packed to standing room with an enthusiastic and wildly appreciative audience. And the young performers *do* get there. They *do* soar. Shannon (on probation for receiving stolen property and now playing Emilia stealing Desdemona's handkerchief) had the chance 'to express all of my uniqueness in a way that people would understand me [...] which is so much fun.'[34] And then there's Coleman's story of the girl, who regularly turned up in the juvenile system and finally ended up in the Courts Project

> and she was always running away. She ran away from home all the time. (Which raises the question: what was going on at home?) And the police would pick her up in Albany [New York] ... in Springfield [Massachusetts] ... Whenever the stress gets high and she can't deal with it any more, she runs away. Over the course of the Courts Project she would miss rehearsals and run away. And the probation officers would find her and bring her back. But as the program went on, she was running away less and less. At the end of the project was the public performance of *Hamlet*. And she was playing Ophelia. She was backstage in a beautiful gown and she looked fabulous: she didn't own clothes like that, her hair never looked that good. – But she had a wastepaper basket in her hands. I said, 'What are you doing with a wastepaper basket?' And she said, 'I'm so nervous, I think I'm going to throw up.' And I thought, 'She's so nervous that she's about to throw up – *but she's not running away!* If *I* was that nervous, *I'd* probably run away!' But she *wasn't* running away. And I thought, 'That's change. Something in her has changed.'
>
> *(Coleman interview, August 2016)*

And it's this kind of change that validates the Courts Project. The participants

> start to perceive themselves differently. They start to value themselves and care about the other kids that they're working with. They become a little more patient and outgoing. A little more interested in others, rather than fixated on the circus that's in their minds. They start to push themselves and are willing to take risks that they would never have been willing to take before. It might be more accurate not to say that they *change*, but that they have *a new experience of themselves* – and they value it. Their perception of themselves gets richer and deeper. They like themselves more, and that changes everything.
>
> *(Coleman interview, August 2016)*

But does it 'fix' them?

That's the perennial question from the funding bodies. And Coleman is really clear that 'Shakespeare in the Courts' *doesn't* fix them:

FIGURE 12.1 Jennie M. Jadow (Education Programs Manager) and MaConnia Chesser (Administrative Director of Training) in *The Merry Wives of Windsor*, dir. Kevin G. Coleman, 2019

Photo: Nile Scott Studios

It *might* fix them, but there isn't a one-to-one corresponding relationship. This project *can't* fix them – for two main reasons. First of all, what needs to be fixed is their home environment: while the little time they spend with us is intense, at the end of it they're back in the environment that needs to be fixed.

Second, the frontal lobe of their brains – which has to do with the ability to make considered decisions, good judgments and see long-term consequences – is still being developed. So they don't yet have the mental ability to consistently control their impulses. They're flooded with hormones that pull them in a thousand different directions, and they're at the mercy of this chemistry-set in their bloodstreams. They get hijacked by their emotional responses and they make terrible decisions. And because their self-knowledge is marginal at best, they also become hijacked by other people's demands on them and expectations and social pressure from their friends.

So this poor little Shakespeare project can't possibly fix all that.

(Coleman interview, August 2016)

Do they reoffend? 'Yes.' Do they make stupid decisions afterwards? 'Yes.' So, if it doesn't fix them, what's the point in doing it? 'Well, the judge will say, "Doing 100 hours of community service doesn't fix them either. Sending them to jail, locking them up, putting them in another horrible environment doesn't fix them either."'[35] But what the Courts Project does provide – beyond a little rain on the oasis of the Best of Themselves – is the juveniles' realization that they have control over their choices and it's okay to participate in something that's good for them. At the close of the performance, as Berkshire Juvenile Court First Justice Joan McMenemy gives the young actors their certificates, she sees the bigger picture of who these teenagers can be: 'We're so lucky in the Berkshires to have Shakespeare & Co. [*sic*] to help show us this'[36] – because it certainly does seem that the young offenders may make better choices.

Take the arsonist renowned for setting Pittsfield on fire: after the Courts Project she registered for Taconic High School, which she knew had a 'Shakespeare in the Schools' program and, when she graduated, she ended up giving the valedictory speech. And for 15-year-old Miranda, who overcame her paralyzing shyness through the Courts Project: 'When I heard I had to come here, I thought I'd be defiant, rude and not do anything. It turned out, I actually enjoy being here. I'll be back, even if it's not court ordered.'[37] Because ultimately she liked performing, and ultimately it's all about *performance* …

Which takes us to the final pillar of Shakespeare & Company …

Notes

1 Mary Hartman cited in Gosselin, L. (2000), 'Teens in Trouble to Tangle with the Bard,' *The Berkshire Eagle*, 17 December 2000.

2 Payne, B. (2007), 'Judge Devises Unusual Punishment for Juveniles: Shakespeare Helps Turn Lives Around,' *The Sunday Republican*, 15 April 2007.

3 Perachi cited in Earls, S. (2008), 'Something's Rotten in the State of these Teen's Lives. Can Shakespeare Lend a Hand?' *Times Union*, 18 May 2008, (my emphasis).

4 Perachi cited in Gosselin (2000).

5 Perachi on NPR's 'Weekend Edition,' with Pippin Ross, 23 April 2003.

6 The venue was the First United Methodist Church in Pittsfield.

7 In 2002, S&Co. received $18,000 from the Massachusetts Cultural Council for the renamed 'Shakespeare Project' to help young people navigate a healthier transition into adulthood. And in 2003, up to 15 participants aged 14–16 were selected by the Berkshire Juvenile Court for the next Shakespeare Project. In time the program expanded to five days a week of after-school sessions for one month, and was renamed 'Shakespeare in the Courts' (or 'the Courts Project').

8 Perachi cited in Gosselin (2000).

9 ibid.

10 Kevin Coleman interview with Bella Merlin, August 2016.

11 Josh McCabe interview with Bella Merlin, August 2017.

12 ibid.

13 Ware cited in Buell, B. (2004), 'Bard's Plays Enrich Troubled Kids: Shakespeare in the Courts Helps Troubled Youths Get on Right Track,' *The Sunday Gazette*, 4 April 2004.

14 Ciara Lee cited in Smith, J. (2013), 'Playing on Punishment: Teenagers Perform in "Macbeth" Tonight at Mill City Theatre,' *The Berkshire Eagle*, 20 March 2013.

15 Coleman cited in van der Kolk, B. (2014), *The Body Keeps the Score: Brain, Mind and Body in the Healing of Trauma*, New York: Penguin, p. 338.

16 ibid.

17 ibid., (my emphasis).

18 Coleman cited in Earls (2008).

19 Coleman notes, July 2019.

236 Education

20 Coleman cited in Kennedy, L. (2010), 'Caught in the Act: Juveniles Sentenced to Shakespeare,' 18 May 2010.
21 Coleman cited in Earls (2008).
22 ibid.
23 ibid.
24 van der Kolk (2014), pp. 344–345.
25 Coleman interview, August 2016.
26 ibid.
27 ibid.
28 Coleman cited in van der Kolk (2014), p. 346.
29 Perachi on NPR's 'Weekend Edition,' with Pippin Ross, 23 April 2003.
30 McCabe interview, August 2017.
31 Coleman cited in Kennedy (2010).
32 Ware cited in Murray, L., 'Shakespeare in the Courts Enters Its Twelfth Year of Working with Young People,' *Berkshire on Stage*, 20 March 2012.
33 Jennie M. Jadow interview with Bella Merlin, July 2017.
34 Shannon on NPR's 'Weekend Edition,' with Pippin Ross, 23 April 2003.
35 Coleman interview, August 2016.
36 Joan McMemeny cited in Smith (2013).
37 Miranda cited in Horwitz, S. (2012), 'Sentenced to Shakespeare: Courts and Theater Company Join Forces,' *Backstage*, 7 May 2012.

ACT IV

Performance

13

THE ART FORM OF PERFORMANCE

'*Performance* is where the chickens come home to roost. That's where the art form lies'[1] (Packer). And the art form at Shakespeare & Company has manifested through hundreds of artists over 40-plus years. So here we focus on a series of questions: What exactly is performance for S&Co.? What is 'truthful' acting? How might *Training* transition into *Performance*? What is directing? What is rehearsing? How has Tina Packer's longevity as founding Artistic Director impacted the performance style? And what draws artists and audiences back year after year? There are a few 'ideal scenarios' within this chapter to pose some provocations along with the questions. Which start with …

What is performance?

'Performance is when the audience comes in and the storytelling circuit gets completed and the whole level of experience goes way up'[2] (Coleman). So basically you could say for Shakespeare & Company, *Performance* is *the actor/audience relationship*.

Performance as actor/audience relationship

As we've seen throughout this book, S&Co.'s original intent was to create a theatrical event in which Shakespeare's language would vibrate between speaker and receiver in a visceral, shared experience. Which means that, once the audience comes in, the stakes for the actor are raised, 'the authenticity is raised. The art form is raised'[3] (Coleman). And the art form is raised because the audience is (ideally) given '*a different experience of themselves*'[4] (Krausnick). As they listen to Shakespeare's words and watch his characters, they're offered new

240 Performance

insights into the human condition. Be it Lady Macbeth's ambition, Demetrius' and Chiron's lasciviousness, Iago's plotting or Juliet's passion, the spectators start pondering, 'At what level does each of *us* murder, or lust, or covet [or love]?'[5] (Packer). And as they contemplate possible answers, they find Shakespeare's words give them deeper insight into their own personalities, unlocking their own story. And 'because each age group will hear the play in a different way – be they 12-year-old or 80-year-old – there'll be 400 stories being told in the auditorium'[6] (Krausnick). And this auditorium full of self-questioning has the potential to collectively manifest something 'mystical,' in that each of those 400 listeners 'will experience themselves as a microcosm in the universal macrocosm, an individual within the collective. And those 400 stories will want to be together – because they're *in community*.'[7] And there's the rub: the audience and actors, mostly strangers,

> form a community as they begin to respond in humor and in emotion together – and that's a pretty intimate thing. When you begin to go through an emotional, intellectual, and artistic experience with somebody that you've never known before, you're immediately more intimate with that person [...].
>
> *(Krausnick cited in Race, N., 'Tina Packer, Shakespeare & Company and the Founder's Theatre,'* The Artful Mind, *July 2001)*

And, within this intimate community, the performance carries the audience along on the human voice of the actors and we 'transcend' our everyday experience[8] (Packer).

From Word to Actor to individual Spectator to collective Audience to Community to Transcendence. That's quite some journey! And while it may sound idealistic – even esoteric – it's actually very direct. And it's exactly what the Elizabethans would have expected:

> The Elizabethans didn't sit *at* a play: they sat *in* a play. And they were in the play because the characters were talking to them. If Hamlet is talking to *me*, it means *I'm* in the play *with* Hamlet. So now I'm much more deeply invested, imaginatively and emotionally. And I'm finding myself having responses to him. I don't have any lines but, because he's talking to me, I'm having emotional, visceral reactions: 'Now I'm with you in this hellhole called Elsinore. And I don't know how to help you, because I don't know what to do. It breaks my heart to hear you say what you're saying. And you're acting horribly towards Ophelia. And I'm not just passively or objectively observing you, I'm responding to you *in my heart* – because I'm in the play *with* you.'
>
> *(Coleman interview, August 2016)*

If we don't forge that immediate *actor/audience relationship* – be it indirectly (in scenes) or directly (in soliloquies) – then arguably 'we're not meeting

The art form of performance **241**

Shakespeare on his own terms, because we're not in the kind of theatre that Shakespeare was creating.'[9] And the kind of theatre Shakespeare was creating could be emotionally intimate because it was *physically* intimate. So meeting Shakespeare on his own terms is very much connected to the architecture of the playing space (as we saw in Chapter 2). And when everyone can see each other, as they can in the Tina Packer Playhouse (inspired in its architecture by the intimacy of Shakespeare's Globe), the theatre has the chance to morph from a place of pure entertainment into a dynamic *debating chamber.*

Performance as debate

'Theatre is about an exchange of ideas,' says Packer. 'I think the very form of plays [is] debate. So ideally you want people to come out of the play asking 'the fundamental questions': 'What does it mean to be alive? How should we act? What must I do?' And those questions 'are relevant regardless of what century you're living in, or even what country; they are the big questions.'[10] So, all the work the actors do on the poetry – as well as on 'the way in which we breathe, the way in which we hold the language' – is for one purpose: for the audience to *experience the language*, rather than hearing it as reportage. And if that can happen, 'they really don't have any choice' but to ask the fundamental questions and engage in the debate of life as they leave the theatre, 'because Shakespeare is so powerful he starts carrying them along himself.'[11] And then all manner of 'human truths' can be explored.

Which prompts the question …

What – for S&Co. – is 'truthful' acting?

It's back to voice and vibration. Packer isn't just looking for the words being true; she's looking for *the place from which they're coming*. And she's also looking for the level at which *the voice can impact the other person*. How is it going to vibrate in the other person's body? How is it going to be picked up on? So as actors (and directors), 'you're trying to make an aural picture, and a visual picture, and a picture that really works on an unconscious level, as well as on a conscious level.'[12] In other words, 'truthful acting' for Shakespeare & Company isn't solely psychological. It's *psychophysical*: in that, the literal, physiological vibrating of the words within and between the speakers and listeners can stir up emotional responses. Which, in many respects, invites actors of a particular propensity …

Actors of a musical soul

When it comes to acting Shakespeare, your ideal actor possesses 'a musical soul': one that 'understands not only the poetry but the implied silences'[13] – just as a musician understands both the notes and the rests.

242 Performance

> In fact, Chopin created a term for this in music: *tempo rubato*. And he used
> it for passages, which were particularly expressive or passionate, and where
> he wanted the musician to absolutely follow the structure, but to breathe
> with it, feel it, be free with it.[14]
>
> *(Packer notes, 22 September 2019)*

When actors possess this kind of musical soul, they can discover moment by
moment

> what it is they are saying. They are amazed by what they think, how they
> react, and it is never the same. The structure of the verse will hold them
> steady, so they can let go and speak each time totally afresh. So this is
> a very particular creative energy that I'm looking for, one that astounds at
> every moment.
>
> *(Packer notebook, 'Notes on Directing,' (early 1990s). S&Co. archive)*

'Astounding at every moment' means being brave as an actor and taking a few
risks in the moment of performance. Because – when the words are really
vibrating on a visceral level, as well as on a psychological and emotion-based
one – you can't really prescribe what you're going to feel. All kinds of unexpected responses may arise (as Rory Hammond touched on in Chapter 6). And
then (*ideally*) you find the courage to go with that response, 'even if it's really
unexpected (you expect this scene to be about tears, but actually you're
laughing)'[15] (Packer). If you can resist the voice in your head telling you, 'This
doesn't make sense: they're being [murdered] and I'm laughing,'[16] you can
experience a connection to language that goes way deeper than your head-led
logic, and into intuition and creative flow. And that partly entails emptying
yourself of any preconceptions. Hence the 'musical soul': you're almost like
a flute, allowing the music of the language to transport you: 'I'm the instrument
[at first]. And Shakespeare's words are igniting responses in me. And as I build
my capacity to take on these experiences, I become the player of the instrument
as well'[17] (Coleman). And when that happens, 'the listener understands more
deeply where the speaker is coming from. It doesn't mean the listener is conscious of the technicalities of "the music," but only of the feeling/thinking state
of the character'[18] (Packer).

Being both the instrument and the player, the music and the musician, reflects
how S&Co.'s *Training* (of your actor's 'instrument') can transition into *Performance* (of the play's 'music'). Your challenge is to expand beyond your personal
experience of the individual 'notes' to Shakespeare's bold navigation of humanity's stories. To put it another way, you rise above your practice of scales and
arpeggios (in rehearsals) to flights of virtuosity (in performance). Now, that can
be quite some elevation – and it doesn't happen without due attention. And
while S&Co.'s Month-Long Intensive (detailed in 'Act II') offers you invaluable
tools, you only have time within those four weeks to focus on one scene in

The art form of performance   **243**

isolation, not on the placement of that scene within the context of a whole play's structure. So let's look further ...

How might aspects of the *Training* transition into *Performance*?

Kristin Linklater succinctly outlines an 'ideal' transition from exploratory *Training* to professional *Performance* in her 'Hypothetical Four-Year Actor-Training Program'[19] (note: four *years*, not four weeks).

She suggests that, in the early stages of training, the scene work focuses on *the personal processes between two people*: 'The text is there to serve the student, so that the accurate interpretation of the scene as the author intended is subordinated to the ability of the student to *personalize* and make the words deeply true for him or herself'.[20] (This is more or less the Intensive's aim.)

However ... As Linklater's hypothetical training progresses,

> the student recognizes that the character in the play may react differently in a given situation from the natural reaction of the person playing it, and ways of *rechanneling that person's raw psychological and emotional material in unfamiliar directions* are examined.
>
> *(Linklater in Evans, 2015: 95, (my emphasis))*

So, it's no longer just a question of unlocking your own, creative thin-skinnedness (though that's certainly still very important): there's now a bigger-picture story to be told. And at this point, Linklater brings in her Stanislavsky-based work. You now 'give flesh and blood, psycho-emotional answers to questions such as "Who am I?," "Where am I going?," "Where am I coming from?," "What do I want?," "What's my objective?," "What's the scene objective?" [and] "What's the plot objective?"'[21] Whether or not Stanislavsky is overtly mentioned in the rehearsal room (be it at Shakespeare & Company or anywhere else), these plot-driven questions can provide invaluable guidelines for how you shift from your self-research to telling the bigger story.

In fact, from here on in, the term '*Performance*' refers to the work of (predominantly) Equity actors paid by S&Co. to share a story with audiences who have paid to watch that story. Of course those performances are no less personalized than in *Training* and *Education*. It's simply that the contract between performer and spectator has shifted from the shared celebration of a personal 'win' to the public's experience of a coherent story in what's ultimately a commercial venture (albeit one that *ideally* 'transcends' daily consciousness). It's worth making this distinction here to clarify that personalization in the professional performances at S&Co. is just the first step. The second step involves acknowledging the playwright's intentions and carefully rehearsing the play's underpinning structure. And it's the combination of the two – the instrument (the personalized connection) and the music (the complete narrative) – that may then 'astound at every moment' in the journey of a whole play.

So let's head into the rehearsal room to see how it all comes together. And the first person we encounter is the *director* …

What is directing?

In Shakespeare & Company's lineage of artistic directors, Tina Packer's long tenure was followed by Tony Simotes (2009–2014); the combined forces of Jonathan Croy and Ariel Bock (2015–2016); and vibrant new visions now vivify the Company with the baton passing in 2016 to longtime Company member and acclaimed actor-director Allyn Burrows. For most of the Company's 40-plus years, Packer's idiosyncratic style and aesthetics have significantly resonated, not least because, for the first five years, she was the sole director of Shakespeare. With her indomitable energy and formidable knowledge, she is arguably the first woman in history to have directed and/or acted in all Shakespeare's canon, completing the works with *Cymbeline* in 2017 (see Chapter 15). And her unique understanding of Shakespeare's female characters has won global acclaim through her book *Women of Will* and her performances of the material, in which she plays roles from Juliet to Desdemona to Cleopatra to Coriolanus to Queen Margaret. And in 2019 she received the Douglas N. Cook Lifetime Achievement Award from the international Shakespeare Theatre Association.

While numerous directors have contributed to the Company's success, Packer has implicitly and explicitly influenced many in her stead. For Kelly Galvin (one of the Company's youngest directors, with *Love's Labour's Lost* [2018] and *The Taming of the Shrew* [2019]) Packer was her 'first real

FIGURE 13.1 Tina Packer and Nigel Gore in *Women of Will*, dir. Eric Tucker, 2011
Photo: Kevin Sprague

The art form of performance **245**

mentor'[22] (see Figures 10.1 and 10.2). As well as taking the *Training*, serving in the *Education* program (2008–2014), pursuing an MFA in Directing at Boston University, working at venues including the Guthrie Theatre and Arena Stage, and founding her own company 'the rig,' Galvin has also assistant-directed Packer. So it's no surprise that Galvin's directing style combines the heritages of both Packer and Kristin Linklater:

> Tina taught me to trust and cultivate the alchemy between actor and text. When a skilled and passionate actor brings their full vocal, physical, emotional and imaginative availability to Shakespeare's text, and when an audience is present to witness it, characters actually come to life. The character is both recognizable (i.e., a character that we know from Shakespeare's play) and simultaneously fresh – rendered vividly and singularly [...] by the actor speaking those words. The Linklater voice work serves as the foundation: by speaking in their natural voices and connecting truthfully to their own humanity, actors can illuminate (rather than indicate) a character and allow us, the audience, to see that character as if for the first time, and understand their humanity anew.
>
> *(Galvin email, 8 July 2019)*

Likewise for Allyn Burrows, a Company member for 17 years, during which he served as an artist manager and Associate Artistic Director (see 'Epilogue'). And now as Artistic Director, he has currents of Linklater's and Packer's legacies rippling through his directing process. Seeking 'the resonance and harmonics within the words,' he aims to create productions that allow the audience to feel they've 'shifted in certain ways over the course of the two hours spent watching a performance.'[23] And by turns masterful and mischievous as a director, he encourages his actors to 'run with the story,' experiment with bold choices and 'live in the characters' extreme situations.'[24] Balancing textual precision with *personal connection*, Burrows' rehearsal environments are crucibles of playful invention and purposeful storytelling (see Figures 2.7 and 13.2).

Because Packer's influence over the years has been so considerable, we'll focus for the rest of this chapter largely on her directing processes (case-studied with *Cymbeline* in Chapter 15).

The 'personal-political' director

Packer has two contrapuntal dynamics to her directing principles. One is inward-flowing and *personal* (the human condition); the other is outward-flowing and *political* (the social condition). And she articulates these in her 1990s' handwritten 'Notes on Directing':

> the actor has to make a whole aesthetic out of verse, prose, silence, listening, stand-up comedy routines (clown), deeply psychological character,

246 Performance

that same character speaking so openly to the audience he [*sic*] is transparent, and a philosopher to boot. [...] ADD to this the POLITICAL and SOCIAL WORLD which the director will choose and we obviously have a mix that transcends any one reality, but which eventually must have a coherence and intensity [so] that it will create its own reality to such a degree that *it will alter the audiences' reality and they will perceive old things anew and say AHA – I see*! And through seeing, the world becomes a lighter place!

[...] It's obviously in the INTERNALITY OF THE ACTORS, the truth the actors make for themselves. For, in the end, all the beautiful pictures, all the wonderful concepts the director creates, count FOR NOTHING once the performance is on. I don't care about Lubimov [*sic*] or Peter Brook or Stanislavsky or Tina Packer. When push comes to shove, it's the actors and the audiences, because they are the only people there. It is the ACTORS and the AUDIENCES and the words they are saying and hearing, which are the only things that count, and I SAY the production lives and dies there!

(Packer 'Notes on Directing,' early 1990s, (my italics))

These 'life-and-death' production imperatives are largely Packer's reaction to the director-*auteurs* she encountered during her early career in Britain. In counterpoint, she essentially 'starts from nothing' in rehearsals (though, as we'll see with *Cymbeline*, that 'nothing' is underpinned by deep research). From there, she tunes into all the information in the room: 'I have two senses, two directions that I'm going in at any given time.'[25]

The first direction involves '*contemplating what's there.*'[26] So this means she listens deeply to the text being spoken and watches closely the actors speaking that text. And since language 'taps into our conscious [and unconscious] minds on all kinds of levels,'[27] there's a 'whole level of understanding of the human psyche that goes on inside the sounds of the words, the DNA of which may have taken 2000 years to evolve.'[28] Then Packer tunes into the musicality of Shakespeare's *dramatic forms*: such as *Structure of the Verse*; poetry; prose; and silence: 'These have different musical [and] psychological levels to them. So [the actors] have to lend themselves back to the old rhythms and forms.'[29] Then there are the *live interactions* unfolding before her in the rehearsal room: what's the relationship between these particular actors saying these particular words at this particular time on the planet?[30] And inevitably a multiplicity of perspectives arises, both through the actors' delivery of the text and the rehearsal-room discussions. Out of all this information she starts 'building the picture of what it is that we're going to do.'[31] In many ways for Packer, 'holding opposite truths – being able to see a wide spectrum of information in the situation'[32] *is* the 'creative process.' And if she and her actors can allow that wide spectrum to resonate through a production, by showing the audience two (or more) sides of a situation, then

The art form of performance   **247**

they might shift their perception of the human condition. Which really takes us to the second direction of her approach to directing.

Since a production 'lives or dies' between the actors and the audience, Packer also listens deeply to what's going on *inside her self*: 'out of what I'm seeing, or out of the moment when I find myself viscerally responding to what's going on, I start building and elaborating.'[33] In other words, she immerses herself fully in *the actor/audience relationship*, always mindful that the discoveries made by actors in the intimacy of the rehearsal room will exponentially blossom once there are multiple audience members in the space. When 400 people are concentrating on you as an actor you find yourself taking imaginative risks that didn't even occur to you before. It's partly due to the actual physics of all that human energy assembled in the theatre space, and partly the intensity of 'being witnessed.' (As Nerissa in Packer's *Merchant of Venice* (2016), which was staged 'in the round,' the 'trial scene' became tangibly more anxious when we were surrounded on all sides by people watching the extreme situation as well as watching *each other* watching the extreme situation. See Figure 3.2 for the scene in rehearsal, before those watching eyes had assembled.)

Packer's bi-directional approach – listening to the text and listening to her visceral experience of that text – is essentially how she proceeds in the complex process of *rehearsing*.

What is rehearsing?

'Rehearsals are a "hot mess,"' says Kevin Coleman, who first played Mercutio in Packer's second (1979) season. 'You're all over the map, you're messy,'[34] as you're trying to align yourself with the character, personalize the language and then contemplate the bigger-picture story. And right from the early days, Shakespeare & Company accommodated this liberating messiness, not least because there were two formidable females at the helm with a host of master-teachers. And all the voices were heard …

The early years of rehearsal

'In most theaters only the director has any input into the play,' said Kristin Linklater in 1983, and they 'tend to get threatened if anybody else feeds in any ideas'; whereas at Shakespeare & Company, 'we have about four different people working on scenes with the actors.'[35] Indeed, Linklater and Packer were part of a pioneering wave of women theatre practitioners in the 1970s, operating 'principally out of relationships' – and 'the aesthetics of the company [were] *based* on relationships'[36] (Packer). They didn't want to impose a directorial concept on the actors; instead, they collectively listened to how Shakespeare's language unearthed relationships, in what was 'a far more messy and female way of working.'[37] Certainly this 'messy' approach brought warm-blooded emotions into rehearsals, which was pretty unusual at the time (maybe due to

248 Performance

a preponderance of male directors in the West). Returning from a trip to London, Linklater noted:

> the actors talked about how cerebral their directors were and how if one of the actors were to happen to cry in the middle of a rehearsal, the director would say, 'Well, I think we'd better stop for a cup of tea, and then when you've all pulled yourselves back together we can get on with the rehearsal.' They would be just terrified of anything irrational, impulsive, or emotional.
>
> *(Linklater cited in Jenkins, 1983)*

And yet these were the very components that gave creative sustenance to the performances that Linklater and Packer sought.

In fact, the experimental rehearsal process was variously described in the early years as 'seeming disorder,' 'controlled lunacy,' 'crazy and wonderful' and full of 'wild ideas.' At that time, there were six to seven weeks of rehearsal, which typically began with three weeks of workshop, including two weeks of *dropping in* the whole play (see Chapter 7). And as the main points of the script emerged, the designers and composers (who were present throughout rehearsals) collectively used their talents 'to emphasize and support the action of the play.'[38] Regular Company designers included Bill Ballou (scenic and lighting) and Kiki Smith (costume).[39] And in the latter three weeks of rehearsal, 'largely expanded building teams' came in 'to get the design elements in place.'[40] Although the actors sometimes felt 'shaking and confused' until the last couple of weeks when everything fell into place, the logistics were arguably no more unconventional than those of pioneering male contemporaries such as Peter Brook, Julian Beck and Joseph Chaikin. The 1970s was a tough time to be a female theatre director.[41] Suffice it to say, many of Packer's early directing practices have galvanized into what has proved to be a highly successful methodology, one which constitutes her typical rehearsal process to this day (albeit on much tighter timelines). So let's look at its components …

What are the components of Packer's rehearsal methodology?

There's actually always a method in Packer's 'mucking about,' as her faith in structure shapes any seeming chaos. The implicit structure of her rehearsal process - or *text progression* - typically begins with *working the play on its feet*.

Working the play on its feet[42]

Packer eschews traditional 'tablework,' believing it locks actors in their heads while the actual table visibly cuts their bodies in half. Indeed, her heart-felt aversion comes from hours of head-led analysis in her early career at the RSC, where (as we saw in Chapter 1) lofty discussions, led by Oxbridge directors,

The art form of performance **249**

paralyzed her creatively. That doesn't mean she doesn't do any detailed text ana-lysis: far from it (as we'll see). It simply means that her own rehearsal process has no sitting round a table and no Day #1 'table read.' Instead she immediately invites her actors' bodies, souls and imaginations to the party by getting you up on your feet, so that you can play on your impulse from the very first moment you meet *this text* with *these partners* in *this space.*

Working the play on its feet is exactly as it sounds. The ensemble sits in a large circle. And if you're involved in a particular scene, you enter the circle and work through the scene on your feet. If your lines mention a character that isn't directly present in the scene, you indicate or actually address the actor playing that character wherever they're sitting in the circle. And thus you can make a visual, energetic connection with the real-life person, which itself ignites a tangible 'face-to-face' experience of what it means to be talking about that character in their absence.

'No blame, no shame' is the main instruction for *working the play on its feet.* If you know your lines – great! If you'd rather have your script in your hand – fine. You can even ask an assistant director to *feed in* your lines (see Chapter 7). It's not about memory-test or performance. It's about immediate, embodied connec-tion with the other actors, as well as with the circled audience. So you can go wherever you want, do whatever you want, respond in the moment however the spirit moves you. And finding the necessary courage to do so is actually quite easy once you realize that no one assumes that what you do while *working the play on its feet* is what you'll ultimately do in performance. It's just playtime! As long as you're listening to each other, you're picturing the images, you're not hurting yourself or each other or the furniture, then anything that arises from this playful experimentation could constitute valuable, raw material for later rehearsals.

This daring first pass through a play is both terrifying and exhilarating (see Chapter 15). And it's usually followed by a healthy discussion of what just hap-pened and what was revealed. The following day the detailed work of *dropping in* the whole play usually begins, and may be followed by scenes being *stood up* and/ or *fed in* if you want to give a scene a heart-felt go without fully knowing your lines yet[43] (see Chapter 7). In the early years, the directive was that, once 'the actors have been fed in, they are asked to learn the scene and they begin a *close textual analysis* both with an individual text coach [...] and with the director'[44] (Packer). The 'text coach' has morphed over time into the voice coaches and assistant directors, who may indeed pursue some *close textual analysis.*

Close textual analysis

Close textual analysis is similar to the *dictionary work* referred to in *Education* (see Chapter 9), and it offers you various avenues of insight. On the most basic level, it explains the *meaning of an individual word or image,* for which the *Oxford English Dic-tionary* 'is our best friend at Shakespeare & Company. We like to know not only what a word actually means to Shakespeare and to his character[s] but also how

250 Performance

a word has evolved.'[45] The process opens up your options, rather than locking in your choices (which comes later). And it's important to remember *dictionary work* typically comes after *dropping in*: 'We're reversing the sequence in which language is usually dealt with in actor training. We're insisting on seeing what the text has to tell us before we make decisions.'[46] And given the enormity of Shakespeare's realm, our own imagination is enhanced when we can tap into his imagination.[47]

Second, *close textual analysis* helps you unlock the *emotional-thought processes of individual lines*. Here the *Structure of the Verse* comes to the fore – particularly with iambic pentameters, as you

> examine the words at the beginning and at the end of each line and try to understand why Shakespeare chose to put them there. The first word of a new line generally introduces *a new thought or sub-thought*. The words at the ends of the line generally build *the spine of a speech*. The actor can make a list of those last words to get a sense of the structure of the speech and construe the emotional direction in which it is going.
> *(Packer in 'Training Shakespeare Actors in A Modern World', 2007: 22)*

Third, *close textual analysis* elucidates for you the *psychological portraits*: 'The characters in Shakespeare are built from the *words* they are speaking and the *order* in which those words are spoken.'[48] So you might note where the ends of thoughts and the ends of lines don't match up: so they 'don't make *logical* sense. However, they do make *visceral* and *emotional* sense.'[49] Take the jealousy-fueled lines of Leontes in *The Winter's Tale*:

> Most dear'st! my collop! – Can thy dam? – may't be? –
> Affection! thy intention stabs the centre:
> Thou dost make possible things not so held,
> Communicatest with dreams; – how can this be? –
> With what's unreal thou coactive art,
> And fellow'st nothing: then 'tis very credent
> Thou mayst co-join with something; and thou dost,
> And that beyond commission, and I find it, –
> And that to the infection of my brains
> And hardening of my brows.[50]

As you can sense from Leontes' speech, *close textual analysis* ultimately *stimulates your feelings*:

> It's not 'this is my part; I need to study it.' It's 'what do these words in this order mean? What do they bring up in me? How are my fellow actors reacting to this? And how am I influenced by how they're reacting to me?'
> *(Packer in 'Training Shakespeare Actors in A Modern World', 2007: 14;*
> *Packer edit, 2019)*

The art form of performance **251**

And in this way, text analysis *synergizes your head and heart*. Far from being intellectual work, you 'remain rooted in the body'[51] with it happening on your feet, in rehearsal and through constantly listening, watching, actively contemplating and *asking questions*.

Directing through questions (and laughter ...)

Acclaimed actress Frances West had known Packer since the mid-1980s, and actually played the lead role in Margaret Edson's *Wit* when she herself was dying of cancer. She was struck by Packer's process of directing through questions – as well as through her laughter: 'Tina does not move you about the stage [...] Instead, she asks a question which stimulates [you] to find an answer. [...] She intentionally leaves a question hanging.'[52] This, and 'her amazing sense of humor which includes an ability to chortle at anyone, including herself, are extraordinary.'[53] And that's just one actor's take. Here's another in a similar vein. Jonathan Epstein has been a celebrated Company member working with Packer since 1988, including as her original partner in *Women of Will: Part 1* (1989), as Shylock (1998 and 2016) and as Cymbeline (2017). He notes that Packer's perceptions are typically 'two orders deeper than everyone else's. She doesn't solve a play's problem but says something about its essence.'[54] In other words, her 'manner is to suggest something [...] to you, the actor, but then laugh it off,' which takes the threat out of the fear of failing.[55] And, as Epstein points out, that's very liberating: 'All of this permits the actor to think about himself, as different parts within [him] come alive.'[56]

Laughing and questioning through her various rehearsal interactions, Packer also turns to her *assistant directors*.

Working with assistant directors

Because she wants to pool knowledge (and mentor young artists), Packer works with assistant directors from a multitude of backgrounds, experiences and perspectives. Typically she has two or three, and they're often recruited through the Drama League Directing Fellowship in New York, which offers yearly fellowships in classical theatre. In recent years, the fellows at S&Co. have included Israeli director Noa Egozi, Syrian director Kholoud Sawaf and African American director Raphael Massie.[57] And since one of her philosophies is 'I listen to what you're saying, I hear what you're feeling and, from that, I create wisdom,'[58] the more *diverse perspectives* she can have in the rehearsal room, the deeper the knowledge can be.

Diverse perspectives

Tackling the difficult questions in Shakespeare's plays is imperative to Packer. Ergo, Noa Egozi was chosen for *The Merchant of Venice* (2016) because 'I

252 Performance

recognize the danger with some of the situations in the play'[59] (Egozi). At the same time, she could 'recognize where in rehearsals we could allow ourselves *not* to be precious about certain elements,' and 'speak freely about the anti-Semitism.'[60] Furthermore, she could offer insights into characters such as Jessica (played by Kate Abbruzzese), who runs away with a Christian: 'Judaism isn't something technical that you just give up: it's about *identity*. So I felt my contribution was to talk to Tina about these issues and work directly with the actors involved.'[61]

Similarly for Raphael Massie, as *Merchant* included Company regulars Thomas Brazzle (Launcelot) and Deaon Griffin-Pressley (Lorenzo), and part of the layering of racial perspectives included dramatized tensions between these two powerful, African American actors:

> As a black man myself I had very specific opinions about how these moments were developing in the play. And that's where I think I made a significant contribution. Early on Tina encouraged us not to shy away from the difficult conversations that develop through rehearsal: otherwise we're not honoring the struggles of the marginalized. So it became very important to me to tell the story between Launcelot and Lorenzo appropriately and clearly. When we're *not* clear about difficult moments surrounding race, religion and gender, that's when people start to feel marginalized or when appropriation, or forms of oppression, [even unintentionally] take place.
>
> *(Massie interview, July 2016)*

With *Cymbeline*, exile and dislocation were important narrative issues. And as a young Muslim woman from Syria, Kholoud Sawaf had important input in rehearsals. Indeed, true inclusion necessitates dialog and, from the moment Sawaf arrived at Kemble Street, Packer was keen to understand, '"What do we need to know to make you feel comfortable here at Shakespeare & Company?" No one had ever asked me that question before in a professional environment and that feeling of being welcomed and seen was wonderful'[62] (Sawaf).

The assistant directors are not only valued for their diverse perspectives on community and dramaturgy: they're also vital for *dropping in*.

Learning about dropping in

Dropping in a whole play is a labor-intensive process requiring all hands on deck. It's also an important way for Packer to disseminate her original practice to young directors. While we've looked at the *Training* principles of *dropping in* (Chapter 7), here the assistant directors offer some practical perspectives for *Performance* – and it's pretty much 'Trial by fire!'[63] (Massie). They're given a brief session in which Packer drops them into a scene from the play, then off they go. And that's how it has to be, because *dropping in* is experiential, not intellectual. Of course, the assistants inevitably ask themselves: 'Can I formulate the questions at pace?'[64] Or: 'Do I understand the

The art form of performance **253**

words well enough to ask the relevant questions?' Or: 'Can I carry the responsibility of helping these actors in their delicate, first navigation of their roles?' The answer to these questions (as with all S&Co.'s work) lies in *breath*. If as a dropper-in you focus on your own breath as well as the breath of the person whom you're dropping in (notes Egozi), 'your mind quiets, you fixate less on the script and instead you note how breath and words are affecting the actors.'[65] In fact, subtle reactions like eye-twitches or smirks (notes Massie) also reveal what's affecting them: 'And once I started paying that degree of attention to the actors – and let them lead me in the *dropping in* – I could navigate the text for them more effectively.'[66]

Being an effective navigator takes some dramaturgical preparation. Sawaf found that, as a dropper-in, she wanted to know in advance, 'How does this scene serve the story? And what's it about in the context of where [the director] is going with this production?'[67] But there's also 'a trick between preparation and no preparation' (notes Egozi):

> I had to know where the words come in the scene, but not really to prepare what they mean to *me*, so that the interpretation could come from *the actor*. It's really about being playful as a dropper-in. And enjoying yourself. And the freer you allow yourself to be, the deeper the process usually goes.
>
> *(Egozi interview, July 2016)*

In other words, 'it's associative rather than linear'[68] (Packer). And if the actor whom you're dropping in is open to the process, 'you actually feel as if you're in their stream of consciousness. They're leading you through their ideas. And then you feel as if you're exploring the scene *with* your actor'[69] (Egozi). So, in many respects *dropping in* becomes a kind of birthing of inspiration, as the dropper-in enables the actor to get to know the play in a very textured way. Yet at the end of the day the dropper-in is only the midwife, not the parent. And when the process is going well, the actor is almost oblivious to the dropper-in, even though the dropper-in is very focused on the actor's experiences. To which end, *dropping in* can be just as important for actor-*director* relationships as for actor-actor relationships: 'I certainly felt more connected to the actors in the cast whom I'd dropped in'[70] (Egozi).

Clearly the assistant directors are invaluable for *dropping in*. And their value is equally important once the scenes are being staged.

Working the scenes

The first time a scene is staged the assistants are present so that they have a clear sense of where Packer and the cast are headed. However, they're not silent witnesses: even in the first pass through a scene, their opinions are valued and frequently followed.[71] As the rehearsal period proceeds, Packer asks them which scenes they want to work on in terms of what they're seeing and how they might help a scene grow. She then entrusts them to go off and rehearse with the actors

254 Performance

on their own, always with the premise that nothing be 'blocked' or imposed. Rather, the guiding principle (as with *Training* and *Education*) is one of curiosity: so the assistants use inquisitive propositions, such as 'Can we try this …? We may find it doesn't make sense but can we see what happens? Now let's try it your way. Let's try it five different ways'[72] (Aspenlieder). Likewise, when they're feeding back to the actors, Packer advises them to use encouragements as much as adjustments. And at the end of every day the assistant directors have their own meeting with Packer in which they *check in* (see Chapter 6) and share how the scenes all went. These meetings form a crucial part of her *mentoring young directors*.

Mentoring assistant directors

Packer's mentoring of assistant directors is multivalent, as articulated here by Massie, Egozi and Sawaf:

First, there's the *seamlessness between life and art*: 'Every conversation I had with Tina was a kind of mentorship moment, a guide as to how she directs. That's just the way she is: she's no different *in* or *outside* the rehearsal room'[73] (Egozi). In fact, one day between rehearsals, Packer said to Sawaf (herself in the throes of prepping a production for her homeland)

> 'Let's get a coffee, then we can talk about taking Shakespeare to Damascus!' For somebody to have the time and will to sit and talk with me for an hour [in the midst of their own rehearsals] about my *Romeo and Juliet* project – and what I want to do with it to heal a place in destruction and war – was true mentorship.
>
> *(Sawaf interview, July 2017)*

Second is Packer's quality of *listening*:

> Tina mentors first by *listening* to what people have to offer; I think that's the most powerful thing she does – for directors, actors, designers, everyone. And that sounds like a very simple thing, but I've never seen anything like it. At every turn, the first thing she does is listen – *all the way*. She doesn't cut you off. She doesn't immediately jump in when she thinks you're done with your point. She waits until you've said everything you have to say. (Which is extraordinary given who she is and how much knowledge she possesses: she could very easily lecture you, explain the situation and move on from there. But she doesn't. She listens.) And then she does her best to take whatever you have to offer and honor your contribution. And that's how she mentors. Of course she imparts her knowledge, but by honoring what you have to offer, she empowers you to continue contributing. Then, when she knows where you're coming from, she can better guide you in the areas where she does have more expertise.
>
> *(Massie interview, July 2016)*

The art form of performance **255**

Third is Packer's willingness to *live through the conflicts* that inevitably arise in any artistic endeavor – especially if you're asking the 'big questions' of human life:

> There were moments in rehearsal when frustrating and difficult things were happening, and Tina would be a quiet presence. When I asked her about this, she said, 'All I do when I'm frustrated is breathe. Sometimes I get very frustrated, but I just let it happen.'
>
> *(Egozi interview, July 2016)*

In fact, Packer believes that the only way for a cast to get to know the fullness of Shakespeare's characters is to live through any difficulty that arises in the rehearsal room and for the director to resist the need to resolve it straightaway: 'She's really watching and engaging with the discussion in a way that she later sees how she can shape it creatively'[74] (Egozi). By witnessing who the team really is and honoring what they bring, Packer allows them to be creatively expressive and 'to make connections between yourself as an artist and yourself as a person'[75] (Egozi). In fact, her ability to collaborate and manifest a vision is 'just magical. I realized how much I'd been disconnected from Shakespeare's words and I've been waiting for the experience to bring the world and the words together. – And here it is!'[76] (Sawaf).

So those are some of the reasons young directors are drawn to the Company. But, of course, Packer is only one of many voices resonating throughout *Performance*. Actors, playwrights, seasoned directors – not to mention stage managers, designers and composers – return year after year. So …

What draws artists back to Shakespeare & Company?

What does it mean to be alive? What must we do? How should I act?

We've seen the premise of Shakespeare & Company was built on asking the 'big questions' – of oneself and of the world. And of the actors in the rehearsal room. And that process of questioning can be very alluring, be it with Packer, Burrows, Galvin or any of the rigorous directors at Shakespeare & Company.[77] Inevitably these 'big questions' can stir up our human complexity. And because they generally don't flinch from asking those questions, the Company becomes (in and of itself) the *debating chamber* that the Elizabethan playhouse offered, a reason why artists seek to return …

Debating the big questions

As creative teams in the Lenox rehearsal rooms tackle Shakespeare's 400-year-old texts, the myriad debates may focus on *historical narratives* (specific to the Elizabethans, relevant to the USA, universal to humanity and local to the Berkshires' community). And since Shakespeare constantly examined what it means to be alive – socially, sexually, culturally, racially, politically – the big questions

256 Performance

often focus on *identity*. So 'What must we do?' invites discussions in the rehearsal room that strive for collaboration, inclusion, diverse processes of personalization, and attention to the dramaturgy of the story being told. Of course, times are always a-changing. And the democratic, multi-racial dynamic on which the Company was founded in the 1970s (notably by two British women) has shifted significantly in twenty-first-century America. Color-conscious casting, approaches to violence and intimacy, discussions surrounding gender identity – these are ever-evolving conversations right across the performing arts, and the Company strives to engage actively in those debates, both with classical and contemporary plays.

All this to say that many artists are drawn back to Shakespeare & Company because it's not just about putting up a production and drawing in the crowds. The messy debates of 'What does it mean to be alive?' put dialog at the center of 'How should we act?' So when Packer took on the difficult material of *The Merchant of Venice* (2016), she brought together a diverse cast, including two Jewish American actors, an Israeli, four African Americans, one Indian American, a Canadian, three Brits and two white Americans, along with assistant directors Elizabeth Aspenlieder, Raphael Massie and Noa Egozi. This 'created a conducive environment for everyone to share their experience,' voiced Company actor Cloteal L. Horne. 'In a room where there's such diversity, there's increased opportunity for all of us to enter into the dialog.'[78] And in 2019 Allyn Burrows cast Deaon Griffin-Pressley and Ella Loudon cross-racially as the twins Viola and Sebastian in his production of *Twelfth Night* inspired by 1959. This created a gritty opportunity, to be further teased out in production, inviting everyone to reflect upon un/conscious biases in the hopes of seeing beyond 'otherness' toward shared humanity. There was one particularly exciting matinee when a multi-racial school-party from Boston whooped with delight as the twins found and embraced each other at the end of the play. The theatre's acoustic was vibrating.

Debating the complex issues also includes sharing *genders*. In fact, cross-gender and multi-role casting have long been a vibrant part of Shakespeare & Company's aesthetic. Lisa Wolpe (longtime Company member and celebrated actor of Shakespeare's males) played four roles in *Coriolanus* (2001), demanding of her a physical, emotional and psychological dexterity: 'The quickness with which I spin around to play someone else challenges my ability to [...] access the thoughts and feelings on a profound level'[79] (Wolpe). And it demanded of the audience a suspension of disbelief 'stretched to its utmost.'[80] Likewise, suspended disbelief was definitely the case with *Cymbeline* (2017), with Ella Loudon cast as Welsh prince Guiderius and I (Merlin, twice Loudon's age) as her younger brother Arviragus. (Now that was stretching disbelief to the utmost ...) When we switch across the genders, we offer up all manner of provocations – to actors and audiences alike – about social norms and gendered behaviors in our increasingly fluid times. And Shakespeare & Company explores gender identities right down to the most localized level of the individual self. With workshops on

The art form of performance   **257**

'Shakespeare and Gender' introduced into the *Training* program in recent years, Shakespeare's plays provide us with thoughtful material, not least because his original actors were all males and many of his characters are gender-fluid. Be it Puck and Ariel; the disguises of Viola/Cesario and Rosalind/Ganymede; the male–male relationships of Cassius/Brutus and Coriolanus/Aufidius; or the 'unsexing' of Lady Macbeth and Queen Margaret in violent circumstances – even the mercurial love-encounters in the sonnets – there are constant challenges to gendered binaries and, therefore, to our own expectations of ourselves. As poet, playwright and Company actor Nehassaiu deGannes notes, 'you come to the cellular knowing of your self and a cellular recognition of the way in which Shakespeare in his brilliance calls to all of us – in all of his characters – to be grappling with gendered, archetypal forms.'[81] And as we grapple with the archetypes, perhaps we have a chance to recognize something in ourselves.

Grappling with the archetypes and ensuring parity between the genders doesn't stop on the stage, but also relates to administrative staff and production teams. In recent years, Shakespeare & Company has featured in the top four-percentile in the USA for representing female directors and playwrights on their stages. And over the years the Company has nurtured a strong team of female directors including Kate Cherry, Kelly Galvin, Rebecca Holderness, Eleanor Holdridge, Cecil MacKinnon, Normi Noel, Nicole Ricciardi and Daniela Varon. There's also a balance in the contemporary repertoire, with local playwrights including Joan Ackermann (*Ice Glen*, which was written for the Company) and international playwrights including Lynn Nottage (*Intimate Apparel*), Lindsey Ferrentino (*Ugly Lies the Bone*) and Lucy Kirkwood (*The Children*). As well, of course, as the Edith Wharton adaptations.

The 'big question' of 'How should we act?' refers not only to our daily lives, but also – as actors – to our professional vocation. And another reason artists return to Shakespeare & Company is the ongoing investment in the *art of acting*.

The art of acting

Vocational mentoring operates in *Performance* as in *Training* and *Education*. Indeed, the 'Values that Unite Us' includes the statement, 'We believe mentoring is integral to a healthy society.'[82] And this holds true for veteran actors and emerging artists alike. When Cloteal L. Horne was cast as Helena in her first professional season, she was surrounded by 'this amazing company of actors, who knew the work and Shakespeare's texts intimately. So, as a young actor, I got to pick their brains and learn from them and watch them and study their craft.'[83] She took text sessions with fellow actors Johnny Lee Davenport and Jonathan Epstein, and sought input from artist-educators Malcolm and Elizabeth Ingram. And she adopted a similar process in 2019 when working as Olivia to the Malvolio of award-winning actor and S&Co. 'newcomer' Miles Anderson.

Veteran actor Nigel Gore is also drawn back to Shakespeare & Company because of the immersion in the work. 'It's where I found my voice. Not only

FIGURE 13.2 Miles Anderson (Malvolio) and Cloteal L. Horne (Olivia) in *Twelfth Night*, dir. Allyn Burrows, 2019
Photo: Daniel Rader

my literal voice, but also my artistic voice. And I began to find out what the work here was all about by watching Company members who are really accomplished.'[84] Gore joined S&Co. in 2006, playing Claudius opposite Packer's Gertrude, as well as partnering her in *Women of Will* from 2009 onwards (see Figure 13.1). And he has returned to Lenox almost every summer since:

> Shakespeare & Company always gives you the opportunity to be better, go further. And you know it'll put you into creative places where you're not necessarily comfortable. […] The fact that we have movement specialists come in during rehearsals; we have text coaches with whom we can go through text; we have voice warm ups before performances … I'd never experienced this before.
>
> *(Gore interview, August 2017)*

Given the Company's commitment to learning, sharing and mentoring, I knew what to do when, in 2017, I was cast as Trinculo in *The Tempest*. I went straight to Kevin Coleman, who has played myriad clowns, fools and jesters at Shakespeare & Company and who generously gave me advice on transferring *Clown* from *Training* (as discussed in Chapter 8) to *Performance*.

The dramaturgy of Clown

Since the clowns were important in Shakespeare's troupe, so too are the clown roles in his plays. And while S&Co.'s *Training* accesses all manner of acting tools through *Clown*, we'll focus for a moment here on the storytelling strategies for clowns in performance. Coleman's first piece of advice was to *understand what type of clown you're playing*. Are they a *clown by nature* (such as Aguecheek, Don Armado or Bottom) or a *professional clown* (such as the jesters Trinculo, Touchstone and Feste, or Lear's Fool)? The professional clowns also have differences: 'A jester is different from a fool, as a jester is always playing *low status* to a king. Whereas the fool has no fixed status, so can play *higher status* than the king.'[85] Coleman's second piece of advice was to *give yourself plenty of permission*: 'Have fun! Run wild! Misbehave!'[86] Which isn't always as easy as it sounds, and yet once you find that (responsible) freedom – with the script, the director, your fellow actors and, ultimately, the audience – not only is the pleasure supreme, but you're also actually serving the dramaturgy of the clown scenes:

> I think Shakespeare knows that's what's needed and he allows the clowns to destroy the seriousness of a scene. The clowns don't worry about the world of the play because they have other extreme concerns. […] If the stakes are too low, the clown-characters become vague, and then the clown-scenes are confusing.
>
> *(Coleman interview, July 2017)*

Just as there are clownmasters at Shakespeare & Company, there are also fightmasters, whose dramaturgical strategies have made a major impact on the Company's performance style.

FIGURE 13.3 (a) Kevin G. Coleman as Touchstone (*As You Like It*), dir. Eleanor Holdridge, 2004; (b) as The Fool (*King Lear*), dir. Tina Packer, 2003

Photos: Kevin Sprague

260 Performance

The dramaturgy of Fight

Tony Simotes (former Artistic Director and fight director) starts with *character*. 'I ask the actors to tell me [...] their story in the play [and] how their character feels in a scene.'[87] And as he listens, he starts imagining how those characters might move on stage and then embodies each role a little to get 'a shape of how physical moves affect emotions or the reverse.'[88] Then there's the *rhythm of the text*, which affects the intensity of the fights: 'If someone speaks in short, staccato bursts, I will find movement to reflect that. [...] Hal is a defensive man. Hotspur, on the other hand, is a charging bull, so I move them that way.'[89] Then, as B. H. Barry points out, there's the storytelling impact of the *actual weapon* being used:

> A weapon is designed to cause harm. How it does this varies with its shape, sharpness and size. Is it going to be used with one hand or two? Will it be used to club, cut, pierce, smash armor or kill a horse?
>
> *(Barry, B. H., Fights for Everyone: The Performer's Guide, Self-published, 2013: 52)*

Which in turn combines with the *nationality of the fighters* and *the historical period*: for *Henry IV, Part 1* (1997), Simotes considered the 'different values of fighting. [...] In my reading, the Welsh are more mystical in their approach to battle while the English are more straightforward.'[90] In *Cymbeline* (2017), Martin Jason Asprey (fight director and lifelong Company member) used similar dramaturgical strategies: for the ancient Britons he incorporated two-handed broadswords and ragtag energy as they bashed their way to defeat at the hands of the Romans, who meanwhile fought in orderly rank-and-file with elegant weaponry. (As you'll see in Chapter 15, the same five actors played both Romans *and* Britons, so we needed all the dramaturgical help we could get!)

Given the range of human knowledge available at Shakespeare & Company, it's clear why artists like to return. But what about the *audiences*?

What draws audiences back to Shakespeare & Company?

Summer after summer, audiences return to Shakespeare & Company. In fact, it only took a couple of years following the founding of the Company for their performance aesthetic to be celebrated – for its physical vitality, theatrical invention, fresh and conversational style of delivery, all while honoring the verse. As loyal audience member and valiant volunteer Sarah Lytle puts it, 'I know I will almost always be surprised and challenged. The core values of the Company stress finding truth in performance and, in my experience, that mandate has come through every year.'[91] 'Invaluable and indefatigable' wrote *New York Times* critic Ben Brantley.[92] 'Among the best Shakespeare performances that I've seen by any company in any country' wrote Ed Siegel of the *Boston Globe*.[93]

And with Allyn Burrows at the helm, the future promises to be 'as spectacular as it is surprising.'[94] What more could you want from a performance?

Notes

1 Tina Packer interview, interviewer KB, PM, Subject #TH-004, 11 May 2000, p. 16. S&Co. archive.
2 Kevin Coleman interview with Bella Merlin, August 2016.
3 Coleman interview, August 2016.
4 Dennis Krausnick interview with Bella Merlin, September 2018.
5 Packer cited in Caffrey, B. (1980), 'Tina Packer: A Passionate Woman With Definite Ideas,' *Evening Independent*, 29 November 1980, (my emphasis).
6 Krausnick interview, September 2018.
7 ibid.
8 Packer cited in Caffrey (1980).
9 Coleman interview, August 2016.
10 'Conversations with Tina Packer,' interviewer unnamed, *newberkshire.com*, 2002.
11 Tina Packer interview, 11 May 2000, p. 17.
12 ibid.
13 Packer in 'Training Shakespeare Actors in A Modern World: Tina Packer Talks to Helen Epstein …,' 24 January 2007, p. 12. S&Co. archive.
14 *Rubato* literally means 'stolen' and, by notating particular passages with *tempo rubato*, Chopin was giving his musicians permission to speed up and slow down as seemed appropriate, robbing some notes of their length in order to make others a little longer, provided the overall rhythm, structure and appropriate pacing were observed. It means the musician could 'linger hesitantly' or 'impatiently anticipate' a moment, almost as if the musician were dialoging with the music, or the soloist were dialoging with the accompaniment. Cf. Rowlands, D. (1994), 'Chopin's *Tempo Rubato* in Context,' in Rink J. and Samson, J. (eds.), *Chopin Studies 2*, London: Cambridge University Press, pp. 199–213.
15 Packer interview, 11 May 2000.
16 ibid.
17 Coleman interview, August 2016.
18 Tina Packer email to Bella Merlin, 22 September 2019.
19 Linklater, K. (2015), 'Hypothetical Four-Year Actor-Training Program' in Evans, M. (ed.), *The Actor Training Reader*, Abingdon & New York: Routledge, pp. 94–97.
20 ibid., p. 95.
21 ibid., pp. 95–96.
22 Kelly Galvin email correspondence with Bella Merlin, 8 July 2019.
23 Allyn Burrows interview with Michael Miller, https://hudson-housatonic-arts.org/2019/01/allyn-burrows-artistic-director-of-shakespeare-and-company-talks-to-michael-miller-about-the-2018-season-directing-acting-and-actors-and-of-course-shakespeare/27 January 2019 (accessed 15 August 2019).
24 Burrows cited in Merlin rehearsal notes, *Twelfth Night*, Summer 2019.
25 Packer interview, 11 May 2000.
26 ibid.
27 ibid.
28 Packer notes, March 2019.
29 Packer interview, 11 May 2000.
30 ibid.
31 ibid.

262 Performance

32 Packer cited in Race, N. (2001), 'Tina Packer: Shakespeare & Co. and the Founder's Theatre' *The Artful Mind*, July 2001.
33 Packer interview, 11 May 2000.
34 Coleman interview, August 2016.
35 Linklater cited in Jenkins, R. (1983) 'As they Like it: A Devoted Young Theater Group Enhances Shakespeare's Words with Motion and Emotion,' *The Boston Globe*, 31 July 1983.
36 Packer cited in ibid., (my emphasis).
37 ibid.
38 Packer document: 'Artistic Director's Statement – Ensemble Grant, S&Co. archive.'
39 Kiki Smith returns regularly to the Company including for Coleman's production of *The Merry Wives of Windsor* (2019).
40 Packer document: 'Artistic Director's Statement – Ensemble Grant.'
41 The main female director at the RSC in the 1970s was Buzz Goodbody, who sadly committed suicide. Joan Littlewood was one of the few female Brits who sustained a powerful career at that time. Cf. Wolff-Wilkinson, L. (1994, 2019), *Buzz Goodbody and her* Hamlet: *A Study*, unpublished DFA thesis.
42 The meat of this section is drawn from a paper entitled 'Creating the Living Word: An Anglo-Russian-American Perspective on Psychophysical Acting' delivered by Merlin at the Shanghai Theatre Academy's 2nd International Forum on Actor Training in November 2018.
43 The first day of rehearsing *The Merry Wives of Windsor* with Kevin Coleman in July 2019 featured *feeding in*, so that from the get-go the actors could be in their bodies on the rehearsal-room floor, in relation to each other and not buried in the script.
44 Packer in 'Training Shakespeare Actors in A Modern World,' p. 15.
45 ibid.
46 ibid., p. 22.
47 ibid., p. 23.
48 ibid., p. 15, (my emphasis).
49 ibid., p. 19, (my emphasis).
50 Shakespeare, W. (1611), *The Winter's Tale*, Act I, Scene ii, 137–146, Leontes.
51 Packer in 'Training Shakespeare Actors in A Modern World,' p. 15.
52 Frances West cited in Cahill, Nunley, Sokol and Banner (2000), 'Muses in Arcadia,' *Frontlist* 2000.
53 ibid.
54 Jonathan Epstein cited in Cahill, Nunley, Sokol and Banner (2000),
55 ibid.
56 ibid.
57 Massie and Egozi assisted on both *The Merchant of Venice* (2016) and *Cymbeline* (2017), with Sawaf joining for the latter. In 2019, Raz Golden assisted both Kevin Coleman on *The Merry Wives of Windsor* and Daniela Varon on *Coriolanus*, again on a Drama League Directing Fellowship.
58 Packer to the assistant directors: Merlin, '*Cymbeline* rehearsal notes,' July 2017.
59 Noa Egozi interview with Bella Merlin, July 2016.
60 ibid.
61 ibid.
62 Kholoud Sawaf interview with Bella Merlin, July 2017.
63 Raphael Massie interview with Bella Merlin, July 2016.
64 ibid.
65 Egozi interview, July 2016.
66 Massie interview, July 2016.
67 Sawaf interview, July 2017.
68 Packer edit, March 2019.

The art form of performance **263**

69 Egozi interview, July 2016.
70 ibid.
71 Massie interview, July 2016.
72 Elizabeth Aspenlieder interview with Bella Merlin, July 2016.
73 Egozi interview, July 2016.
74 ibid.
75 Egozi interview, July 2016.
76 Sawaf interview, July 2017.
77 Including in recent seasons Regge Life, Nicole Ricciardi, Daniela Varon and James Warwick, with both contemporary plays and classics.
78 Cloteal L. Horne interview with Bella Merlin, August 2016.
79 Lisa Wolpe cited in Race (2001).
80 ibid.
81 Nehassaiu deGannes interview with Bella Merlin, August 2017.
82 'Statement of Values that Unite Us,' c. 2000. S&Co. archive.
83 Horne interview, August 2016.
84 Nigel Gore interview with Bella Merlin, August 2017.
85 Kevin Coleman interview with Bella Merlin, July 2017.
86 ibid.
87 Tony Simotes cited in Borak, J. (1997), 'Accepting the Rigors of Action: Shakespeare & Co. Fight Director Fits Movement to Character,' *Berkshires Week*, 31 July 1997.
88 ibid.
89 ibid.
90 Simotes cited in Bass, M. (1997), 'Battling away at The Mount,' *Berkshires Week*, 24–30 July 1997.
91 Sarah Lytle email to Bella Merlin, 30 July 2019.
92 Ben Brantley cited in Siegel, E. (2007), 'Conjuring Magic at Shakespeare & Company,' *Berkshire Living*, July 2007.
93 Siegel (2007).
94 St Clair, A. (2019) 'Review of *Twelfth Night*,' *The Berkshire Edge*, 15 July 2019.

14

TALK #3

Theatre, Therapy and Theology

A man is praying at an altar, eyes upturned to the heavens.

A man is sitting at the crossroads, surrounded by earth and grass and breezes, becoming one with the universe.

A teenage girl is sitting in her therapist's office, inarticulate about why she cuts herself every day.

A teenage boy sits in a group of other boys, supervised by a fatherly 30-year-old, stumbling toward some understanding of why the boy won't eat, or if he does, why he has to vomit – knowing he will die if he doesn't find the answer, feeling he will die if he has to ingest food.

A group of people enact a story about a man who yearns for God,[1] starves himself and sits in a cave through a long winter. On the surface of the man's hands and feet, globs of blood begin to appear. The group of people talk to the birds and animals as the man did, but can only gaze at pictures of the stigmata: they cannot re-enact that. Nor can they sit in the cave through the long winter.

A Christian man in Egypt tries to understand why he is targeted to die. A Muslim woman and her mother in Syria pray that they and the children won't be hit by bombs from the sky. A soldier from Senegal is walking by himself across the Sahara desert, towards a promised land. A Rashidi woman from Myanmar now knows that a fellow countryman will rape her, though he is a Buddhist and Buddhists eschew violence. None of this makes sense. But it is real.

A woman is lying on her back, screaming as hard as she can, bearing down in long, hard rhythms, trying to push the child out from between her legs. A baby's crown appears, bloody and miraculous. She births life.

Men have been dancing for 12 hours, collectively and individually, shifting minds, bodies, earth, rhythms, stomping to make the rains come. The rain comes.

Talk #3: Theatre, Therapy and Theology **265**

The Bride walks down the aisle dressed in flowing, virginal white. The father gives her away, though she hasn't done what he told her to do since she was 12 years old. And he certainly knows she's not a virgin. And so does the man to whom he's giving her. And so does she! They are all happy this moment has come.

A sailor weeps as his lips say, 'In sooth, I know not why I am so sad.'[2] But he does know why he is so sad. The words make him weep. The water flows down his cheeks.

A person who identifies as neither man nor boy, woman nor girl, struggles to find a place, knowing the body and mind can fill any identity, if the voice is strong enough to claim it. But who will hear?

Theatre, Therapy and Theology: joined since time began, words were formed, questions asked, answers sought.[3] The places where we seek to find insight into our own behaviors and the actions of the world. So let's take ourselves back to ancient Greece … then dart to the present … maybe flit between the two and around …

In order for us to understand the relationship between the gods, nature and the community, an amphitheatre has been carved into the hillside so that earth, air, fire and water are consciously part of this story. The dimensions of the seating, the curve of the perimeter, the acoustics of the stone and brass, all measured and duplicated so that, when the whole community comes to hear the story, the telling will be amplified *externally* so the meaning will be connected *internally*. The vibrations can go up to the gods so the universe is kept in harmony. The play takes place on the *surface* of the earth, but the stomping of the dancing feet of the chorus resonates *into* the earth.

Beside the theatre in Ephesus we have dug a chamber deep into the earth where we can tell our personal dreams. We fill a pit with snakes, whose poison in small drops immunizes the body, and in large portions kills. The priest listens as a man lies on an elevated slab. Deep in the earth, the unconscious mind can be known; what can't be seen in daylight can be revealed in the dark by this skilled therapist. The dream, which is performed like a play in the sleeping, human mind, has messages for the human who dreamed. Or maybe there's a message from the gods to the whole community. The therapist will know. He is adept in the 'healing of god.'

As the play is performed, a person belonging to all genders guides the story, seeing the future and the past, eschewing sexual identity for a greater knowledge, and thereby surrendering gender as a place to blame for the sins of the world. Tiresias does not attribute blame, only sees cause and effect, chaos and form. But *we* blame. We think that if we could get rid of a person, we'll get rid of the hurt. So Tiresias will be blamed by everyone and be sacrificed by Apollo, carrying all our projections. And Tiresias is now mourned ('twere the cheaper way …').[4] Tiresias is the embodiment of Theatre and Therapy and Theology. Tiresias will die in order to be born again; be genderless until he becomes she, she becomes he, they become they, and a new form is born.

266 Performance

THEOLOGY is the 'study of God' (however we choose to interpret that concept … in ancient times, now, or in between …). We study God, gods, forms of worship, sacred texts, our own and other people's.

THERAPY is the 'healing of God.' In the dark chamber, someone more skilled than yourself can see patterns in your daily behavior, the relationships you build and destroy, and what truth your unconscious mind is revealing in dreams. (In ancient times the therapist would advise if this was your personal dream or whether it should be told to the whole community; in our times only you and your therapist will know.)

Finally, THEATRE is 'the place where God is found.' Some say theatre is 'the place where God is *heard*.' And so the amphitheatre is built into the hillside: the sky, the mountains, the crevices reminding the whole community where the gods live; the playing space below is the altar for Dionysus, god of theatre, wine and madness. The sounds of the people playing the chorus – half-singing, half-speaking, hovering between this world and the next, between sanity and madness – reveal, through the story, those things which are hidden in our memory. Hidden because they are not spoken. Hidden because it is forbidden to speak of them. But in this sacred space they *will* be spoken. This is an *amphi*-theatre: it *amplifies* the message through the sound, the rhythms of the dancers, the voices of the story. In this space we can expand ourselves – to be in touch with the largest elements, to have the power to contain and understand – and celebrate the twisted pathways of our smaller selves.

And we must *know* the gods. We must listen to nature, listen to the theosophist. We must let our vibrations guide the whole city-state: with messages about family life; about our interaction with the stranger at the crossroads; the foreigner who led us out of the labyrinth; the meaning of the plague; the sacrifice of the daughter. The psychological and political must both find their common ground. And he that hides from the Bacchanalia does so at his peril. For healthy individuals means a healthy society.

And so we have a *desire* for 'God,' some kind of unifying principle that makes sense of our lives. That makes us whole. That isn't random. That proves there is something greater than simply 'our bodies' and 'our desires.' And the very yearning for that unifying principle is our *soul*, which links us to the eternal. The drive to understand the way our organs, nervous system, blood circulation, impulses to think, feel, act, all work: all these together make up our spirit. Of course our sensory perceptions – those attributes that allow us to gather knowledge through taste, touch, smell, hearing and sight – don't always lead us to *wise* choices. And so, if a good marketing campaign can persuade us that 'this dress,' or 'those shoes,' or 'that car' can complete our life, then maybe for two or three days we can remain on a high as we indulge our pleasure. But then the big questions – the important questions – return. And by then we've already wasted two or three days. And now these big questions are even more urgent. In this way we're entertaining ourselves to death. Slowly killing ourselves like the frogs in the water, not noticing it's gradually coming to the boil.

Talk #3: Theatre, Therapy and Theology

But We Must Survive …

Survival in the past has often meant 'my tribe, not your tribe.' But now we have to get beyond this feeling of threat. If we continue to obey our primitive knee-jerk reaction of 'this person doesn't look like me. They must be the enemy, so I'll drive them away,' we're not going to evolve.

And We Must Evolve …

We now have bombs that could obliterate the whole world several times over. We're already killing the planet at a rapid rate. If we don't get beyond our unconscious drives and our titillating desires, we simply will not survive. Our evolution may come with the help of a religious or spiritual impulse that tells us, 'We are all God's creatures.' It may come from the curiosity to welcome interaction with people who *don't* look and sound like us. It may be a realization that survival, creativity, production, all work better when the gene pool is larger – and certainly much larger than our own immediate tribe, as the ancient Greeks realized when ten tribes came together to make 'Athens.' But in order for us to build community with 'strangers,' *empathy* must be aroused. Common stories must be found. Food, music, children joyfully co-mingled. Creativity, rather than fear, must become the dominant impulse. Because fear closes all doors, except to survival: yet acting out of fear often means you *won't* survive.

Theatre, Therapy and Theology. Recognizing their common roots can play their part in helping us shift the pictures, engage our minds, and eschew superficial entertainment. If *fear* is the tool for present danger, *love* is the tool for future empowerment. Understanding the connections between one human being and another not only evaporates fear, but also brings a shared understanding, which

FIGURE 14.1 Dennis Krausnick as King Lear, dir. Rebecca Holderness, 2012
Photo: Kevin Sprague

268 Performance

in turn opens the door to all kinds of other connections: both the visceral and the intellectual, the spiritual and the sexual (which includes companionship, love, laughter, intimacy).

Theatre, with its unique tool set, can make these connections. Adelheid Roosen, a theatre visionary from Holland, arranged in one theatre happening for middle-aged women in the audience to ride on the back of the motorcycles of young Muslim men through the streets of the Hague and Amsterdam. In another happening, she had people of all religions sleep overnight together on the floor of a school. She felt that enabling her young actors and audience to do something so basic yet so intimate together would break down divisions and they would find out what they needed to say to each other. Is this really theatre? I don't know. It certainly asks the big questions: 'What does it mean to be a human being? How should we act? What must I do?' In fact, one of Adelheid's most seminal pieces was 'The Veiled Monologues.' It was based in form on *The Vagina Monologues* only it concentrated on clitoridectomies within the Muslim communities of myriad countries. She had no shortage of women willing to come forward to tell their stories, but she could only get Turkish-born actors to perform the play: the others were too scared. Nevertheless, the piece went forward and, despite death threats, shed light on important semi-religious, semi-social practices that needed to be addressed, discussed and changed.

Sharing stories like this through *language* is how we connect ourselves with other people. Language is the glue that binds – whether in love or hatred. With our natural desire to understand the 'big moments' in life, language is the means by which we formulate our perceptions, and then share that understanding with others. Whether it's Birth. Death. Sex. Love. Family. Infidelity. Rejection of Family Power Structures. Desire for More Status. Murder, Rape, Violence. Pitting Bravery against Death. Climbing the Mountain. What makes us grow, expand, see more? What makes us bond with others, feel outrage, be in awe of human behavior – good or bad? What makes us write a constitution that future generations can aspire to? How do we know ourselves and others? *Language.* Our means for sharing and connecting is language.

Yet we're living in conflicted times. On the one hand, the bombardment of fake news breeds the angry, 'me-not-you' instincts: 'My tribe is right, yours is wrong.' And the television images that illustrate these moments, excite our blood, dull our brains, reinforce our tribalism, and divorce us from the idea that we might actually have something in common with this 'enemy.' What begins at a political rally or a soccer match might end up on the battlefield, or with the women and children dead under a bombardment. On the other hand, live theatre can offer a small antidote to that fake news. It can take the same dramatic moment and gather people together to examine why this moment is so. Take *Macbeth*: a story of excess: it makes us ask the big questions. And although the bloodiest events aren't shown, the build-up, the triggers, the causes, and the resulting consequences *are* there on the stage for everyone to experience. The suffering of a whole nation at the end of the chain of events ... The human culpability in allowing this to happen … We watch and hear all this as it unfurls on the stage in front of us.

And so Theatre has this opportunity to ask the big questions collectively, to make the connections. To bring together (if I can put it like this) the dimensions of spiritual practice and therapy. The burning question is how to make the experience on stage so deep, that we can truly learn from it? How can we understand in the present moment what's actually going on? How can we ensure that the audience is not only reacting and being triggered, but also seeing *why* they're reacting and being triggered? And 'being triggered' can be an important teaching tool: it's nature's way of asking, 'What's this about? Is this experience pleasurable or horrifying or maybe both?' So we shouldn't necessarily shut down the triggering: we should use it.

It's certainly true that therapy can effect some healing after a long period of time. We can work with our bodies to gently release the traumatized areas. Or at least, we can learn to recognize the physical symptoms of the trauma as they come in, and educate ourselves not to react as if our survival were under threat. That's the function of therapy. (But it comes *after* the event; whereas our dreams, as the ancients knew, are the means by which our unconscious mind gives up its secrets, so that perhaps we can be forewarned *before* the event.) And this therapy will be undertaken *in private*, one person at a time. But might it not be possible to speak of these traumas *in public*, so that 500 people at a time can start finding a way through them – a collective therapy? A collective asking? A theatre healing? We know that the world is made up of trauma and joy and growth – from ourselves, our parents and grandparents, way back into our ancestry. We're living the consequences of those who came before us, passed on through economic patterns, genetic information, psychic damage, institutional structures. And that collective trauma has to be addressed, whether it's war, slavery, exploitation or genocide. We can let it go *only* through recognition, acknowledgment and regret; and thereby let go of the hatred, anger and shame.

And for me that's the primary role of Theatre: in large pictures and small, through humor, song, rage and, above all, through connection. Through insight. Insight through *sight*. The Greeks, Romans and Elizabethans knew that going to the theatre was not just about *seeing the gods* or the spiritual. In theatre – the place where the community gathers – the audience *saw each other*. You were a part of the whole gathering. The seating wrapped around the playing space, so that you knew, you *felt*, you were a part of something much larger than the individual self. And the Elements were present: the light, the wind, the stunning landscape. (Even though in Elizabethan times they painted the heavens on the stage ceiling – and you could only see part of the real sky above the Wooden O – its whole presence was there nevertheless.) We get little of this now in the theatre. We're lucky if we can even see our fellow audience members. Yet we're still coming together to build our sense of community. Together, we watch and listen to a story that will take us out of ourselves and, at the same

270 Performance

time, offer us something relevant that helps us answer the big questions and understand what life is about.

This very act of collectively asking questions about our existence lifts us out of ourselves. It gives us delight. A mental delight. A sense of wonder and mystery. Whether we enter a cathedral built specifically to allow us to experience that mystery (with its Rose window shining ancient secrets of color and form) or we're sitting in an amphitheatre (looking up to the mountain tops in a great landscape of earth and sky), we feel the wonder of this universe that's so much larger than ourselves. A *spiritual presence*. And this is where Theatre can transcend real life. Here's how ...

In real 'life-and-death' events, there's a point where we can feel that *presence* and absorb it – and there's a point where we can't. If something is happening for real – say, a mob is surrounding a person and they're going to kill them – we might not actually believe what we're seeing. Or we might know it's true and run away as fast as we can. Or we might stand mesmerized unable to move. Or a few of us, a rare few, might actually run into the crowd and try and stop the killing. (A mother watching her son, for instance, would probably run into the fray.) But whatever the situation and whatever the reaction, your reaction in that real-life moment would be automatic, autonomic. You wouldn't be asking *why* is this happening? Nor what you could do about it. Nor why you were behaving in the way you were behaving. You might reflect on it later, of course, but in the actual moment, your body is going to take over and you'll act in the way your automatic (autonomic) nervous system dictates you should act.

Now let *Theatre* take that same dramatic moment ...

The mob has surrounded Cinna and they're going to kill him (even after they've registered he's Cinna the *poet*, not Cinna the *conspirator*). And the danger, the violent actions, the building of the frenzy, the mob mentality, the manner of the death, the knives, the kicking, the tearing, the sounds, shrieks, grunts, are going all to be the same as in real life – except the actor playing Cinna is *not* going to be killed and the actors playing the mob are *not* going to kill him. They *are* going to make it so realistic the audience reacts as if they *are* killing him. So then the audience can allow themselves to register their own emotions and feelings. And the actors can allow themselves to plug into the mob mentality *because* they know they're not going to kill Cinna – but they willl certainly make it look as if they are! And it's essential that the truth of this situation can come through, because then we have the opportunity of collectively asking, 'What just happened? Why did those human beings behave like that? And how can we *not* behave like that in those circumstances?' It's a conversation that comes out of reality and responsibility, rather than dismissing it with an, 'Oh, I'd never behave like that,' or 'That could never happen to me.' It's by recognizing that it *could* happen to any one of us: that's what unites actors and audiences in this 'ritual.' ('Ritual,' because it's choreographed and repeatable, and each step is precisely executed.) And it excites a reaction *as if it were true*. It's traumatizing and cathartic. It's a life cycle about which we can perhaps come to a deeper understanding, rather than addicting our audience to more violence. But, like the therapeutic powers of inserting one drop of poison so that the body produces the antibodies to repel the sickness, we can recognize what we've just *avoided* and we can be wiser in building our social structures. In other words, we can know both the danger *and* the way out of that danger.

For over 3,000 years we have been groping our way toward understanding why we behave the way we do as human beings. We've come a long way. The stories of human behavior and their consequences are buried in our myths – and those myths both illuminate and offer wisdom about our ways of doing things. We want to know the actions of our forefathers and foremothers. And we may want to *repeat* those actions; or we may feel we are *stuck* in them whether we like it or not; or we may feel our *validity* comes from doing them in the same way that they were done before – or *not* doing them in the same way that they were done before. In any case, we want to *be conscious of* what we're doing, so that we can validate ourselves both from without and within. We want both the satisfaction of deep love for another and the ability to say, 'I am myself alone.' Or, 'This lives after me.' What we *don't* want to feel is that our lives made absolutely no difference to anyone whatsoever. Which is all to say: we want to feel power in our everyday lives. Some kind of 'authenticity.' That doesn't mean having dominance over others so that they don't have any power in their own lives (though we often mistake it for that). It does mean embodying our own life force *consciously*.

And this is what actors do. They fill every cell in their body with life; they alert the spirit; they joyfully use the voice. And they strive to be as conscious as possible of everything around them. Our collective understanding of why we do

FIGURE 14.2 Allyn Burrows (Coriolanus) and Tina Packer (Volumnia), *Coriolanus* workshop production, dir. Daniela Varon, 2019

Photo: Emma Rothenberg-Ware

272 Performance

what we do has to be present in the act of Theatre. Because in the act of Theatre we're performing our lives; we're understanding why we're performing our lives; and we're spiritually exulting in the fact that we *can* perform our lives.

So how do the three disciplines of Theatre, Therapy and Theology come together?

Well, at their heart are *moments of truth*. And it's in those moments of truth that all three disciplines merge into one. Those moments come when the actor (or rabbi, or priest, or shaman or 'therapee') owns what they are saying deeply (acknowledging his/her/their *personal connection*). Then the words – because of their 'poetic' form – go far beyond personal ownership and pass into the universal; and the members of the audience (or congregation or therapist) can feel the truth of what's being said. And they all know they are in the presence of a *revelation*. That revelation is sacred *because* it is true; it holds intellectual perception, empathetic connection, and deep knowledge in the body. The poetic form generates sensations – even creativity – in the listener by the very DNA of the words, the sounds, the atavistic structure, the rhythm. And in those moments lies great theatre, as well as healing therapy and a palpable presence of something more than us. That spiritual presence? A 'higher power'?

And wouldn't it be wonderful if theatrical performances of this power were made in every town and village, zip code and battleship, homeless shelter and presidential palace? The same plays *and* different plays. I suggest that every part of the country has the responsibility to understand the history of that land: Whose blood was shed and how? Why was that blood shed and are we still doing it? What might be the understanding gained from our common events – whether we're the inheritors of the conquerors or the vanquished – so that we can acknowledge that past and move forward into the future? Not least it means understanding how technology is cutting us off from each other ... while superficially connecting us ... while distancing us from the deeper connections absolutely necessary for our spirits to flourish and our children to grow up.

Therapy and Theology, I argue, are both necessary ingredients of Theatre – though both can, and should, be used separately from Theatre. But for Theatre to truly work, we need to train our actors and our playwrights not only to understand deeply our human behavior, but also its possible consequences, its influences both for growth and for destruction. The small picture connected to the big picture. The rites that unite us. The sense of belonging. Let's learn from indigenous cultures. The rhythms, sounds and calls that live in the cells of our bodies, stir our spirits, call us to our larger selves: this is Theatre.

My own dream is that all plays ask Shakespeare's three great questions: 'What does it mean to be a human being? How should we act? What must I do?' Those are the questions whether we're trying to make sense of gun violence in America, xenophobia in Hungary, a child washed up on a Greek shore, the life of a boy soldier in Angola, the rise of Kim Kardashian, the opioid crisis or the death of an unarmed person in an unmarked grave. The spirit, the heart, the viscera, the connection between us, infuse every answer. And those answers can be *felt* as well as *understood*. Yet catharsis cannot take place if we don't *surrender*. And we can't surrender if we don't know what the matter is. ('What's the matter?' Coriolanus asks the working people.[5] 'What's the matter?' Hamlet asks his mother.[6] 'What's the matter?' we ask ourselves until we go deep enough to find an answer.) And we don't know what the matter is if we haven't asked the right questions.

So, even if only 50 people see the performance: Has the play asked the right questions?

Have the actors worked hard enough on themselves and their craft that they can touch the atavistic depths of the words? That they're funny enough to create laughter together? Strong enough to fight? Conscious enough to keep everyone safe?

Has the playwright developed a script that has evolved the structure and scenes in such a way that we can respond to the tiny, individual moments of truth and understand the larger, social political landscape the play lives in?

And how does it connect to the past?

And what will be the trajectory into the future? …

Notes

1 While 'God' is talked about a lot in this chapter, you're invited to interpret the word, as you will. It essentially means whatever we might believe in beyond the three dimensions, if indeed we want to believe in anything at all.

2 Shakespeare, W. (1597), *The Merchant of Venice*, Act I, Scene i, line 1, Antonio.

3 In 1997 longtime Company actor Peter Wittrock wrote a dissertation for the School for New Learning entitled 'A Discussion of the Ritual Roots of Theater' (S&Co. archive). In it he notes that 'theology' comes from *theos* (God) and *logos* (science of, or study of). *Therapeia* means 'to tend or to treat (as in healing) originally 'to tend in the sense of worship or sacrifice' and only used in the modern, psychological sense in the late nineteenth century. And *theatron* means 'the seeing place' and may also be related to *thauma* ('wonder' or 'miracle'): so the theatre 'is both a place from which you see things but also something special that is seen – a wonder or a miracle.' (p. 2). Wittrock notes in his dissertation that, although etymologically 'theology' doesn't have the same prefix as either 'theatre' or 'therapy,' healing for the Greeks was very much to do with the gods.

4 Shakespeare, W. (1604), *Measure for Measure*, Act II, Scene iv, line 172, Isabella.

5 Shakespeare, W. (c.1609), *Coriolanus*, 'What's the matter, you dissentious rogues,' Act I, Scene i, line 170, Coriolanus.

6 Shakespeare, W. (1599–1601), *Hamlet*, 'Now, mother, what's the matter?,' Act III, Scene iv, line 8, Hamlet.

15

CYMBELINE

A performance case study

Tina Packer had never paid much heed to *Cymbeline*. With its higgledy-piggledy plot (see Appendix 3) and echoes of many other Shakespeare plays,[1] she knew from her work on *Women of Will* that he wrote it when he was sick and had left London for Stratford to be with his daughter Susannah. She also knew that the narrative obeyed the rules he'd set for himself in the late plays:[2]

> Some man in charge [Cymbeline] did terrible things at least 10 to 20 years ago or at the top of the play. And all these sins have to be redeemed and it's the daughter [Imogen] who'll redeem them. There'll be some kind of witch [The Queen] or magical person [Doctor Cornelius]. There'll be a servant who's really honest and straightforward [Pisanio]. But by and large it's the daughter – through her fortitude, love and ability to see the larger picture – who makes the play come out right in the end.
>
> *(Packer in Arden Group discussion, S&Co., August 2017)*

On the few occasions Packer had seen or read *Cymbeline* it hadn't made much aesthetic sense. And apart from 'O! For a horse with wings'[3] and 'Fear no more the heat of the sun' (probably her 'favorite song in the whole of Shakespeare's canon with such lyrical depth and simplicity'),[4] there seemed to be little great verse. So with no real instinct for where the play lived on a deeper level, she was actually 'scared' of it – especially that strange dream scene in Act V, Scene iv (so often cut or deliberately staged to be ludicrous) when Posthumus is visited in prison by his dead family and Jupiter. Having never directed, acted or taught it,[5] *Cymbeline* for Packer 'was like looking through a glass darkly.'[6] However …

When Allyn Burrows decided to open his first season at Shakespeare & Company with *Cymbeline*, he offered Packer the opportunity. Almost despite herself she said, 'Yes!' It was the last play in the canon for her as a director and/or actor, which in itself was significant – if not historic – given the paucity of directors (let alone females) who have achieved such a task. And so the work began …

Pre-production considerations

Packer started by asking questions …

Tina: *I have a kind of map in my head about different frames I look through when I'm directing a Shakespeare play. He tells stories on multiple levels that all add up aesthetically, but it's easy to miss one of them if you're not alert. Fortunately all the frames begin with P – so they're easy to keep track of. First, there's the* political *situation, how the country is being ruled, who is being discriminated against: is part of the story about changing this system? Second, what's the* poetry *saying: how is it coloring the scene? Third, what is the* psychology *of the characters, and in* Cymbeline's *case, what's the psychology of the symbols?* [More anon.] *Fourth, there's the* physicality *– both the physical action and energy of the scenes, and of each individual person. Fifth – what's Shakespeare saying* philosophically*: either directly in the words of the text, or in the overall action of the play? Finally, how does it live on a* personal *level – for the actors, the characters and the audience? I ask questions from all those points of view: it helps me clarify and know where to put the emphasis.*[7]

Then Tina turned to a trusted friend …

Tina: *Eleanor Holdridge (who directed us in* Hamlet *and whom I admire a lot) said* 'Cymbeline *is my favorite play!' Which made me sit up. 'It's a real play for our time. It's about Brexit – with the Brits wanting Britain for Britain without this European influence. It's about the refugee crisis: everybody's on the road. And it's about ignorance prevailing.' So this gave me a handle on how to look at* Cymbeline.[8]

Then came the *storytelling logistics* …

Storytelling logistics

Shakespeare & Company was founded on the idyll of long rehearsal periods and large casts. Yet over the years, production budgets had incrementally decreased, leaving *Cymbeline* with four weeks' rehearsal and just nine actors (to play some 30 roles). With this 'nightmare' scenario, how was Packer going to tell the story coherently, let alone stage the battles? If Shakespeare inserts a battle, 'you have

276 Performance

to do it because the stage needs that energy. So, I couldn't just say, "Well, I can't do it because I've only got nine people!""[9] (Packer). So she had to make some early decisions about the storytelling style.

Cymbeline starts with six servants gossiping. But what would happen, thought Packer, if this scene were reconfigured as a group of actors telling a story? Well, it would immediately establish the convention of actors fluidly swapping between roles. Not to mention some fluidity with genders. Given that she'd have to cast women as the Welsh boys Guiderius and Arviragus (a.k.a. Polydore and Cadwal), might she also find moments when the males might play females? What if – on the flick of a fan and the spin of a heel – actors momentarily morphed from their designated characters (Posthumus, Pisanio, Iachimo, etc.) to female court attendants in a bold, theatrical wink to the audience? Thus, a 'budgetary necessity' could be used to highlight a topical conversation:

> What sets Shakespeare apart from other playwrights is that he works for every age, for every country, for every time. [...] We're at a point now where [...] gender identity and gender fluidity have come to the forefront as one of the revolutions of our time. A Shakespeare play addresses that head on.
>
> *(Packer in Arden Group discussion, S&Co., August 2017)*

And so would Packer. With the overt theatricality of actors telling a story – and the logistics of shifting from one character to another, as well as from one gender to another (sometimes mid-sentence) – a clear aesthetic for the production was emerging. Which would of course impact the *design* …

Design

Kris Stone (scenic) had worked with Packer before and understood that her design concepts emerge organically:

Tina: *When I told Kris I hadn't yet made up my mind what the play was about and, therefore, couldn't visualize it, she said, 'Why don't we put dressing tables upstage to remind the audience there's a whole life going on in the theatre that they don't normally see?' This visual metaphor quickly propelled me towards the idea of 'What can you – and can't you – see in life?'[10]*

Stone also knew that Packer wanted a sense of people migrating, so a red road would be painted down the middle of the stage. And because there are lots of alchemical symbols in the play – ending with the Soothsayer's interpretation of Posthumus' dream and a cedar tree – the set would also incorporate those. The masculine symbol of Jupiter would be represented center stage by the wings of an eagle (also the symbol of Rome and America), and the feminine symbol of Britannia (with subtle reverberations of Lady Liberty) would manifest as a statue. A Book of Law would also be in view, along with a ladder (the alchemical symbol for ascension into heaven) and a compass:

Tina: *Guiderius and Arviragus are very precise about how they want to bury Fidele/ Imogen with the head towards the east. So I felt a compass was very important: the center of the universe, by which we're trying to align ourselves.*[11]

Whether the audience would consciously comprehend these images didn't matter: they might resonate unconsciously.

Tyler Kinney (costume) – a Packer 'favorite' – works in a similarly organic way and could accommodate each actor having multiple costumes. Meanwhile, Deb Sullivan (lighting) and David Reiffel (composer/sound) were colleagues of Burrows from his previous company ASP. Sullivan's skill at painting with lights would come into its own during technical rehearsals, particularly with the battle scenes to disguise the Roman and British armies comprising fewer than five apiece. And for the soundscape …

Tina: *I said to David, 'I know this play is about storytelling. I know it's about the past and the future, and it's very much in the present. It's also about magic and people trying different ways to solve problems. And it's about nature: so, we'll need all kinds of calls – owls and the like. And we'll need heroic music under the battles. But that's all I know right now.' I then sent him a script with 'the past' scribbled at various points and 'the future' at other points, and 'the present' at particular moments (such as Iachimo creeping into Imogen's room: is he or isn't he going to rape her?)*[12]

Completing her team were Company regulars Kristin Wold (*Movement*), Martin Jason Asprey (*Fight*), Gwendolyn Schwinke (*Voice/Text*) and assistant directors Raphael Massie, Noa Egozi and Kholoud Sawaf.

The actors

The cast comprised three women (Tamara Hickey, Ella Loudon and Bella Merlin) and six men (Martin Jason Asprey, Thomas Brazzle, Jonathan Epstein, Deaon Griffin-Pressley, Nigel Gore and Josh McCabe). We'd all taken S&Co.'s *Training* and/or worked with Packer previously, so there'd be a shared understanding of her vocabulary and *text progression* (see Chapter 13). And time would typically be reserved each day for discussion:

Tina: *It's so necessary for me to have a meeting* at the top of the day – *'Thoughts from yesterday, insights, ideas'* – so that I can hear what everybody is thinking or what came up for them in the night. And at the end of the day: 'What are the insights that came out of the day's rehearsal?' And it's important to have these discussions as a collective, in a circle, with everybody having equal time – unless

278 Performance

> *they don't want to talk, which is fine, too. This feedback enables everyone to see where everyone else is in the process. So we're feeling the whole, as well as deeply honing in on individual roles. My directing comes out of these common insights and gets back to why Shakespeare was writing these words in the first place.*[13]

Prior to rehearsal, Packer sent out an edit of the play (divided into 43 beats) and a list of provocations for the actors' imaginations:

> How does the past effect the present? What can we see and what is invisible (but still affects us)? What is unconscious, what is conscious? What are the journeys we take? Love is the power that can transcend barriers and gives the courage to go on journeys. Jealousy is a driving force as potent as love, and activates destructive behaviour. The Gods look after us whether we know it or not. Dreams and Soothsayers are the keys to unlocking hidden knowledge. The Tree of Knowledge is the image of the Oracle. The daughter redeems the father (and a load of other people too). Every situation is joyful and painful, or trying to squash joy and avoid pain. People are ridiculous and very funny.
>
> *(Packer introductory letter to* Cymbeline *team, May 2017)*

Pondering these provocations, we headed into rehearsals …

Week 1: mapping the landscape

Days #1–6: Tuesday 30 May–Sunday 4 June 2017

Tina's collaborative way of directing examines how 'what we're working with in scenes is reflecting in our own lives, and *vice versa.*'[14] Although at the start of Day #1 she candidly confessed she didn't yet know what *Cymbeline* was about, she shared her initial thoughts on the *esoteric elements* ('What does it mean to *not* know something and what lives on an unconscious level?') and the *contemporary reverberations* (domestic and political manipulation, Brexit, exile and how these themes might influence the production). Then she flagged up some *given circumstances of the script* and its three realms of 'higher' (gods, with Jupiter as the dominant presence); 'middle' (people); and 'lower' (ghosts). And within that middle realm were three, tangibly different worlds: the wild simplicity of the Welsh cave; the ordinariness of the British court; and the elegance of Rome. Given this mini-Elizabethan World Picture, how might these realms be manifested physically? Which led to *Body Work, Voice Work* and *Text Work* …

Movement and Voice workshops

Place a body on stage and the space is instantly activated: how the audience perceives that activation is the essence of theatrical storytelling. So Kristin Wold explored with us *actual movement* (journeying, marching and simple dance steps) and *metaphorical movement* (escaping from constraints and physicalizing emotions: such as anger, love, revenge). From bodies to voices, Gwendolyn Schwinke took us through the Linklater *Voice* progression, and since each actor in this production took multiple roles – how might our acting instruments be evocatively played?

Then into Tina's *text progression* …

Working the play on its feet

Working the play on its feet avoids those awkward first rehearsals where actors aimlessly wander around the stage, noses in scripts, oblivious to the impact of their words on their partners or their partners' impact on them. Instead with *this* process, your whole being is instantly recruited into the creative research, time-efficiently activating discoveries that might otherwise take days (see Chapter 13). As Arviragus, for instance, I was genuinely excited when my 'dad' Morgan/Belarius (Nigel Gore) recounted the tale to me and my brother Polydore/Guiderius (Ella Loudon) of what happened to him 20 years earlier when he was exiled by King Cymbeline (Jonathan Epstein): my innocent Cadwal/Arviragus was struck by the weirdness of all the treachery at court compared to our simple life in the mountains. Pragmatically, we also got a sense from this 'work through' of quickly flipping from one character to another.

The next stage in Tina's *text progression* was to reflect on the discoveries made …

'Checking in' experiences, 'reinforcing' discoveries[15]

Tina's directing process foregrounds *the actor/audience relationship* (as we saw in Chapter 13). So the prompts for discussion after *working the play on its feet* were two-fold: What did we *experience* (as actors in a scene) and what did we *feel* (as audience watching the scenes)? This reinforced that the choices we made about our characters came from an experiential (rather than a head-led) place. And thus Day #1 concluded.

Curiously Day #2 began with another *checking in* discussion. At first, this seemed strange ('What can we possibly add this morning that we didn't share last night?'). Actually, it was canny. Time between rehearsals is a murkily creative time when you're rehearsing a role, as your imagination and your rational mind begin to whirr. And many discoveries about a play can actually emerge when you're not consciously thinking about them … even when you're asleep … So Day #2's discussion started with the dramaturgical questions: 'Where does my character's journey begin? What do they learn? Where do they end up?' – and then the prompts went deeper: 'What might our *dreams* reveal?' Curiously, the outcomes of this discussion were multi-faceted: we collectively shared how Shakespeare's language was working on us in mercurial ways, and we realized that, because the plot consists of multiple, interconnecting storylines, we may be playing two or more characters with differing (even contradictory) positions in the story. The dramaturgy was emerging …

Day #3 took us to the next step in Tina's *text progression*: *dropping in* …

280 Performance

Dropping in the Welsh family

We've seen the *Training* of *dropping in* (Chapter 7) and the nub of the practice for assistant directors (Chapter 13). So here are some concrete examples from the actors' perspectives, starting with the Welsh family – comprising Nigel (Morgan/ Belarius), Ella (Polydore/Guiderius) and myself (Cadwal/Arviragus). Because every breath with *dropping in* can invite a new impulse … thought … image – which in turn stirs a new emotional response – there's a subtle shift from left-brain rationale to right-brain creativity. You find yourself, in the process of *dropping in*, building a matrix of choices as an actor, which inspire new possibilities when you return to the rehearsal-room floor. So, as Kholoud Sawaf, Noa Egozi and Gwendolyn Schwinke dropped in the Welsh family, an enormous sense of history imaginatively evolved between us, informed by the mix of: Shakespeare's imagery; the actual vibrations of the words; the droppers-in's suggestions; the myriad impressions from each other's faces; and the shared energy between us. One moment we burst out laughing. The next moment tears sprung to our eyes. The idea of racing up the mountains was exhilarating. And it was almost spooky how natural it felt for me and Ella to be 'sons' to Nigel's 'father.' This unlikely bond endured from that first *dropping in* session till the final curtain of the last performance: looking at Ella was always like gazing with pride into my own brother's eyes; holding Nigel's hand was always like clasping the firm grip of my own grandfather. And for Kholoud, 'I think the beautiful relationship of the Welsh family came as a result of *dropping in*: I don't know if we'd have arrived there otherwise.'[16]

It was during the *reinforcement* discussion at the end of Day #3 that Tina said something strange: 'These alchemical symbols are bothering me!' …

Alchemical symbols

Tina had been talking a lot about 'the things we can't see.' (I didn't particularly understand what she meant at this stage). And now she was asking about the alchemical symbols in the play (which I hadn't really thought about, either). We'd been so focused on the complex plot and how to clarify what *is* there, it hadn't crossed my mind to consider what *isn't* there. Especially because 'Shakespeare usually says all the things he wants to say'[17] (Packer). And I hadn't even noticed the symbols … But once she brought them into the room, it was almost as if they alchemically started working their magic. But what had inspired Tina's line of enquiry? Her answer takes us right back to Chapter 1 and her joining the Research Into Lost Knowledge Organization (RILKO) …

Tina: *A key figure in RILKO was Trevor Ravenscroft. Everyone knew and revered him. We met him every Monday night and he'd hold forth. During World War II he'd worked for Winston Churchill, advising him where Hitler's Kabbalistic thinking may be taking him. And previously he'd been employed as the tutor to the Shah of Persia's children because the family very much believed in alchemical things. Trevor was quite old by the time I met him, and I learned about the lay-lines of Europe, and how cathedrals were built on lay-lines, and how Franco had actually built his mausoleum where two lay-lines crossed because he wanted his legacy to live on. And the idea that there were energetic power-lines across Europe really fascinated me. That's just one area of the Research Into Lost Knowledge. Another is flowers and their properties. And the soil. And numbers. Where the sun rises and sets is also very important. So when I was in India, I went to Ganeshpuri, Swami's ashram, which is built exactly where the sunlight falls between two huge mountains. (As a young girl, Stonehenge and the Rollright Stones – which were close to where I'd gone to school – fascinated me, how the sunlight comes up and goes down, and how the earth is centered.) And I was always interested in where the voice fitted in to all this, because what is the voice but the external expression of our body and breath? Alchemy for me was a way of approaching things in the world that I didn't understand. Posthumus more or less says it: 'I don't understand it, but there's a sense to it. And that comforts me.'[18] And I'd say it's like that for me. In the January Intensive when we do the* Elizabethan World Picture Day, [see Chapter 8] *we send the participants out into the natural world to look at the harmony in a leaf, and then between the leaf and the branch. And at the end of* Cymbeline *there's the image of the cedar tree, whose branches have been lopped off: and now we're going to put them back on – and then what will happen? I don't know exactly what it means but, once we put the branches back on, there's (what I'm going to call) a 'parallel universe.' It's a universe that we're not brought up to be conscious of in our Western culture – but that doesn't mean it's not there.*[19]

The 'parallel universe' seemed particularly resonant for that strange 'dream scene' with Posthumus' dead family … Could it be that *that* scene, with Jupiter's peculiar prophecy, held the key? Tina's rehearsal process was in many ways reflecting what was unfurling in the play: she was asking us to let our unconscious set to work so that she could find the role of the unconscious in the play.

That night, I ordered two books on alchemy and symbols, plus a collection of Welsh fairytales for Arviragus and Cicely Mary Barker's 1920s' watercolor flower-fairies for the Queen. Then I began some character work …

Arviragus

For Arviragus, the warrior seemed relevant. The Elizabethans had a renewed interest in chivalry, in reaction against 'the adulterous love condoned by the twelfth and thirteenth centuries.'[20] Which raised the questions: 'What is loyalty? How does *romantic* loyalty compare to *patriotic* loyalty? What's considered honorable?' For some reason I'd brought to Lenox a translation of *The Bhagavad Gita*, which I now opened:

> There is no greater good for a warrior than to fight in a righteous war … But to forgo this fight for righteousness is to forgo thy duty and

282 Performance

honour ... [T]o a man who is in honour, dishonour is more than death ... Prepare for war with peace in thy soul.

(Vyasa (trans. Mascaró, J.), (Mascaro, J.) The Bhagavad Gita, London, 1962: Penguin: 51)

(More on peace anon ...)

I then dipped into an online version of *The Mabinogion*, compiled in Middle Welsh in the twelfth and thirteenth centuries, full of fantastical tales of tragedy and romance. And I was struck by the tale of the king who received a mortal wound, after which his courtiers lopped off his head and bore it on their travels for the next 87 years. Maybe Cadwal/Arviragus was brought up on this tale; so, seeing Polydore/Guiderius holding the head of the Queen's son Cloten which he has severed in a fight would be like seeing my brother transformed into a legend right in front of my eyes. As for the world of the court? The final scene of *Cymbeline* shows the court riddled with dishonor. As I sat in Apartment D in Lawrence Hall on the Kemble Street campus, the deposition of former FBI leader James Comey was unfurling on the television. 'I expect loyalty,' demanded Donald Trump. 'I will be honestly loyal,' replied Comey. So what is loyalty to an elected political leader or a birthright king? Or indeed to a husband? Which takes me to the Queen ...

The Queen

'[A]n impossible fiction composed of the silliest elements,'[21] say the scholars. And certainly the character of the Queen is problematic. Shakespeare was representing James I as both Cymbeline and Caesar (uniting the Britons and Romans, as James united England and Scotland). But it would've been highly unseemly for the wicked Queen to be seen by Shakespeare's audience as James's virtuous consort, Anne of Denmark. And so it's thought 'the Queen is made conventionally grotesque after a fairytale fashion in order to counteract the temptation to find a real-life analogue.'[22] Over the next few days my research into alchemy proved lucrative. The Queen definitely dabbles in alchemy, collecting flowers dappled with dew (a sacred liquid for alchemists) and peddling potions with Doctor Cornelius. And then I discovered that the *chemical* alchemists (pragmatists, who strove for material gold) fell out with the *theosophical* alchemists (spirituals, who believed the real gold was the soul). So while the Queen might represent the chemical alchemists (seeking material gain until her son Cloten is beheaded and her value-system collapses), Arviragus (for whom gold and silver are 'dirty gods')[23] is the epitome of the golden soul. Finding these two characters at alchemical opposites was tantalizing to the imagination ...

With many thoughts percolating through conscious brains and unconscious dream-states, our collective discussions bookended most days. And that 'dream scene' wouldn't stop bugging us ...

Cymbeline **283**

The dead Leonati: a scene that holds the key

On Day #5 we *dropped in* the 'Dead Family' dream scene, with Josh McCabe (father), Tamara Hickey and Deacon Griffin-Pressley (the two brothers), myself (mother) and Thomas Brazzle (the living Posthumus). And much was revealed, not least because *dropping in* interweaves imagination, autobiography and ensemble exchange with little coercion. *Imagination* was ignited for me in realizing this is the first time I've ever seen my son Posthumus because I died in childbirth. *Auto-biography* was touched through the complexity of not being a birth-mother myself. The *ensemble exchange* between the five actors was activated with a sense of ancient legacy and connection, perhaps because all the characters are dead except Posthumus. And the oracle placed on Posthumus' chest by Jupiter suddenly seemed absolutely necessary. The discoveries made from *dropping in* this scene galvanized Tina's intuitions:

Tina: *Because this scene with the dead parents visiting Posthumus Leonatus is often cut from productions, you don't really get the point of the ghosts. But it's key for me. What I saw was that, first, the dead parents left Posthumus when he was a baby, and then Cymbeline abandons him. So no wonder he thinks Imogen has been unfaithful: he's acting out the patterns of his childhood! And once I started realizing that, other things began falling into place. For example, Cymbeline's boys were stolen and brought up in the countryside, yet their adopted father keeps saying, 'I can't keep the nobility out of them. They keep being the noble people that they really are.'[24] I started to see that Shakespeare was actually trying to point to things, which are underneath – psychologically and philosophically.[25]*

While these ideas would continue to crystallize in time, Week 1 had involved *working the play on its feet*, improvising various scenarios, *dropping in* scenes, and many a discussion (not least surrounding the bizarre drama-turgy of Imogen taking what she thinks is the Queen's restorative potion, losing consciousness, waking beside the beheaded body of Cloten and thinking it's her husband Posthumus). True to Tina's exploratory process, however, we hadn't 'staged' anything yet. Wherever our own heads were at (and they were most squarely on our shoulders), there was still much road to travel …

Week 2: finding our bearings

Days #7–12: Tuesday 6–Sunday 11 June

Week 2 revealed Kris Stone's road and compass now painted on the floor. These visuals sharpened our awareness of metaphorically keeping the moral compass,

284 Performance

finding our bearings and marking the road upon which we walk. Then, when we came to *dropping in* the final, very long 'Beat 43' (of Tina's script breakdown) – in which myriad revelations are made – something potent happened …

Dropping in the revelations

Partly due to the length of the scene, partly due to the powerful imaginations of all involved … when it came to the reveal in Cymbeline's court of the exiled Posthumus – followed by Iachimo's detailed revelation of his almost rape of Imogen in her bedchamber – a major shift occurred in the ensemble. With Raphael Massie and Noa Egozi as their 'droppers-in,' Thomas Brazzle (Posthumus) and Tamara Hickey (Imogen) became so connected to the language that, when it was revealed that Posthumus was actually Imogen's husband *and* he hadn't been beheaded after all *and* her honor had been toyed with *and* her beloved servant Pisanio had unintentionally poisoned her with the Queen's 'restorative' potion, they were both inundated with feelings. The enormity of the given circumstances, the commitment of the actors and the focus of the whole ensemble *dropping in* for two hours made for an intense experience. The process demonstrated what a remarkably textured alternative to 'tablework' *dropping in* can be, and how working with breath and keeping 'on voice' (ergo, vibration) during the process can access imaginative reservoirs.

Designers' stagger-through

Once all the scenes were dropped in (though still nothing formally 'staged'), the play was 'staggered through' for the designers at the end of Week 2. While many elements were incomplete – not least the battles – it provided a valuable opportunity for them to see (in a rough, raw fashion) the precipitous storytelling. Tyler Kinney (costume) witnessed how physical everyone was, how quickly we changed from one character to another and, therefore, how robust the actual construction of the costumes needed to be. David Reiffel (music) could sense where instrumentation or sound or song was needed. Kristin Wold (*Movement*) could intuit the physical vocabulary, noting, for example, that in the final scene – when the revelations from the past become present-tense experiences – Time could be accentuated by collectively describing circles clockwise and anticlockwise round the stage. And Gwendolyn Schwinke (*Voice/Text*) could hear when voices were vibrating effectively (or not), accents were accurate (or not) and consonants were articulate (or not). And there were other significant realizations such as the mercurial juxtaposition of styles in *Cymbeline*: 'Head straight into each different world! Don't worry about them being in tension – just let them exist!'[26] (Packer).

One of the most important epiphanies from this stagger-through was the play's final image. Previously Tina had thought the Soothsayer's interpreting of Posthumus' dream via Jupiter's oracle-tablet was an odd way to end the play. Now she realized that the message in the tablet was the message of the play:

Cymbeline **285**

Tina: It's about Cymbeline, the cedar [seeder] of power, who has 'lopped off' two of his branches: the 'lion's whelp' (Posthumus Leonatus) and the 'tender air' surrounding him (Imogen). Now it's all going to start coming right because – 20 years after it all went wrong – the cycles of life have come full circle. People have done terrible things, but Imogen has righted many of them – even when she didn't know what was happening and even when she thought all was lost.[27]

Seeing the patterns and images emerge, Tina now realized that *Cymbeline*, 'often with very simple poetry, was pointing to profound truths.'[28] So the task now was to decipher and then manifest those truths …

Week 3: the landscape reveals itself

Days #13–18: Tuesday 13–Sunday 18 June

Week 3 took the next step in Tina's *text progression*: the detailed staging of each scene. While in a typical rehearsal process this might feel nervously late for such work, Tina isn't typical. And the discussions, improvisations and entire *dropping in* of the play had uncovered significant treasures. So, in parallel groups (using the assistant directors), we sought direct avenues between those riches and the logistics of nine bodies on a thrust stage. The week also entailed *Movement* sessions (with Kristin), *Voice* and accent work (with Gwendolyn) and *Fight* choreography (with Martin Jason). And through this blend of *close text analysis*, physical storytelling and collectively shared insights, we were beginning to hear the play's tone. And at the end of Week 3 …

A stumble-through

Now the whole production started to reveal itself: the flow of scenes; the choric speaking; and the story of the battles. The most striking 'seen' element was how the costume changes established the English court, Roman court, Welsh countryside, battlefields, let alone the disguises and reveals. Yet for all these discoveries, Tina was insistent that the story would only be clear if we honored the *Structure of the Verse* and allowed articulation to be a motivator, not a distraction: 'Let the consonants deepen your intelligence.'[29] In terms of deciphering the 'unseen' elements, the end-of-the-week stumble-through also revealed: the *nature images*; *Posthumus' psychology*; and the *ending of the play*.

Nature images revealed

Tina: It was probably a week before going into tech that the nature images really resonated. Jupiter's prophecy comes down with the sunbeams; and the eagle; the cedar; the branches that are lopped off: it's all in nature images. Then there's the image of the flowers on Imogen/Fidele's dead body. So the question at every turn seems

> to be: 'How can nature reveal and heal?' I think this is because Shakespeare had
> gone back to Stratford at this time and his son-in-law was the leading physician,
> John Hall: the Elizabethans thought of 'man' as being part of nature and the
> immune system could be healed by natural means. [...] I also think that Shake-
> speare's leaving London and going back to live in the country brought into focus
> all the elements he knew as a boy and how much he loved animals and nature.
> He saw himself as part of the natural world. So the sense I get from Cymbeline
> (and the other late plays) is that Shakespeare himself is at another spiritual level;
> in other words, he can see 'man' in nature; he can see 'man' as part of a whole;
> and what one person does over here affects what another person does over there.[30]

The natural and alchemical symbols had always informed Tina's scenic vision for *Cymbeline*, with the cedar tree at the center. Indeed, the tree is a fundamental symbol in alchemy, depicting the inner development that enables a person to awaken to new life.[31] And the Kabbalistic Tree of Life is a symbol for finding harmony and balance within ourselves.[32] And harmony and balance were essentially what Tina's *Cymbeline* subtly sought, not least regarding Posthumus' psyche ...

Posthumus' psychology revealed

Tina's hunch about Posthumus' dream really started to pay off after the stumble-through. For the alchemists, the small world of 'man' (*microcosm*) – comprising body, soul and spirit – had a corresponding 'cosmic soul,' which dwelled in the realm of the stars (*macrocosm*). And 'man' communicates with the *macrocosm* through prophecies in dreams ...[33]

Tina: It all started falling into place with a kind of resounding thud. Though the dream
        sequence had previously made no sense to me – and Jupiter just seemed ludicrous –
        I now realized Shakespeare was bringing that bit of Posthumus' past from 20 years
        ago onto the stage to say something really relevant. It wasn't just that Posthumus was
        abandoned by his family – with his brothers (killed in battle) and his father (dying of
        grief): it was that his mother had actually died in childbirth. I had a sense of how
        hard that is because the mother of one of my closest colleagues, Kevin Coleman, had
        died very shortly after his birth and I knew how much it had affected his life.[34]

In other words, Tina realized the grief in Posthumus' psyche lay at the heart of the whole play. And having cast Thomas Brazzle in the role – an African American – all manner of other resonances began to resound:

Tina: I'd already thought how much the opening of Cymbeline is like Romeo and
        Juliet with the lovers being banished as the parents forbid the match. But then
        I saw the narrative turn into Othello with the jealous rage and Imogen's hand-
        kerchief and the 'Kill her – because she's unfaithful to me!' mentality. So
        I started putting these patterns together. On the one hand, Shakespeare seems to

FIGURE 15.1 Dead Family and Jupiter visit Posthumus, sleeping
Photo: Stratton McCrady

> understand that the loss of parents means you suffer from that in some way all your life. On the other hand, in Othello we have this incredible love story with one lover destroying the other. And it seemed to me that Shakespeare was trying to work out through the late plays how this story could end differently. Does it have to end in destruction? This was the first big clue for me in Cymbeline of 'What is it that couldn't be seen and that is now being revealed?' I saw it was the root cause of Posthumus' behavior that was being revealed.[35]

Following Posthumus' psyche through to the end of the play and 'Does it have to end in destruction?' takes us to the third major revelation of Week 3 …

The play's ending revealed

The end of the play is complex on many levels. First – in this production – there's the multiplicity of roles, with Nigel Gore switching between Doctor Cornelius, Morgan/Belarius and Caius Lucius, sometimes mid-sentence. Apart from being a theatrical *tour de force*, this mercurial style of acting reflects the mercurial state of our own, confusing world, raising issues of 'the characters' own understandings and misunderstandings of who and what they are.'[36]

288 Performance

Second, the narrative can't be completed by any one person: we only see our own place in the story once everyone else shares theirs:

Tina: *One after another, each character comes out and says, 'Let me finish the story' but then says, 'But I don't know what happened after that.' So somebody else steps forward and says, 'Let me finish the story …' And thus the 9/10ths of what we don't see can only be completed once everybody comes together at the end and the whole story can be revealed.*[37]

Third is the issue of peace. On the one hand, 'Rome' in *Cymbeline* seems to be a collective for the whole world: Britain pays its dues (a monetary 'tribute') to Rome at the end of the play like the United States, say, must pay its dues to the global community. On the other hand, the chaos of Brexit unfurling on the news raised serious questions about the disintegration of Europe and the troubling rise of nationalistic fervor. The end of *Cymbeline* shows a Britain reintegrated with honor into the civilized world of the Roman empire, ennobling it and revealing how its 'national identity depends on a continued identification with Rome.'[38] But what on earth are the ramifications for Britain in 2017 … 2019 … and beyond?

So while the stumble-through at the end of Week 3 was terrifying in many respects, it was elucidating in many others.

Week 4: the northern star guides

Days #19–24: Tuesday 20–Sunday 25 June

In our ongoing discussions – as we shared our discoveries – we were increasingly struck by the brutality towards Imogen. Although Imogen's centrality had always been clear, every time we ran the play her impact on the narrative came into sharpening relief. Indeed, Tina acknowledged that if she were to go back to *Women of Will*, she would include much more on Imogen, 'because she's shown me a lot of things that I've discovered through *doing Cymbeline* rather than *reading it.*'[39]

Imogen awakens us

Imogen is the ultimate healing force in the play. At first she seems to be everyone's plaything – separated from the man she loves, almost raped by her husband's abettor, accosted by the clottish Cloten, nearly poisoned by her stepmother, almost killed as a Roman captive. Yet throughout it all she strengthens.

Tina: *Imogen is the only person who doesn't shift her moral ground. She remains straight and true, never losing sight of what she herself wants – which is a relationship with the man she loves (Posthumus) – and she's going to do whatever it takes to have it. Her inner life comprises a very strong sexual and spiritual state of being. And I think Shakespeare is saying there's another way for the world to work: we just have to have enough people strong enough inside themselves to keep on doing the right thing. And we need leaders who see that there's a different way other than the old patriarchal structures of subjugation and war. So Imogen's story is one of human evolution and awakening consciousness.*[40]

In fact, Arviragus calls Imogen a 'bird,' and the bird 'is almost universally seen as a symbol for the soul or anima,' the breath of the world's soul 'hidden in matter.'[41] As it awakens us each morning, the bird forges 'a link between heaven and earth, conscious and unconscious.'[42] And as the play revealed itself to us in the rehearsal room, it was as if Imogen was calling us to consciousness, not least because of Tamara Hickey's integrity and playfulness. Tina had cast Tam 'because she needed someone whom she knew could be the moral compass for the play,' while 'delivering a strong sense of fun' in light of everything that happens to Imogen.[43] Indeed, as Tam herself recalled after one performance,

> I was waiting to come on for the final scene and I found myself thinking, 'Oh my god! I'm going back to the man who banished me! I'm going home disguised as a boy! I've fought with the Roman Army (as a Brit) against my dad! What do I play? What do I play?' And I think that's *Imogen's* experience: she's overwhelmed, but she's actively pursuing what she wants. And it says so much about the power of love: love allows you to stay on course in spite of and regardless of what's happening. I think that's how powerful Imogen's love is: so all I try to do every performance is go onstage and fill her heart.
>
> *(Hickey in Arden Group discussion, August 2017)*

FIGURE 15.2 Tamara Hickey (Imogen) and Thomas Brazzle (Posthumus Leonatus)
Photo: Stratton McCrady

290 Performance

Week 5: final journeying

Days #27–30: Thursday 29 June–Sunday 2 July

Technical and dress rehearsals are Tina's 'favorite time,' as all the components come together and she can shape the theatrical experience. With *Cymbeline*, there was a heady mix of cast excitement and abject terror at the enormity of the production. The backstage rhythm of grabbing props and costumes, ably corralled by the assistant stage manager Matthew Luppino. The challenge facing the nimble-fingered dressers Ashley Hutchins and Brooke Arthur, zipping zippers, popping poppers and jamming wigs on pates as part of the onstage action. The insane battles, one moment in Roman helmets and breastplates, the next in furs and machetes as marauding Britons. The gasps of horror as Imogen (Tamara) awoke to the headless Cloten (albeit a mannequin marvelously made by props-master Patrick Brennan). The tangible fizz as we suddenly transformed into Tyler Kinney's flamboyant Queen, King, lady's maid or villain. The artistic mystique of Deb Sullivan's lighting and the Kabbalistic symbols of Kris Stone's set. The evocative vibrations of David Reiffel's score, with birdcalls, thunderclaps, patriotic drumming, lyrical Welsh melodies and haunting harmonies to 'Fear no more.' The constant cueing held together by consummate stage manager Hope Rose Kelly … It's magical …

Time to let it live – in *the actor/audience relationship* …

Week 6: homeward bound – and into performance

Previews provide the opportunity to find the true life of a production: 'From the moment the curtain opens and we face out front for our collective storytelling, my in-breath is the audience: their energy comes into my body. And it's a palpable physical sensation'[44] (Hickey). With the energy of 400 people, 'it starts to become a living experience and there's nothing like it: you get as high as a kite'[45] (Packer).

One of the biggest discoveries made in the previews (as a result of the audience reactions) was the robustness of the tonal changes.

Tonal changes

'What's unusual about this production,' said Jonathan Epstein (Cymbeline), 'is the alternation between high drama, melodrama, tragedy and a kind of goofy comedy':

> It's a conventional idea that Shakespeare puts comedy next to drama all the time – but he rarely does it *within* a scene as often as he does in *Cymbeline*. Most directors try to fix it. […] But Shakespeare is saying that you can have the sublime next to the ridiculous and it doesn't diminish either. Tina has a lot of goofy stuff going on – and I think that any production that tries to fix the

FIGURE 15.3 Opening storytelling tableau
Photo: Stratton McCrady

> goofiness is disrespecting Shakespeare. He's writing at the end of his life: he's not making accidental mistakes. If he's alternating goofiness and drama, he's doing it on purpose.
>
> *(Epstein in Arden Group discussion, S&Co., August 2017)*

Indeed, many goofy moments were confirmed by the audience, not least the macabre visuals, such as Imogen (Tamara) awaking beside the headless Cloten and believing it's Posthumus, asking, 'Where is thy head?' and then scrabbling on the floor searching for it: 'It's very funny. And you can't do Shakespeare and not have people laugh'.[46] (Packer). Likewise with the last scene of riotous revelations. One moment it's ridiculous, the next moment it's heart-rending – all garnering the audience's satisfaction that these multiple plotlines can be neatly tied up. And it demands nimbleness in the acting to keep the options open for that emotional rollercoaster:

> When I'm on stage with Thomas as Posthumus at the end – touching his head in disbelief that he's alive and has his head on – there's a lot of audience laughter. And the duality is incredible: *I'm* having one experience and the *audience* is having a wholly different experience – and they're both legitimate and they can both coexist. It fuels the conviction that we *make* theatre and *go* to theatre because it's completely different than sitting at home and reading the play. […] As valuable as the words on the page are, it's only when we collectively give them breath that we can then truly experience them. […] And that's what makes it a human experience as opposed to a scholarly analysis.
>
> *(Hickey in Arden Group discussion, S&Co., August 2017)*

292 Performance

FIGURE 15.4 Final revelations
Photo: Stratton McCrady

That *Cymbeline* 'manages to embrace tragedy, comedy, and romance' is ultimately 'a reminder that the love has to be spread around'[47] (Packer).

And so the play comes to rest ...

Peace to all

Cymbeline 'has many contemporary echoes: Britain for the British; banishment from the country of birth; leaders breaking treaties; the forever-bloody handkerchiefs; the chaos of selfish ambition' – but 'fortunately it all comes right in the end'[48] (Packer). Despite winning the battle, Cymbeline decides to pay Rome the pecuniary tribute because peace is ultimately more important:

Tina: *When Cymbeline says, 'Pardon's the word to all,' I believe Shakespeare is really saying, 'If you can keep operating from love and generosity then things will come round. You'll be forgiven. Other people will be forgiven. You will be able to forgive.' [...] And I think that's why the audience really responds to the play.*[49]

Indeed, through working on *Cymbeline*, Tina had taken a complete about-turn:

Tina: *I now think it's one of Shakespeare's most profound plays. Through telling a fairytale, he's actually trying to point the way in which the world moves forward. You need to act out of an understanding of what another person is going through, and he illustrates this through people not understanding at all what the other people are going through. The fight between Britain and Rome is about who has ascendancy as a war-like state. And, although this time the Britons actually beat the Romans, Cymbeline recants, saying, 'We promised we'd pay the tribute – so we'll pay it.' In other words, he shifts his moral ground in a profound way. In the end, a Shakespeare play for me is about the collective energy onstage and what the audience is invited to share. And, no matter which play you're doing, it's about the relevance of what's going on today. And* Cymbeline *comes out with quite a few things that are very relevant for today.*[50]

Yet for me the ending of *Cymbeline* was always deeply poignant as Ella and I strode the stage as Guiderius and Arviragus, respectively brandishing our Union Jack and European Union flags, with Brexit hovering in the ethersphere. Isn't 'peace to all' the most fanciful fairytale?

Tina: *Maybe ... And then you turn to our two assistant directors Kholoud and Noa, who have become so close they can see how it could work for them as a Syrian and an Israeli. So why on earth can't it work for everyone else? Because it needs their kind of consciousness to do that. And not to be afraid that somebody's going to take everything away from you. And – even if they do take things away from you – there's a way to redeem the situation beyond rage and helplessness.*[51]

So maybe 'peace' and 'pardon' really could be the words to all ...?

The proof of the potion

'Packer brews a magic potion [...] this production is out of this world.'[52] '[B]reathtaking,'[53] 'magnificent and energetic,'[54] 'robust and intoxicatingly funny.'[55]

While any spectator has as valid a response as a seasoned critic, it tends to be the published responses that form an archival record. And because it's always satisfying when a story finishes with a happy ending, I'll leave it to two longtime theatre critics:

> Until now nobody quite knew what to make of [*Cymbeline*]. Is it a tragedy, romance or comedy? Packer has conflated all of the above in a manner that has us rolling in the aisles. [...]
>
> While Packer is credited as director, [...] this was truly a team effort and indeed it takes a village of artists to create such a vivid and enduring masterpiece.
>
> The actors [...] are flawless and compelling. The language is fluid, articulate and suitably poetic. One feels the magic of the writing set onto the performers with stunning clarity. [...]
>
> The costumes of Tyler Kinney are well suited to the quick-change transitions [...]. The sound design of David Reiffel expands our imagination of time and space. The props [by Patrick Brennan], including a severed head,

294 Performance

are terrific [...]. With the fight coaching of [Martin] Jason Asprey and choreography of Kristin Wold there was fluid action and movement that kept us absorbed and diverted. [...]

What an abundance of riches.

(Guiliano, C., 'Review of "Cymbeline," Berkshire
Fine Arts, 9 July 2017')

And from Ed Siegel:

Packer is not only one of the most thoughtful Shakespeare directors around, she's one of the most exciting Shakespeare directors around. There are echoes of contemporary politics bound up with creative feminism, strong humor, beautiful movement and melt-in-your-mouth acting [...].

And in almost every case I can think of, her interpretations don't bend Shakespeare out of shape – she convinces you that he and she are theatrical soulmates. [...]

Though Packer's politics lean toward the pacificist [...] she's not afraid to get her hands bloody. Can a beheading be humorous in this day and age? Packer's not afraid to go there and you'll be laughing too hard at the consequences in the plot to be offended.

What a fitting end to Packer's traversal of the canon. [...] I'm ready for her to start all over again.

(Seigel, E., The ARTery, 26 July 2017)

Notes

1 Echoes include *The Taming of the Shrew, Romeo and Juliet, The Two Gentlemen of Verona, Othello, King John, Much Ado About Nothing, Titus Andronicus, The Rape of Lucrece, Henry VI Part 2, Hamlet, Richard III* and *Pericles*.
2 The late plays are *Pericles, The Winter's Tale, The Tempest* and *Cymbeline*.
3 Act III, scene ii, line 50, Imogen.
4 Packer in Arden Group discussion with Tamara Hickey and Jonathan Epstein, S&Co., August 2017. 'Fear no more the heat o'the sun' is sung by Polydore/Guiderius and Cadwal/Arviragus over Fidele's body, Act IV, scene ii, lines 258–281.
5 Packer, T. (2015), *Women of Will: Following the Feminine in Shakespeare's Plays*, New York: Alfred A. Knopf, p. 277.
6 Packer and Merlin conversation, August 2017.
7 Packer edit, September 2019.
8 Packer and Merlin conversation, August 2017.
9 ibid.
10 ibid.
11 ibid.
12 ibid.
13 Packer and Merlin conversation, December 2018.
14 Packer in Arden Group discussion, August 2017.
15 See Chapter 6 for *checking* in and *reinforcing* practices.
16 Kholoud Sawaf interview with Bella Merlin, July 2017.
17 Packer in Arden Group discussion, August 2017.

Cymbeline **295**

18 'Tis still a dream, or else such stuff as madmen/Tongue and brain not; either both or nothing;/Or senseless speaking or a speaking such/As sense cannot untie. Be what it is,/The action of my life is like it, which/I'll keep, if but for sympathy.' *Cymbeline*, (1611), Act V, Scene iv, lines 146–151, Posthumus Leonatus.

19 Packer and Merlin conversation, August 2017.

20 Laurence, W. W. (1969), *Shakespeare's Problem Plays*, London: Penguin, p. 170.

21 Foakes, R. A. (1971), *Shakespeare: The Dark Comedies to the Last Plays: From Satire to Celebration*, London: Routledge and Kegan Paul, p. 100.

22 Palmer, D. J. (ed.) (1971), *Shakespeare's Later Comedies: An Anthology of Modern Criticism*, London: Penguin, p. 261.

23 Shakespeare, W. (1611), *Cymbeline*, Act III, Scene vi, line 53, Arviragus.

24 'How hard it is to hide the sparks of nature' (line 79), 'The princely blood flows in his cheek' (line 93), Belarius describing Polydore/Guiderius and Cadwal/Arviragus, Act III, Scene iii.

25 Packer and Merlin conversation, August 2017.

26 Packer cited in Merlin, *Cymbeline* rehearsal notes, 11 June 2017.

27 Packer in Arden Group discussion, August 2017.

28 ibid.

29 Packer cited in Merlin, *Cymbeline*, rehearsal notes, 18 June 2017.

30 Packer and Merlin conversation, August 2017.

31 Ronnberg, A. and Martin, K. (eds.) (2010), *The Book of Symbols: Reflections on Archetypal Images*, Cologne: Taschen, pp. 128–130.

32 ibid, p. 142.

33 Roob, A. (2014), *Alchemy and Mysticism*, Bonn: Taschen, 2014, p. 19, 20, (my emphasis).

34 Packer and Merlin conversation, August 2017.

35 ibid.

36 St Clair, A. (2017), '"Cymbeline" at Shakespeare & Company: A Play for Our Time,' *The Berkshire Edge*, 2 July 2017.

37 Packer in Arden Group discussion, August 2017.

38 Kingsley-Smith, J. (2003), *Shakespeare's Drama of Exile*, Basingstoke: Palgrave Macmillan, p. 161.

39 Packer in Arden Group discussion, August 2017, (my emphasis).

40 Packer and Merlin conversation, August 2017.

41 Ronnberg and Martin (eds.) (2010), p. 238.

42 ibid., p. 240.

43 Byrne, T. (2017), 'To Tina Packer, "Cymbeline" is much more than a Shakespeare Medley,' *The Boston Globe*, 29 June 2017.

44 Hickey in Arden Group discussion, August 2017.

45 Packer in Arden Group discussion, August 2017.

46 ibid.

47 Packer cited in Byrne (2017).

48 Director's Notes, Tina Packer, *Cymbeline* program, July 2017.

49 Packer in Arden Group discussion, August 2017.

50 Packer and Merlin conversation August 2017.

51 ibid.

52 Siegel, E. (2017), 'With a Terrific "Cymbeline," Shakespeare & Company's Tina Packer has Now Done It All,' WBUR, *The ARTery*, 26 July 2017.

53 Fanger, I. (2017), 'Review of "Cymbeline,"' *TheaterMania*, 12 July 2017.

54 Sorokoff, S. (2017), 'Review of "Cymbeline,"' *Broadway World*, 9 July 2017.

55 Plemmons, C. (2017), 'Review of "Cymbeline,"' *Curtain Up*, July 2017.

EPILOGUE

'On such a full sea are we now afloat'[1]

We've voyaged through the life of Shakespeare & Company over the past 40 years, seeing the heritage of its three pillars: *Training, Education* and *Performance*. And we've viewed some of the pitfalls along with the peaks of success. 'You know, the most difficult thing about creating a theatre company,' says Packer, 'is the constant question, where is the money going to come from?' That question is followed by

> is this the best way to organize this? Plunging into the world of a Shakespeare play gives some answers and builds a lot of strength. But how to get each activity to become the well-spring of the other – that's the question I'd like to answer.
>
> *(Packer notes to Merlin, 16 September 2019)*

Somehow – as we've seen throughout this book – Shakespeare & Company keeps managing to answer that question, even if it has sometimes been on a wing and a prayer. And while much terrain has been covered, there's still much to see. Certainly over the past two decades, there has been a concerted effort to ensure the Company's legacy endures beyond its three lifelong, founding members, Packer, Krausnick and Coleman. Across the three areas, they've been mentoring more teacher-trainees, training more education artists, and recruiting actors from further afield. They've been seeking more online resources; creating the Oral History Archive Project; and indeed, galvanizing the writing of this book. The Company's legacy bears other ripe fruit through entrepreneurial artists, who over the years have honed the skillsets and garnered the confidence to create their own theatres.[2] There are also troupes and projects in Israel, India, Australia, Canada and the Czech Republic, and professors in institutions across the globe teach S&Co.-inspired work. Meanwhile,

Packer and her fellow Company members deliver lectures, workshops and performances, nationally and internationally. And loyal patrons return each year to share the work in Lenox. But that's just part of the story.

As we said in the Prologue, this Epilogue is really Act I of a whole new play. So we conclude by celebrating the phase into which the Company entered in 2016 when, alongside Adam Davis as Managing Director, Allyn Burrows became Artistic Director, joining General Manager and loyal colleague Steve Ball.

Burrows unto the breach

Allyn Burrows (as previously noted) was steeped in the work of Shakespeare & Company long before he took up artistic directorship. Following a degree in International Relations from Boston University, he studied acting at the National Theatre in London, where among his teachers was Anthony Hopkins. In 1988, while playing Oliver in *As You Like It* at Merrimack Rep, Massachusetts, he received a call from Packer asking him to perform in an adaptation of Primo Levi's *Survival in Auschwitz*. The following January he took the Month-Long Intensive, having been cast as Cassius in the Northeast Regional Tour of *Julius Caesar*. And thereafter he stayed on to become a full-time Company member.

S&Co. was just ten years old at the time and Burrows found himself in the midst of a 'dynamic, explosive, searing, intriguing'[3] group of artists who were very demanding of themselves and each other. They were collectively engaged in synthesizing the principles proposed by Packer, Linklater and the master-teachers into a practical methodology:

> And I think this is what differentiates Shakespeare & Company from other companies. There's an understanding that there's a single imperative that we're trying to achieve [i.e., Shakespeare's *language as experience* between actor and audience]: it's just defined actively and differently by different people.
>
> *(Burrows interview, July 2017)*

And Burrows remained in this active, investigative environment for 17 years, playing many roles to great acclaim both in the Wharton adaptations at The Mount (including Percy Lubbock in *Duet with Variations* [1989]) and Shakespeare's canon (including Hal in *Henry IV Part 1* [1997] and Henry V [2002]).

As an artist manager, his initiatives included The Elephant pub at The Mount where they sold company merchandise and concessions. Later he became an Associate Artistic Director responsible for programming seasons. And throughout his time at Shakespeare & Company, 'the pursuit of the true artist' was always 'a fascinating phenomenon.'[4] In 1989 he prophetically stated in a press interview, 'In twenty years I would like to be able to say that if it had not been for Shakespeare & Company I couldn't have done all this.'[5] Stepping away on other ventures (among them as one of the founders of ASP in Boston, where he was Artistic Director from 2010 to 2016), little could Burrows have known that

FIGURE E.1 Allyn Burrows as Henry V, dir. Jonathan Epstein, 2002
Photo: Kevin Sprague

almost 30 years after he first came to Shakespeare & Company, he would be leading them into their 40th season.

It's Burrows' history with S&Co., along with his vision for their future that renders him such an apt director. He understands the Company's aesthetic, and at the same time he appreciates what visitors to the Berkshires might be seeking in their theatrical fare. At Kemble Street

> you have to create a destination. People have come for the summer to Berkshire County: the Arden to New York. So tourism has to affect choices. People are escaping from something, so we can't simply repeat what they'd expect to see in an urban environment. I like to say we do productions *in reflection of* rather than *in reaction to*. And in some ways the experience has to be richer, because we don't do something for *effect*: we do it for *impact*. And we constantly have to take into consideration our local environment as well as our global environment.
>
> *(Burrows interview, September 2018)*

So, when it comes to programming and directorial choices, Burrows seeks to manage the 'pleasure quotient' alongside the 'provocation factor':

FIGURE E.2 Gala 2018: Kenneth E. Werner (Chair), Kevin G. Coleman, Tina Packer, Michael A. Miller (longtime Chair), Annette Miller (Company member), Dennis Krausnick, Adam Davis and Allyn Burrows

Photo: Christina Lane

> When you're dealing with something as fluid, malleable and subjective as theatre – so dependent upon people's reception and view of it in order for it to persist – you have to walk the line between doing something *substantive* and something *festive*. You want to do what you feel is right, to say what's important about life through this set of words, mainly Shakespeare's; you want the audience to think and feel. Yet people also come to have a really good time, and they may just want to be transported into a story that helps them to put aside their daily lives and the global news. So you have to hit a note, which is inclusive of both *their* existence and *your* thoughts, and *your* voice and all the *people's* voices around you – because there's also a collective voice at work here at Shakespeare & Company.
>
> *(Burrows interview, September 2018)*

That collective voice is perhaps where Burrows' background in International Relations comes in:

> When you're running a theatre company you have to make decisions very quickly – and they have to be right. They're not necessarily life-and-death situations, but because everything has a ripple effect and everything is

interconnected, no decision lives in a vacuum. Every decision affects a budget and programming and people's perception and reception of the work. So every decision affects people's lives.

(Burrows interview, September 2018)

At the same time, he's mindful of the lives of the three people, who (as this book details) have affected the Company throughout its existence. Although many individuals – especially Kristin Linklater – have contributed to the Company's success, he understands the 'collective commitment to take what has now become an ideal and form it into something people want to deepen with each other.'[6] To which he says, 'Look what's been created by Tina, Dennis, Kevin and all these people here. Let's figure out how it has fermented over the years and how we can honor it, synthesize it and further it.'[7] And Burrows seeks to sustain, revivify, celebrate and evolve this vision through all manner of productions, scripts, actors and audience experiences across all three pillars of *Training*, *Education* and *Performance*:

We're fortunate to have this raw material of Shakespeare to work with. And we're all tradespeople in that way. We're working our trade and we're working it hard. And we do it under confined time periods and in intense ways. But the amount of goodwill here is startling. Everyone keeps doubling down on their willingness to give of themselves. And that's our lifeblood here at Shakespeare & Company.

(Burrows interview, September 2018)

FIGURE E.3   Cast of *Lovers' Spat: Round Two*, dir. Allyn Burrows, 2018

Photo: Carolyn Brown

And the lifeblood of this resilient theatre company – with its heart in the Berkshires and its limbs reaching far across the world – continues to pump with creative oxygen under Burrows' artistic directorship. As they head into their next 40 years, there may be little more to say in our story here than: 'Heaven give [them] many, many merry days!'[8]

Notes

1 Shakespeare, W. (1599), *Julius Caesar*, Act 4, Scene iii, line 221, Brutus.
2 Longtime artist manager Dan McCleary left in 2006 to found Tennessee Shakespeare Company in Memphis. In 1995, Jim Andreassi (a notable Petruchio) founded the open-air, free-admission Elm Shakespeare in New Haven, Connecticut, handing over the artistic directorship in 2016 to another S&Co. member Rebecca Goodheart. Company education artists Brian and Nikki Weaver left to create the Portland Playhouse in Oregon, whither Kevin Coleman returns regularly to train their education artists for their own Fall Festival of Shakespeare. Other American-based companies over the years include Kristin Linklater's and Carol Gilligan's Company of Women and Company of Girls in the 1990s; Lisa Wolpe's LA Women's Shakespeare; Eric Tucker's and Andrus Nichol's Bedlam; Rory Hammond's Animus; Ray DuBois' Black Shakespeare Project; Daniel Boudreau's Praxis Stage; Alec Lachman's, Andy Montano's and Jake Thompson's Voices Found Repertory; and Andrew Borthwick-Leslie's and Michael F. Toomey's Humanist Project.
3 Allyn Burrows interview with Bella Merlin, September 2018.
4 Burrows cited in Plemmons, C. (1989) 'Conversation with an Actor: Allyn Burrows,' *Citizen News*, 13 September 1989.
5 ibid.
6 Burrows interview, September 2018.
7 ibid.
8 Shakespeare, W. (c.1602), *The Merry Wives of Windsor*, Act V, Scene v, line 266, 'Heaven give you many, many merry days!' Mistress Page.

APPENDIX 1: AN ABRIDGED PERFORMANCE HISTORY

See www.shakespeare.org/about/performance-history for more details. Throughout the Company's history an original DibbleDance has been staged most years from 1987 onward, along with performances by STI, SSI, SPI, PIP and/or Shakespeare & Young Company Conservatories, and – from 1990 – the Fall Festival. There are also the annual Northeast Regional Tours and winter playreading festivals.

Tina Packer, Artistic Director

1978

A Midsummer Night's Dream
(*Mainstage*)
Three Voices of Edith Wharton (*Salon*)

1979

An Afternoon with Edith Wharton
(*Salon*)
The Winter's Tale (*Mainstage*)
Romeo and Juliet (*Mainstage*)

1980

A Very Special Afternoon (*Salon*)
The Tempest (*Mainstage*)

1981

A Very Special Evening (*Salon*)
As You Like It (*Mainstage*)
Duet with Variations (*Salon*)
Twelfth Night (*Mainstage, Toronto Theatre Festival*)

1982

Edith: An Intimate Portrait (*Salon*)
Macbeth (*Mainstage*)
Twelfth Night (*Mainstage, Brooklyn's Prospect Park*)

1983

The Comedy of Errors (*Mainstage*)
The Mount: A Turning Point (*Salon*)

Appendix 1 **303**

1984

A Midsummer Night's Dream (*Mainstage/Tour*)
The Custom of the Country (*Salon*)
Romeo and Juliet (*Mainstage/Tour*)
Songs from the Heart (*Salon*)

1985

The Comedy of Errors (*Mainstage*)
In One Door and Out the Other (*Salon*)
Much Ado About Nothing (*Terrace*)
Songs from the Heart (*Salon*)

1986

Antony and Cleopatra (*Mainstage, co-produced with Cleveland Playhouse*)
Roman Fever (*Terrace*)

1987

A Midsummer Night's Dream (*Mainstage*)
All's Well That Ends Well: (*Mainstage*)
Autres Temps (*Terrace*)
Othello (*Tour*)
The Other Two (*Terrace*)

1988

Afterward (*Salon*)
As You Like It (*Mainstage*)
Confession (*Salon*)
Hamlet (*Tour*)

1989

Duet with Variations (*Salon*)
Expiation (*Salon*)
Julius Caesar (*Tour*)
Roman Fever (*Salon*)
The Temperate Zone (*Salon*)
The Tempest (*Mainstage*)

1990

The Aspern Papers (*Salon*)
As You Like It (*Mainstage*)
Daisy Miller (*Salon*)
The Descent of Man (*Salon*)
Duet with Variations (*Salon*)
Edith: An Intimate Portrait (*Salon*)
The Legend (*Salon*)
The Old Maid (*Salon*)
Roman Fever (*Salon*)
Romeo and Juliet (*Tour*)
Songs from the Heart (*Salon*)
Women of Will 1: From Violence to Negotiation (*Stables*)

1991

The Aspern Papers (*Salon*)
The Descent of Man (*Salon*)
Hamlet (*Salon*)
The Last Asset (*Salon*)
The Legend (*Salon*)
Macbeth (*Tour/Mainstage*)
Shirley Valentine (*Stables*)
Tearsheets (*Stables*)
Twelfth Night (*Mainstage*)
Women of Will 1: The Warrior Women (*Stables*)
Xingu (*Salon*)

1992

A Life in the Theatre (*Stables*)
A Love Story (*Salon*)
Berkeley Square (*Salon*)
Custer Rides (*Stables*)
Duet for One (*Stables*)
The Inner House (*Salon*)
Julius Caesar (*Stables*)
Maisie (*Salon*)
The Mission of Jane (*Salon*)
Much Ado About Nothing (*Stables*)
Romeo and Juliet (*Tour/Mainstage*)
Shirley Valentine (*Stables*)
The Tale of the Tiger/Eve's Diary (*Stables*)

304   Appendix 1

The Taming of the Shrew (*Mainstage*)
Women of Will 1: The Warrior Women
(*Stables*)

1993

A Midsummer Night's Dream (*Mainstage*)
A Memory of Splendor (*Salon*)
Autres Temps (*Salon*)
Berkeley Square (*Salon*)
The Custom of the Country (*Salon*)
Duet for One (*Stables*)
Julius Caesar (*Stables*)
Kerfol: A Ghost Story (*Salon*)
The Landscape Painter (*Salon*)
On the Open Road (*Stables*)
Roman Fever (*Salon*)
The Spirit Warrior's Dream (*Mainstage*)
Troilus and Cressida (*Stables*)
Twelfth Night (*Tour/Stables*)
Virginia (*Stables*)

1994

The Comedy of Errors (*Mainstage*)
The Custom of the Country (*Salon*)
The Fiery Rain (*Salon*)
Hamlet (*Tour/Stables*)
The House of Mirth (*Salon*)
Kerfol: A Ghost Story (*Salon*)
Laughing Wild (*Stables*)
Macbeth (*Stables*)
Mrs. Klein (*Stables*)
New Land'scapes (*Stables*)
Richard II: Deposed (*Stables*)
Souls Belated (*Salon*)
The Winter's Tale (*Stables*)
Xingu (*Salon*)

1995

A Memory of Splendor (*Salon*)
Afterward (*Salon*)
Expiation (*Salon*)
The Fiery Rain (*Salon*)

Fortune and Misfortune (*Salon*)
Goodnight Desdemona (Good Morning
Juliet) (*Stables*)
Laughing Wild (*Stables*)
Much Ado About Nothing (*Mainstage*)
New Land'scapes (*Stables*)
Othello (*Stables*)
Shirley Valentine (*Stables*)
The Turn of the Screw (*Salon*)
Women of Will 2: Going Underground
(*Stables*)
Women of Will 3: The Maiden Phoenix
(*Stables*)

1996

A Love Story (*Salon*)
The Death of the Father of Psychoanalysis
(& Anna) (*Stables*)
Ethan Frome (*Stables*)
Faith and Hope: Edith at War (*Salon*)
Madame de Treymes (*Salon*)
The Merry Wives of Windsor (*Mainstage*)
Measure for Measure (*Stables*)
Mercy (*Stables*)
The Monkey's Paw (*Salon*)
Women of Will, Parts 1, 2, 3, (*Stables*)

1997

Betrayal (*Salon*)
Brief Lives (*Salon*)
The Death of the Father of Psychoanalysis
(& Anna) (*Stables*)
Ethan Frome (*Stables*)
Henry IV, Part 1 (*Mainstage*)
The Lady's Maid's Bell (*Salon*)
Off the Map (*Stables*)
The Pretext (*Salon*)
The Verdict (*Salon*)
The Winter's Tale (*Stables*)

1998

A Room of One's Own (*Salon*)
All's Well That Ends Well (*Stables*)

The Dilettante (*Salon*)
Glimpses of the Moon (*Stables*)
The Lear Project (*Stables*)
The Merchant of Venice (*Mainstage*)
The Millionairess (*Stables*)
The Mistress (*Salon*)
Private Eyes (*Salon*)
The Triumph of Darkness (*Salon*)
Wit (*Stables*)

1999

A Room of One's Own (*Salon*)
Glimpses of the Moon (*Salon*)
Richard III (*Duffin Theatre at Lenox High School*)
Love's Labour's Lost (*Mainstage*)
Private Eyes (*Salon*)
Summer (*Stables*)
The Woman in Black (*Salon*)

2000

The Compleat Works of Wllm Shkspr (abridged) (*Duffin*)
Coriolanus (*Stables*)
Jack & Jill (*Stables*)
Romeo and Juliet (*Mainstage*)
Twelfth Night (*Duffin*)
The Wharton One-Acts (Oh! Mr Chekhov, The View Beyond) (*Salon*)

2001 Final Year at The Mount and First Year on Kemble Street

A Midsummer Night's Dream (*Mainstage*)
A Tanglewood Tale (*Spring Lawn*)
Collected Stories (*Founders'*)
The Comedy of Errors (*Stables*)
The Compleat Works of Wllm Shkspr (abridged) (*Stables*)
Coriolanus (*Founders'*)
King John (*Stables*)
The Tempest (*Founders'*)
The Turn of the Screw (*Founders'*)
The Wharton One-Acts (The Rembrandt, An International Episode) (*Spring Lawn*)

2002

Edith Wharton Centennial Celebration (Summer, Ethan Frome, The Fiery Rain) (*Founders'*)
Henry V (*Founders'*)
Macbeth (*Founders'*)
Golda's Balcony (*Spring Lawn*)
The Scarlet Letter (*Founders'*)
The Valley of Decision (*Spring Lawn*)
The Vienna Project: Wittgenstein Vs. Popper (*Mass MoCA*)
The Wharton One-Acts (Roman Fever, The Other Two) (*Spring Lawn*)

2003

The Chekhov One Acts (*Spring Lawn*)
The Compleat Works of Wllm Shkspr (abridged) (*Founders'*)
Ethan Frome (*Founders'*)
The Fly-Bottle (*Spring Lawn*)
King Lear (*Founders'*)
Lettice and Lovage (*Spring Lawn*)
Much Ado About Nothing (*Founders'*)
A Midsummer Night's Dream (*Rose Footprint*)
SLaW (*Rose Footprint*)
Vita and Virginia (*Spring Lawn*)

2004

As You Like It (*Founders'*)
The Comedy of Errors (*Founders'*)
Full Gallop (*Spring Lawn*)
Lettice and Lovage (*Spring Lawn*)
The Othello Project (*Founders'*)
SLaW (*Rose Footprint*)
Vita and Virginia (*Spring Lawn*)

2005

Ice Glen (*Spring Lawn*)
King John (*Founders'*)
The Taming of the Shrew (*Founders'*)
The Tell-Tale Poe (*Founders'*)
The Tamer Tamed (*Rose Footprint*)

306 Appendix 1

Wild and Whirling Words (*Rose Footprint*)
The Tricky Part (*Spring Lawn*)
The Wharton One-Acts (The Promise,
The Mission of Jane) (*Spring Lawn*)

2006

Enchanted April (*Founders'*)
Hamlet (*Founders'*)
The Merry Wives of Windsor (*Founders'*)
Martha Mitchell Calling (*Founders'*)
No Background Music (*Founders'*)
The Servant of Two Masters (*Rose Footprint*)
Wild and Whirling Words (*Rose Footprint*)
Kerfol: A Ghost Story (*Founders'*)

2007

A Midsummer Night's Dream (*Founders'*)
Antony and Cleopatra (*Founders'*)
Blue/Orange (*Founders'*)
Rough Crossing (*Founders'*)
Scapin (*Rose Footprint*)
The Secret of Sherlock Holmes (*Founders'*)
SLaW (*Rose Footprint*)

2008–2009

All's Well That Ends Well (*Founders'*)
Bad Dates (*Winter, EBT*)
The Canterville Ghost (*Fall, EBT*)
The Goatwoman of Corvis County (*EBT*)
The Ladies' Man (*Founders'*)
The Lear Project (*EBT*)
The Mad Pirate and the Mermaid (*Rose Footprint*)
Othello (*Founders'*)

2009–2010

Cindy Bella (or the Glass Slipper) (*Founders'*)
Devil's Advocate – American Premiere (*EBT*)

Diva Series: The Actors Rehearse the
Story of Charlotte Salomon (*EBT*)
Diva Series: Shirley Valentine (*EBT*)
Diva Series: Golda's Balcony (*EBT*)
The Dreamer Examines His Pillow (*EBT*)
Hamlet (*Founders'*)
The Hound of the Baskervilles (*Fall, EBT*)
Les Liaisons Dangereuses (*Winter, EBT*)
Othello (*Founders'*)
Pinter's Mirror (*EBT*)
Romeo and Juliet (*EBT*)
Twelfth Night (*Founders'*)
White People (*EBT*)

Tony Simotes, Artistic Director

2010–2011

The Amorous Quarrel (*Rose Footprint*)
Bad Dates (*EBT*)
Julius Caesar (*EBT*)
Mengelberg and Mahler (*EBT*)
The Mystery of Irma Vep (*Winter, EBT*)
The Real Inspector Hound (*Fall, EBT*)
Richard III (*Founders'*)
The Santaland Diaries (*Christmas, EBT*)
Sea Marks (*EBT*)
The Taster (*Founders'*)
The Winter's Tale (*Founders'*)
Women of Will (*Founders'*)
SLaW (*EBT*)

2011–2012

As You Like It (*Founders'*)
The Hollow Crown (*EBT*)
The Hound of the Baskervilles (*Founders'*)
The Learned Ladies (*Winter, EBT*)
The Memory of Water (*EBT*)
Red-Hot Patriot: The Kiss-Ass Wit of
Molly Ivins (*EBT*)
Romeo and Juliet (*Founders'*)
The Santaland Diaries (*Christmas, EBT*)
SLaW (*EBT*)

The Venetian Twins (*Rose Footprint*)
War of the Worlds (*Fall, EBT*)
Women of Will: The Complete Journey: Parts 1–5 (*EBT*)

2012–2013

The 39 Steps (*Fall, EBT*)
Cassandra Speaks (*EBT*)
Endurance (*TPP*)
King Lear (*TPP*)
The Liar (*Winter, EBT*)
Parasite Drag (*EBT*)
The Santaland Diaries (*Christmas, EBT*)
Satchmo at the Waldorf (*TPP*)
SLaW (*EBT*)
The Tale of the Allergist's Wife (*EBT*)
Tartuffe, the Imposter (*Rose Footprint*)
The Tempest (*TPP*)

2013–2014

A Midsummer Night's Dream (*The Dell at The Mount*)
Accomplice (*Fall, EBT*)
The Beauty Queen of Leenane (*EBT*)
Heroes (*EBT*)
Kaufman's Barbershop (*Upstreet Barbershop*)
It's a Wonderful Life: A Live Radio Play (*Christmas, EBT*)
Leap Year (*McConnell Theater at Simon's Rock College*)
Les Faux Pas (*Rose Footprint*)
Love's Labour's Lost (*TPP*)
Master Class (*EBT*)
Mother Courage and her Children (*TPP*)
None But the Lonely Heart (*EBT*)
Private Lives (*Winter, EBT*)
Richard II (*TPP*)
SLaW (*EBT*)

2014–2015

A Midsummer Night's Dream (*TPP*)
The Compleat Works of Wllm Shkspr (abridged) (*TPP*)

Henry IV Parts I and II (*TPP*)
Julius Caesar (*EBT*)
It's a Wonderful Life: A Live Radio Play (*Christmas, EBT*)
Private Eyes (*Fall, EBT*)
Romeo and Juliet (*The Dell at The Mount*)
Shakespeare's Will (*EBT*)
The Servant of Two Masters (*Rose Footprint*)
Vanya and Sonya and Masha and Spike (*EBT*)

Ariel Bock & Jonathan Croy, Interim Artistic Directors

2015–2016

The Comedy of Errors (*TPP*)
Cry Havoc! (*TPP*)
Hamlet (*The Dell at The Mount*)
Henry V (*EBT*)
The How and the Why (*EBT*)
An Iliad (*Fall, EBT*)
It's a Wonderful Life: A Live Radio Play (*Christmas, EBT*)
Mother of the Maid (*EBT*)
Red Velvet (*TPP*)
SLaW (*Rose Footprint*)
The Unexpected Man (*TPP*)

Ariel Bock & Jonathan Croy, Artistic Directors

2016–2017

Cry Havoc! (*EBT*)
The Emperor of the Moon (*Rose Footprint*)
Henry VI 6 Marathon (*TPP/Rose Footprint/Shakespeare's Garden*)
It's a Wonderful Life: A Live Radio Play (*Christmas, EBT*)
The Merchant of Venice (*TPP*)
Or, (*TPP*)
Sotto Voce (*EBT*)
The Taming (*EBT*)

308 Appendix 1

The Two Gentlemen of Verona (*TPP*)
Ugly Lies the Bone (*EBT*)
Twelfth Night (*The Dell at The Mount*)

Allyn Burrows, Artistic Director

2017–2018

4000 Miles (*EBT*)
Cymbeline (*TPP*)
God of Carnage (*EBT*)
Intimate Apparel (*EBT*)
A Midsummer Night's Dream (*The Dell at The Mount*)
Miss Bennet: Christmas at Pemberly (*Christmas, EBT*)
Shakespeare Valentine Surprise (*EBT*)
Storytellers and Songwriters (*TPP*)
The Tempest (*Roman Garden*)
An Evening of Wharton One-Acts (Roman Fever & The Fullness of Life) (*EBT*)

2018–2019

As You Like It (*Roman Garden*)
Creditors (*EBT*)

Heisenberg (*TPP*)
Hir (*EBT*)
Love's Labour's Lost (*The Dell at The Mount*)
Lovers' Spat: Round Two (*EBT*)
Macbeth (*TPP*)
Morning After Grace (*EBT*)
Mothers and Sons (*EBT*)
Pride and Prejudice (*Christmas, EBT*)

2019–2020

The Children (*EBT*)
Coriolanus (Workshop production) (*EBT*)
Julius Caesar (Rehearsed reading) (*TPP*)
The Merry Wives of Windsor (*Roman Garden*)
Sense & Sensibility (*Christmas, EBT*)
Shakespeare Valentine Surprise (*EBT*)
The Taming of the Shrew (*The Dell at The Mount*)
Time Stands Still (*EBT*)
Topdog/Underdog (*TPP*)
Twelfth Night (*TPP*)
The Waverly Gallery (*EBT*)

APPENDIX 2: AN ABRIDGED *DRAMATIS PERSONAE*

Core leadership and staff (2019)

Administrative: Allyn Burrows (Artistic Director), Adam Davis (Managing Director), Tina Packer (Founding Artistic Director), Stephen Ball (General Manager), Ariel Bock (Producing Associate), Catherine E. Wheeler (Executive Assistant), Brittney Holland (Company Manager, Regional Tour and Intern Program Coordinator), Al Hiser, Eddie O'Toole & Robert Pelliciotti (Facilities Associates), Mary Budzn (Receptionist). **Center for Actor Training:** MaConnia Chesser (Administrative Director), Susan Dibble (Workshop coordinator). **Costumes:** Govane Lohbauer (Costume Director), Michelle Benoit & Toby Kreimendahl (Drapers), Mary Boyce & Lezlie Lee (Stitchers), Stella Schwartz (Designer, draper, stitcher). **Development:** Natalie Johnsonius Neubert (Senior Development Officer), Elizabeth Aspenlieder (Business Sponsorship and Events), Alexander Zaretsky (Development Strategist), Kristen Moriarty (Individual Giving Associate), Zoe Wohlfeld (Individual Giving Assistant). **Education:** Kevin G. Coleman (Director of Education), Jennie M. Madow (Education Programs Manager), Megan Marchione (Educations Program Administrator). **Finance and IT:** Richard Martelle (Director of Finance), Laura Taylor (Finance Assistant), Tim Auxier (IT & Business Systems Director). **Housekeeping:** Bonnie Wilson (Housekeeping Manager), Gina Squires (Housekeeping Associate). **Marketing, Public Relations and Patron Services:** Jenne Young (Director of Marketing & Communications), Molly Merrihew (Press & Publicity Director), Katie McKellick (Graphic Designer/Marketing Associate), Kevin Lempke (Patron Services Manager). **Production:** Kevin Harvell (Production Manager), Hope Rose Kelly (Production Stage Manager), James W. Bilnoski (Master Electrician), Patrick Brennan (Properties Master), Bob Lohbauer (Weapons Master), Patrick Kilgore & Hayley Wenk (Carpenters), Devon Drohan (Scenic Charge Artist), and Danny Irwin (Sound Supervisor).

310 Appendix 2

Board of trustees (2019)

Kenneth E. Werner (Chair), Jeffrey B. Konowitch (Vice Chair), Barry R. Shapiro (Vice Chair), Suzanne Werner (Treasurer), Michael A. Miller (Clerk), Allyn Burrows (Artistic Director/President), Jerome Berko, Sandra Bourgeois, George Camarda, MaConnia Chesser, Kevin G. Coleman, Nancy Edman Feldman, Gerald Friedman, M.D., Ph.D., Michael Fuchs, Phoebe L. Giddon, Michael Helfer, Beverly Hyman, Jennie M. Jadow, Erick J. Lucere, Barri Marks, Maureen O'Hanlon, Helga S. Orthofer, Tina Packer, Claudia Perles, Andrew D. Rothstein, Scott Rubinow, William M. Ryan, David A. Smith, Robert B. Strassler and John Douglas Thompson.

Advisory board (2019)

Kevin Bartini, Helene Berger, Roberta Berry, Gail and Stanley Bliefer, Roxanne and Scott Bok, Janet Carey, Linda Colvin, Michael and Shawn Leary Considine, Ruth Dinerman, Janet Egelhofer, Randall Frank, Audrey Friedner, Sonya Hamlin, Jennie M. Jadow, Eleanor Lord and Margaret Wheeler, Marybeth Mitts, Dr. Carolyn Newberger, The Honorable Paul Perachi, Carol Seldin, Howard and Natalie Shawn, Thomas and Maureen Steiner, Dr. Harriet Vines, Marian Warden, Dorothy Weber, Rhea Werner and Leone Young.

Training faculty members

Over the years they have included (among others): (*Voice*) Christine Adaire, Zoë Alexander, Claudia Anderson, Mary Baird, Christopher von Baeyer, Fran Bennett, Brent Blair, Ariel Bock, Anne Brady, Adele Cabot, Louis Colaianni, Paul D'Agostino, Mary Coy, Paul D'Agostino, Dave Demke (longtime Associate Director of Training), Timothy Douglas, Keeley Eastley, Dianne Eden, Tom Giordano, Rebecca Kemper Goodheart, Debra Hale, Andrea Haring, Melissa Healey, Margaret Jansen, Isobel Kirk, Dennis Krausnick, Paula Langton, Kristin Linklater, Cecil MacKinnon, Mary Mayo, Michael Morgan, Julie Nelson, Normi Noel, Antonio Ocampo-Guzman, Natsuko Ohama, James Goodwin Rice, Rebecca Schneebaum, Gwendolyn Schwinke, Robert Serrell, Judith Shahn, Leigh Smiley, Sarah Weatherwax, Frances West, Kimberly White, Walton Wilson, Peter Wittrock; (*Movement/Dance*) Trish Arnold, Sarah Barker, Karen Beaumont, John Broome, Susan Dibble, Charls Sedgwick Hall, Sarah Hickler, Elizabeth Ingram, Tod Randolph, Victoria Rhoades, Kristin Wold; (*Clown/Play*) Michael Burnet, Kevin G. Coleman, Merry Conway, Jane Nichols, Virginia Ness Ray, Michael F. Toomey; (*Fight*) Martin Jason Asprey, B. H. Barry, Ted Hewlett, Mark Ingram, Edgar Landa, Corinna May, Ellen Salland, Tony Simotes, Claire Warden and Ryan Winkles; (*Text*) Sarah Kate Anderson, Andrew Borthwick-Leslie, Jenna May Cass (Sonnet), Jonathan Epstein (Sonnet), Neil Freeman, John Hadden, Michael Hammond, Rebecca Holderness, Elizabeth Ingram, Malcolm Ingram,

Tom Jaeger, Tina Packer, Clare Reidy, Rocco Sisto, Daniela Varon, Kevin Vavasseur, Bob Wicks. While each faculty member has one or two areas of specialty (*Voice, Movement, Fight, Clown, Dance, Sonnet,* etc.), they all come together for classes such as *Basics* and *Scene Work*.

Education artists and administrators

They have included over the years (and among many others): Kate Abbruzzese, Zoe Archer, Ellie Bartz, David Bertoldi, John Beale, Ariel Bock, Gregory Boover, Andrew Borthwick-Leslie, Dara Brown, Allyn Burrows, Kaia Calhoun, Caroline Calkins, Victoria Rhoades, Jenna May Cass, Ken Cheeseman, Candace Clift, Gregory Uel Cole, Jonathan Croy, Jeff Deutsch, Emily Ehlinger, Lori Evans, Allison Galen, Kelly Galvin, Colin Gold, John Hadden, Rory Hammond, Andrea Haring, Luke Haskell, Fiona Herter, Kaileela Hobby, Hannah Gellman, Tom Jaeger, Jennie M. Jadow, Margaret Jansen, David Joseph, Marcus Kearns, Caitlin Kraft, Zoë Laiz, Lezlie Lee, Paula Langton, Madeleine Rose Maggio, Jordan Mann, Conor Moroney, Nick Nudler, Devante Owens, Kirsten Peacock, Isabella Pelz, Lisa Anne Porter, John Sarrouf, Douglas Seldin, Dara Silverman, Enrico Spada, Steven Sylvester, Sarah Jeannette Taylor, Patrick Toole, Michael F. Toomey, Karen Torbjornsen, Carrie Upton, Jo Ann Valle, Jenna Ware, Josie A. Wilson, Ryan Winkles, Mark Wollett, Lisa Wolpe.

Oral History Archive Project volunteers (2016–2019 and onwards)

Sarah Lytle, Kristen Lochrie, Melody Mason (Current and previous co-chairs), Sandy Bourgeois, Gail Kotler, Jean Leif, Selina Morris, Julie Quain, Frank Speizer, Jeanne Speizer, Nancy Walters, Sharon Brecher, Esse Dean, Rachel Donner, Phyllis Gormezano, Carol Laban, Phil Laban, Scott Rubinow, Mara Winn, Randy Winn and Susan Wozniak.

APPENDIX 3: A POTTED PLOT OF *CYMBELINE*

Once upon a time, King Cymbeline ruled over ancient Britain: *guardian* to his dead friend's son Posthumus Leonatus (whose mother died in childbirth), *father* to Imogen (who loves Posthumus), *husband* to his second wife the (wicked) Queen and *stepfather* to the foolish Cloten. As our story opens, Cymbeline is threatening war with Rome, who 20 years earlier conquered Britain. Meanwhile … Posthumus clandestinely marries Imogen (destined for stepson Cloten) and Cymbeline banishes him to Italy. There Posthumus wagers his new wife's fidelity with the cunning Iachimo, who sets sail for England to test Imogen's honor. Meanwhile … in the mountains of Wales two lads, Polydore and Cadwal, live with their assumed father Morgan ('Assumed' because Morgan is actually Belarius, a general exiled by the boys' father Cymbeline, so in revenge ran away with the boys when they were babes and their real names are Guiderius and Arviragus.)

Many long stories short (and not necessarily in this order) … *Iachimo* falters in seducing Imogen, but lies about it on his return to Italy. … In jealous rage, the exiled *Posthumus* swears vengeance on his wife and returns (disguised) to England. … *The wicked Queen* plots to poison *Imogen*, who – disguised as a boy ('Fidele') – runs off to seek Posthumus and, exhausted from her travels, secretly shelters in the Welsh cave-home of Belarius and the boys. There she drinks the Queen's 'restorative' potion, given to her by Posthumus' trusty servant *Pisanio*, and falls into a dead faint. … *Cloten*, in the garb of Posthumus, heads to Wales in search of Imogen and is beheaded in a fight by Polydore. (Gruesome, to say the least.)… *Imogen/Fidele*, deemed dead of the poison by Belarius and the boys, awakes alone beside the beheaded body of what she takes to be her husband Posthumus. (Frightening, to say the least.) She (or is it he?) is discovered, a-grieving, by Roman ensign *Caius Lucius*, who is marching through Wales to attack Cymbeline, and so he recruits 'Fidele' as his page. … The battle between the Romans and the Britons ensues. *Cymbeline* is about to be captured, when he

Appendix 3 **313**

is rescued by *Polydore* and *Cadwal*, aided by a third (unknown) soldier. *Posthumus* the unknown soldier is mistaken for a Roman and thrown into jail. There, he is visited in a dream by his dead family and by Jupiter, who drops a prophecy on his sleeping body. ... *'Fidele'* is captured when the Britons defeat the Romans. ... The *Queen* dies of fevered remorse (though nobody gives a tuppenny fig). ... *Belarius and the boys* are honored for their valor at Cymbeline's court, where the boys are revealed by Belarius to be Cymbeline's sons, Guiderius and Arviragus ... *'Fidele'* is about to be slain by his (or is it her?) British captors when he (she) is revealed to be Cymbeline's daughter Imogen. She's reunited with *Posthumus* (revealed to be the unknown soldier), who is likewise now at court being noted for his bravery in battle. And *Iachimo*, about to be slain as a captive, confesses his sins and is pardoned. A *Soothsayer* interprets Jupiter's prophecy and it turns out that Posthumus is of royal descent. All these plots are threaded together by the trusty servant, *Pisanio*. *Cymbeline* – in beneficent mood – declares he'll pay Rome the tribute after all, even though he has beaten them in battle. So Rome and Britain are united in peace. And they all live happily ever after.

The End!

INDEX

1789 109

Abbruzzese, Kate 252
Ackermann, Joan 257
'An Actor at Work' 30, 172
actor/audience relationship 12, 15–18, 19, 24,
    42, 45, 85, 86, 96–100, 116, 206, 247,
    290; *Basics* 126, 128–129; *Clown* 30–31,
    152, 154–155; curiosity 90; *Cymbeline*
    279; *Education* 186, 190; Fall Festival
    202; final scenes 163–164; Ground
    Rules 118; Kemble Street 52–55;
    Movement 150; pauses 111; *Performance*
    239–241; Riotous Youth 217; *Scene
    Work* 136; Talk #1 66–67, 77; Talk #2
    107–115
Actors' Shakespeare Project 58, 277, 297
Adizes, Ichak Kalderon 118, 129n6
air broadswords 185, 199–200, *200*
alchemy 107, 121, 153, 245, 282;
    alchemical symbols 276–277,
    280–281, 286
Alexander Technique 124
alexithymia 99
Alon, Ruthi 26
Altshuler, Donald I. 35, 39, 40
American Association of Fight
    Directors 22
American Center for Shakespeare
    Performance and Studies 54
Anderson, Dion 16
Anderson, Miles 257, *258*
Antony and Cleopatra 244

Apprentice/Intern program 210, 218–219;
    Performance Internship Program (PIP)
    222n24
Arnold, Trish 19, 22–23, 24, 30, 31, 41,
    84, 87, 119, 124, 149; *see also* Pure
    Movement
Arthur, Brooke 290
articulation 94, 122–123, 285; consonants
    94, 122, 217, 284, 285
artist manager xi, 54, 58, 218, 245, 297
Art of Logic 74, 96
Art of Rhetoric 55, 74, 76, 96, 133, 149n9
Aspenlieder, Elizabeth 142, 143, 254, 256
Asprey, Laurie 11
Asprey, Martin Jason 11, 22, *59*, 260, 277,
    285, 294
Associate Artistic Director 58, 245, 297
As You Like It 10, 60, 137, 141, 174, *203*,
    257, *259*, 259, 297
audiences 124, 150, 155, 157, 185, 201,
    220, 245, 246, 259, 260–261, 269, 291,
    299; *see also actor/audience relationship*
Avari, Erick 30

Bacchanalia 266; function 110
Ballou, Bill 248, 60n10, 61n11
Ball, Steve xvi, 4, 297
'Bare Bard' productions 43
Bargh, Gillian 43, 60n10, 61n11
Barry, B. H. 19, 21–22, 27, 30, 41, 60n10,
    84, 156, 159, 185, 222n25, 260
Barton, John 10, 18, 19–20, 22, 95, 123,
    132, 133

Bartz, Ellie *203*

Basics 112, 116, 124, 125–131, 132, 135, 146, 150, 157, 163, 216

Beale, John 209

Beaumont, Karen 23, 31, 37n66, *150*

Behan, Brendan 109–110

Bennett, Fran 42

Berenson, Mitchell 34–35, 37n77, 38, 40, 47, 60n10

Berhle, Leila 40

Bernstein Center for the Performing Arts 53–54, 148; *see also* Elayne Bernstein Studio (EBT)

Bernstein Schwartz, Elayne Polly 53–54

Bhagavad Gita 281–282

The Bible Speaks 49, 50

the "big" questions (What does it mean to be alive? How should we act? What must I do?) 46, 76, 78, 79n3, 100, 231, 241, 255–257, 266, 268–269, 270, 272

Black Power movement 110–111

Bock, Ariel 58, 174–175, 221n22, 244

Body Work 83, 98–100, 129, 148–160; *Cymbeline* 278–279

Borak, Jeffrey 85, 163

Borthwick-Leslie, Andrew 87, 90, 128, 129, 144, 154, 163, 300n2

bouffon 31, 152, 155–156, 161

Bowsher, Julian 206

Brantley, Ben 260

Brazzle, Thomas 252, 277, 283, 284, 286, *289*, 291

breath 15, 24, 60, 94, 95, 98, 99, 108, 111, 113, 119, 121–123, 124, 128, 134, 184, 241; *Body Work* 149; *dropping in* 139, 142, 144, 153, 253, 283; *Fight* 157; *Sonnet* 135; *Structure of the Verse* 133–134

Brennan, Patrick 290, 293

British-American company 1, 16–18, 22, 34, 45

Britons 260, 275, 278, 288, 289, 290, 292–293; Brexit 278, 282, 288, 293; Britannia 276

Brook, Peter 26, 84, 246, 248

Broome, John 19, 20–21, *21*, 22, 41, 60n10, 84, 148, 151, 200

Burbage, Richard 95

Burrows, Allyn xiv, xvi, 3, 4, 42, 58–59, *59*, 60, *140*, 244, 245, 255, 256, 258, 261, 275, 297–301; *Coriolanus 271*; *Cymbeline* 275; Gala 2018 *299*; Henry V *298*; *Lovers' Spat 300*

Calhoun, Kaia 27, 42, 60n10, 188n2

Calkins, Caroline 204, 211, 212, 213, 214, 215–216, 217, *220*, 221

Cannon, Taylor 199

Carmichael, Stokely 110–111

Carson, Eliza *220*

Cass, Jenna May 135–136

catharsis 14, 69–70, 72, 86, 99–100, 114, 115n3, 270, 273

Center for Actor Training 28, 83

Chaikin, Joseph 14, 248

checking in 118, 198, 211–212, 213, 214, 254, 279

Chekhov, Michael xiv, 124

Cherry, Kate 257

Chesser, MaConnia 87, *234*

Clipston Grange 51

close textual analysis 249–251, 285; *see also* textual analysis

closing circle 165

Clown 30–31, 108, 148, 151–156, *154*, 163, 187, 209, 219, 221, 245, 258–259, *259*; fool 31, 259, *259*; Sacred and Profane 155–156; *see also bouffon*

Cole, Gregory Uel 27, 45, 60n10, 61n11, 188n2

Cole, Maria 40

Coleman, Kevin G. xv–xvi, 3, 14, 27, 28–30, *31*, 41, 49, 60, 94, 110, 121, 128, 152–153, 163, 171, 173–176, 178–187, *182*, 191, 211, 221n22, *234*, 242, 286, 296, *299*, 300; adolescence, understanding 179–180, 225; awards 178, 224; *Clown* 258–259, *259*; Courts Project 223, 225–229, 231–234; Fall Festival 193, 194–206; *Performance* 239–240; rehearsals 247; Shakespeare & Young Company 218; three levels of being 180–181

Coleman, Wolfe 197, 221n22

comedy 65, 111; *Cymbeline* 290–292, 293

The Comedy of Errors 31, 218

Common Classes 199–200; Elizabethan Movement/Dance 199, 200; Performance 199, 200; Stage Combat 189n55, 199–200, *200*, 224; Technical Production 199

community 55, 64, 66, 68, 73, 75, 77, 83, 91, 171, 178, 179, *182*, 195, 204, 215, 240, 252, 265–266, 267, 269

Condell, Henry 95

consciousness 65–67, 70, 78, 109, 271, 273, 289

316 Index

Conservatory Training Program 45; *see also* Shakespeare & Young Company conservatories

Conway, Merry 23, 30–31, 84, 119, 149, 152, 155, 222n25; Mindbody Perception, Physical Awareness 31

Coriolanus 1, 102, 244, 256, 257, *271, 273*

Courts Project *see* Shakespeare in the Courts Program

Crane, Joyce 40

Crean, Patrick 21

Croy, Jonathan 41, 58, 175, 176, 183, 184, 224, 244

curiosity 25, 26, 45, 75, 99, 103, 119, 121, 210, 213, 254, 267; pedagogy of 89–90

Cymbeline 244, 245, 246, 252, 256, 260, 274–295, *287, 289, 291–292*; design 276–277, 283–284; Linklater; Voice progression 279; potted plot 317–318; rehearsals 278–290

'Danger Process' 104n9, 111

Davenport, Johnny Lee 257

Davis, Adam xvi, 4, 58, 297, *299*

debate, theatre as 75, 78, 124, 241, 255–256

deGannes, Nehassaiu 257

The Dell 44, 60, 191, *191*

Demke, Dave 61n44, 87, 88, 89, 118

Devoti, William 173, 176

Dibble, Susan 20, 21, 34, 149, 150–151, *151*, 160–162, 166n53, 221n22, 222n25

dictionary work 186, 198–199, 249–250

Dildine, Rick 58

Dillon, Janette 206

DiMaggio, Richard 204

directing 244–255; 'Artistic Director's Statement' 46; assistant directors 214, 249, 251–255, 285; Courts Project 229, 230–231; director's role 45, 112, 200; directorial 'frames' 275; Fall Festival 196–197, 200; 'Notes on Directing' 245–246; personal-political director 245–247

Director-in-Residence 192–193

Douglas, Timothy *140*

Dovydenas, Betsy Dayton 49

dropping in 24, 96, 116, 132, 137–147, 248, 249, 250, 252–253; *Cymbeline* 279–280, 283–284, 285

DuBois, Ray *150*, 300n2

Dukakis, Olympia 26, 46, 112

Edith Wharton Restoration, Inc. (EWR) 47, 55

Education 3, 21, 30, 31, 34, 110, 159, 169–236, 243, 245, 296; on campus 209–222; funding 55; the ; mission 44–45, 46; practical pedagogy 171–189, 210, 212, 214, 224, 225; schools 171–187, 190–208; Shakespeare in the Courts 223–236; Shakespeare in the Schools 190–208

Egan, Michael 206

Egozi, Noa 205, 251–252, 253, 254–255, 256, 262n57, 277, 280, 284, 293

Elayne Bernstein Theatre (EBT) 54, 148, 232; *see also* Bernstein Center for the Performing Arts

Elements 149, 161, 162, 269

Elizabethan playhouse *see Elizabethan theatre*

Elizabethan theatre 2, 18, 23, 24, 30, 33, 41, 42, 52, 56, 75, 84, 86, 124, 149, 150, 201, 206, 240, 255, 269, 297

Elizabethan World Picture 20, 40, 132, 149, 160, 161, 166n52; Chain of Being 40–41, 160; *Elizabethan World Picture Day* 116, 134, 151, 155, 156, 160–163, 281; Elizabethan values, principles 44, 54

El Petitui, Mohamed 202

empathy 17, 33, 78, 98, 101, 102, 108, 113, 114, 181–182, 199, 212, 267, 272; *see also* mindfulness

ensemble 11, 46, 219, 224, 249, 284

Epstein, Jonathan 30, 41, 58, 129, 134, 146n7, 251, 257, 277, 279, 290–291

Erhard, Werner 85–86

'essentialized' self 152–153

est training xiv, 26, 32, 85–86, 104n9, 111, 137

experiential authority 193

Fall Festival of Shakespeare 175, 176, 177, 190, 193–205, *203*, 215, 216, 218

Farrell, Aileen 39

feeding in 137, 144–145, 228–229, 249

Feldenkrais, Moshe 26, 124

Ferrentino, Lindsey 100, 257

Fight Work 18, 21–22, 99, 108, 148, 151, 156–159, *159*, 163, 172–173, 259–260; Courts Project 223, 229–230; *Cymbeline* 260, 285; *Education* 184–186, 219, 221; Stage Combat common class 199–200, *200*; Stage(d) Violence 156

Index **317**

First Folio 23, 95–96; *The Applause First Folio of Shakespeare* 96
Fletcher, Rachel 56
Ford Foundation 2, 14, 16, 18–19, 20, 23, 25, 40, 88, 137, 156
Founders' Theatre *see* Tina Packer Playhouse
Foxhollow School 35, 39, 40
Freeman, Neil 23, 95–96
French, Darrin 198
Funches, Ashli *220*
function of the theatre 15, 22, 28, 60, 89, 99; Talk #1 63–79, 132
Futterman, E. 202, 203

Gale, William 226
Galvin, Kelly 60, *191*, *192*, 244–245, 255, 257
Gaulier, Philippe 152
gender 92, 96–98, 101, 102–103, 136, 221, 252, 256–257, 265, 276
Geometry 56
Gestalt therapy 137; bodymind gestalt 93
Gilligan, Carol 96–98, 100–101, 102, 105n48, 205, 300n2
Gilligan, James 100–103, 157–158
God, gods, goddess *see* religion
Goodbody, Buzz 20, 262n41
Goodheart, Rebecca Kemper 146n7, 301n2
Goodman, Nelson 177
Gore, Nigel xiii 60, *244*, 257–258, 277, 279, 280, 287
Grassle, Karen 12, 36n21
Greek theatre, drama 14, 26, 38, 67–70, 99, 100, 101, 108, 114, 122, 168, 265–266, 267, 269, 270, 273n3
Green, Stefan 54
Gregory, André 27, 29, 46
Griffin-Pressley, Deaon *59*, 252, 256, 277, 283
Grotowski, Jerzy xiv 29, 129; *via negativa* 129
Ground Rules 117–118
Gurr, Andrew 206

habits 23, 89, 117, 119, 120, 124, 217, 220
Hadden, John 34, 60n10, 61n11, 142, 172, 190, 221n22, 222n24
Hall, Charls Sedgwick 23
Hall, Peter 18, 19
Halpern, Herb 40
Hamlet xvi 5, 91, 107, 111, 112, 141, 143, 180, 181, 193, 200, 206, 224, 228, 233, 240, 258, 273

Hammond, Michael 58, 61n44, 221n22
Hammond, Rory 4, 123–124, 211, 212, 215, 217, *220*, 221, 221n22, 242, 300n2
Hartman, Mary 176, 188n2, 192–193, 206, 223
Haring, Andrea 188n2
Harvard University 177–178, 195
healing 5n2, 14, 18, 22, 28, 34, 94, 99–100, 172, 269, 272, 273n3, 278n3, 285; *see also* Theatre, Therapy, Theology
Heilbron, Lorna 37n67, 60n10, 61n11
Heminge, John 95
Henry IV, Part 1 100, 206, 260
Henry V 27, 111, 297, *298*
Henry VI Parts, 1, 2, 3, 27, 101, 150, 164, 257, 297
Hickey, Tamara 60, 277, 283, 284, 289, *289*, 290–291
Hildy, Franklin 206
Hobbs, Bill 21–22, 159
Hoffman, Ted 14
Holderness, Rebecca 257, *267*
Holding the space 213, 214
Holdridge, Eleanor 257, *259*, 275
Hook, Maeve *164*
Horne, Cloteal L. 256, 257, *258*
Horst, E. 203
The Hostage 109–110
Humours 149
Hutchins, Ashley 290
Hyslop, Austin 25

iambic pentameter 20, 95, 133, 149, 250
'The Idea Behind the Plan' 16–18
identity 96, 103, 255–257, 265; *see also* gender, multi-cultural, multi-racial
Ingram, Elizabeth 105n48, 257
Ingram, Malcolm 41, 257
intimacy 30, 52, 88, 96, 97–98, 108, 127, 157, 177, 240–241, 256, 268
invitations, pedagogy of 90–92
Irvin, William 177

Jadow, Jennie M. 187, 226, 231, 232, *234*
Jaeger, Tom 219, *220*, 221
James, Henry 11, 28, 43
Jesuits, Society of Jesus 14, 27, 28, 29, 49
Johnstone, Keith xiv, 152
Jones, Mark 54
Jooss-Leeder 20, 22
Joseph, David 43
Journaling 132, 134,146n2, 210

318 Index

Julius Caesar 111, 137, 257, 270, 296, 297
'Juvenile Youth Project' 223–224

Kapp, Richard 16, 18, 25–26, 32–34
Kass, Peter 14, 26, 112,174
Kelly, Hope Rose 290
Kemble, Fanny 48
Kemble Street 5, 48–60, *50*, 209, 217, 252, 298
Kennedy, Ted 55
King John 20, 92, 123, 127, *220*, 221
King Lear 28, 30, 32, 47, 103, 108, *259*, *267*
Kinney, Tyler 277, 284, 290, 293
Kirkwood, Lucy 257
Kobler, Donald 176–177
Kraft, Caitlin 211, 212, 213, 215, 217
Krausnick, Dennis xv–xvi, 2, 3, 14, 23, 27–30, *31*, 38, 47, 49, 52, 83, 87, 88–89, 90, 93, 124, 125–126, 137, 148, 163, 185, 239–240, *267*, 296, *299*, 300; *bouffon* 155; *Clown* 153, 154, 156; death 5; *dropping in* 142; Elizabethan World Picture Day 160–161, 162; feeding in 145; Fight 156; *Sonnet* 134–135, *136*; *Three Voices of Edith Wharton* 43

Laban, Rudolf 149
lamentation rites 69
Landa, Edgar 22
Langton, Paula 105n48
language 16, 19, 28, 32–33, 75, 76, 86, 99–100, 108–109, 123, 126, 127, 128, 143, 149, 157, 161, 164, 165, 172, 174, 176, 177, 180, 181, 183, 184, 186, 191, 192, 199, 202, 209, 210, 211, 214, 216, 226, 228, 229, 242, 246, 268, 279, 284, 293; atavistic roots 18, 86, 272, 273; language as experience 33, 34, 84, 103, 116, 120, 132, 140, 162, 239, 241, 247, 297
Lawrence Hall 49, 51, 93, 282
Leavis, F. R. 19
Lecoq, Jacques 31, 152, 155
Leeder, Sigurd 20, 22
Lee, Lezlie *203*, 204
Leibowitz, Judith 124
Lenox Boys' School 48–49, 50, 52, 54
Lindenmaier, Ava 202
Linklater, Hamish 14, 221n22
Linklater, Kristin xv, 1, 2, 9, 12–16, *15*, 19, 24, 25, 26, 28, 34, 40, 41, 45,

60n10, 84–87, 97, 112, 116, 119–124, 125, 129, 132, 134, 174, 184, 221n22, 245–246, 297, 300; 'An Actor at Work' 172; *dropping in* 137; emotion map 167n66; hypothetical training 243; Kristin Linklater Voice Centre 15; rehearsals 247–248; *Voice* progression 119–124, 279
listening 77, 97, 99, 212, 245, 246–247, 254; dynamic listening 144
Littlewood, Joan 109–110, 262n41
Lohbauer, Bob 194
London Academy of Music and Dramatic Art (LAMDA) 12–13, 16, 18, 19, 20, 21, 22
Loudon, Ella *59*, 256, 277, 279, 280, 293
Lovers' Spat: Round Two 300
Love's Labour's Lost 11, 60, *191*, 244, 259
Lowry, W. McNeil 25
Lubarr, Josh 166n52
Luppino, Matthew 290
Lytle, Sarah 260

McBain, Kenny 37n67,172, 60n10
Macbeth 21, 101, 109, 111, 112, 141, 186, 200, 206, 218, 230, 240, 257, 268–269
McCabe, Josh *59*, 157–158, 200, 201, 220, 226, 230, 232, 277, 283
McCurdy, Peter 56
MacKinnon, Cecil 58, 257
Mackintosh, Iain 52
McMenemy, Joan 235
Mainstage *31*, 41–43, *42*, 44, *48*, 52
Maltz, Maxwell 85, 104n7
Marshall, Henry 22
Marsh, George E. 52, 61n47
Massie, Raphael 251, 252, 253, 254, 256, 262n57, 277, 284
May, Corinna 22, 43, *44*, 61n15, 159
Measure for Measure 126, 209, 265
Medea 68
mentoring 4, 22, 188, 210, 213, 244–245, 254–255, 257–258
The Merchant of Venice 42, *53*, *76*, 247, 251–252, 256, 265
The Merry Wives of Windsor 60, *234*, 297
A Midsummer Night's Dream 40, 41, 48, *48*, 135, 185, 213, 257, 259
Miller, Annette 51, *299*
Miller Building 51
Miller, Michael A. 51, *299*
mindfulness 89, 103, 179, 214; bodymind-fulness 88; compassion 78, 113, 175, 179, 215, 217; generosity 177, 187, 204;

Index

kindness 187, 188; mind/body connection 120; *see also* empathy

mission statement 44–47; Young Company 219

Mitchell, Gary 58

Mnouchkine, Ariane 109

Month-Long Intensive xiii, 3, 28, 31, 83–106, 112, 132, 164, 175–176, 184, 187, 205, 242–243, 297; *Basics* 112, 116, 225–131, 132, 135, 157, 163, 216; *Body Work* 148–167, *150–151*, 154–155, *154*, 160–165, *164*; evolution and influences 83–106; function of the theatre 63–79; Riotous Youth 210, 212; *Text* ; *Work* 132–147; *Voice Work* 116–131

Monologues 92, 127, 132, 163, 198, 210, 216; *see also* soliloquies

Morton, Joe 41

The Mount 2, 31, 35, 38–44, *42, 44*, 47–48, *48*, 51, 52, 54, 55, 57, 58, 60, 171, 191, *191*, 194, 218, 297

Movement/Dance 18, 84, 86, 124, 148–151, 159, 199, 200, 206; cosmic dance 20, 161; *Cymbeline* 209, 219, 224, 278–279, 285; Pure Movement 23, 24, 31, 149

multi-culturalism 1, 26, 174

multi-racialism 1, 32, 34, 45, 174, 221, 252, 256

Mumford, Hilda 39

musical soul 241–242; *tempo rubato* 241, 261n14

Nakamura, Midori 42

National Institute on Teaching Shakespeare 177

National Music Foundation (NMF) 49–50, 57

nature images 277, 281, 285–286

New York University (NYU) 14, 26–32, 96, 112, 125

Nichols, Jane 31, 96, 152, 153, 154, 176, 208n33

Noel, Normi 257

Northeast Regional Tours 44, 190–191, 220, 297

Nottage, Lynn 257

Nunn, Trevor 18

Oedipus 68, 75

Ohama, Natsuko 42, 60n10

opening circle 117–118, 211–212

Oral History Archive Project xv, 4, 296

Othello 139–140, 233, 244, 286–287

Outreach Study Program 45

Oxford Court 43

Pack, Roger Lloyd 32

Paquette, Mimi 199

Parks, Suzan-Lori 100

participation, pedagogy of 87–88

Partridge, Caitlin 201

pedagogy, principles of 183–187

Perachi, Paul E. 172–173, 174, 223–225, 229–230

Performance 31, 159, 171, 191, 205, 237–295; art form 239–263; Courts Project 231–233, 235; *Cymbeline* ; case study 274–295, *287, 289, 291–292*; Fall Festival 199, 200; the mission 44–45, 46; Riotous ; Youth 216; Talk #3 264–273

personal connection 10, 92, 98, 112, 126, 129, 135, 136, 184, 197, 198, 226, 245

personalization 19, 115n3, 129, 181, 186, 243, 247

Physical Awareness 119, 121

'playing with the story' 212–213

Play 157, 184–185, 211, 249; playfulness 119, 145, 178, 186, 188, 214; training 152

political 1, 4, 9, 14, 54, 117, 142, 245, 255, 273, 294

Poretsky, Rebecca *154*

practical pedagogy *see Education*

practice-based research 13, 18, 22, 25, 33, 34, 88

presence 153–154, 177, 270

previews 290

professional development 205–206; the art of acting 257–260

project-based learning 183–184, 192

Project Zero 177–178, 183, 186–187, 195

'Protect the Cookie' 153, *154*

Prusha, Diane 43, 61n44, 221n22

Pujic, Ilija 94

Puma, Nicholas J. 54

Pure Movement 23, 24, 31, 149; *see also* Arnold, Trish

Quakers, Religious Society of Friends 9, 49

Rain Dance 64–65, 101

Randolph, Tod 42

320 Index

Ravenscroft, Trevor 280–281
Reeves, Keanu 3, 83
rehearsals 107, 145, 163, 247–256; Fall
  Festival 198–199, 201; *Cymbeline*
  277–290
Reiffel, David 277, 284, 290, 293
reinforcing 91, 118, 165, 211, 212, 214,
  279–280, 181
religion 55, 62n49, 71–75, 252, 264–273,
  273n1; gods 55, 64, 65, 66, 68–70, 73,
  75, 110, 162, 278
Renbourn, John 161
Research Into Lost Knowledge
  Organization (RILKO) 26, 280–281
responsibility, social 185–186, 270, 272;
  personal 192
revelation 16, 24, 86, 108, 109, 111, 112,
  115n3, 118, 121, 214, 249, 272; *Cymbeline* 285–288, 291, *292*
Reverence 202–203, 207n26
Rhoades, Victoria 21, 105n48, 150, 151,
  207n26, 219, 221
Ricciardi, Nicole 257, 263n57
Richard II 27, 171
Richard III xiii, 27, 101
Richards, Lloyd 24
Riotous Youth 57, 191, 209–218, *218*,
  219; Riotous Company 216
rites of passage 183, 184, 197
rituals 64, 65, 67, 69, 72, 73, 78, 99, 114,
  116–119, 129, 146, 270
Rogal, Bruce 118, 129n5
Rogal, Rachel 118, 129n5
Roman Garden Theatre 58–60, *59*
Romans 70–71, 79n3, 108, 110; *Cymbeline*
  260, 269, 277, 278, 282, 288, 289, 290,
  292–293
Romeo and Juliet 30, 102, 175, 190, 193,
  194, 240, 244, 247, 254, 286
Roosen, Adelheid 268
Rose Footprint 56, 57–58, 209, 216, 218,
  220, *220*
Rose Playhouse 54–58, *57*, 206; Institute
  206; Project 176
Rose Renaissance Village 55, 57
Royal Academy of Dramatic Art (RADA)
  10, 20, 22
Royal Shakespeare Company (RSC)
  10–11, 12, 19, 20, 21, 22, 148, 248
Rylance, Mark 111
Rylands, George 'Dadie' 19

St. Martin's Hall 51, 59, 60

Sacred and Profane *see Clown*
The Salon 43, 51
Saukiavicus, Tim 174
Sawaf, Kholoud 251, 252, 253, 254, 255,
  262n57, 277, 280, 293
Scene Work 135, 136–137, 144–146
schools 171–187, 190–208
Schools Residencies 190, 192–193
Schwinke, Gwendolyn 277, 279, 280,
  284, 285
Seidel, Steve 178, 184
self-knowledge 182, 199, 225, 229,
  231, 234
self-observation 112, 113
Shakespeare & Young Company
  conservatories 57, 175–176, 210,
  218–221, *220*
Shakespeare and the Language that Shaped
  a World (SLaW) 190, 191–192, *192*
Shakespeare in the Courts 176, 178,
  223–236, *234*
Shakespeare in the Schools 174, 190–208
'Shakespeare Off the Wall' 174
Siegel, Ed 260, 294
sighing 121–122
Simotes, Tony 22, 27, 30, 58, 60n10, 156,
  157, 158, 159, *159*, 244, 260, 60n10
Sink, Christopher 51
Sisto, Rocco 30, 41
Slade, Peter 176, 188n16
Smith, Kiki 248, 262n39
Smuckler, David 12
Society of British Fight Directors 22
'Socratic discussions' 2
soliloquies 92, 108, 111
Sonnet 24, 92, 132, 134–136, 150, 162, 163
'Sonnet Fest' 134, 162
Sound and Movement 24, 124,
  149, 161
Spada, Enrico *192*
spiritual xiv, 4, 18, 21, 28, 29, 51, 54, 55,
  66, 73, 83, 91, 159, 163, 165, 165n11,
  266, 268, 269, 270, 272, 286, 288;
  physio-spiritual14
Spring Lawn 51
the Stables 43, 44, 54
Stage(d) Fight/Violence *see Fight Work*
stagger-through 284–285
standing the scene up 137, 144, 145, 249
Stanislavsky, Konstantin xiv, 14, 26, 84,
  112, 125, 129, 154, 165n11, 243, 246;
  state of 'I am' 129
'Statement of Values that Unite Us' 2

Stevens, Carl 49
Stone, Kris 276, 283, 290
Storm Dance 151, *151*
structure 20, 21, 116, 117, 132, 135, 153, 211, 243, 250, 268; management 32; social 78; *see also* artist manager
Structure of the Verse 18, 19–20, 22, 132–135, 242, 246, 250, 285
Sugarman, Paul 96
Sullivan, Deb 277, 290
Summer Institute on Teaching Shakespeare 205–206
Summer Performance Institute (SPI) 43, 175, 222n24
Summer Shakespeare Intensive (SSI) *see* *Summer Training Institute*
Summer Training Institute (STI) 3, 43, 83, 87, 94, 103, *136*, *150*, *159*, 184, 187, 210, 233
'Sun, Moon and Stars' 151, 161, 166n3

The Taming of the Shrew 18, 24, 25, 60, 194, 244
Taylor-Williams, C. 198
The Tempest 59–60, *59*, 95, 258, 257, 259
Tesher, Ellie 143
text analysis 206, 249–251, 285
text progression 246–247, 248–251, 277; *Cymbeline* 279–280, 285
Text Work 83, 84, 86, 95–96, 116, 132–147, 153, 163; *Cymbeline* 278–280; *Education* 184, 186–187, 209, 219, 221, 224
Theatre, Therapy, Theology 65, 66, 132, 264–273
Thompson, John Douglas 3, 41
Tillyard, E. M. W. 41, 161
Timon of Athens 20
Tina Packer Playhouse (TPP) 52–53, *53*, 56, 59, 163, 191, 195, 201, 219, 241
Tiresias 265
Titus Andronicus 240
TPP *see Tina Packer Playhouse*
Toomey, Michael F. 31, 152–153, 154–155, 156, 301n2
Tucker, Eric *244*, 301n2
Torbjornsen, Karen 209
touch 92, 99
Training 21, 31, 34, 81–167, 171, 186, 191, 205, 219, 242–243, 245, 252, 258–259, 277, 296; the mission 44–45, 46; Talk #2 107–115; *see also Body Work*; Month-Long Intensive; *Text Work; Voice Work*
transcendence 67, 109, 240, 243, 278

transformation 11, 86, 88, 94, 116, 118, 163, 165, 171, 174, 224, 232; pedagogy of 88–89, 99
truth 19, 22, 26, 28, 31, 34, 45, 47, 69, 86, 107, 111, 113–114, 120–121, 125–126, 144, 172, 177, 228, 231, 239, 241, 245, 272, 285
'Truth Process' 104n9
Twelfth Night 155, 180, 256, 257, *258*, 259

unconscious 16, 17, 25, 33, 53, 78, 86, 89, 109, 120, 141, 143, 160, 241, 246, 266, 269, 278, 281, 282, 289

'vacuuming your lungs' 122
'Values and Ethic' 46
'Values that Unite Us' 257
van der Kolk, Bessel 98–100, 227, 228
Varon, Daniela 257, 262n57, 263n77, *271*
'The Veiled Monologues' 268
vibration 14, 17, 24, 25, 68, 108, 119, 122, 124, 128–129, 184, 239, 241, 242, 265, 266, 280, 264
violence 5, 21, 22, 27, 30, 66, 88, 96, 99, 100–103, 156, 157, 158, 174, 180, 185–186, 229–230, 256, 271, 272
vesica piscis 53
vocabulary 119–120, 151, 184, 186, 211, 277, 284
Voice Work 12–15, 19, 83, 84, 85, 86, 96–98, 99, 108, 112, 116–131, 163, 257–258, 299; *Cymbeline* 278–279; *Education* 184, 197, 206, 209, 219, 224; psychology 96–98; self relationship 97; truthful acting 241

Waldren, Bill 9
Warden, Claire 22, 157, 159, 166n41
Ware, Jenna 175, 183, 184, 186, *192*, 199, 224, 232
warming up 119, 184, 185, 192, 210, 211, 227, 258
Warren, Iris 12, 13, 23
The Wars of the Roses 27, 32, 37n50
'We Hold These Truths' 219
Werner, Kenneth E. *299*
West, Frances 105n48, 251
Wharton, Edith 2, 28, 35, 39, 43, *44*, 48, 57, 61n6, 257, 297
White, George 24
Whitman, George 10; Shakespeare and Company bookshop 9–10
Wicks, Bob *154*, 164
Williams, Eric C. 198

322 Index

Winkles, Ryan 192, 205
The Winter's Tale 1, 141, 250
Wit 94
Wittrock, Peter 41, 175, 221n22, 273n3
Wold, Kristin 21, 23, 61n15, 149, 277, 278–279, 284, 285, 294
Wolfert, Stephan 100, 105n61
Wolpe, Lisa 175, 256, 301n2

Women of Will 244, *244*, 251, 258, 274, 288
Woolly Mammoth Hunt 64, 65, 75, 101
working the play on its feet 248–249, 279, 283
Wu, Shirong *164*

Youngerman, Jim 58, 59, 60
Youth Bridge Global Project 94, 105n37